THE LANDS BETWEEN

Zones of Violence

General Editors: Mark Levene and Donald Bloxham

THE LANDS BETWEEN

CONFLICT IN THE EAST EUROPEAN BORDERLANDS, 1870–1992

ALEXANDER V. PRUSIN

OXFORD
UNIVERSITY PRESS

OXFORD

UNIVERSITY PRESS

Great Clarendon Street, Oxford OX2 6DP

Oxford University Press is a department of the University of Oxford.
It furthers the University's objective of excellence in research, scholarship,
and education by publishing worldwide in

Oxford New York

Auckland Cape Town Dar es Salaam Hong Kong Karachi
Kuala Lumpur Madrid Melbourne Mexico City Nairobi
New Delhi Shanghai Taipei Toronto

With offices in

Argentina Austria Brazil Chile Czech Republic France Greece
Guatemala Hungary Italy Japan Poland Portugal Singapore
South Korea Switzerland Thailand Turkey Ukraine Vietnam

Oxford is a registered trade mark of Oxford University Press
in the UK and in certain other countries

Published in the United States
by Oxford University Press Inc., New York

British Library Cataloguing in Publication Data

Data available

Library of Congress Cataloging in Publication Data

Library of Congress Control Number: 2010927241

Typeset by SPI Publisher Services, Pondicherry, India

Printed in Great Britain
on acid-free paper by the
MPG Books Group, Bodmin and King's Lynn

ISBN 978–0–19–929753–5

5 7 9 10 8 6 4

Acknowledgements

While working on the subject, I received help from many individuals. First of all, I am grateful to the editors of the series, Donald Bloxham and Mark Levene, who read the entire manuscript several times and provided invaluable feedback, tactfully putting up with my proclivities to narrative.

Amir Weiner, Gabriel Finder, Eric Weitz, Omer Bartov, Peter Holquist, Norman Naimark, Jerzy Borzecki, Michael Gelb, Martin Dean, and Scott Zeman questioned my conclusions and accorded me helpful comments and suggestions. I am deeply indebted to John Staples and my friend and research companion Vadim Altskan for their generous help.

I am pleased to recognize the most important contribution of the staff members of the John Skeen Library at New Mexico Tech, especially Tom Irion, Peter Martinez, Sandra Licata, Tony Telles, and George Tavarez, without whom the research for this book would have been impossible.

The workshop 'National Politics and Population Migrations in Central and Eastern Europe' at the University of Minnesota in April 2006 and the international conference 'Borderlands: Ethnicity, Identity and Violence in the Shatter-Zone of Empires since 1848' in Marburg, Germany, in May 2007 provided a propitious intellectual environment for the exchange of ideas.

Matthew Cotton of Oxford University Press tolerated my lateness in submitting the manuscript, while copy-editor Veronica Ions stoically corrected my numerous errors and omissions.

Finally, I owe much to my wife Elena, who supported me through the entire process of completing the project.

Contents

List of Maps

List of Tables

Abbreviations

AK	Home Army (of the Polish government-in-exile)
KPZB	Communist party of western Byelorussia
KPZU	Communist party of western Ukraine
LAF	Lithuanian Activist Front
LANC	League of National Christian Defence (Romania)
LAS	Union of Lithuanian Activists
LVR	Lithuanian Auxiliary Formation
MGB	= NKGB after March 1946
MVD	= NKVD after March 1946
NKGB	People's Commissariat of State Security (USSR)
NKVD	People's Commissariat of Internal Affairs (secret police, USSR)
ONR	National Radical Camp (Poland)
OUN	Organization of Ukrainian Nationalists
PKWN	Polish Committee of National Liberation
POW	Polish Military Organization
PPS	Polish Socialist party
RKO	Reichskommisariat Ostland
RKU	Reichskommisariat Ukraine
UPA	Ukrainian Insurgent Army
UVO	Ukrainian Military Organization
ZUNR	West Ukrainian National Republic

Book Abbreviations in Notes

(For full details, see Bibliography)

Baltic States R. J. Misiunas and R. Taagera, *The Baltic States: Years of Dependence, 1940–1980*

Baltischen Provinzen A. Ezergailis and G. Pistohkors, eds, *Die Baltischen Provinzen Russlands zwischen den Revolutionen von 1905 und 1917*

Homelands N. Baron and P. Gatrell, eds, *Homelands: War, Population and Statehood in Eastern Europe and Russia, 1918–1924*

Postroenie sotzialisma A. D. Pedosov et al., *Postroenie sotsializma v Sovetskoi Pribaltike: istoricheskii opyt kompartii Litvy, Latvii, Estonii*

Społeczeństwo polskie R. Kotodziejczuk, ed., *Społeczeństwo polskie w dobie pierwszej wojny światowej i wojny polsko-bolszewickiej 1920 roku*

Tygiel K Jasiewicz, *Tygiel narodów: stosunki spoteczne i etniczne na dawnych ziemiach wschodnich Rzeczypospolitej, 1939–1953*

Introduction

Historical destiny placed Eastern Europe between Russia and Germany.
Hence, the most popular form of the East European travelling is to escape
either from the Russians to the Germans, or from the Germans to the
Russians.[1]

Taking a tour along the land-strip that once was Russia's western
frontiers and today separates it from the rest of Europe a modern
traveller would certainly notice many signs of a diverse and fascinating
history. From Estonia to Moldova one would be dazed by a variety of
languages, confessions, and architectural styles that testify to the coexistence
of different cultures, customs, and traditions. At the same time, medieval
castles, military cemeteries, and monuments to national martyrs and heroes
convey impressions of continuous crises, social upheavals, ethnic conflicts,
and frequent boundary changes that affected these lands through the centuries.

East European history in general has exhibited historical continuity,
stemming from its ill-fated location between the more organized and
powerful neighbours. Yet, though hardship is certainly no novelty to
Eastern Europe, the 'Lands Between'[2] that by the mid-nineteenth century
constituted the frontier zones between the German, Austrian, and Russian
empires stand out as particularly volatile. Mainly a flat land, traversed by the
river-systems in the Baltic, the Pripiat' marshes and forests in Byelorussia,
and the Carpathian Mountains in the south, it was a passageway for frequent
raids, incursions, and invasions from the west and from the east. At different
times the Danish and Teutonic crusaders, the Mongol horsemen, the
Swedish and Polish kingdoms, and the Russian and Ottoman empires had
dominated and relinquished some regions of the borderlands, with each

successive conqueror attempting to mould them according to his vision of administrative and ideological uniformity.

Yet, the multi-ethnic texture of the borderlands militated against such measures. Located on the threshold of Europe and Russia, they served as a point of contact and conflict between different cultures that shaped their political and economic structure and affected their relationship with the administrative power-centres. In time, the latter evolved into more rich, industrialized, and centralized entities, while most of the borderlands remained poor, predominantly agricultural, culturally conservative, and being contested by the neighbouring states, continuously unstable. As a result, they were in a constant state of flux, characterized by blurred ethnic boundaries, frequent population migrations, and amorphous border-lines, until in the early nineteenth-century Austria, Prussia, and Russia incorporated them into their respective imperial domains. For more than a century the borderlands remained in peace although official concerns over the sensitive border-areas translated into attempts to detect and diffuse potential irredentist tendencies through state assimilation.[3]

The First World War turned the borderlands into a huge battlefield whose contours expanded and contracted in accordance with the fortunes of the opposing armies and the war ravages, economic deprivation, and refugee crises replicated themselves in quick succession. The totality of the war on the Eastern Front gained momentum in 1915, when the Russian army deported or expelled more than a million residents to Russia-proper. The tendency to treat civilian populations as legitimate targets and the geographical and political vulnerability of the borderlands revealed themselves again during the Second World War, when the two expansionist states, the Soviet Union and Nazi Germany, subjected the occupied territories to brutal 'social engineering', deporting and murdering hundreds of thousands of people.

The patterns of conflicts and violence in the borderlands suggest a particular case study worthy of examination. For example, the Russian deportations of 1915 largely affected the subjects of the Tsar and were beyond replication in the European theatre of war, comparable only to the Turkish deportations of Armenians. Barely had the First World War ended than the polities that emerged on the ruins of the three empires claimed the disputed territories through military force. Between 1918 and 1920 the borderlands lived through the vicissitudes of several foreign occupations and civil wars, compounded by refugee and economic crises. During the interwar period some regions still remained 'hot spots', causing frictions and undermining stability and the defensive capacity of the involved parties. For instance, having wrested the city of Vilnius from Lithuania in 1920, Poland incurred its neighbour's implacable enmity that consistently inhibited Polish efforts to form a military alliance with the Baltic countries. During the Second World War most of the borderlands again followed a different trajectory from the more homogeneous 'core'—lands of Eastern Europe and Russia. Subjected to two foreign occupations—by the Soviets in 1939–41, by the Germans and their allies in 1941–4—and then again reconquered by the Soviets, they became a huge laboratory for the Soviet 'socialist reconstruction' and the Nazi 'New Order' that resulted in massive fatalities. The war between the two totalitarian regimes generated a series of civil wars that involved competing ethnicities and ideologies and eventually extended well into the late 1940s. Simultaneously, substantial segments of the population took an active part in the Holocaust that heralded the end of the Jewish communities in the borderlands. Finally, it took almost a decade for the Soviets to pacify the reconquered territories, using well-tested methods of mass terror and deportations of entire ethnic groups. Only the introduction of the more flexible governing system after Stalin's death—in the form of the Soviet 'affirmative action' state[4]—ushered in a long absence of politically inspired violence until the early 1990s, when the Soviet government's ability to keep its subjects in check faded away.

★ ★ ★

Why did the situation in the borderlands, relatively tranquil under imperial rule, become so volatile between 1914 and 1953? Under what circumstances were conflict and violence in the borderlands most protracted and intense? The historiography of the borderlands—here the term refers to the regions that in the course of the twentieth century changed hands several times, namely the modern Baltic republics (Estonia, Latvia, and Lithuania), the western provinces of Byelorussia and Ukraine, and the republic of Moldova—has been firmly situated within the framework of general Eastern European studies, offering various interpretations of the instability of the region. Most authors have stressed the conflation of the biased state ethnic policies and the relatively inflexible or slow-to-react Eastern European economies that fuelled internal conflicts. The 'bogeyman' of modernity—nationalism—is most frequently named as a dominant factor that put some ethnic groups on a collision course with the state and/or their neighbours.[5] Certainly, a logical explanation for the tumultuous past of the borderlands

could be ascribed to their geopolitical situation as the bone of contention
between the major powers or to the exigencies of the *Age of Extremes*—the
twentieth century as the epoch of particular instability, intolerance, and
brutality.[6] Two studies that specifically focused on the borderlands have
tendered a more nuanced analysis of the borderlands' particularities. Kate
Brown accentuated the state efforts to establish tighter control over the
diverse populations of the sensitive frontier-zones (Brown defines the entire
right-bank Ukraine as a borderland area), as the major cause for political and
economic instability. On the other hand, Timothy Snyder has contextual-
ized the integrative role of the former Polish-Lithuanian Commonwealth in
the development of the 'subordinate' Ukrainian, Byelorussian, and Lithuanian nations, with the implicit conclusion that the general trend of ethnic
discourse in the borderlands—at least until the First World War—was
coexistence rather than conflict.[7]

The present study aims to examine the causes and mechanisms of conflict in
the borderlands and partially subscribes to the notion that socio-economic
cleavages and ethnic rivalries—most common patterns of the East European
landscape—were at its root. Its dominating thrust, however, is predicated
upon the opinion that the borderlands' ethno-cultural diversity was in basic
conflict with the nationalizing policies of a state—understood here as a major
functioning political and military-fiscal power. In peacetime, when the
state's control over all forms of social relations was unchallenged, it acted as
the highest arbitrator, manipulating the conflicting claims of rival groups
and maintaining relative stability in its domain. To be sure, until 1914 the
borderlands were predominantly violence-free, for the imperial states
accorded their subjects a modicum of stability and relative (by the East
European standards) political equilibrium. Hence, despite occasional erup-
tions—the Polish uprising of 1863 and the 1905–7 revolutionary turmoil in
Russia's western provinces were the most serious—the borderlands hardly
resembled what a prominent historian called the 'caldrons of conflict'.[8]

At the same time, it should be noted that although imperial rule in the
borderlands was fully consolidated, the Russian, Austrian, and German
authorities were concerned over the loyalty of the diverse populations in
the vulnerable border-areas. Historically, collective identities in the borderlands were based on the commonality of language, religion, culture, and
ethnicity, or in other words on ethno-communal rather than national
associations. Consequently, connections between ethnic groups across
state borders raised suspicions that their allegiances and identities were not

necessarily, or at least not always, compatible with those envisioned by the state. For example, although many Baltic Germans had faithfully served in the Russian imperial administration and military, their potential collusion with Germany made the Russian political and military establishment increasingly apprehensive. As international tensions in Europe heated up, the Great Powers' geographical proximity and strategic interests turned the borderlands into a large security complex and the opposing governments increasingly worried that a national movement within or across the border could set in motion a dangerous chain reaction, undermining the integrity of the state.

The state officials, therefore, strove to impose some sort of supranational identity upon the patchwork of ethnically mixed settlements and such efforts became a standard through the nineteenth and the early twentieth centuries. In wartime the traditional imperial modes of the peaceful conflict resolution were replaced by the more militant ideologies and aggressive military structures, accelerating the conflict between the state and the population and making the potential for extreme violence so much greater. As economic and human resources became strained to the limit, suspicions of the groups deemed less loyal to the state blurred the concept of internal and external enemies and entailed reprisals against the allegedly 'corrosive' elements. From 1920 similar concerns dominated the policies of the inter-war 'successor-states' that attempted to impose the national-state blueprint on the territories marked by linguistic, religious, and ethnic cleavages. Such policies created generic conditions under which simmering feelings of insecurity, resentment, or collective aggression could detonate in suitable time. The Soviet and German rule in the borderlands followed the same pattern of enforcing homogenizing policies, but by much more radical methods of eradicating 'class-enemies' or the racially 'inferior' ethnic groups. Both states greatly facilitated internal conflicts by encouraging latent hostilities and creating an environment in which inter-communal violence was conceived as legitimate means and could assume a genocidal character.

This study, accordingly, accentuates the role of the state as the main instigator of violence, which comprised two major elements. First, the state—whether the Russian empire, the interwar Poland, or the Soviet regime—aimed at the nationalization of the borderlands by expropriating the economic and financial assets that belonged to the allegedly disloyal communities. Second, claiming legitimacy in governing a specific disputed territory the state endeavoured either to 'improve' it by assimilating the groups deemed worthy of assimilation or by removing those that were considered intractable. Although imperial policies tended to be relatively lenient albeit biased towards particular ethnic groups—the discriminatory anti-Jewish policies in Russia are a case in point—in wartime, when the integrity of the state was threatened, the government used all means at its disposal to render potential enemies harmless. As the war weakened the state's ability to maintain a monopoly on violence, such policies lit the fuse to the local conflicts, whether strong or dormant, and the nationalist agitators became more assertive in claiming the territories they considered as 'historically' their own. Consequently at the end of the First World War and in the midst of the Soviet–German war, violence was sustained and exacerbated by popular participation, acquiring its own destructive logic and mutating into a vicious cycle of multi-sided clashes. In other words, while the state initiated violence, it mobilized—often deliberately as well as unintentionally—local grievances. One objective of this study is to examine the process by which violence mutated from the legitimate state domain to a violence of masses as a vehicle to secure access to political power and economic resources.

Importantly, internal conflicts that exploded in wartime were rooted in the lack of social cohesion in the borderlands, for the majority of the population had limited access to employment, education, and politics. To put it another way, the state consistently failed to integrate most of its subjects into the collective decision-making process. On this account, notwithstanding regional differences, which at times were profound, at least until the late 1930s the borderlands were part and parcel of the larger Eastern European pattern characterized by similar modes of distress: predominantly agricultural societies, small elites dominating economies and politics, a middle class of different ethnic or religious background than the population at large, and limited opportunities for social mobility.

Nationalism remained a subordinate factor in regional politics and was the prerogative of relatively small groups, concentrated in urban areas. It reached its maturity predominantly at the end of the First World War, when the national states, suddenly propelled into existence by the collapse of the three empires, faced a difficult task to forge their respective multi-ethnic societies into nations. Therefore, although through the nineteenth century nationalism remained an important force in the Eastern European political discourse, it acquired momentum only when large groups of people found its appeals meaningful and corresponding to their social and economic interests. Between the two world wars most of the interwar 'successor-states' faced political and economic instability and increasingly prioritized the interests and values of their 'core' ethnic constituencies over the minority groups. Such attitudes effectively placed diverse populations, which did not share similar extraction with the dominant ethnic groups, into the categories of 'outsiders'. Correspondingly, large segments of the disaffected minorities supported the nationalist or communist movements and, once the war broke out, mutual animosities were reflected in different affiliations and allegiances. Thus, in sharp contrast to the summer of 1914, when the majority of the imperial subjects flocked together under their respective state-colours, in September 1939 many Byelorussians, Ukrainians, and Jews welcomed or at least remained indifferent to the collapse of the Second Polish Republic. In June 1941 the populations of the borderlands (with the exception of Jews) displayed a similar unity in welcoming the German army. The convergence of interests in regards to the elimination of political or economic rivals between the state on one hand and the population at large on the other entailed large-scale collaboration, essential for the Soviet 'socialist re-construction' and the Nazi implementation of the 'Final Solution'.

Psychological environment in the borderlands is crucial for understanding popular behaviour. The majority of the population had no control over political and social processes, and this promoted tendencies to see rapidly changing situations through an emotional prism. Anticipated threats generated a 'double-bind' process, in which assumptions—frequently wide of the mark—about the potential power-resources of a potential enemy became overwhelming and often provoked a pre-emptive strike.[9]

* * *

The main methodology employed in this study can be dubbed 'integral'—namely, it neither attempts to provide a detailed description of each borderland region, nor to illuminate all political and socio-economic changes that transpired in the borderlands as a whole. Rather it intends to create a larger synthetic narrative and analytical framework that encompasses all the borderlands as a specific region, giving it the appearance of a particular zone, beset by recurrent and often extreme instances of conflict and violence within a specific time-frame and across whatever arbitrary and usually quite provisional international borders that had been determined by external or internal forces. Such an approach warrants a symmetrical pattern of examination—concentrating on several dominant themes and providing several detailed examples as paradigms characteristic for the entire area in question. Accordingly, this study is built up primarily on the foundation of existing literature; archival materials are introduced when the author felt they were necessary to complement other sources.

The suggested time-span is approximately set between the era of modernization of the Russian and Austrian empires (and the evolution of the latter into a dual monarchy) and the break-up of the Soviet Union. The evolution of the Austrian empire into a dual monarchy and Russia's reforms of the 1860s are marked as the starting points because they profoundly impacted the political, national, intellectual, and economic development later inherited by the interwar 'successor-states' and the Soviet Union. The main emphasis, however, is placed on the 'era of conflict' between the outbreak of the First World War and the Soviet pacification of the borderlands in the early 1950s. Throughout the period in question the Jewish communities were consistently singled out as targets, and therefore a special effort is made to analyse the ideological, socio-cultural, and psychological factors associated with the ritualization and mechanisms of anti-Jewish violence as the harbinger of a new political order.

Since internal conflicts in the borderlands were derivative of profound internal cleavages, Chapter 1 serves as a background narrative, highlighting the socio-economic, ethno-linguistic, and cultural diversity of the borderlands that stemmed from and affected imperial nationality and security policies. Chapter 2 situates the borderlands in wartime, considering the circumstances under which the opposing armies in the First World War resorted to repressive measures against civilian populations. More precisely, it analyses the motives and factors that compelled the military regimes—given the massive population displacement initiated by the Russian army, it receives a primary attention—to employ draconian methods against entire ethnic groups. Chapter 3 shows the effects of the collapse of the three empires and conditions that generated civil wars and national conflicts, ultimately resulting in the new territorial settlement in the borderlands. Chapter 4 begins with an overview of the political, socio-economic, and ethnic problems faced by the 'successor-states' in the borderlands with special emphasis on state policies towards ethnic minorities, the circumstances that radicalized inter-communal enmities, and the activities of the revisionist states that ultimately destroyed the peace settlement. Chapter 5 focuses on the Soviet invasion and the integration of the borderlands into the USSR in 1939–41. It analyses the Soviet application of 'class' policies as the catalyst for the mobilization of ethnic animosities and the gestation of ethnic violence that erupted during German occupation. Chapter 6 shifts to examine the circumstances that contributed to the extreme brutality of the Holocaust, largely focusing on the role of local collaboration in the genocide of Jews. Chapter 7 concentrates on the causes and dynamics of the civil wars and ethnic conflicts within the context of the Soviet–German conflict. Chapter 8 explores the reimposition of Soviet control over the borderlands and methods of reintegrating them into the Soviet Union, and Chapter 9 traces the evolution of Soviet policies from the death of Stalin to the break-up of the Soviet Union and the new territorial rearrangement in the borderlands.

★ ★ ★

Because the borderlands have belonged both to the Russian and Eastern European geopolitical space, frequent references to both are made to highlight connections between national and regional histories. All names are transliterated in accordance with the system adopted by the Library of Congress. Most localities have changed names several times and, to avoid confusion, here all geographical names appear in modern spelling accompanied by a contemporaneous spelling in parenthesis, except those which have been integrated into the English language such as 'Kiev' instead of the Ukrainian 'Kyiv' or 'Transcarpathia' instead of the Ukrainian 'Zakarpattia'.

According to the Russian imperial administrative system, the term 'Baltic provinces' until 1918 will be applied to Estonia and Latvia, but not to Lithuania. However, after 1918 the designation of the 'Baltic region' or the 'Baltic states' will relate to Estonia, Latvia, and Lithuania because of their common historical experience. The term 'western Byelorussia' is applied to the modern Hrodna (Grodno) and Brest oblast' of the Republic of Belarus' in addition to the western parts of Vitebsk oblast' west of Western Dvina River and the western counties of Minsk oblast'. The term 'Western Ukraine' refers to the historical regions of East Galicia, northern Bukovina, Transcarpathia, and the present-day Rivne and Volhynia oblast'. Today East Galicia is divided between the L'viv, Ivano-Frankivs'k, and Ternopil' oblast' of Ukraine, whereas Bukovina and Transcarpathia approximately correspond to the boundaries of the Chernivtsi and Transcarpathia oblast' respectively. Today the Russian imperial province of Bessarabia is split between the Republic of Moldova and the secessionist 'Transdniestria' republic. Although the Russian imperial and Soviet administrations used the term 'Moldavian'—in contrast to Romanian—to denote a different ethnicity of the majority of the population in the region, in this study the term will be used in reference to the Romanian-speaking population of Bessarabia/Moldavia/Moldova.

The term 'borderlands' here is applied in a geographical rather than in an ethnographic sense and implies as a spatial concept, a zone of overlapping, co-habitation, and contact between different polities, cultures, and peoples. In comparison, the more ideological term 'frontier' would denote a fluid zone within or outside of the state-organized society, even if bounded by clearly marked political boundaries. The generic term 'violence' applies to all forms of deliberate infliction of harm, including combat, but particularly directed against civilians. State violence, which receives special attention in this study, is understood as the use of force by the agents and institutions of the state and carried out in a comparatively organized and systematic manner.

The term 'nationalism' refers to an ideology or movement that promotes an idea of an autonomous or independent state for a particular ethnic group. Since the mid-nineteenth century in Western Europe the term 'nation' has been associated with the state, implying a well-delineated geographic space, where a complex government structure stands at the top of the politically, linguistically, and ethnographically united society. In Eastern Europe, until the formation of independent states, the term traditionally delineated a socially and politically mobilized group that sought self-determination in the form of independent statehood. The term 'ethnicity'—as opposed to 'nation'—is used to denote various communities bound by a common ethno-linguistic, historical, and cultural background, but not necessarily living within the same spatial limits, while the derivative term 'nationality' implies a higher degree of social organization such as an educated and politically engaged elite and a middle class and substantial population segments conscious of their common origins and destiny.[10]

I

The Land and the People

Historically the borderlands have been the areas of contact and conflict between different cultures and religions and between the power-centres and peripheries. Consequently, they tended to retain some degree of autonomy from the administrative core-areas, which, in turn, aimed at establishing a firmer control over their peripheries. As time passed, the core-areas evolved into more centralized and developed regions, whereas the borderlands remained largely agricultural, poorer, and innately unstable as a buffer-zone between more powerful polities. After the incorporation into the three imperial domains—Prussia, Austria, and Russia—the ethno-religious diversity of the borderlands' populations still remained a source of concern for their new masters, who were always seeking more efficient methods of detecting, diffusing, or suppressing potential separatist or irredentist tendencies.

The following is a brief excursion through the history of the borderlands, with special focus on the interplay between the internal divides such as ethnicity, culture, and socio-economic status and the security concerns of the imperial powers. Since in the nineteenth century the bulk of the borderlands belonged to the Russian and Austrian empires—approximately two-thirds and one-third respectively—special attention is accorded to the historical circumstances that led to the distinctive state policies and patterns of inter-ethnic relations in the two imperial domains. The main contention of this chapter is that the relations between the state and the populations of the borderlands were deeply rooted in the structural incompatibilities of the two entities. Particularly from the 1850s, when international developments exposed the weaknesses of Austria (Austria-Hungary) and Russia in the face of more advanced Western European powers, the ethno-cultural diversity of the borderlands evolved into a security complex for the imperial

Map 1. The Borderlands before the First World War

governments. Consequently, the latter strove to impose ideological and administrative uniformity upon the strategically important regions. However, while the Russian and Austrian policies in the borderlands were driven by similar economic and strategic interests, the methods of controlling their vast and diverse realms varied, reflecting different ideologies and political organizations of the two empires.

The 'classic' borderlands

The political and territorial organization of the borderlands was shaped by their experiences as frontier zones (Map 1). Situated between more powerful neighbours, these territories changed hands numerous times. In fact, only Transcarpathia and Klaipėda (the coastal region in western Latvia) remained within the same polities until the end of the First World War— the former since the eleventh-century as a part of the Hungarian kingdom and the latter since the thirteenth century as the Memel province under German domination. The rest of the borderlands had followed a much more turbulent trajectory. In the thirteenth century the Danish and German Crusaders colonized the Baltic region. They founded important cities and trading centres such as Tallinn and Riga (in the fourteenth century the Danes sold their rights in Estonia to the Teutonic Knights) and eventually Christianized the local population. As a crucial trade and strategic area, the Baltic coast attracted Sweden, Poland-Lithuania, and Russia, which in the sixteenth and seventeenth centuries fought each other in a series of wars that devastated the region. The final showdown took place during the Great Northern War of 1700-21, from which Russia emerged as the ultimate victor and integrated the Baltic region into the imperial administrative system. In the nineteenth century northern Estonia made up the province (*gubernia*) of 'Estland' and southern Estonia and northern Latvia were joined in the province of 'Lifland'.

Continuous warfare weakened the once mighty Polish-Lithuanian Commonwealth and between 1772 and 1795 it was partitioned by Austria, Prussia, and Russia. Austria came into possession of Galicia (in the fourteenth century Poland wrested it from medieval Russia) that was divided into two halves demarcated by the San River. Russia's share included Lithuania, Byelorussia, Ukraine, eastern Latvia (known as Latgalle), and Kurland. These acquisitions constituted new administrative units:

Table 1.1. Ethnic Structure of the Russian borderlands in 1897

Ethnic group	Baltic provinces		Lithuania-Byelorussia		Suvalki		Bessarabia	
	Pop.	%	Pop.	%	Pop.	%	Pop.	%
Bulgarians & Gagauz							55,800	3.0
Byelorussians	79,000	2.8	2,691,300	46.8	4,200	1.1		
Estonians	906,100	32.7						
Germans	165,267	5.9	49,073	0.9	19,000	4.9	60,200	3.3
Jews	62,686	1.24	364,700	6.4	42,000	10.8	228,200	12.4
Latvians	1,326,600	47.8						
Lithuanians	24,400	0.8	1,661,000	28.9	296,000	76.7		
Moldavians							1,009,400	54.7
Poles	70,000	2.5	482,800	8.4	21,000	5.4	11,700	0.6
Russians	200,000	7.2	96,000	1.7	3,600	0.9	330,600	17.9
Ukrainians			347,100	6.0			123,100	6.68
Others			53,700	0.9			24,900	1.4
Total	2,834,053		5,745,673		385,800		1,843,900	

Note: The population of the entire Volhynia province was 2,940,000. Correspondingly, by the author's calculation, western Volhynia had about 550,000 residents.

Sources: Henning Bauer, Andreas Kappeler, and Brigitte Roth, eds., *Die Nationalitäten des Russischen Reiches in der Volkszählung von 1897* (Stuttgart: Franz Steiner Verlag, 1991); Piotr Eberhardt, *Ethnic Groups and Population Changes in Twentieth Century Central-Eastern Europe: History, Data, and Analysis* (New York: M. E. Sharpe, 2003), Louis Roman, 'The Population of Bessarabia during the 19th Century: The National Structure', *Romanian Civilization* 3/2 (1994): 53-66.

Lithuania-Byelorussia made up the Vilnius (Vil'na), Kaunas (Kovno), and Hrodna (Grodno) provinces, a part of Lithuania on the left bank of the Neman River was integrated into the Kingdom of Poland (*Tsarstvo Pol'skoe*) as the Suwałki (Suvalki) province, and the province of Kurland encompassed most of Latvia's western seaboard; a large portion of the right-bank Ukraine became the province of Volhynia.

Russia and Austria also benefited from the decay of another great power—the Ottoman empire—whose fortunes declined simultaneously with those of Poland-Lithuania. In 1774 the Austrians annexed northern Bukovina that alongside Galicia became the easternmost outpost of the Austrian empire. In 1812 the Russians annexed the eastern part of the medieval principality of Moldova. The new possession was named the province of Bessarabia (it also included some Ukrainian counties on the right bank of the Dniester River).

Table 1.2. Ethnic structure of the Austro-Hungarian borderlands in 1910

Ethnic group	East Galicia		Bukovina(northern)		Transcarpathia	
	Pop.	%	Pop.	%	Pop.	%
Germans	38,000	(0.9%)	105,200	(13%)		
Hungarians			10,000	(1.3%)	115,000	(21.9%)
Jews	573,500	(13.6%)	88,000	(10.9%)	77,000	(14.7%)
Moldavians			36,000	(4.5%)		
Poles	875,200	(20.7%)	36,000	(4.5%)		
Romanians			229,000	(28.6%)		
Ukrainians	2,711,400	(64.3%)	297,800	(37.1%)	295,000	(56.3%)
Others	18,900	(0.45%)			37,000	(7%)
Total	4,217,000		802,000		524,000	

Sources: Piotr Eberhardt, *Ethnic Groups and Population Changes in Twentieth Century Central-Eastern Europe: History, Data, and Analysis* (New York: M. E. Sharpe, 2003); B. Stopnevich, 'Naselenie Galitsii', Ukrainskaia zhizn', 11–12 (1914): 43–54; G. Piddubnyi, *Bukovyna. Ii mynule i suchasne: suspil'no-politychnyi narys iz maliunkamy i mapoi Bukovyny* (Chernivtsi: Zelena Bukovyna, 2005).

The Russian expansion brought together four relatively well-defined historical areas—the Baltic region, Lithuania-Byelorussia, right-bank Ukraine, and Bessarabia, inhabited by a variety of people who spoke at least eight different languages, used three scripts (Latin, Cyrillic, and Hebrew) and practised five religious rites (Orthodox, Protestant, Roman Catholic, Greek Catholic, and Jewish). The distribution of ethnicities and cultures reflected an amazing heterogeneity of the borderlands. In the Baltic provinces the Estonians and Latvians made up 80 per cent and the Russians, Germans, Byelorussians, Poles, and Jews, about 20 per cent of the total population. A roughly similar proportion characterized ethnic divisions in Lithuania-Byelorussia, where the Polish, Ukrainian, Jewish, and Russian minorities lived amidst much larger Lithuanian and Byelorussian communities. In Bessarabia the Romanian-speaking Moldavians constituted almost 55 per cent of the total, followed by the 25 per cent of Russians and Ukrainians, 12 per cent of Jews, and much smaller other ethno-linguistic groups such as Bulgarians, Gagauz, and Roma (see Table 1.1).[1]

The situation was analogous on the Austrian side of the border. In East Galicia the Ukrainians made up a majority of the population—64 per cent; the Poles and Jews respectively constituted approximately 21 and 13 per cent. More than half the population of Transcarpathia was also of Ukrainian descent, while in Bukovina the Ukrainians and Romanians made up 65 per cent of the total; Jews and Germans represented 11 and 13 per cent (see Table 1.2). The only exception for the borderlands' ethno-cultural mosaic was the Klaipėda (Memel) district in the German empire, inhabited by roughly 68,000 Germans and 68,000 Lithuanians.[2]

There were also enclaves of smaller minorities such as the Czechs in Volhynia, while others such as the Rusyns of the Carpathian region were related to a larger linguistic family, but spoke regional dialects and constituted distinct ethno-cultural entities. Religion reinforced ethnicity and simultaneously transcended ethno-linguistic, socio-economic, and political borders. The Germans, Estonians, and Latvians were Protestants (though most Latvians in the Latgalle region were Roman Catholics), the Lithuanians and Poles were predominantly Roman Catholics, and the Russians and Moldavians practised Greek Orthodoxy. Religious allegiances of the Byelorussians were divided between the Greek Orthodoxy and the Greek Catholic (Uniate) rite. Similarly, the Ukrainians in Volhynia and Bukovina were largely Orthodox, whereas their kin in East Galicia and Transcarpathia belonged to the Greek Catholic Church.

Such diversities could not obscure the most 'classic' common feature of the borderlands—they were highly stratified and rigid societies, in which ethnicity and religion were interrelated with each community's socio-economic status and whose economic interests were at variance with each other. Since the imperial policies on both sides of the border were to maintain the supremacy of the government and to transform their subjects into obedient and loyal subjects, the state methods of control sustained and amplified the socio-economic and ethnic divisions. The top of the social hierarchy was occupied by the representatives of the 'imperial' nations— Russians and Germans—who dominated the administration, the army, and the police. Their numbers, however, were too small, for qualified Russian and German officials preferred service in the administrative centres to the posts in the remote and less 'civilized' border-regions. For example, ethnic Russians in the Baltic provinces constituted about 7 per cent of the total population; the German minorities in East Galicia and Bukovina made up 1 and 13 per cent respectively.

The Russian and Austrian governments, therefore, were perforce to delegate the middle-level administrative and managerial positions to the reliable 'titular' groups that possessed the legacy of historic kingdoms in the past, preserved a vernacular language and distinctive culture, or were valued for their particular economic and administrative skills. In East Galicia the Austrian government accepted the traditional political and economic dominance of the Polish nobility; in Transcarpathia the Hungarian magnates and the gentry had long enjoyed similar privileges. However, if the Polish and Hungarian nobles were grudgingly reconciled to the superiority or at least the equality of German culture to their own, the Russians were painfully aware that some of their new subjects were more advanced and sophisticated than their conquerors. The annexation of the Baltic region brought under Russian rule skilled and educated Protestant groups, particularly the Germans, who contributed to the growth of cities and industries, possessed better agricultural methods, and enjoyed the highest literacy level in the empire. Interested in the development of trade and commerce, the Russian government retained and extended the privileges of the German landowning nobility that constituted a separate estate, *Ritterschaft*, formed provincial diets, and dominated the regional and local administration, court, and education system. Conversely, the Germans appreciated such a social contract and many became loyal and efficient servants of the state—until 1917 one-eighth of top imperial officials came from the German-Baltic nobility and the middle class.[3] Strategic and economic considerations in Lithuania-Byelorussia that formed the central sector of the Russian defence against a potential threat from the west also induced the Russian government to preserve the Polish nobility's dominance in regional and local politics and economy. For the imperial governments, however, such practices revolved around a painful dilemma—how to make concessions to the 'titular' groups and at the same time keep them under control.

★ ★ ★

The 'dual revolution'—the term applied by Eric Hobsbawm to the nineteenth-century French political and British industrial transformations—posed a serious challenge to the three East European empires, where the major indices of economic growth such as industrialization, urbanization, and literacy lagged far behind. The socio-economic backwardness of the borderlands revealed itself in the following statistics—by the late nineteenth century 70–80 per cent of Estonians, Latvians, Lithuanians, Byelorussians, Ukrainians, and Moldavians made their living by agriculture and their opportunities for upward social mobility were extremely limited. Even in the Memel district, a part of the highly industrialized German empire, 82 per cent of the labour force were agricultural workers. Another particular East European pattern was a small middle class. This 'gap' position (by Karl Marx's definition) was filled by numerically small ethnic groups, particularly Jews, who dominated petty trade, commerce, and artisanship. Although these 'middlemen' lived in the borderlands for generations, the population at large still considered them aliens due to their distinct culture, religion, socio-economic status, and linguistic differences.

The economic and military successes of Britain and France provided an attractive socio-economic model worth emulating, but at the same time caused great concerns for the Prussian, Austrian, and Russian governments, which sensed that they were gradually losing in the European competition for power, prestige, and influence. In fact, although the defeat of Napoleon seemingly represented the apex of the East-European empires' military prowess, the growing strength of their main rivals pushed Prussia, Austria, and Russia to exertion in maintaining a major-power status. To this end, the imperial governments attempted to modernize their administrative and economic structures, achieving various degrees of success. Austria was first to begin the age of reforms in the late eighteenth century, when concerns over the rising power of Britain, France, and Prussia compelled Austrian rulers to partially emancipate the serfs and modernize the army. Similarly, in 1808-16 the Prussian government emancipated the serfs and began restructuring its administrative, judicial, and military systems. The drive to reforms in East Europe also affected the Russian empire—Poland received an autonomous status as the Kingdom of Poland, joined to the empire through the Russian monarch, and by 1819 the Estonian and Latvian serfs were emancipated and received full legal rights.[4] Outside the Baltic region, however, the Russian political and military establishment was determined to rigidly maintain its political and socio-economic system and particularly its most odious institution, serfdom, exactly at the time when Western Europe was going through rapid political and socio-economic transformation.

The second age of reforms was spawned by crushing military defeats that shook the Austrian and Russian empires. In 1847 a revolt by the Polish nobles in West Galicia, suppressed by a peasant counter-revolution, forced the Austrian government to promise the abolition of labour-rent (which was not enforced). The revolutions of 1848–49 forced further concessions: the government initiated the complete emancipation of peasants, introduced a national assembly, and upgraded the judicial system. Another series of reforms followed the humiliating military defeats suffered by Austria in the wars against France and Piedmont-Sardinia in 1859 and against Prussia in 1866. Similarly, shaken by the disastrous Crimean War of 1853–56 and the humiliating peace terms, in February 1861 the Russian government under Alexander II realized that Russia's weaknesses were rooted in the country's socio-economic system and abolished the institution of serfdom; peasants were granted personal freedom and the right to own property.

While the empires had suffered military reverses before—the memories of the catastrophic defeats at the hands of Napoleon were relatively fresh— the novelty of the situation was reflected in the profound psychological stress and international repercussions of the wars in the 1850s–1860s. The revolution of 1848–49 in Hungary, suppressed only after the intervention of the Russian army, revealed the inadequacy of the Austrian military and political system, whereas the defeats in 1859 and 1866 indicated that the entire state apparatus needed an overhaul or Austria would lose its status as a European power. For Russia the impact of the Crimean defeat was of equal consequence. The deficiencies in armament, especially the abysmal performance of the Russian sailing vessels against the French and British steamships, confirmed the backwardness of Russia's economy. Not only did the war effectively annul Russia's major-power status that it achieved between 1815 and 1850, but the humiliating peace terms were accompanied by an economic crisis, caused by the disruption of American cotton supplies to Russia's textile industries. When, in search of alternative sources of supply, Russian commercial interests shifted to Asia, they were blocked by the British. Hence, in the short and long run the Crimean War demonstrated that rivalry with the West remained crucial for Russian domestic and international policies.

The reforms in Austria and Russia thus followed a similar pattern: military defeat necessitated the adjustment of the state's economic and political machinery. Consequently, the reforms initiated in the 1860s were bound to deeply affect the two states' political and industrial development. Seeking to stem the rise of the national movements and to placate the powerful Hungarian nobility, to whose hostility Vienna attributed its defeat in the war with Prussia, in 1867 the Austrian government conceded an agreement—*Ausgleich*—that made Austria and Hungary a dual monarchy joined through the single monarch, the emperor of Austria. The Hungarian kingdom became autonomous in all but foreign and military affairs. A similar 'appeasement' policy effectively handed Galicia over to the Polish nobility, who received a virtual monopoly over the provincial state apparatus, the economy, the education system, and the main legislative provincial body, the *Sejm*. The modernization of the political system was followed by the drive to industrialize imperial economy. In Galicia and Bukovina these efforts spawned a relatively well-developed rail network and the increase of industrial enterprises (especially in food and lumber processing) that by the late nineteenth century employed about 35,000 workers. The rail expansion, however, exposed traditional agricultural economy to the realities of the new market system, for the influx of manufactured goods from Austria and Bohemia dealt a harsh blow to the much weaker Galician and Bukovinian industries.[5]

In Russia the emancipation of the serfs was followed by the restructuring of the legal and educational systems; cities and towns received limited self-government rights and in 1874 the government introduced universal military service that effectively turned the armed forces into a mass con-script-army. Due to the high level of mechanization, managerial skills, and literacy in the Baltic provinces (in comparison to the rest of the empire), they gradually evolved into the main sites of Russia's metalworking, wood-working, textile, chemical, and food-processing industries. About 67 per cent of the industrial production of Estland, Lifland, and Kurland was absorbed by Russia, reflecting their weight in the imperial economy. By 1900 the Baltic region's industrial output reached an unprecedented level of 8 per cent annual increase and its factories and plants employed 110,000 industrial workers—the two largest industrial sites of the empire, Warsaw and Łódź (Lodz´) had 186,500 and 132,900 workers respectively—indicating a relatively high degree of social mobilization.[6]

The Baltic success-story, however, simultaneously underscored incom-plete patterns of modernization. A century-long population explosion—the population in Lithuania-Byelorussia almost doubled between 1800 and 1900—far outstripped agricultural and industrial development and caused unprecedented land-scarcity. By 1897 in Lifland alone there were 600,000 landless agricultural labourers. In contrast to large German estates that owned between 500 and 2,500 hectares (one hectare equals 2.47 acres), the Estonian and Latvian peasants on average owned 50 hectares. Similarly, while in Bukovina a number of peasant households grew from 38,100 in 1847 to 109,200 in 1902, more than 56 per cent owned less than 2 hectares, and the largest estates belonged to the Polish and Romanian nobles. Landlessness generated the emergence of a peasant sub-class, which drifted between towns and cities and worked as unskilled industrial and seasonal labourers.[7]

Industrial progress was also too slow to produce large metropolises. By 1900 only four of the cities in the borderlands—Riga, Vilnius, Chişinău (Kishinev), and L'viv (Lwów)—respectively had the populations of 282,230, 154,532, 108,483, and 206,113 and were comparable to large Western European cities. Socio-economic backwardness was also reflected in the scarcity of medical personnel and high death rate. In Transcarpathia one doctor and one nurse had to provide medical services for five thousand people, whereas in Chişinău six doctors and twenty-five medical assistants served 500,000 people. Consequently, in Transcarpathia and Bessarabia the sickness and mortality rate, especially among infants, was among the highest in all Europe.[8]

The national challenge

The transformation of agricultural economy to a market system was con-comitant with lively educational and intellectual activities that profoundly affected the social and political status of the borderlands. In contrast to Western Europe, where the concept of the state as an expression of supra-national identity had become prevalent by the end of the eighteenth century, nationalism in Eastern Europe was embedded in ethno-cultural and religious identities. The ideas that these identities could evolve into national communities, united by culture, language, historical background, and a common destiny originated in the late eighteenth and early nineteenth centuries. According to the classic formula of Miroslav Hroch, impressed by the formation of modern Western nations, the Romantic literati and artists in Eastern Europe embarked upon recovering or 'reinventing' the ethos of their ethnic constituencies such as language and folklore. Once this process was under way, the native intelligentsia aimed at imbuing the masses with the sense of common identity and destiny; the third stage of national evolution involved mass political mobilization.[9]

Several particular features of the borderlands bolstered the development of the national movements. In traditional agricultural societies ethno-linguistic and communal affiliations were much more comprehensible than secular connections such as class, party, or ideology prevalent in Western societies. Ethnic differences in fact mirrored the socio-economic disparities between 'imperial', 'titular', 'middlemen', and 'agricultural' groups. For example, Estonian and Latvian peasants detested their 'German' landlords, Lithuanian peasants felt exploited by the 'Polish' nobles, and Ukrainian and Moldavian peasants shared enmity towards the 'Jewish' tradesman or merchant. The correlation of the same ethnicity, religion, and socio-economic status hence facilitated the formulation of national identity and consciousness. Official censuses, which were compiled according to religion and language, also helped the national agitators construe common ethno-cultural modes. But most importantly, the ideologies and political structures of the Austrian and Russian empires facilitated—often unwillingly—the rise of nationalism.

From its inception in the sixteenth century until its demise in 1918 the Habsburg empire remained a conglomerate of separate territorial units that possessed deep-rooted and unique historical identities and the administrative authority was exercised by the landowning elites bound to the Emperor by a form of social contract. To rule and keep together its diverse domains, the Austrian government used flexible policies that allowed it to maintain a relative equilibrium between different nationalities. The co-optation policies of the 'titular' groups facilitated the formation of 'nobility-nations' among Poles and Hungarians, who embraced romantic nationalism and construed their histories as an uninterrupted process of struggle against foreign hegemony. The legacies of medieval statehood and strong cultural traditions legitimized their demands for autonomy and broad political participation. At the same time, such claims engendered the sentiments of moral and cultural superiority, especially in regard to the 'agricultural' people, for while the *Ausgleich* benefited the nobles, the situation of Polish and Hungarian peasants was no better than that of their Ukrainian, or Slovak counterparts. Fears of absorption by more numerous co-nationals, conflated with wishful thinking that 'superior' Polish and Hungarian culture would attract 'inferior' ethnic groups, spurred an aggressive assimilation campaign. Between 1874 and 1906 the Hungarian administration in Transcarpathia reduced the numbers of the Rusyn-language elementary schools from 479 to twenty-three; the 1907 education law eliminated them altogether. Conversely, facing the aggressive 'Magyarization' campaign and attracted by the opportunities of social advancement many Rusyns, Ukrainians, Germans, and Jews willingly assimilated into Hungarian culture.[10]

Similarly, zealous to preserve its dominance in East Galicia, the Polish elite invariably opposed any expressions of Ukrainian national identity, despite the fact that Ukrainians constituted the predominant demographic majority in the province. The Polish claims to supremacy, however, did not

go unchallenged. Concerned about Polish irredentism—the Polish rebellion in West Galicia in 1847 was the case in point—the Austrian government encouraged Ukrainian literary and educational activities as a lever
against the Poles. Although there was no Ukrainian statehood in the past,
the history of the Cossacks (a political-military organization that between
the sixteenth and eighteenth centuries fought the Turks, Tatars, Russians,
and Poles) provided the Ukrainian Romantic writers with a starting point.
In the late eighteenth century the popularization of the Cossack and peasant
culture coincided with the Austrian government's reforms that introduced a
combination of the Church Slavonic and Ukrainian vernacular in village
schools; the Greek Catholic Church received equal status with its Roman
Catholic counterpart. Peasant emancipation contributed to the proliferation
of Ukrainian cooperatives, schools, libraries, and theatres. From the 1860s
Ukrainian deputies entered the regional and imperial parliaments and the
last decade of the nineteenth century witnessed the formation of the first
Ukrainian political parties. The introduction of universal suffrage in 1907
intensified the Polish–Ukrainian political rivalry and a year later Ukrainian
voters won a quarter of the seats in the imperial Parliament. Alarmed by
these developments, the Polish political elite supported the Russophile
faction—the Ukrainians' rivals in regional politics—and attempted to ma-
nipulate the dietary elections. The Polish–Ukrainian confrontation erupted
in April 1908, when a Ukrainian student assassinated the Polish Viceroy of
Galicia and violent clashes between the two groups took place in several
localities.[11]

In Bukovina, which in 1861 became a crown-land ruled directly by
Vienna, the Austrian government also catered to the Romanian and Polish
nobility, but more even ethnic distribution than in Galicia fostered equally
vibrant development of national cultures. The search for the 'forgotten past'
generated numerous literary works and theatrical performance in native
languages; German, Romanian, and Ukrainian schools grew in numbers;
and all ethnic groups were proportionally represented in the civil service,
education system, and trade. The political representatives of these groups
also cooperated in the provincial diet. In 1890 the Romanians, Poles, and
Ukrainians formed a united bloc against the Germans and Jews; in 1892 the
German, Jewish, Ukrainian, and Polish deputies joined forces against the
Romanians.[12]

Austrian traditions of ethnic tolerance were particularly noticeable
in regard to Jews. Most Jews in the borderlands lived in close-knit

communities, where their cultural, religious, and linguistic heritage made them a distinct minority. They dominated in urban areas, especially small towns, and made their living by petty trade, inn keeping, and artisanship. Educated Jews also constituted the largest ethnic group engaged in free professions and were well represented in the regional administration, court, and educational system. Yet, since the mid-nineteenth century the industrialization drive portended a gradual decline of Jewish trade and commerce. Large businesses and corporations gradually took over domestic and foreign trade and the growth of Polish and Ukrainian cooperatives made the role of Jewish middlemen in the countryside increasingly obsolete. At the same time, impoverished by industrialization, many Polish gentry turned to local commerce and trade; the influx of peasants into towns and cities further intensified economic competition. Anti-Jewish sentiments among the nascent Polish middle class and the clergy were exacerbated by the conspicuous indifference of Jews towards Polish national aspirations. The majority of religious Jews adhered to Orthodoxy and refrained from politics, while the Jewish intelligentsia was split between the Zionists, Socialists, and Social-Democrats. However, regardless of religious preferences and political affiliations, the Austrian Jews pledged their loyalty to the Emperor, whose majestic figure symbolized the rule of law and order extended to all subjects regardless of their ethnicity, social status, or religion.[13]

In sum, due to the Austrian nationality policies the crucial fundamentals of Polish, Ukrainian, Romanian, and Jewish national life—language, cultural and educational organizations, religion and political participation— were firmly established in East Galicia and Bukovina. In contrast, in Transcarpathia the eight centuries of Hungarian rule had kept the Ukrainians and Rusyns at a low level of socio-economic and cultural development and severely checked the evolution of national identity and consciousness. Also, though the Austrian government tolerated the primacy of the Hungarian and the Polish nobilities, it simultaneously allowed the coexistence of multiple loyalties—a person could be a Polish or Ukrainian nationalist and a loyal Habsburg subject. The incitement of ethnic hatred was a criminal offence and the *Pax Austriae* was certainly preferable for most Ukrainians, Romanians, and Jews to a state dominated by a 'titular' nationality.[14]

* * *

In comparison to more flexible Austrian nationality policies, the Russian government perceived the nascent national movements as an ultimate threat to the integrity of the empire. To fully appreciate such concern, it is necessary to place it into proper historical prospective. To begin with, the ideology of the Russian state and the diversity of the borderlands militated against each other as two irreconcilable concepts. A huge military-fiscal state, imbued with its Orthodox and Pan-Slavic 'civilizing' mission could hardly be forbearing towards 'alien' Roman Catholic, Protestant, Greek Catholic, and Jewish populations. The Russian rulers were particularly concerned with the borderlands' proximity to potentially hostile foreign neighbours and strong national traditions, especially among the Poles and the Germans. Therefore, the borderlands were governed as a defensive barrier against a potential enemy thrust to the Russian core-areas. For this purpose, the regions that seemed particularly vulnerable to the enemy attack were grouped into special administrative units—the military general-governments. The three western military general-governments encompassed Lithuania-Byelorussia, the right-bank Ukraine, and Poland (with the Suwałki province). The General-Governors were military commanders of high rank, who were granted extraordinary powers such as the right to deport or expel potential troublemakers without due legal processes.[15]

Contrary to highly patronizing attitudes towards the peoples of the Caucasus and Central Asia, the imperial policies in the Baltic and Lithuania-Byelorussia were partially affected by a sense of cultural inferiority towards the Germans and Poles, who were more sophisticated—by Russian standards—in terms of education, culture, and economic skills. For instance, despite their subservience to the German landlords, the Estonian and Latvian peasants were more literate and enjoyed higher living standards than their Russian or Ukrainian counterparts. Consequently, the Russian politicians and government officials worried that 'intrinsic' Russian qualities such as passivity, lack of intelligence, and poor entrepreneurial abilities were no match for highly entrepreneurial and aggressive attitudes of the non-Russians, especially the Germans, Poles, and Jews.[16]

In general, the Russian nationality policies in the western borderlands could be characterized as 'defensive-reactive', rarely displaying uniformity and fluctuating from assimilation attempts to outright repression. Initially, the co-optation policies towards the socio-economic and ethnic elites in the newly acquired territories were deemed most effective. Until the late 1820s the Russian government allowed Bessarabia to retain a substantial degree of autonomy that it had enjoyed under the Ottoman empire. However, the war with the Ottomans in 1828 provided a convenient pretext to fully integrate Bessarabia into the imperial administrative system as a regular *gubernia*. If these measures were to 'level' the new possession within the imperial socio-economic system, other changes were propelled by international developments in the mid-century. As an outcome of the Crimean War Russia lost three southern districts of Bessarabia to Romania, where the authorities established Romanian schools and subordinated the Russian Orthodox Church to the Bucharest patriarchate. After the 1878 Berlin Congress returned south Bessarabia to Russia, the Russian administration again curtailed the province's political and cultural autonomy and replaced the Romanian landed nobility (*boyars*) with the Russians in the administration, finances, and the court system. The Romanian language was excluded from publications, administration, the school system, and church services, although it remained prevalent in the countryside. The Romanian-language newspapers had a short life span, for the majority of Moldavians were illiterate, whereas the *boyars* and the Romanian-speaking intelligentsia adopted the Russian language and culture and were co-opted back into state service.[17]

Similarly, while in the lands of the former Polish-Lithuanian Commonwealth the Russian government initially tolerated the dominant position of the Polish nobility, after the Polish uprising in November 1831, it abolished regional self-rule and confiscated rebels' land-estates. After a period of relative political relaxation in the 1840s and 1850s, the uprising of 1863 entailed more repressions. Although defeated militarily, the Polish political elite never gave up hopes for independence, and such aspirations were manifested in various forms, from armed uprisings to gradual 'positivist' policies, aiming to gradually recover lost positions and foster national unity among Poles across social divides. Formed in 1892, the Polish Socialist party (PPS) promoted the link between social revolution and national independence among industrial workers, while its main rival, the National Democrats (*Endeks*) advocated the replacement of the traditional nobility-dominated system with a strong, nationally conscious middle class that would lead the Polish masses to national sovereignty. The *Endeks* were particularly popular among peasants outraged at the Russian persecution of the Roman Catholic Church and the nascent middle class locked in a ferocious competition with German and Jewish merchants.[18]

The Russian government also attempted to limit Polish influence among the 'agricultural' people—Lithuanians, Byelorussian, and Ukrainians—by banning the Uniate Church. Other measures included the introduction of the Russian language in the education and justice system; Cyrillic replaced the Latin alphabet in Lithuanian textbooks. Jews and Poles in Lithuania-Byelorussia were prohibited from buying peasant holdings, whereas the administration provided landless peasants with small allotments. In contrast to Russia-proper, peasants in Suwałki received manorial land without redemption payments. Similar stick and carrot policies were deployed in the Ukrainian provinces, where the use of the Ukrainian language was prohibited, but the administration encouraged the influx of Ukrainian settlers as a counterbalance to the Polish nobility.[19]

Still, an all-out attack on the Polish nobility never eventuated since it entailed the assault on the established socio-economic order. In addition, Russian policies were highly decentralized, for though St Petersburg issued general guidelines to the administration in the borderlands, various ministries responsible for finances, education, and land issues quarrelled over primacy in the decision-making process. Nor did the personal aspirations of military governors, who held supreme power in the borderlands and tended to act independently, help maintain a coherent policy, which to all intents and purposes was impossible, given the discrepancies in economic and cultural developments in different regions. Imperial anti-Polish policies simultaneously affected the fledgling Lithuanian, Byelorussian, and Ukrainian national movements, whose attempts to revive native languages and cultures were interpreted as Polish subversion. In 1863 all three languages were banned (the Russian authorities consistently brushed off the Byelorussian and Ukrainian languages as the 'lost' Russian dialects), and a year later the Russian government prohibited the use of Latin in church services in Lithuania and Byelorussia. Approximately 60,000 Byelorussian Catholics were forcibly converted to Orthodoxy (the Uniate Church was banned in 1839).[20]

To monitor the nascent national movements, however, proved to be a Sisyphean labour, for pressure on one specific ethnic group inevitably resulted in relaxation policies towards the others, allowing the resumption of nationalist agitation. Traditionally, Russian officials assumed a highly paternalistic attitude towards the 'agricultural people', who were to be protected from the 'harmful' German and Polish influence. In the late 1860s, egged on by the nationalist press that accentuated the 'Germanization' effect on Estonians and Latvians, the Russian government turned against the traditional German dominance in the Baltic. In 1867 the Russian language replaced German in the administration and education system; ten years later a new statute stipulated the formation of municipal self-governments in which Estonians, Latvians, and Russians received a number of seats. More pressure was applied in the 1880s, when the police, judicial, and education systems were 'levelled' with other Russian provinces (Russian became the dominant language in courts and schools). Although the Estonian and Latvian intelligentsia resented the language policies, they utilized the opportune moment to campaign for the adoption of the native languages in schools and universities. The official permission for the publication of Estonian and Latvian newspapers became a milestone in the Baltic national movements. The Estonian and Latvian literary societies began advocating the historical distinctiveness of the Baltic region and its people. For example, a prominent Estonian activist, Jaan Tõnisson, argued that the countryside with its cultural and linguistic traditions provided a vital element for the common Estonian national identity, while the Latvian Literary Association promoted the unification of Lifland and Kurland as the homeland for the united Latvian nation. The government limitation on the size of large estates stimulated the growth of Estonian and Latvian households—between 1871 and 1912 the numbers of the Estonian-owned estates grew from 18 to 69 per cent. Anti-German policies corresponded with the influx of the native students and industrial workers to urban areas, gradually changing their composition and encouraging social and political mobilization. Between 1871 and 1913 the Latvian population in Riga rose from 24,000 (24 per cent) to 187,000 (40 per cent), whereas the numbers of Estonians in Tallinn increased from 16,200 (52 per cent) to 93,900 (72 per cent).[21]

★ ★ ★

Arguably, no other issue pertinent to the Russian nationality policies was as pressing as the 'Jewish question'. From the first glance its significance could be explained in mere demographic terms. At the end of the nineteenth century the Russian borderlands were the abode of the second largest (after the Kingdom of Poland) Jewish enclave in the world—1,811,443 people. Spread from the Baltic to the Black Sea the Jewish communities predominated in towns and cities (on average they made up 40 per cent of the urban population) and represented a gamut of cultural orientations and economic potential. The most numerous were the 'eastern' Jews—predominantly Yiddish-speaking and Orthodox—who lived in close-knit communities in the Pale of Settlement which included Lithuania, Byelorussia, Bessarabia and most of Ukraine, specifically designated for Jewish residence. Not only did they, in the words of Czesław Miłosz, live 'within the same walls, yet as if on separate planets [with their Christian neighbors]',[22] but they were the world apart from the middle-class German-acculturated Jewish communities of Tallinn, Riga, and Kurland. Two-thirds of the Russian Jews were occupied in commerce, trade, artisanship, and free professions and although the overwhelming Jewish majority in the Pale lived in abject poverty, in the Kaunas, Vilnius, and Bessarabia provinces the Jews owned about 50 per cent of enterprises and small industries.[23]

The 'otherness' of the Jewish culture and socio-economic profile informed Russian policies that fluctuated according to the changing political, social, and economic situation in the country. Attempts to assimilate Jews at the beginning of the nineteenth century corresponded with more liberal nationality policies, which, in turn, were sidelined by various restrictions during the reign of Nicholas I. Concerns about the unreliability of Jews translated into a special decree that prohibited them to reside within 50 kilometres of the western frontier. Although the era of reforms in the 1860s opened up new opportunities for the Jews in professional and educational spheres, further restrictions were imposed in the 1880s.[24]

Still, inside the Pale the Jewish communities enjoyed substantial autonomy, fully regulating their religious and cultural life. Jewish schools and religious establishments became the flourishing centres of cultural and educational activities, while relations between Jews and Gentiles were marked by relative tranquillity. However, the imperial policy of 'containment' to keep Jews inside the Pale and the industrialization drive aggravated the situation. Overpopulation in the villages and labour opportunities in cities and towns generated the migration of peasants to urban areas, where competition for employment became increasingly fierce and quickly acquired ethnic coloration. Mass social dislocation became the breeding ground for political radicalism among different ethnic groups, including Jews, especially educated ones who joined and became prominent in the revolutionary movements. The participation of a Jewish female revolutionary in the 1881 assassination of Alexander III provoked widespread pogroms, whose scale depended on the willingness of the regional administration to intervene. Anti-Jewish violence erupted in Vilnius, Kaunas, and Hrodna provinces, but was prevented from spreading by the energetic actions of the Russian administration. In 1882 the 'temporary regulations' prohibited Jews to move to villages and buy or lease land. Further regulations established quotas on the numbers of Jews in colleges and universities and legal and medical professions.[25]

In 1903 a large-scale pogrom in Chişinău made headlines around the world. In this city, where Jews made up about 50 per cent of the population (about 50,000) and owned most of the businesses and small industries, economic competition between them, the Moldavians, and the Greeks was especially intense. Such rivalries were heightened by the only daily newspaper in the province, *Bessarabets*. Run by a notorious anti-Semite and partially funded by the Russian administration, the newspaper called for the emulation of the Romanian anti-Jewish policies across the border and blamed Jews for poor harvests and industrial unemployment. In spring 1903 *Bessarabets*' allegations of ritual murder sparked a pogrom that lasted two days and claimed the lives of forty-seven Jews; more than four hundred were wounded. The assailants hailed from different social sections—artisans, industrial workers, peasants, and the city rabble—and the conspicuous passivity of the administration and the police that stood by gave credibility to the allegations of their complicity in violence. The pogrom was paradigmatic, demonstrating the universality of anti-Semitism as a uniting platform for competing ethnicities and different social classes.[26]

State anti-Semitism also fortified the worldviews of the Roman Catholic clergy, traditionally ill-disposed towards Jews, and corresponded with the aspirations of the Polish National Democratic Party (*Endeks*) that advocated the removal of Jews from the socio-economic sphere as a crucial step on the road to national independence. The *Endeks* rejected Jewish assimilation as a device to dominate Polish society—such arguments mirrored subconscious anxieties over 'pure' but innately weaker Polish culture succumbing to the Jewish cunning and ingenuity—and carried out vehement anti-Semitic propaganda and the economic boycott of Jewish businesses.[27]

By the beginning of the twentieth century the Russian Jews found themselves in the most perilous situation since the partition of Poland. Accused of revolutionary turmoil and the capitalist onslaught of traditional agricultural economy, they had become Russia's convenient lightning rod for the country's economic misfortunes and political instability, detested by the state and living among large segments of the antagonistic population.

The borderlands as a security complex

Although by the turn of the twentieth century the Baltic, Polish, and Ukrainian national movements had gained substantial popular support, unless 'internationalized' or coinciding with an acute internal crisis, they were in no position to challenge imperial rule. At the same time, the diversity of the borderlands made them fragile from the official point of view, for ethnic minorities led by determined elites with well-developed national consciousness could become a potential source of trouble, especially if encouraged by similar developments across the border or by the deliberate actions of a hostile state.

The revolutionary upheaval of 1848–49 taught the Austrian government a valuable lesson that even the defeated revolutionary and national movements could not be ignored as a power-potential. Indeed, it was in the post-revolutionary era that the Hungarian and Polish nobilities acquired their power-bases in the government, administration, judiciary, and educational system. Hence, until the outbreak of the First World War the monarchy laboured to promote the cohesion of its domain, pursuing relatively tolerant ethnic policies and maintaining a multicultural state-machinery.

Security concerns over the borderlands were much more acute for Russia particularly because in the second half of the nineteenth century its military and diplomatic fortunes inexorably declined. The suppression of the Hungarian revolution in 1849 hardly counted as a significant military success, particularly in comparison to German triumphs against Austria and France. Even the fruits of the victorious Russo-Turkish war of 1877–78 that resulted in the re-annexation of southern Bessarabia were nullified by the Berlin Congress that denied Russia's gains in the Balkans. Such a situation strengthened the position of the Pan-Slavists who promoted the inevitability of the Russian–German conflict. In this context, any social or national unrest, especially when it transpired at the time or in the immediate aftermath of international crises, caused alarm in St Petersburg. The 'Polish question' is illustrative, for during the Napoleonic Wars the Polish troops fought side by side with the French army against Russia. In the era of Romantic liberalism the Polish revolutionaries found sympathetic audiences and supporters in Britain and France. The Polish uprising of 1863 also came in the wake of the disastrous Crimean War and the aggressive Russification policies in Lithuania-Byelorussia had to be contemplated in conjunction with a possible reaction of the powerful Polish nobility in Austrian Galicia. The contagion of nationalism across the border also revealed itself in the form of publications smuggled by the Lithuanian intelligentsia from East Prussia into Lithuania. The Ukrainian organizations in Galicia carried out similar activities in Volhynia, while literary works in Byelorussian were published and then smuggled to Russia from Galicia and Poznań.[28] Equally worrying for the Russian government was the realization that it could not use the Lithuanian, Ukrainian, and Byelorussian nationalisms against its enemies because it had nothing to offer to its subjects. Instead, stringent school and language policies were conceived as the tools to blunt the nationalist agitation, while the influx of Russian and Ukrainian settlers was to strengthen the pro-Russian elements in the border-areas (for example, between the Crimean War and the end of the nineteenth century the Russian and Ukrainian populations in Bessarabia rose from 146,000 to 453,700).[29]

The revolution of 1904–5 explicitly demonstrated the connection between foreign adventures and combustible domestic issues, deepening a sense of Russia's vulnerability. Although the socio-economic and political grievances were the main driving forces of the revolutionary explosion, they were also linked to the nationality question. In fact, the revolution proved most violent in the imperial peripheries, where the industrialization made deep inroads and where the national and socio-economic grievances conflated. Already in 1895–1900 out of the fifty-nine street demonstrations and strikes that occurred in the empire, twenty-five took place in the Kingdom of Poland, nine in the Baltic, and nine, seven, and six in Ukraine, Byelorussia, and Finland respectively.[30]

The national factor was especially palpable in the Baltic region, which alongside Poland and Transcaucasia became the site of the most intense revolutionary upheavals. Social mobilization in Estland, Lifland, and Kurland was especially facilitated by a high literacy rate—by 1897 78 per cent of Estonians and 70 per cent of Latvians could read and write— and the appeal of Social Democracy, which was rooted in the influence of German culture in the Baltic. For instance, in October 1905 the Latvian Social Democratic Workers' Party had in its ranks 18,200 members—more than the Russian Bolsheviks and Mensheviks together. Lenin admitted that such strength derived from the advanced capitalistic development in the region, the fully-crystallized 'class antagonism', and the more advanced culture of the Latvian proletariat. On the eve of the revolution the Estonian and Latvian Social Democrats organized a number of strikes, and ethnic and social tensions intensified as Estonians and Latvians competed with the Germans in municipal elections. In 1904 the Estonians gained a majority in the municipal council in Tallinn and the Germans were barely able to hold a majority in Riga.[31]

After the beginning of the Russo-Japanese War, the shift from the production of consumer goods to military hardware coincided with the drop in wages and economic shortages. Anti-war resentment erupted when the news of 'Bloody Sunday'—the massacre of the peaceful demonstration in St Petersburg on 9 January 1905—reached the borderlands. Strikes and demonstrations grew in intensity in Tallinn and Riga, where the troops fired on the crowds, killing more than seventy workers. The Social Democratic parties responded with a call to arms. Strikes, demonstrations, and clashes with police swept through the Baltic provinces and Lithuania. In the spring–summer unrest spread into the countryside, where peasants refused to pay taxes and rent and demanded higher wages and shorter working hours. Attacks on German manors that followed soon had all the appearance of a rural revolt against the old order, represented by the German landlords and officials. Violence assumed socio-ethnic connotations as the attackers burned land-estates and government offices, but also destroyed the German libraries, museums, and reading rooms. The traditional social hierarchy seemed to be in collapse, for the Germans and Russians were in full retreat. Since the government was unable to suppress the revolution, the German nobles organized their own self-defence forces and carried out random reprisals against Estonians and Latvians. By mid-summer 1905 the situation in Estland and Lifland resembled a full-blown civil war, and in August martial law was declared in Kurland. By the end of the year more than five hundred German estates were destroyed and eighty-two German nobles, priests, and landowners were murdered.[32]

In urban areas, where socio-economic disparities were the major driving force of violence, political demands and ethnic identification became conspicuously conflated. The demonstrators and petitioners demanded freedom of press, assembly, and religious practices, and the introduction of the native language in schools. Revolutionary committees were formed in cities and the countryside, and anti-German sentiments translated into demands for autonomy and the expansion of self-government bodies at the expense of the German deputies. The All-Estonian Congress demanded national and cultural self-determination, unification of Estland and Lifland, the introduction of the Estonian language in urban and rural elementary schools, and the abolition of all privileges for landowners.[33]

In predominantly rural Lithuania the influence of Roman Catholicism— in comparison to the social-democratic ideology in Latvia and Estonia— impacted the character of the revolution. Sporadic attacks were directed against the Orthodox clergy, perceived as the main vehicle of the official anti-Catholic policies. Nevertheless, the activist groups demanded that Polish and Lithuanian be taught in public schools and that passages that stressed the benign role of Russian domination be removed from textbooks. At the same time, the Lithuanian demands for national autonomy entailed the intensification of the conflict with the Poles, who claimed Lithuania as the 'historic' homeland.[34]

The situation in the Baltic forced the government to reverse its policies and to side with the German nobility. In turn, deeply affected by the Russification policies that endangered their privileged status, the Baltic Germans had long viewed the Latvians and Estonians as the accomplices of the Russian government. Nevertheless, they had a limited choice of action and once the latter unleashed a reign of terror, they became prominent in the counter-revolutionary reprisals. In November 1905 the Russian military committed large numbers of troops to the region with instructions to suppress the revolution by all necessary means. Martial law was established in Estland and Lifland and the punitive units acted as if in an occupied country. The fact that the Germans featured among the commanders of the punitive units was firmly imprinted in the collective psyche of the Estonians and Latvians, whereas the scale of state-terror demonstrated that the government appreciated the danger of the revolution in the strategically and economically important border-region. The intensity of the revolution and counter-revolution was attested to by the following numbers: out of two thousand estates burned in the empire, 460 (almost 25 per cent) perished in Latvia and 120 in Estonia. From December 1905 to June 1906 the troops killed about 2,500 people; about 600 were executed by drumhead courts-martial. The remaining rebels took to the forests, where they formed the so-called forest brothers bands (named after the medieval guerrillas) that carried out about 900 assaults on local administrative offices, post and telegraph facilities, and manors. The resistance finally petered out in 1908.[35]

Although defeated, the revolution fortified the national movements and forced the government to concede some reforms. The language restrictions in the Baltic were lifted, discrimination against non-Orthodox denominations abolished, and the 'October Manifesto' guaranteed civil rights, effectively facilitating national education and propaganda. The Estonian and Latvian delegates participated in the Duma (the Russian parliament) proceedings even after 1907 when a special electoral law drastically reduced the numbers of non-Russian delegates. In Byelorussia and Volhynia, where the

largely agricultural nature of the economy held back successful social mobilization, the Social Democratic groups published revolutionary proclamations in Byelorussian and Ukrainian, and the 'thaw' period after the
revolution witnessed the appearance of Byelorussian libraries, publications,
schools, and credit societies. In Bessarabia, where small Romanian nationalist circles were formed at the turn of the century, a group of activists
demanded the introduction of Romanian in education, forcing the government to allow Romanian-language newspapers. In May 1906, in the wake of
the revolution, the administration allowed the appearance of the first
Romanian-language newspaper in Cyrillic, *Basarabia*. It called for full language rights, a democratic parliament, and autonomy for Bessarabia (eventually, after nine months the authorities closed the paper).[36]

The revolution was also accompanied by the most violent anti-Jewish
pogroms that in magnitude and ferocity exceeded anything that the Russian
Jews had experienced before. Carried out by the most radical monarchist
groups, who blamed Jews for the breakdown of social order and political
turmoil, violence was conceived as a tool to restore the traditional status
quo. The pogrom wave spread from the left-bank Ukraine to Volhynia and
Bessarabia, leaving behind a trail of destruction. In Bessarabia, which had
already gained notoriety during the Chișinău pogrom, the pogroms erupted
in sixty-seven localities; 110 Jews were murdered and many more were
wounded. Supported by Russian officials, the anti-Semitic press alleged that
Jews spearheaded the revolution and dodged military service. Such allegations gained wide credibility, especially after the October Manifesto that
guaranteed all Russian subjects full civil and political rights. Headed by
anti-Semitic agitators, unemployed industrial workers, petty traders and
artisans—who competed with Jews in the regional economy—targeted
Jewish shops and warehouses. In June 1906 the participation of the troops
and police in a large-scale pogrom that erupted in Białystok (Belostok) set a
pattern of violence that mutated from its traditionally civilian to a military
mode.[37]

As horrible as the pogroms were, they were not driven by consistent and
systematic policies, although the assailants found sympathetic support
among the middle- and low-level Russian officials. There were several
small-scale attacks on Jews in the Baltic region, but anti-Semitic traditions
in the Protestant Estonia and Latvia were traditionally weaker than in the
Roman Catholic and Eastern Orthodox borderlands and mitigated by much
stronger anti-German enmities. In early November an attempt to organize a

pogrom in Riga was successfully thwarted by the Social Democratic self-defence units that clashed with the 'Black Hundreds'.[38]

★ ★ ★

Since the formation of the two military power-blocs in Europe—the Entente and the Central Powers—the borderlands had become a strategic area, in which the national security of Germany, Austria-Hungary, and Russia clearly overlapped. Contemplating a potential confrontation with the Central Powers, the Russian government appreciated the danger posed to the western borderlands. Foreign invasion would threaten the industries of the Baltic region, the agricultural and timber enterprises in Suwałki, Hrodna, and Vilnius provinces, and the grain industries in Bessarabia (the latter accounted for 10 per cent of Russia's grain exports).[39] Also, enemy attack through Volhynia and Bessarabia exposed south Ukraine, which since the late 1880s had became Russia's primary centre for mining and metallurgical industries.

Conversely, the Russian military planners considered the borderlands a crucial salient, from which an attack on East Prussia could secure access to the Baltic Sea, whereas a successful offensive from Volhynia into Galicia and Bukovina would secure Galicia's oil industries and Bukovina's salt mines and open an accessible route to Austria-proper and the Hungarian plains. Placed within these considerations, the diversity of Russia's subjects became an important issue related to the country's defensive abilities. Since the late nineteenth century the Russian military deployed comprehensive statistical data to establish the demographic and ethnographic make-up of the population of the empire. Military statisticians determined that ethnicity was the key criterion to evaluate political loyalty, for the imperial spatial core was judged more 'healthy and reliable', whereas the diverse populations on the fringes of the empire were 'undesirable and unreliable'.[40] The Russian High Command especially anticipated that in case of war Jews would become the most willing and dangerous spies and saboteurs. In 1912 a survey among fifty top generals, who would later head Russian armies in the First World War, revealed deep-seated anti-Semitism, and since the potential theatre of war against Austria-Hungary and Germany included most of the Pale of Settlement, such attitudes boded extremely ill for its Jewish population.[41]

The traditional mobility of borderland residents across provincial and state borders—in summer-time agricultural labourers from Lithuania and Byelorussia sought employment in the Kingdom of Poland and East

Prussia—had also come under serious consideration of the regional administration and the police. Already in 1887 the Russian government forbade
foreigners to buy property in the twenty-one provinces, including Bessarabia, Volhynia, and the North-Western Region which included Lithuania
and most of Byelorussia. Similarly, concerned over the 'German predominance' in the Baltic, the Russian government had contemplated restrictions
for Russian Germans, especially in regard to owning and buying land. The
cooling Russian–German relations in the 1880s generated a number of
official reports that stressed how Germans separated themselves from Russian society by the wall of language and culture. The involvement of the
émigré Baltic-German organizations in anti-Russian propaganda and espionage further fuelled anxieties over a potential threat brewing up in German
estates and colonies.[42]

To counter centrifugal tendencies among the ethnic minorities, the
Russian nationalist and liberal circles attempted to cultivate a sense of ideological unity, reflected in the Pan-Slavic movement. Since the 1870s the
Russian Pan-Slavists had established contacts with Galician and Bukovinian
Russophiles—a group of intellectuals who argued that Ukrainians are kin to
the Russians—and promoted the annexation of Galicia, Bukovina, and
Transcarpathia as 'primordial Russian lands'. Joined by the Holy Synod,
the Pan-Slavists helped set up 'Russian-Galician' societies that emphasized
the common roots of all Slavs, especially between Russians and Ukrainians.
Various interest groups supplied these societies with money, books,
and newspapers in Russian; a number of the Ukrainian youth received
scholarships to study in Russia. In turn, the Russian military planners hoped
that such activities would undermine the potentially contagious Ukrainian
national movement and facilitate successful prosecution of war in the
Austrian borderlands.[43]

The Chełm (Kholm) issue also indicated that the Polish question remained one of the cornerstones of the Russian nationality policies, especially
sensitive at the time of international tensions. A part of the Lublin province
on the west bank of the Bug River, the region was inhabited by a sizeable
Ukrainian population, predominantly of the Greek Catholic (Uniate) faith.
In 1875 the Russian Orthodox Church marked the region for forcible
conversion, thus eradicating the last Uniate diocese in Russia. However,
after the Tolerance Edict in 1905 the majority of the converts returned back
to Greek Catholicism. Alarmed over the similar prospects in Vilnius *gubernia*, the Russian nationalist factions convinced the government and the
Duma that a territorial 'adjustment' was necessary. In May 1912 the region

was removed from the administration of the Kingdom of poland and made into a separate province within the North-Western Region.[44]

Although Austria-Hungary's main concerns were with the situation in the Balkans, fearing Russian influences in Galicia, Bukovina, and Transcarpathia, the Austro-Hungarian government counteracted by tacitly supporting the anti-Russian Polish and Ukrainian national organizations. After the Russian revolution of 1904–5 the Polish émigrés from the Kingdom fled to Galicia, where under the auspices of the Austro-Hungarian intelligence services they set up paramilitary groups ready to be deployed in wartime. During the Balkan Wars some Ukrainian agents from Galicia penetrated into Russian Ukraine on missions of propaganda and sabotage. Vienna was also concerned about pro-Russian influences among the Ukrainian and Rusyn populations—the Austrian government remembered that in June 1849, when the Russian army poured into Hungary via the Carpathian passes, they were enthusiastically greeted by the Rusyns. Before the outbreak of the war, the government staged several trials, in which a number of alleged Russophiles and the Ukrainians who had converted to Orthodoxy were charged with high treason. The Austrian Gendarmerie compiled lists of potentially unreliable individuals that included those who had visited Russia, the Russophiles, and pro-Russian sympathizers, all to be arrested in case of war. The Russian–Austrian confrontation reached its peak during the Balkan Wars, when the two sides accused each other of subversive activities. In November 1912 the Russian Ambassador to Vienna, Nicholas Girs, plainly stated that as long as Galician–Polish and Galician–Ukrainian questions were unresolved, friendly relations between the two states were not foreseeable.[45]

Summary

By the turn of the twentieth century approximately 16,352,000 people lived in the borderlands, including 10,809,000 on the Russian and 5,543,000 on the Austro-Hungarian side of the border. Situated on the fringes of the empires, the borderlands were 'incomplete societies',[46] where modernity coexisted with the outdated socio-economic structures and socio-economic inequalities coincided with ethno-cultural categories, often defined in terms of religion. Outside the Baltic region the economic patterns remained essentially the same—the majority of the population was suffering acute land-hunger, the industrial force remained small, and economic and political power was still wielded by the economic and political elite. At the same time, the late nineteenth century witnessed the growth of cultural and national awareness of the 'subordinated' people as their national movements began to emerge. However for the predominantly agricultural and ill-educated communities, social and economic reforms proved to be more attractive than the dim vision of national independence. In fact, socio-economic interdependence in the borderlands—across provincial and state borders—provided the environment in which different ethnic groups became closely connected to each other, by performing their respective social functions.

The military and strategic concerns spurred the Austro-Hungarian and Russian governments to begin an overhaul of the countries' socio-economic and military apparatus. In an attempt to emulate the 'dual' revolution in Western Europe, the industrialization process in the borderlands generated an impressive economic growth. Although the Austro-Hungarian and Russian governments aimed at the same objectives—keeping together their diverse domains—their methods reflected different imperial ideologies. In the nineteenth century the Austrian (Austro-Hungarian) empire was transformed into a highly bureaucratic state that operated on the basis of *Aufklärung*—the idea that a content and prosperous population constituted the foundation for a strong state. Hence, the imperial 'live and let live policies' or, in the words of an Austrian statesman, keeping everyone in the state of 'bearable dissatisfaction',[47] were to guarantee that all subjects would carry out their civil and military duties and to mitigate the potentiality of ethnic conflict. In contrast, the Russian government consistently resisted any constitutional experiments, and the concepts of autocracy, rigid Orthodoxy, and the estate-based order remained the key foundations of the imperial order. A few years after the revolution of 1905–7, once the government felt secure enough, it reversed its concessions and resumed its traditional policies, demonstrating that any substantial political changes in Russia could not be achieved through democratic processes.

Although in the course of the nineteenth century a number of ethnic groups had 'rediscovered' their national identity and the rigid social order caused deep frustrations and antagonisms, traditional social barriers, a low literacy rate, and limited urbanization delayed the process of nation-building. In addition, serious antagonisms among the most advanced national groups helped the imperial governments maintain the status quo. The

Estonians and Latvians looked for Russian protection against the Germans, the Ukrainians in Galicia sought Vienna's support against assimilatory Polish practices, and even the Russian Jews preferred the 'normality' of everyday official anti-Semitism to the fury of a mob.

In sum, despite profound socio-economic divisions and ethnic animosities, with the exception of the Polish uprisings and the first Russian revolution, the borderlands remained largely violence-free. Even the Polish national movement that had managed to attract to its banners large numbers of workers and peasants, exercised limited political power. The future Prime Minister of independent Lithuania, Augustinas Voldemaras, admitted that 'to strive for complete separation from Russia in 1905 would have been madness. Nobody would have made such demands, not even the Poles, even though a Polish problem was [officially] recognized'.[48] However, the increased state reliance on repressive methods to deal with civilians and the fusion of social and ethnic conflicts, especially in the time of deep political and economic crisis, had the potential to expedite the third stage of the national awakening—mass political mobilization along ethnic lines—and transform latent animosities into violent conflicts.

2

The Reign of the Generals,
1914–1917

'The war, which could have been holy and honourable, has instead become a raid of some wild horde, into a mockery of all law and honour' lamented a Russian official upon hearing of the violence visited upon East Galicia by the Russian troops in the summer–autumn 1914.[1] Although the First World War with its predominant trench warfare on the Western Front is rarely identified with a total war against civilians, a much longer and fluid front line in the east exposed masses of the civilian population to the vicissitudes of brutal fighting. This was especially true in the borderlands that from the outbreak of the war became a huge battlefield, which eventually spilled over to the regions that lay far behind the front lines.

In addition to the flat terrain, conducive to the rapid movement of troops, other factors conditioned the severity of war in the borderlands, such as the departure from the nineteenth-century rules of warfare that were established to ameliorate violence against civilians. These rules faded away when the efficient prosecution of war demanded the total mobilization of economic and human resources and the centralization of political control. The militarization of the state necessitated more concerted efforts of political and administrative institutions such as the bureaucracy, army, and police; more sophisticated peacetime methods of population control were replaced by reprisals, hostage-taking, and mass deportations.

This chapter aims to examine the function and meaning of violence inflicted upon the borderlands by the opposing armies. It begins with the analysis of spy-mania that gripped the Austro-Hungarian and Russian armies and were translated into campaigns against specific targets. The focus then shifts to the activities of the military regimes that between 1914 and 1917 governed large parts of the borderlands from southern Latvia to East Galicia and Bukovina. Before the outbreak of the war the Austro-Hungarian and Russian governments granted their respective armies and military administrations vast powers that superseded civil authorities. Such overreaching jurisdiction imbued the military regimes with the vision that the territories under their jurisdiction had to be secured militarily and politically. Since military policies were shaped by the belligerents' official war aims, the crucial ingredients of national unity such as ethnicity, race, and religion became the catalysts for loyalty and patriotism. Consequently, the military regimes exacerbated the pre-existing ethnic tensions by targeting allegedly 'hostile' and privileging 'friendly' ethnic communities in regard to religion, language, education, and property ownership. Such 'mobilization of ethnicity' became a rudiment of the total war, expanding it far beyond the areas of combat. At the same time, these policies boosted the pre-war national movements and ultimately precipitated the disintegration of the Austro-Hungarian and Russian empires.[2]

The anti-spy campaign on the Eastern Front

At the outbreak of the war the multi-ethnic subjects of the Kaiser and the Tsar turned up en masse at the recruiting stations. In the Austrian borderland provinces the populations joined in patriotic demonstrations professing loyalty to the ruler. The Jewish communities donated large sums for war effort, while the Polish and Ukrainian volunteers flocked to the banners of the national units—the Polish Legions and the Ukrainian Sharpshooters—which took part in ferocious frontier battles. In Russia the multi-ethnic population acted in a similar fashion. Some protestations of loyalty were certainly genuine, but each ethnic group also hoped that loyalty in the time of crisis would win more concessions, ease restrictions, or inaugurate more liberal government policies.[3]

If popular response to the call to arms should have pacified the imperial governments' concerns over the loyalty of their subjects, persecution of alleged spies and saboteurs soon nullified initial enthusiasm. Accusations of espionage, resistance, and collaboration with the enemy that were proffered against entire ethnic groups eventually became a source and a tool of policy-making in the borderlands. Such evolutions, however, were not confined solely to the Eastern Front, for since the beginning of the war spy-mania affected all the belligerent countries and reached as far from the battlefields as Australia and Canada.[4] Nevertheless, in the countries immediately affected by fighting the speedy militarization of society and the drive for national unity generated the cultivation of the sense of insecurity and fear. The diversity of the borderlands, where particular 'stimulus qualities' of 'outgroups' generated suspicions or hostility and dated back decades or centuries, was a crucial factor. Accordingly, the state that practised persecution in peacetime was prone to behave in more extreme manner during the war. Such an argument, however, seems less applicable to Austria-Hungary, known in peacetime as the 'Rechtsstaat' (the state based on law) and yet first to display an obsessive fear of spies and saboteurs lurking behind the front lines. Hence, a structural commonality—unpreparedness for war that entailed military setbacks—might help to explain the brutal conduct of the two armies.

In the Austrian case, the confusion of priorities between the Russian and the Balkan fronts created chaos on communication lines and transfer of troops to the two theatres of operations lagged far behind the schedule. The defeats suffered by the Austrian armies in East Galicia and Serbia in the summer–fall 1914 reverberated in rumours of sabotage. When the Austrian intelligence intercepted pro-Russian proclamations issued by several Russophile groups, the military decided that they had enough grounds to launch a large-scale preventive action. The military, the police, and the Gendarmerie shut down the Russophile organizations and clubs, confiscated their property, and froze financial assets. Simultaneously, individuals suspected of connections with the Russophiles were arrested and detained; many spent months in prison without being interrogated. Soon, however, suspicions of treason and disloyalty were cast on all the Rusyns and eventually, Ukrainians.[5]

Although reprisals were mounted by army commanders, it was the rapid militarization of the state that removed legal barriers for collective punishment. Shortly before the war the Austrian government issued special decrees that placed the potential front-zones under the military regimes that were empowered to deploy extraordinary measures against individuals who displayed pro-Russian, pro-Serbian, or anti-military orientations.[6] In turn, the inability to stem the Russian advance fuelled the tendency of the military to ascribe its failures to the ill-deeds of internal enemies. Contrary to peacetime state policies that strove to preserve a relative balance between different nationalities of the empire, the official propaganda spread public hysteria, all the more malicious since it was directed against Austria-Hungary's own citizens. For example, the Minister of the Interior accused the 'entire Ukrainian peasantry led by the popes' in treachery, and in some instances government officials tolerated lynch-justice as raging mobs assaulted the arrested suspects. In such atmosphere the latent ethnic or personal animosities were bound to surface, especially after the military offered financial rewards for information on suspicious activities. The Ukrainian national activists hastened to blame the Russophiles for collaboration with the Russians, whereas the Polish political elite used the opportune moment to accuse all Ukrainians of disloyalty. For the Austrian commanders, especially those of Hungarian background, the proximity of the Ukrainian language and the Rusyn dialect were a subtle nuance. Acting upon these denunciations, they launched mass arrests of the Ukrainian intelligentsia, priests, and completely apolitical individuals, who became victims of blanket military justice. Investigation and court procedure were limited to a minimum and the testimony of one witness sufficed for a verdict of guilty; even the Parliament members of Ukrainian descent were denied immunity.[7]

Extraordinary measures reached their peak simultaneously with the progression of the Russian offensive. On 31 August 1914, the Supreme Court of Galicia suspended jury trials and prohibited the functioning of civic organizations. The police were empowered to search premises and make arrests without warrants, and civilians became liable to courts martial in the districts where mobilization was under way. In early September, after the Austrian army abandoned L'viv, the commanders in Galicia and Bukovina received extraordinary powers to execute on the spot any suspicious individuals. Gallows were erected in Ukrainian and Romanian villages—since most Romanians were Eastern Orthodox it sufficed to generate suspicions of treasonous activities—and hundreds of individuals whose guilt was never established were hanged and left on trees along streets and roads. In October 1914, when the Russian army entered Transcarpathia, the Austrian troops began reprisals against the Rusyn population, whose cultural and linguistic proximity to the Russians was a sufficient ground for suspicions of disloyalty. Eventually, to stem a growing number of arrests and executions, the Austrian military was compelled to issue a circular, reminding the troops that they *were not* in the enemy's territory. Altogether about 30,000 individuals, including women and children, were executed in Galicia or sent to concentration camps in Austria and Bohemia, where they lingered in appalling conditions until the spring 1917 amnesty.[8]

As brutal as Austrian reprisals were, they targeted particular political groups and individuals—vaguely defined—rather than Ukrainians and the Rusyns as entire ethnic communities, and displayed a mixture of severity and restraint. Eventually, by the winter of 1915, the wave of reprisals subsided. That such measures were extraordinary, propelled by specific circumstances, was attested to by Ukrainians continuing to serve in the administration and the Parliament. The Ukrainian military personnel fought with distinction in the ranks of the imperial army until the end of the war— a clear indication that, disgusted as they might have been at the persecution of their kin, they perceived it as an aberration rather than a rule.

★ ★ ★

Similarly to its Austro-Hungarian counterpart, Russia was woefully unprepared to wage a long, modern war. Although the government began a large-scale rearmament programme before the war, Russia's military-industrial capacity was still below the level of the major European powers. Contrary to conventional wisdom, the imperial industries produced a sufficient volume of military hardware, but there was not enough railway rolling-stock to timely deliver troops and munitions to the front. Despite a number of well-trained and capable senior officers, the Russian high command in general proved inefficient in conducting large-scale military operations. These factors had profound psychological consequences upon the army and Russian society at large, and from the beginning of the war generated ever-growing anxieties over shadow forces undermining the country's war efforts.[9]

Immense powers invested in the Russian military also became a main source of gross abuses and violence in the front-zone. On 29 July 1914 the Tsar signed a decree entitled 'The Regulations for Field Administration of the Army in Wartime' that placed the entire territory west of St Petersburg and Smolensk and south along the Dnieper River to the Black Sea— including the borderland provinces—under the jurisdiction of the Supreme Command (*Stavka*). The military establishment thus evolved into a virtually independent entity, operating outside the framework of any peacetime authority and treating the civilian population according to its own conceptions of rules of warfare.[10]

Determined to avoid what it considered the counter-intelligence failures in the Russo-Japanese War, the army became the driving force of 'vigilantism'— a euphemistic term for the persecution of alleged internal enemies that especially gained momentum after the two Russian armies were wiped out in East Prussia. The defeat profoundly shocked Russian society and dispelled popular hopes for the speedy and victorious termination of the war. Because the Austro-Germans were able to intercept Russian radio messages, the Russian military's anxieties over enemy agents in and outside the front-zone became overwhelming. Such attitudes were fraught with consequences, since according to the 'Regulations' all matters of intelligence and counter-intelligence were Stavka's direct prerogative (handled by its Quartermaster-General) and its guidelines on combating spies were received by the army commanders as direct orders. Consequently, as Stavka insisted upon more stringent security measures, the troops' propensity to believe that at any given moment they could be ambushed mutated into a penultimate concern. The conjuncture of vigilantism from the top and lower echelons of the military created a psychological context in which violence was conceived as a prevention measure and developed into a dominant theme. Such attitudes were bound to affect the borderland areas, where the diversity and the professional occupation of many residents as traders, peddlers, and smugglers made them particularly suitable for intelligence activities.[11]

The wave of reprisals against alleged saboteurs began in the occupied districts of East Prussia, where the Russian commanders threatened to punish entire communities for any act of resistance; in some instances Russian units executed suspicious individuals and burned houses from where the alleged shots were fired. In content, such measures did not contravene the provisions of the 1899 Hague Convention that obliged irregular combatants to wear clearly identified uniforms and insignia. The Russian army's logic, therefore, was that if these rules were not followed, the Convention lost its power.[12] Indeed, the Germans deployed similar practices in Belgium, where the activities of the franc-tireur resisters generated mass reprisals against civilians. In their form, however, the Russian reprisals deviated from the conventional definition of reprisals, for they almost immediately evolved into random pillaging of the occupied localities under the pretext of 'searches' for potential resisters and hidden arms. German civilians also suffered casualties—according to different sources between 1,620 and 6,000 civilians died during the two Russian occupations (in February–March 1915 the Russian troops briefly captured several districts of East Prussia), although many may have fallen victim to actual combat. During retreat the Russians burned houses and buildings, whose destruction was designed as a strategic tool to deprive the enemy of valuable resources.[13]

If in East Prussia the brevity of Russian rule spared the population from the worst abuses, in East Galicia and Bukovina violence against civilians immediately assumed ethnic dimensions. The Russian troops specifically targeted the German settlements, which were plundered; individuals who resisted or delayed giving up goods were flogged. The worst cruelties, however, were exacted upon the Jewish communities, which suffered a series of devastating pogroms from Lithuania to Bukovina. In contrast to pre-war anti-Jewish violence, the military pogroms were carried out in the form of punitive expeditions and were better organized, more thorough, and more destructive. Certainly, combat fatigue, anxiety over the enemies lurking in the shadows, and the inability to comprehend a population that spoke different languages caused psychological distress and engendered a propensity to release frustrations in the form of violent outbursts. Also, most contemporaries recalled that plunder and looting, especially by the Cossacks, who traditionally practised robbery and plunder as an inseparable part of warfare, were the most ubiquitous element of the pogroms. In this regard, the Russian commanders followed a tradition of letting troops go on the rampage as a reward for capturing a town or a city. Practised by many armies since antiquity and known as the 'tax of violence',[14] such easy and fast methods made up for supply shortages, especially as the Russian communication lines were extended to the limit and the troops often remained hungry and poorly clothed. Hence, the pogroms evolved along a 'classic' formula—alleged shots were more often than not registered from the most affluent houses and shops, which were then subjected to plunder. Violence became a highly profitable enterprise—for example, after the occupation of Chernivtsi (Chernowitz) in early September 1914, the Cossacks and soldiers plundered the town for an entire week and then sold their loot on a market square under the conniving eyes of the officers.[15]

While the Russian commanders were willing to tolerate the predatory instincts of their subordinates for practical reasons, ideological aspects of violence made it more systematic and brutal. From the beginning of the war *Stavka*, particularly its Chief-of-Staff Nicholas Yanushkevich, became a major source of virulent anti-Semitic propaganda actively cultivating the fears of Jews as the most resilient, wily, and dangerous foe. The Russian military had long conceived that the Pale of Settlement would be the breeding ground for spies and saboteurs, and numerous situational reports to and from *Stavka* referred to Jews as enemy spotters, agents, and guides. For example, the court martial of the 10th Army Corps in Galicia sentenced fifteen Jewish 'arsonists, robbers, and spies' to flogging—a clear indication that the court possessed no incriminating evidence, for such crimes were as a rule punished by death.[16]

Significantly, *Stavka* did not just blame Jews for carrying out diversionary activities, but charged them with coordinating a huge network of anti-Russian resistance. To this effect the anti-Russian propaganda carried out by the Jewish organizations in Germany and Austria-Hungary and the German army's appeals to Russian Jews served as ample proof of international Jewish conspiracy. Hence, the official vilification of Jews effectively exonerated any violent act committed against them. Accordingly, many Russian officers and soldiers came to believe that the war against the Central Powers was also a war against the Jews. A Jewish doctor who spent a night with a group of Russian officers recalled that they were obsessed with the vision of the 'traitorous Jew', which dominated all conversations.[17] Although anti-Semitic propaganda was conspicuously crude, it fitted perfectly into the mindset of the predominantly peasant army, which easily absorbed anti-Jewish imageries since they correlated with traditional superstitions and biases against Jews. In Galicia and Bukovina the Cossacks and soldiers conveyed to the population that they had come to free them from the 'Jewish yoke'. In some instances, the Russians incited the population to anti-Jewish excesses and frequently, having looted Jewish stores and houses, distributed the booty to the Christian populace. If assaults on German settlements were mostly limited to robbery, rape and murder in the Jewish communities also became a frequent occurrence. The ideological character of war against the Jews translated into a whole cluster of rituals of degradation and humiliation. The troops forced Jews to dance, ride on pigs—insulting the sensibilities of religious Jews—crawl, or run naked. Such behaviour symbolized the end of the old Austro-Hungarian order, from which Jews putatively derived most benefits.[18]

Anti-Jewish violence also involved local residents, who, egged on by the Russian troops, turned against their neighbours. Although some assailants may have acted out of the desire to settle scores with individual Jews, especially those who during the Austrian reprisal campaign displayed a conspicuously hostile attitude to alleged traitors, in all likelihood the opportunity to rob with impunity was the most prevalent impulse. Groups and individuals guided the soldiers to Jewish houses and shops, where they received part of the loot. At the end of September 1914, inflamed by rumours of shots fired from a Jewish-owned house, the troops and the local rabble descended upon the Jewish quarters in L'viv and subjected them to vicious pillaging and destruction; between twenty and fifty Jews were murdered and more than a hundred wounded. Conversely, once Poles and Ukrainians realized that their ethnic credentials could protect them from undesired intruders, they adorned their houses and apartments with icons and crosses.[19]

By autumn 1914, with the establishment of the military administration in Galicia and Bukovina, 'wild' violence visibly subsided. While the Russian command consented to the troops' rampages for a short spell, it could not afford to tolerate them indefinitely, for the pogroms compromised military discipline, especially since the official propaganda accentuated the 'liberating mission' of the Russian army. As important were *Stavka*'s political objectives of the integration of Galicia and Bukovina into the Empire and the consequent appropriation of the provinces' economic and financial assets. In this context, the troops' 'misbehaviour' was certainly counterproductive.

The Russian nationalization campaign

Throughout the war the borderlands lived under two opposing military regimes that bestowed upon themselves the combined task of military conquest and administration of the occupied territories. To this effect, the military regimes established a far-reaching system of population control, acting upon the preconceived ideological and cultural notions in regard to each ethnic group. Although the Russian and the Austro-German military administrations differed in their methods of achieving these objectives, they were similar in conceiving their overriding objectives as of a military and political nature.

As the generals mapped the geography and ethnicity of the future war-zones, they expected the civilian populations to provide services and supplies, but also envisioned that the war offered an unprecedented opportunity to blend the borderlands ideologically, administratively, and economically with the rest of the Empire. The Russian government thought in the same vein, contemplating the logistical necessity to utilize the borderlands' economic, material, and human resources. Such convergence of interests between the military and civil administration, did not, however, produce a uniformity of opinion. Whereas the government advocated a more cautious approach, the military pressed for immediate 'Russification', for the ethno-cultural diversity of the borderlands and the secure home front were irreconcilable political and cultural constructs and inhibited the successful prosecution of the war. Consequently, each ethnic group was to be judged upon its usefulness or potential danger to the state's war efforts, while a determined and comprehensive campaign against allegedly danger-ous groups would permanently situate the borderlands within the pattern of Russian national domination.

A massive nationalization campaign involved a systematic assault on specific targets, initially the nationals of the Central Powers, but eventually it engulfed Russian citizens as well. The first attempts to 'remould' the borderlands began in the Baltic provinces that were made subject to the 'Regulations'. Owing to the economic vitality of the region, however, the civil administration was left intact although the military retained priorities in defence and security matters. In August 1914 *Stavka* and the Ministry of the Interior proposed the expulsion of the Baltic-Germans, arguing that the German communities' 'detached existence from the Russian population' made them a potential base for subversive activities. The Russian right-wing press echoed such accusations and launched a slanderous campaign presenting all Germans as implacable enemies of the Empire, while extolling Estonians and Latvians as the most loyal subjects of the Tsar. The new 'Russification' cycle ensued, following the pattern established at the end of the nineteenth century, when the government temporarily encouraged Estonian and Latvian national aspirations at the expense of the Germans. The German schools were closed, and professional unions and cultural organizations were shut down. Such policies, however, immediately revealed the potential for ethnic conflict far behind the front line, for, sensing an opportune moment, the Estonian and Latvian press vehemently attacked the Germans; some articles called for 'revenge', invoking the images of the punitive expeditions of 1905–7. A number of Latvians and Estonians became voluntary detectives and informants for the Russian police, providing deliberately falsified information about the alleged espio-nage among the Germans. The Russian defeat in East Prussia spawned a new spiral of anti-German hysteria and the press spread stories about the subver-sive activities of the Baltic Germans. Orders to remove German shop and street signs and the banning of the German language in public places were accompanied by police searches and arrests of prominent Germans. Since German landowners used their influence to avoid the army's requisitions of cattle and horses, these were extracted from Estonian and Latvian peasants, fuelling their hostility to the Germans in general. By mid-November the Council of Ministers had banned German publications and assemblies. These measures corresponded with the army's confiscations and sequestration of property belonging to the German nationals in East Galicia and Bukovina, where the military began the process of 'nationalizing' the provinces.[20]

Still concerned about potential unrest in the time of war—certainly the memories of the revolutionary turmoil were still fresh—the Russian civil administration conducted a thorough investigation and concluded that the accusations of espionage and treason among the Baltic Germans emanated from wartime 'nervousness'. Russian authorities issued several ordinances that explicitly qualified any act of inciting national tensions as criminal. Realizing that anti-German measures would stimulate Estonian and Latvian national aspirations, the government decided to shelve the nationalization campaign until the end of the war. It displayed a similar caution when the 'Liquidation Law' signed by the Tsar in February 1915 eliminated land-ownership by Austro-Hungarian and German subjects within 160 kilometres of the front line; the Russian Germans were prohibited from purchasing property and had to give up their property located in the countryside. Since the implementation of the law entailed an assault on the two-century old socio-economic tradition, the Council of Ministers specified that the Law applied only to those Germans who had received Russian citizenship after 1880.[21]

Russian policies in the occupied Austrian provinces also revealed the contradictions between nationalist ideology and imperial expansionism. Since the military conquest was conducted under the slogans of 'liberation', after the outbreak of the war the Supreme Commander Grand Duke Nicholas and the Tsar issued appeals to the Poles that vaguely promised the fulfilment of Polish national aspirations under Russian rule. The Grand Duke made a similar appeal to the 'Russian people' (the term applied to the Ukrainians and Rusyns) of Galicia, Bukovina, and Transcarpathia, and the Russian press hailed Russian victories as the final stroke in the unification of these 'primordial' Russian lands. Issuing the appeals, however, failed to produce the desired result of winning over the two communities, for making Galicia 'Russian' effectively implied the end of the Polish dominance in the province and entailed the treatment of the Ukrainians as the inferior 'lost tribe'.[22]

Meanwhile the *Stavka* and the government disagreed on immediate policies in regard to the new territorial acquisitions. The military pressed for immediate integration of Galicia and Bukovina into the imperial administrative structure, whereby the Poles would temporarily retain their traditional privileges and the Ukrainians would be subjected to a systematic 're-education' campaign that would turn them into pliant imperial subjects. The government, however, objected on the grounds that any territorial changes were premature and had to be coordinated with the Allies; Russian statesmen were also concerned that the annexation of Bukovina would alienate Romania. In November a compromise was reached: it was decided that Galicia and Bukovina would be fully integrated into the Empire, but only after the war. For the time being all political measures had to be subordinated to immediate war aims.[23]

Nevertheless the government consented to the idea that some preparatory steps could be implemented instantly. On 18 September 1914 the Russian military administration—the General-Government—took over power in Galicia and Bukovina and the army retained its jurisdiction over the immediate 50-kilometre front-zone. Such division of authority was deemed optimal for governing the occupied territories. Initially, the army and the military administration advocated conciliatory policies towards the Ukrainians, who were conceived as 'duped' by the pre-war Austrian policies. The 're-education' campaign began with the requests for government subsidies for Ukrainian peasants and promotion of individuals known for pro-Russian sympathies to positions in the administration. The Russian language was made mandatory in schools, and the Orthodox Church launched a forcible proselytizing campaign that affected entire Ukrainian villages; by November about 30,000 Ukrainians had been converted. At the same time, the military administration tried to appease the Poles by retaining most of the Polish civil employees, allowing Polish publications (albeit under strict censorship), and outward forbearance of the Roman Catholic Church.[24]

These attitudes, however, did not last long. Ideological objectives of winning over the Slavic populations came under pressure from the field commanders, who were unable to feed their troops via regular supply lines and conducted constant confiscations and requisitions that soon alienated the countryside. Suspicions of 'corrosive' elements, acting to the detriment of the Russian rule, were heightened by the activities of the 'Union for the Liberation of Ukraine' (SVU)—a Vienna-based Ukrainian organization that waged anti-Russian propaganda. In autumn 1914 suspicions of 'Mazepism' (the label derived from the name of the Ukrainian Cossack leader Ivan Mazepa, who sided with the Swedes during the Russo-Swedish war of 1700–21) translated into the ban on the Greek Catholic Church; its property was taken over by the Orthodox Church. Armed police confiscated the property of the Ukrainian educational and cultural institutions. A number of prominent Ukrainian politicians and civic leaders, including the head of the Greek Catholic Church Metropolitan Andrej Sheptyts´kyi, were arrested and deported. Repressions also affected Polish politicians and officers suspected of anti-Russian orientation. These measures coincided with police repressions in eastern Ukraine, acquiring the trappings of all-out assault on the Ukrainian national movement.[25]

Ethnically tainted economic restrictions were also devised as the tools for the nationalizing of the borderlands. In September 1914 the army began sequestering the land belonging to Poles and Jews who had fled from Galicia and Bukovina and the property of the German businesses and cultural organizations. *Stavka* in particular was determined to 'solve' the Jewish question and insisted that the application of imperial laws in the occupied territories was the ultimate solution to this thorny issue. To this effect, it pressed the government to impose Russian citizenship upon the Galician and Bukovinian Jews. Such a step would make Jews liable to the confiscation of land and the deportations deep into Russia-proper, effectively eradicating Jewish economic and cultural influence as the paramount vestige of the Austrian rule; simultaneously, similar measures would be launched throughout the Empire. *Stavka* was echoed by the right-wing press that called the war a godsend opportunity to eliminate the Jews altogether as a socio-economic force. In contrast, the Russian nationalists argued that the Jews should be stripped of citizenship, deprived of property, and expelled from the country altogether. Meanwhile in Galicia and Bukovina the army banned publications and schooling in German and Yiddish; public use, artistic performances, and exhibitions in these languages were prohibited.[26]

Although the November 1914 government decision prevented the realization of *Stavka*'s plans, the military succeeded in destroying the socioeconomic foundations of Jewish life in Galicia and Bukovina. In February 1915, shortly after the introduction of the Liquidation Law, the Grand Duke issued an order that limited the movement of Jews in the frontzone, severely affecting Jewish trade. By spring 1915 the nationalization campaign in Galicia and Bukovina had eliminated Jews from any positions of influence; random requisitions and confiscations by the troops devastated most Jewish communities. A prominent Jewish civic activist, Solomon An-Ski, during his passage through Galicia in autumn and winter 1914–1915 found that Jews travelled only at night on country roads, circumventing larger towns and often under the paid protection of a soldier. Jewish shops, synagogues, and warehouses were plundered or appropriated by the local garrisons, and the population took over empty Jewish houses or dismantled them for firewood. Jewish life came to a standstill and, correspondingly, so did economic life in the borderlands. A Bukovinian contemporary described this situation succinctly 'no Jews, no shops'.[27]

★ ★ ★

Perhaps the most cruel feature of the military operations on the Eastern Front was the mass relocation of civilians. To begin with, rumours of Russian atrocities generated the flight of up to 800,000 German refugees from East Prussia. During the Austrian retreat in August–September 1914 between 250,000 and 300,000 people left Galicia and Bukovina. Desperate to stem the enemy's advance and deprive him of supplies, the Austrian military burned entire villages, forcing out hundreds of residents. Droves of cold and hungry refugees trudged alongside retreating troops, succumbing to hunger and epidemics.[28]

In contrast to the Austrian high command that conceived such measures as extraordinary and temporary, the Russian military conducted mass relocations of civilians as tactical and strategic measures—'cleansing' (*ochishchenie*) the front-zone from potentially unreliable elements and a part of the nationalization campaign to alter permanently the socio-economic profile of the borderlands. Accordingly, between 1915 and 1917 the Eastern Front witnessed one of the largest forcible migrations in modern history.

The Russian army had considerable experience in the removal of large masses of civilians. During the conquest of the Caucasus and the Crimean War it deported or expelled entire 'unredeemable' Muslim communities to the Ottoman empire. These campaigns achieved their objectives of 'clearing' the strategically important Black Sea coastline and severely strained the economic resources of Russia's arch-enemy. On the eve of the First World War the Russian contingency plans also included the removal of certain ethnic groups from the strategically sensitive areas. In late July 1914 the Russian General Staff and the Ministry of the Interior issued orders to the army to deport German nationals from several areas in Kurland, around

Riga and from Suwałki. On 1 August, the day Russia entered the war, the Russian General Staff authorized the commanders of the military districts to deport the subjects of the Central Powers east of the Volga River.[29]

Initially, the military aimed to prevent able-bodied foreign males from being drafted into enemy armies. While such measures were not exceptional—enemy-nationals were interned in other countries affected by the war, including Australia and the United States—the Russian deportations engulfed women, children, and the elderly, who clearly did not constitute potential manpower for the enemy. Already in early August 1914 *Stavka* ordered deportations of any suspicious individuals from the front-zone, and the army targeted specifically Russian nationals of German and Jewish background, who represented a crucial socio-economic cross-section in the national economy. In late August about 1,500 'unreliable' Jews from the Khotin district of Bessarabia were expelled to Podolia; in September deportations and expulsions affected Jews and Germans in the Kingdom and Lifland. In Galicia and Bukovina the army deported a number of the German intelligentsia, Jews, and Poles suspected of anti-Russian disposition. As the deportations gained pace, an Evangelist priest recalled that the population lived in constant fear, for 'everybody lost any sense of security'. Increasingly, the Russian military began referring to the deportations as 'cleansing' or 'clearing' the territory under its jurisdiction, implying the intended totality of such operations.[30] If the first wave of forcible migration in the summer–autumn of 1914 affected several regions, the second, more systematic and coordinated, began in winter 1915 along the entire front line. Between February and May 1915 the army deported about 160,000 Jews from the Kaunas province. The fundamental principle for defining who was liable to deportation was landholding—the army specifically targeted property-owning Germans and Jews, pushing for the socio-economic homogeneity of the borderlands.[31]

In early May, after a massive Austro-German offensive shattered the Russian front, *Stavka* ordered a general retreat. Simultaneously, orders were given for a scorched earth policy in the path of the enemy, a tactic successfully practised by the Russians on several occasions, most recently during the French invasion of 1812. People, machinery, grain, and cattle were to be evacuated to the east; from Kurland to Bukovina the Russian troops burned and destroyed bridges, railroads, locomotives, and oil wells, while special detachments forced the population, especially draft-aged men, eastward. The evacuation was accompanied by wholesale expulsions of the

Germans and Jews from Kurland and Kaunas provinces and in June–July from Volhynia and Bessarabia. Fearful of Austro-German brutalities against the Slavic people—such rumours were deliberately disseminated by Russian propaganda—thousands of Ukrainians, Rusyns, and Byelorussians also made up huge columns of refugees, who in search of food stripped the fields and gardens along the roads. Meanwhile a wall of fire rose behind as the Cossack units burned the abandoned houses and barns. An eyewitness recalled that the columns trudged eastward 'beset by moaning and crying . . . Human and animal corpses littered the roads, and fresh graves stared at us with wooden crosses'.[32]

The 'Great Retreat' severely debilitated Russia's war effort. The mass influx of the largely destitute people produced a colossal economic crisis that soon engulfed entire provinces in Russia-proper, rapidly depleting food supplies and financial resources. The government was overwhelmed by the wave of protests from the provincial authorities, who faced insurmountable problems of housing and feeding the multitudes of new arrivals. In some provinces the urban population doubled and tripled as the towns and cities were flooded by human waves. For example, by the end of the summer 80,000 refugees were encamped at Roslavl', a small town in Smolensk province with a pre-war population of 28,000. The imperial railroads were overburdened with transporting the masses of refugees instead of troops and military hardware. Combined with the devastating defeats at the front, epidemics, economic shortages, and social tensions created an acute atmosphere of panic and the sense of impending doom. In distress, the Council of Ministers warned that a 'huge human wave is spreading over Russia, heightening [negative] tempers', while a prominent statesman predicted that 'this second Great migration of the people' had the potential to drag Russia into the 'abyss of revolution and destruction'. Although the Russian ministers vehemently protested against the heavy-handed rule of the military—even the Tsarina pleaded with her husband to intervene with *Stavka*—the latter remained aloof.[33]

Stavka clung all the more to the idea that the deportations helped the attempted nationalization campaign. When the deportations of the German colonists began from Volhynia, they were given ten days to sell their property or otherwise lose it without compensation. Their land was slated for distribution among the Slavic refugees from Galicia and Poland (the army used the same ethnically orientated practices in 1916, when about 7,000 Germans were deported from Lifland and their property, schools, and hospitals were passed over to the Latvians). However, not only did the deportations divest the land of a skilled agricultural work force at harvest time, but the accretion and distribution of the collected economic assets—a principal objective of deportations and expulsions—eventually ended in failure. While some members of the Russian-'friendly' ethnic groups were allowed to buy abandoned goods and property and prospered at the expense of their neighbours, the confiscated livestock and agricultural implements were stolen by local residents or sold off by corrupt Russian officials, who made fortunes.[34]

The deportations and expulsions sparked a new cycle of pogroms. In contrast to the 'wild' violence in 1914, now the Russian troops had direct orders to destroy anything of value and thus had a free hand to loot and burn at will. The Jewish communities again were singled out as the troops acted more like bands of thugs than regular units. Indeed, once the orders to remove the populations were given, it was natural that the Cossacks and soldiers plundered houses and shops before setting them on fire. Rape and murder became rampant since the commanders could not control the actions of their subordinates; some tolerated the violence as inevitable. Concerned over the breakdown of military discipline, the Grand Duke was compelled to issue an order that subjected commanders who incited pogroms to courts martial. The military violence also sent a powerful signal to the population that the assaults on Jews and Germans were officially sanctioned. Consequently, town dwellers and peasants frequently appeared near the communities marked for expulsion; sometimes they waited for the refugees to leave or attacked their houses and murdered residents who stayed behind after the Russian withdrawal.[35]

Although the Great Retreat could potentially assume genocidal proportions, it was far different from the horrors inflicted upon the Armenians. The Russian military never conceived the assault on Jews or Germans as an initial stage for physical destruction (although, given different circumstances, individuals like Yanushkevich could have attempted to carry it out). Despite prevalent anti-Semitism in the army, some Russian commanders and many civil officials doubted the practicality of the persecution of Jews, which stirred negative public opinion in Russia and abroad. The government admitted that the deportations and expulsions overburdened communication lines and national finances and even forced the Ministry of the Interior to expand Jewish settlements into areas far outside of the Pale. Since American, British, and French loans and credits were paramount for

Russia's war economy, the government also worried that the mistreatment of Jews would limit Russia's access to foreign financial aid, allegedly controlled by the Jewish banks.[36]

By the end of 1915 the Great Retreat left behind huge swathes of destruction. The Russian deportations and expulsions affected approximately 1,500,000 civilians, who were displaced or fled the ravages of war and became homeless refugees and exiles far away from their homes. Kurland alone lost about 700,000—two-thirds of the population. Half a million Jews or almost a quarter of the pre-war Jewish population of the borderlands were expelled or deported. By December 1915 there were 2,706,309 officially registered refugees in Russia (including those from the Caucasian Front).[37]

Besides economic and psychological damage, another outcome—certainly unplanned and undesired by the Russian military—was the facilitation of stronger national ties among the affected minorities. The refugee and exile communities became the most propitious grounds for national activities, since common suffering engendered the sense of common destiny and convictions that ethnic affiliation and ethnic identity overrode political or social cleavages. Organized by the native intelligentsia, various relief organizations collected money and food for refugee communities, but also stressed the need for cultural and political autonomy for their ethnic constituencies, emphasized necessity of more liberal imperial policies, and cultivated the sense of national identity. These organizations operated on both sides of the front lines and gradually evolved into the focal points of nationalist and revolutionary activities. The Tallinn branch of the All-Russian Union of Cities became the centre for the Estonian liberal and democratic elements. Simultaneously, the committee leaders gained necessary political and management experience. Janis Čakste, a leader of the Latvian Central Welfare Committee, was destined to be a future president of Latvia; the Russian lawyer Martynas Ycas, a principal personality of the Lithuanian Welfare Committee in Petrograd, would become a minister of finance in independent Lithuania; and Antanas Smetona, the last president of pre-Second World War Lithuania, ran another relief committee in Vilnius. Initially, the leadership of these organizations promoted ideas of autonomy for their native lands within democratic Russia. For example, the Lithuanian committees envisioned culturally and politically autonomous Lithuania (including the Suwałki *gubernia*) with its own parliament in Vilnius.[38]

Although such activities definitely contradicted pre-war official policies, the critical situation at the front forced the Russian government to tolerate the national aspirations of its subjects as long as the latter helped facilitate the war effort. To counter the formation of the Polish and Ukrainian national units by the Central Powers, in January 1915 the Russian military conceded the formation of a Polish Legion. In July the Polish soldiers under the Russian and Austrian banners met in a battle near Białystok. Emboldened by the good performance of the Legion and heeding the pleas of the Latvian national activists, in August the military also ordered the formation of the Latvian national battalions that eventually expanded to 130,000 men and evolved into crack units of the Russian army.[39]

The Central Powers in ascendance

By autumn 1915 the Central Powers had occupied huge tracts of Russian territory, including the Kingdom of Poland, almost all Lithuania, parts of Latvia (the front line ran just west of Riga), and western Byelorussia and Volhynia; the Austrians recaptured East Galicia, where the Russians clung to a narrow land-strip around Ternopil', and Bukovina. The bulk of the conquered territories—the Russian provinces of Kurland, Suwałki, Vilnius, Hrodna, and Białystok—were placed under the German military administration known as the *Ober-Ost* and nominally headed by the German Supreme Commander in the east, Paul Hindenburg, but in actuality by his deputy, General Erich Ludendorff. The Austro-Hungarian army governed Galicia, Bukovina, Volhynia, and the western districts of Podolia.

The Central Powers had not elaborated any definite plans in regard to the borderlands. The Austro-Hungarian government was primarily concerned with recovering its lost territories and weakening Russia by re-establishing its hegemony in the Balkans. A number of political groups in Germany, alarmed by the high birth rates among the Polish and Jewish minorities in the German western provinces, advocated turning the borderlands into a gigantic ethnic dump, where Poles and Jews would be resettled. Other groups promoted the 'cleansing' of the borderlands for German settlers, but the failure of Bismarck's 'Kulturkampf' in the late nineteenth century merited caution against direct annexation. The idea of '*Mittel-Europa*'—a chain of puppet buffer states erected between Russia and Germany—was first discarded as impractical, but was revived in August 1915, after the

German government exempted the Kingdom of Poland from the jurisdiction of the *Ober-Ost*. Ludendorff was outraged and decided to establish what he called a 'Kingdom in Kurland and Lithuania' that was to serve as a salient for the further prosecution of war against Russia. Such a plan reflected far-reaching aspirations of creating a buffer state that would separate Russia from Europe and simultaneously provide agricultural resources and a labour force for the German military machine.[40]

In contrast to the Austrians, the Germans possessed limited knowledge about the lands and people they came to dominate. They literally felt lost in space in the huge territory traversed by flat lowlands, forests, rivers, and bogs. German propaganda, therefore, compared the German army to the Teutonic Knights as the carriers of the superior German culture 'civilizing' the East in the struggle against the hordes of barbarians. Some Austrian and German officials, who had already served in the administration of occupied Poland, decided that their experience dealing with the 'backward' Poles could be transplanted to the east. A neat partition of the borderlands into administrative units and the cataloguing of inhabitants into specific categories seemed the most viable solution for economic and security matters.[41]

Initially, the prospects for the new regime seemed quite promising. After the horrors of the Russian retreat the population welcomed and admired the discipline of the German troops and their propensity to order and cleanliness. The military regimes issued several declarations that guaranteed all ethnic groups civil equality and liberties and allowed the publications of Polish, Yiddish, and Lithuanian newspapers, and encouraged the opening of theatres, schools, and gymnasia. In Lithuania-Byelorussia the *Ober-Ost* published decrees in native languages and issued identification cards in the native language of the bearers. The mandatory introduction of German in local schools and the expansion of native educational organizations, theatrical performances, and cultural exhibits were to facilitate the integration of the borderlands into the German cultural and political domain. The ideological conversion of the natives, through German guidance, was conceived as a symbol and guarantee of the local acceptance of the new order, and the occupation system was officially presented as the completion of the 'civilizing' German mission in the East. All these measures, however, dovetailed and barely concealed political and economic imperialism, for the German military and administration operated on the assumption that the needs of the army superseded those of the occupied populations. As a result, the

Ober-Ost effectively mutated into an oppressive colonial state with its own administration, tax system, and police forces.[42]

The notion that the land was to pay for the army's expenses became the overriding objective as the war dragged on and translated into more systematic exploitation of people and resources. In autumn 1915 the extended communication lines compelled the German and Austro-Hungarian armies to begin a merciless requisition campaign of agricultural products, horses, and cattle and the confiscations of houses, shops, and commercial enterprises; forests were cut down for lumber and sold to private German firms. In Lithuania alone the Germans requisitioned 90,000 horses, 140,000 cattle, and 767,000 pigs. The borderlands' economy suffered another severe blow after the *Ober-Ost* introduced its own currency—the 'East money'—that devalued the Russian rouble and was deeply resented by the residents. A multiplicity of taxes, toll, and labour duties depleted the already meagre local financial and economic assets, leaving the population bitter and destitute. In addition, the passing troops lived off the land, robbing the residents or leaving receipts that the administration refused to honour.[43]

Accordingly, by the end of 1915 the German military regime became a close replica of its Russian predecessor and fully dissipated the initial goodwill of the population. As a result of rationing of agricultural products, flourmills, bakeries, and butcher shops ceased to function, markets emptied, hunger and epidemics spread, and throngs of sick and exhausted people overcrowded towns and cities. The military was horrified, but refused to change its economic policies. Ludendorff bluntly stated that easing economic pressure in the *Ober-Ost* 'at the cost of the homeland out of false feelings of humanity would have been an absurdity'. In similar vein Hindenburg stressed the primacy of the army and the German state over the native population. Such views were supported and implemented by German officials, who acted as satraps in their own domains and were convinced that local residents were 'parasitic', incapable of creative and productive work, and 'ungrateful' not to appreciate the fruits of German culture. Physical abuse, forced labour, arbitrary imprisonment, and executions became a routine punishment for the failure to deliver agricultural quotas.[44]

Expectedly, popular resentment evolved into resistance. Forested and marshy terrain in Kurland, Lithuania, and Byelorussia proved a suitable area for guerrilla warfare. Initially, small Russian details carried out actions behind the German lines and were aided by local residents. Deteriorating economic conditions and desertion on both sides of the front line resulted in the proliferation of armed gangs, who were joined by escaped Russian POWs and labour force dodgers. The gangs grew in strength and audacity attacking villages, killing German officials and soldiers, and imposing their own taxation system in some remote areas. The ranks of the 'Forest Brothers' swelled as more destitute and desperate residents fled to the forests. The German Gendarmes, who were responsible for security, were few and far between—a single Gendarme patrol often guarded the area of more than 170 square kilometres and several thousand inhabitants. By early 1918 in Lithuania-Byelorussia about 12,000 Germans had to control an area of 87,000 square kilometres inhabited by more than 2.5 million people. To undermine the resistance, the German administration issued orders limiting movement in the occupied areas, but it only put an additional burden on the economic activities of the population. Hence, the army increasingly thought that brutality was the only viable solution to suppress the resistance. Punitive expeditions and guerrilla attacks often followed each other in waves, while the population found itself at the receiving end of requisitioning, looting, and killing. German control over the countryside gradually eroded.[45]

The situation was no different in the Austro-Hungarian zone, where the administration treated the liberated and occupied territories as a bread basket and a source of raw materials. Requisitions, the mandatory delivery of food quotas, and mobilization for labour units exerted tremendous pressure on the civilian population in Galicia, Bukovina, and Volhynia. Economically drained and psychologically exhausted communities faced starvation and epidemics.

★ ★ ★

A distinctive feature of the Central Powers' rule in the borderlands was the nationality question. From the beginning of the war all belligerents used the 'liberationist hyperbole' that was intended to undermine the national unity of the opposing side by fostering national grievances of the disgruntled subjects.[46] The *Ober-Ost* efforts to promote schools in native languages and the proliferation of cultural and educational institutions were designed to create a relatively homogeneous administrative unit, which would be easier to govern. All residents were to perform a variety of tasks for the ultimate objective—winning the war.

However, the lack of a uniform ideological concept resulted in the application of different and often contradictory nationality policies. Although the administration encouraged the expansion of Lithuanian schools, they were to operate according to a German curriculum, while strict censorship was imposed on Lithuanian publications. As a result, an underground educational network began operating under the auspices of the Lithuanian Refugee Aid Committee; the national agitators propagated the creation of a Lithuanian state that would embrace the 'historical Lithuania'—the Suwałki and Hrodna provinces, southern Kurland, and Vilnius (despite the fact that the Lithuanians made up only 4 per cent of the city population). Similar policies were pursued towards the Byelorussians, who received the status of a distinct national group. The *Ober-Ost* authorized the opening of the Byelorussian teachers' courses and increased the numbers of Byelorussian language-schools, especially in Białystok and Hrodna regions. German functionaries and censors, however, closely scrutinized the activities of the Byelorussian clubs, teachers' unions, and publications.[47]

While German policies encouraged national aspirations in the occupied territories, they simultaneously facilitated ethnic discord. To maintain an efficient administration apparatus, the *Ober-Ost* retained the Polish employees, including those who had previously served in the Russian civil administration. In the eyes of the Lithuanians, Byelorussians, and Ukrainians these officials became the proxies of the occupation regime and incurred popular hostility. In December 1915 a German-sponsored conference that discussed the re-creation of the old Grand Duchy of Byelorussia-Lithuania as a German protectorate revealed an unbridgeable gap between the Lithuanians and Poles. While the Lithuanian delegates promoted the 'historical' Lithuania as the core area of the future Grand Duchy, the Poles, who in such a scenario would lose their traditional dominance, vehemently objected. Their recalcitrance, in turn, outraged the Germans, who decided to limit Polish influence. In the Kaunas district the administration partially supplanted the Polish language with Lithuanian, closed a number of Polish schools, and arrested and deported a number of Polish politicians, teachers, and priests. The distribution of food supplies that was conducted according to ethnicity further inflamed ethnic relations, compelling an observer to make a fateful prophecy that 'political myopia destroyed a potential for a common [Polish, Lithuanian, Byelorussian, and Jewish] future'.[48]

If the Germans were willing to lend assistance to the Polish, Lithuanian, Byelorussian, and Ukrainian groups that sought independence from Russia, different policies were pursued in the Baltic region, where the establishment of imperialist hegemony required the suppression of all national trends. Considering the Latvian national movement inimical to German political

interests—and the strong anti-German sentiments among the Latvians certainly gave validity to such views—the administration, which included a
number of the Baltic-German émigrés, suppressed the use of the Latvian
language and closed most cultural and educational organizations.[49]

A common denominator to the *Ober-Ost* nationality policies in the
borderlands was an unexpected and undesired outcome. Namely, they
facilitated the tendencies of all communities to identify themselves in ethnic
terms. As a result, the longer the war continued and the administration had
to make concessions to the groups it considered reliable, the bolder national
activists became in demanding more rights in the fields of education,
language, and broader political participation. Eventually, these demands
crystallized in the requests for autonomy under the auspices of the Great
Powers.[50]

By 1916 the Austro-Hungarian peacetime policies of co-optation of the
Polish and Ukrainian national movements seemed no longer effective, for
the two peoples became increasingly reluctant to fight merely to preserve
imperial hegemony and wanted guarantees that their contribution to the
war and sacrifices would be rewarded. Such aspirations were especially
strong among politically active Poles. Indeed, the Polish question seemed
highly complex, since the front lines divided Poland between the German,
Austro-Hungarian, and Russian military zones, making any coordination
between different Polish political groups all but impossible. At the same
time, the division of Poland accorded Polish politicians an opportunity to
manoeuvre between the three powers. The PPS leader Józef Piłsudski and
his followers considered the struggle against Russia as the main stage on the
road to independence. To this effect, Piłsudski opted for a temporary
alliance with the Central Powers and was instrumental in the creation of
the Polish Legions that were to serve as a nucleus of the future Polish army
and a rallying symbol for a mass uprising against the Tsar. When in response
to the Grand Duke's appeal in August 1914 the Central Powers issued their
own declarations—vague as they were regarding the political status of the
future Poland—they initially galvanized Polish public opinion. However,
the Central Powers' refusal to unite Galicia with the Kingdom and to create
the 'Trialistic' state of Austria, Hungary, and Poland confirmed Piłsudski's
suspicions that the Austro-Germans viewed the Legions merely as cannon
fodder. He, however, was willing to bide his time and pushed for the
expansion of the Legions, while his supporters in Poland formed underground cells that were fused into the Polish Military Organization (POW)

that ran secret training camps and prepared caches of arms. Roman Dmowski, on the other hand, who believed that Poland's re-emergence was possible only through territorial expansion, considered Germany the main enemy and banked on the victory of the Entente, hoping that after the war Russia, prodded by France and Great Britain, would be willing to concede Poland's independence. Russia's military debacle in 1915, however, delivered a crippling blow to Dmowski's orientation and he left for France, hoping to gain more support in French and British political circles.[51]

The war also generated a powerful impetus to the Ukrainian national movement. The SVU members waged active anti-Russian propaganda and with the approval of Austrian authorities oversaw the formation of a Ukrainian crack unit, the Sharpshooters, which took part in battles against the Russians in the Carpathians. Thousands of Ukrainians also fought in the ranks of the Austro-Hungarian army on all fronts of the empire. Ukrainian aspirations, however, that Galicia, Bukovina, and Transcarpathia would eventually become a single autonomous unit within the Habsburg monarchy, put them on the collision course with the Poles in Galicia and the Chełm region, with the Romanians in Bukovina, and with the Hungarians in Transcarpathia.[52]

The Polish–Ukrainian tensions heated up in the summer–autumn of 1915, when the Polish administration in Galicia spearheaded a witch-hunt for the alleged traitors among the Ukrainians; the campaign of persecution continued after the Russian retreat. Considering such a situation unacceptable and concerned that the Poles accrued too much political power, in April 1915 the Austrian government replaced the Polish Viceroy of Galicia, Witold Korytowski, who advocated sterner measures against the Ukrainians, with an Austrian general. The Austrian administration also reintroduced Ukrainian into public institutions, encouraged the proliferation of Ukrainian political, cultural, and educational organizations, and enlarged the Ukrainian Legion. To add insult to injury, the government appointed a Ukrainian as deputy-governor and the Ukrainian representation in Vienna announced that it would never recognize Polish predominance in the post-war Galician political establishment. When in August 1915 the government decided to make the Chełm region a part of the General-Government of Lublin, the General Ukrainian Council formed in May in Vienna vehemently protested, arguing that the region should be joined with the Ukrainian territories. The Council also warned the government that any preferential treatment of the Poles would compel Ukrainians to look more favourably towards alliance with Russia.[53]

Still, the military situation dictated the Central Powers to stake on the better organized and more sophisticated 'titular' nationality—the Poles. In the wake of a powerful Russian offensive in the summer of 1916, the German and Austro-Hungarian emperors issued a declaration that provided for the creation of a Polish state under German and Austrian auspices and the formation of an advisory state council that seemingly heralded the formation of the national government. Although the future state was deprived of the most important historical and economic regions such as Poznań, the Baltic Coast, Silesia, Galicia, and the Białystok area, the state council provided the Poles with the nucleus of a political infrastructure, whereas the Legions and the POW constituted armed formations, crucial for claiming power at an opportune moment. At the same time, the *Endek* leaders—Dmowski in Paris and the famous pianist Ignacy Paderewski in America—successfully promoted the Polish cause on behalf of the National Committee founded in Switzerland. In September 1917 the Entente recognized the Committee as the representation of Poland in the Allied camp.[54]

Concomitantly with the Polish–Ukrainian conflict, Polish–Jewish relations rapidly worsened during the war. After the hardships of Russian rule, the Jewish communities accorded the most enthusiastic welcome to the Austro-German armies. In turn, the Central Powers hoped to use Jews as a political force in the war against Russia and allowed Jewish cultural and political organizations to resume their activities, and encouraged the expansion of Yiddish and Hebrew schools. Although the German and Austrian administrations did not grant the Jews the status of a national minority (as many Jewish activists had hoped), they fully restored Jewish civil rights. Such policies facilitated the evolution of an institutional framework that would constitute the foundation of the Jewish life in post-war Poland. Jews were excited over these developments, but initial hopes turned to bitter disappointment. Although the economic policies of the *Ober-Ost* did not single out Jews for harsher treatment, they brought about a rapid pauperization of the Jewish communities; German officials often confiscated or openly robbed Jewish businesses. Because of linguistic proximity of Yiddish and German, many Yiddish-speaking Jews found employment in the Austro-German administration as low-level officials, interpreters, and clerks. Having become a part of the administrative structure, Jews drew popular resentment upon themselves. Polish political groups were alarmed in particular by the activities of the Zionist organizations that propagated close links between Jewish and German cultures and advocated the introduction of German in Jewish schools. For the Poles such steps seemed to portend the beginning of the Germanization process in the east and by autumn 1915 the image of Jews as Austro-German proxies became predominant in the Polish press, and the Polish administration in Galicia began the 'de-judaization' of the provincial civil service by replacing the Jewish employees, who had been reinstated after the Russian retreat, with Polish officials. Conflicts over property, stolen or plundered by the local population during the Russian occupation and claimed by returning Jewish refugees, heightened popular resentment and led to violent clashes and mutual denunciations.[55]

The impact of the February revolution

The revolution in February of 1917 in St Petersburg reverberated through the borderlands. The population at large welcomed the events in the Russian capital in the hope that it was the beginning of monumental social reconstruction of the entire country. Such hopes were fortified after the first decrees of the new Provisional Government, which authorized the abolition of all imperial restrictions imposed on ethnic minorities and granted full civil and political rights to all Russian subjects. Emboldened by these developments, democratic and liberal circles advocated the introduction of a democratic form of government, autonomy, and the principle of self-determination that corresponded with the aspirations of the national leaders in Russia and in the territories occupied by the Central Powers. The declarations of the Allies seemed to herald the Western powers' commitment to the transformation of Europe on the principle of self-determination. Accordingly, politically minded Estonians, Latvians, Ukrainians, and Byelorussians formed committees, calling for self-government, autonomy, and the introduction of native languages in schools. For instance, the Byelorussian National Committee—founded on the basis of the relief committee in Minsk—demanded that the Provisional Government recognize Byelorussia as a distinct territorial unit and open schools with Byelorussian as the language of instruction. In March the representatives of all major Lithuanian organizations and parties in Russia formed the 'Provisional

Committee for Administration of Lithuania' that claimed to speak for the Lithuanian people.[56]

The Ukrainian activists in Kiev formed a national council (*Rada*) that initially contemplated autonomous Ukraine within democratic and federal Russia and acted as the representative of the Provisional Government. The position of the *Rada*, however, became increasingly precarious as it was ignored by the Provisional Government and challenged by the Bolshevik-dominated Soviets. In addition, the national consciousness of the Ukrainian peasantry, mostly concerned with land reforms, was still at an embryonic stage. To put it differently, peasants conceived the new political freedoms as a blanket permission to redistribute land. As the Russian defences at the front collapsed, a peasant war—harbinger of times to come—against the old order gradually engulfed the countryside. Galvanized by revolutionary agitation and led by soldiers who had deserted, peasants burned manor houses, cut down forests, and killed estate-owners. Despite the frantic appeals of the administration, the command of the South-Western Front was helpless, for the troops, egged on by the Bolshevik agitators, refused to obey orders.[57]

Political power in Bessarabia was as fragmented. The commissars appointed by the Provisional Government clashed with the civic committees, which acted as advisory bodies, and were dominated by the Socialist-Revolutionaries and the Mensheviks. The committees promoted the autonomy of Bessarabia within the Russian Federation and the official use of the Moldavian (Romanian in Cyrillic) language. Since the political programmes of the Socialist-Revolutionaries and the Moldavian National Party included extensive land reforms, they enjoyed popularity among the peasantry. In contrast, the influence of the Bolsheviks was minimal—during the provincial conference of the Soviets in September 1917 there were only five Bolsheviks among the thirty-three delegates.[58]

Faced by the German advance and deteriorating conditions at home, the Provisional Government had perforce to offer concessions to the national aspirations of the 'subject people'. In April 1917 it decreed the unification of northern Lifland (it remained in Russian hands) and Estland, which came under the authority of the Estonian and Latvian rather than Baltic-German government commissars. The traditional political subordination in the Baltic was hence reversed. In June democratic elections in Estland resulted in the formation of *Maapäev*, a council dominated by Estonian peasant representatives that acted as the legislative assembly and the government of autonomous

Estonia. Similarly to the Ukrainian *Rada*, the *Maapäev* did not aspire to independence, but considered Estonia a part of the Russian Federation.[59]

However, the Provisional Government dragged its feet on the issue of the introduction of the Estonian language in schools, and Russian officials still controlled school funds. Meanwhile, the deepening political crisis and deteriorating economic conditions played into the hand of the Estonian Soviets, who consistently agitated against the war. The Soviets showed their disposition on 1 May, when the Russian soldiers, sailors, and the Estonian Bolsheviks tore up Estonian national flags. The Bolsheviks were particularly popular among industrial workers and soldiers, and in demanding the confiscation of German-owned land holdings they enjoyed support among the peasantry. In the summer the Bolsheviks won provincial elections in Lifland, where they received more than 70 per cent of votes. The visible weakness of the Provisional Government forced the hand of the *Maapäev*, which after the German capture of Riga in early September 1917 hastened to declare itself the representative of the Estonian nation abroad, overriding the mandate granted by St Petersburg.[60]

The Latvian Refugee Aid Committee in Russia and the émigré-organized National Committee in Switzerland also promoted Latvia's autonomy within the Russian Federation, a national parliament, and universal suffrage. However, in the parts of Latvia unoccupied by the Germans it was the Bolsheviks who became the most powerful political force. They enjoyed mass support among Latvia's industrial workers and especially among the Latvian riflemen, who, brutalized by the experiences in the war, became most susceptible to Bolshevik propaganda. Already in March 1917 in a newspaper article the leader of the Latvian Bolsheviks Pēteris Stučka indicated that, although the Bolsheviks supported the principle of self-determination, they would seek a more 'practical' solution for the 'small states'—a union with Russia. The German offensive and the Bolshevik threat forced the Latvian Social Democrats, the Farmer's Union (led by Kārlis Ulmanis), and the National Democratic Party to form the Latvian National Council, which became the umbrella group for all Latvian political parties.[61]

Summary

The war transformed the borderlands into a testing ground for imperial ideological and economic experiments, and violence and repression became

the ubiquitous tools of the opposing armies in dealing with civilian populations. Russian deportations and the policies of the military regimes undermined the socio-economic fabric of the borderlands, divesting them of
human, economic, and material resources. Some provinces lost two-thirds
of their socio-economic infrastructure.

The Russian methods of governing the borderlands aimed at the security
of the strategically sensitive areas and nationalizing the socio-economic
space in the western provinces and in the occupied territories. These
policies succeeded in severely debilitating the more economically successful
and sophisticated minority groups—the Germans and Jews. Simultaneously,
the influx of the masses of deportees and refugees in Russia-proper effectively 'unsettled' the Russian empire, draining limited economic resources
and heightening social and ethnic tensions.

The political and strategic expectations of the Central Powers also proved
faulty, for the attempts to win over the populations and to govern the
occupied territories in colonial fashion, particularly in the area under the
Ober-Ost, were bound to fail. Although the Austro-German nationality
policies lay the groundwork for mutually beneficial cooperation and initially the population seemed amenable to the new regimes, the ignorance of
local conditions under the *Ober-Ost* and the economic exploitation in the
Austro-Hungarian and German occupation zones eventually dissipated
popular good will.

The war facilitated the state's application and association of the group
reliability criteria with ethnicity. Such an approach fuelled existing antagonisms, which became especially combustible at the end of the war. The
Estonians and Latvians supported the Russian anti-German campaign that
portended the reversal of the traditional imperial order, while the Poles and
Ukrainians cherished different visions about the future of the Austro-Hungarian empire. The situation of the Jews, who in the Russian war-zone were
effectively eliminated as the dominant socio-economic force, became particularly precarious, since war ravages generated increasingly vicious competition in social and economic spheres.

The attempts of the belligerent armies to transform the borderlands into
uniform administrative, political, or cultural constructs contributed to the
consolidation of national identities as a basis for collective action. The
creation of political infrastructures—in the form of the civil and national
committees and national units—became a crucial stage in the bid for
national autonomy and, eventually, independence. Consequently, the Feb-

ruary revolution in Russia became a focal point for nationalists, who, emboldened by the situation, demanded more political freedoms for their ethnic constituencies and claimed autonomy for the territories they considered to be ethnographical or historical 'cradles' of their respective nations.

Crucially, the end of the war witnessed the evolution of some ethnic communities into nationality groups, whereby many Estonians, Latvians, Lithuanians, Poles, and Ukrainians, led by the highly engaged political elite, conceived themselves as members of ethno-cultural kinships. Although in the final analysis none of these people—the Poles might be considered an exception—had been formed into a nation, the war mobilized, organized, and armed hundreds of thousands of people. Hence, by late 1917 national aspirations, traditionally in the realm of dreams, had become a reality. The implementation of these aspirations, however, depended on the will of the Great Powers and on historical opportunities created by the collapse of the Russian empire.

3

The Frontier Wars, 1918–1920

On 11 November 1918 Winston Churchill wrote to Lloyd George that 'the War of the Giants has ended; the quarrels of the pygmies have begun'.[1] Such a condescending remark referred to a horrid tangle of conflicting claims presented to the victorious Entente by multiple nationality groups of the former Russian, German, and Austro-Hungarian empires. As various national committees and émigré communities argued and pleaded for the 'fair' territorial settlements—more often than not at the expense of their immediate neighbours—drawing permanent borders in Eastern Europe's ethnic patchwork became a nightmare for the peacemakers in Paris.

Ultimately, however, the new borders were not settled at diplomatic tables, but were imposed by force of arms. For two years after all became 'quiet on the Western Front', in a pattern similar to the domino-effect of the 1848–9 turmoil in the Austrian empire, the borderlands were caught up in the vortex of imperial collapse, national revolutions, and armed conflicts. In contrast to the two-sided warfare between the Entente and the Central Powers, the frontier wars involved multiple contestants and ideologies. Foreign interventions and local insurgencies defied the self-proclaimed provisional governments, shaped national identities, and polarized large segments of the population, leaving behind permanent feuds and resentments.

This chapter examines the causes and dynamics of the frontier wars that raged from the Baltic to the Black Sea from the Bolshevik revolution in November 1917 to the termination of the Soviet–Polish war in autumn 1920. Historians of the Russian Civil War have traditionally treated the events in the borderlands as a sideshow to the much more consequential 'Red–White' war in Russia. While in terms of sheer numbers of participants and the intensity of conflict such views may be justifiable, they neglect the importance of the frontier wars in changing the political profile of the former imperial provinces and in establishing the national states, which blocked the Soviet advance into Europe.

A particular nature of the frontier wars derived from two factors. First, the collapse of the German, Austro-Hungarian, and Russian empires exposed the borderlands to two revolutionary currents. One was the revolution of national self-determination, fuelled by the wartime nationality policies of the warring states and particularly by the Allied and Bolshevik slogans of self-determination. Similarly, the social revolution was the offspring of the competition and convergence of the Bolshevik and the western-liberal ideologies, both pledging a more fair distribution of national wealth. Second, the severity of the conflicts in the borderlands depended upon and fluctuated according to the ability of the two main protagonists—Germany and Soviet Russia—to maintain a monopoly on violence. As the two powers weakened, the war in the borderlands lost its 'normative' character, for no conventional rules regulated the multi-sided conflicts. The 'cost of violence'—previously controlled by the imperial governments—declined and the multiple protagonists were able to make their own rules of warfare.

Exporting the revolution

Although in 1917 the borderlands were in deep economic and political crisis, it was the Bolshevik seizure of power in November that set different political factions on the course of inevitable collision. If until this point the social-democratic and liberal forces hoped that national and social aspirations such as autonomy, the redistribution of land, and the introduction of the native languages in schools was possible within the Russian federation system, they perceived the Bolshevik coup as the penultimate threat to the recently won liberties and freedoms. Indeed, while Lenin and his close associates were willing to utilize nationalism to achieve social revolution, they paid lip service to the principle of self-determination, accentuating that it was applicable and practical only in its 'proletarian' form.

In contrast to the better-organized Bolsheviks, whose increasing strength made them serious contenders in the race for power, the national parties did not possess substantial armed forces and were divided by the front lines that made coherent national policies extremely difficult. The patronage of the Entente was also highly problematic, for although its leaders publicly supported the national revolutions, their primary concern was the prosecution of the war in the west. The Allies' ambivalence towards the national movements in the east was manifested in January 1918, when President Woodrow Wilson's famous 'Fourteen Points' declaration stipulated the formation of the independent Polish state, whose borders were to be consistent with the territories inhabited by the 'indisputably Polish populations'. In regard to other groups, the declaration simply promised them free opportunity for autonomous development. Even less forthcoming were the Central Powers, which effectively controlled the situation in Eastern Europe. Since the Estonian, Latvian, or Ukrainian national movements' political platforms included both national and social reforms and were predicated upon reversing the imperial social and political order, such objectives were totally unacceptable to Germany and Austria-Hungary.

The fragility of the national movements revealed itself immediately after the Bolshevik revolution. When a week later the Estonian *Maapäev* declared itself the 'sole bearer of supreme power' and called for the convention of a Constituent Assembly, the Bolshevik-organized Military-Revolutionary Committee (VRK) proclaimed itself the sole governing body in the country. The confrontation between the two contenders intensified in January 1918 during the elections to the Constituent Assembly, when the Estonian national and social-democratic parties won by a large margin. The VRK responded by declaring the results void and banning the Assembly. Simultaneously, the VRK followed the pattern established in Russia and launched a terror campaign against the 'class' enemies—the nobility, landowners, politicians, officers, and priests. In the German-occupied areas the Estonian national units, organized with the approval of the German command, retaliated by executing or detaining in concentration camps alleged communist sympathizers. The civil war in Estonia was hence in its opening stage.[2]

In the parts of Latvia unoccupied by the Germans the confrontation between the national and Bolshevik forces followed a similar trajectory. However, in contrast to Estonia, where ethnic Russians made up the bulk of revolutionary forces, most Russians had evacuated from Latvia during the German advance and the conflict, therefore, increasingly assumed a 'native' character. The Bolshevik-dominated 'Executive Committee of Latvia' (the so-called *Iskolat* Republic) defied the Latvian National Council and introduced the Latvian language in official and public life. This measure and particularly the distribution of land at the expense of the Baltic Germans attracted the poorer strata of the population to the Bolshevik cause. The first shots of the civil war were fired in December 1917, when the Soviet–Latvian units began confiscating the German-owned estates and clashed with armed German landowners. The 'revolutionary terror' began in January–February 1918, when the *Iskolat* ordered deportations of political prisoners to Russia.[3]

In February, when the Bolshevik delegation stalled at the peace talks in Brest-Litovsk, the Central Powers launched an offensive and occupied all of Latvia, Estonia, Byelorussia, and Ukraine. Facing defeat, on 3 March 1918 the Bolsheviks signed the Brest-Litovsk peace treaty that effectively truncated the former Russian empire. The treaty fused the First World War, the national revolutions, and the Russian civil wars into a single context, since from now on the military, political, and diplomatic situation in the borderlands depended upon the relations between the three warring powers—Germany, Russia, and the Entente. The treaty provided a crucial respite for the German High Command that transferred most of its combat units to the west; the 'Brotfrieden' (bread-peace) agreement with the Ukrainian *Rada* also granted the Central Powers access to Ukraine's raw materials and grain supplies. The Bolsheviks also received a breathing space to strengthen their political gains and to concentrate the bulk of their forces against the White armies in south Russia and Siberia. Lenin, however, realized that the treaty was but a temporary let-up and that the Central Powers could resume hostilities at the first opportunity.

The Brest-Litovsk treaty forced the Entente to pay closer attention to the borderlands, where it made sense to undermine the Central Powers by supporting the national movements. Germany, however, was far ahead of the Entente. Already in September 1917 the *Ober-Ost* sponsored the convention of a National Lithuanian Council in Vilnius, *Taryba*, which declared Lithuania an independent state under German auspices.[4] Similarly, in March 1918 the Germans set up a puppet Byelorussian government in Minsk that declared an independent Lithuanian-Byelorussian state that appealed to the Kaiser for support. Finally, in April, exasperated with the Ukrainian *Rada*'s inability to control the country and to maintain a steady flow of supplies to the Central Powers, the Germans replaced it with a puppet government. The same month the *Ober-Ost* authorized the creation of the so-called Baltic Dukedom, carved out of Kurland, Lifland, and Estland. Since Russia was effectively out of the war, the goal of making the Baltic region a German colony seemed to be at hand. Plans were made for the arrival of 50,000 German settlers from East Prussia and Germany-proper and in June the former Russian provinces of Estland and Lifland were joined in a new administrative unit called 'Baltikum'.[5]

The Armistice in November 1918 was greeted with relief and anxiety by all warring parties, though for different reasons. For the national governments the end of the war meant the fulfilment of national self-determination as the cornerstone of Woodrow Wilson's 'Fourteen Points'. Still, the independence of the new states rested on extremely shaky foundations threatened by the two aggressive neighbours, Germany and Russia. In turn, the Entente realized that if previously military intervention in Russia (in March–April the Allied troops landed in Archangel and Vladivostok) was to forestall the German occupation of Russia, now it supported two opposed forces—the Whites, who fought for 'one and indivisible Russia', and the nationalists, who struggled to break away from Russia—and faced the Bolsheviks who seemed to be on the verge of filling the political vacuum in the borderlands. Determined to create a *cordon sanitaire* against Soviet Russia and Germany, in November 1918 the Entente recognized de facto Lithuania, Latvia, and Estonia as independent republics. By doing so, the Entente effectively became involved not in one, but in many civil wars raging in the former Russian empire.

The Bolshevik reactions to the Armistice combined exaltation and anxiety. Ever a pragmatist, Lenin fully realized the economic and strategic potential of the borderlands. As a dedicated communist, he and his close associates never fully abandoned dreams of igniting an all-European revolution launched from the Baltic, Poland, and Bessarabia. Therefore, anticipating Germany's collapse, in September 1918 the Soviet government formed the 'Central Bureau of the Communist Organizations of the Occupied Territories', which was to coordinate the activities of the communist groups in the borderlands with the Red Army. In October 1918 at a public rally Trotsky stressed that Lithuania, Poland, Ukraine, and even Finland soon 'will be united under the banner of the RSFSR'. At the same time, the Bolsheviks appreciated that, relieved from the burdens of the First World War, the 'imperialist' powers could concentrate on defeating Soviet Russia. On 8 November 1918 Lenin warned the All-Soviet Congress that although the international proletarian revolution was close as never before, the Bolsheviks faced the most critical moment of all and had to act quickly and decisively. Five days later Soviet Russia unilaterally abrogated the Brest-Litovsk treaty; on 17 November the Red 'Western' army in Byelorussia crossed the Soviet–German demarcation line and advanced towards Minsk and Vilnius. In December the Soviet troops crossed over into Estonia and Latvia.[6] The race for the borderlands had begun.

The Baltic wars, 1918–1919

By the end of 1918 the situation of the nascent Baltic republics looked critical, for in the wake of Germany's collapse the Soviet offensive faced no organized military opposition and certainly looked like a 'triumphal march' (the conventional Soviet reference to the Bolshevik successes after the November revolution), since in the prevalent conditions of chaos, war weariness, and hunger the Bolsheviks seemed the only organized force capable of restoring law and order in the war-ravaged land. The Bolsheviks also counted on the strong leftist traditions among industrial workers, especially in Tallinn and Riga, and the Red Army's advance was spearheaded by the Estonian units and nine Latvian regiments, which were the most reliable of the Soviet forces.

The military offensive was accompanied by an ideological one. On 24 December 1918 the Soviet government officially recognized the independence of the 'Soviet' Estonian, Latvian, and Lithuanian republics, promising them full political and economic support. Although the Soviet advance in Estonia ran out of steam twenty miles east of Tallinn, the Red Army (assisted by the Bolshevik insurgents) captured Riga on 4 January 1919; two days later Soviet troops entered Vilnius. Lenin's vision of the European revolutionary conflagration seemed at hand. In March the Soviet government authorized the creation of the Communist International that was to coordinate the activities of the Bolshevik party in and outside of Russia.[7]

The Bolshevik successes seemed so much more decisive in contrast to the situation across the frontline, where the national governments found themselves in a desperate situation. Although national appeals found receptive grounds among the Estonian, Latvian, and Lithuanian intelligentsia and educated workers, the idea of independence found little response among peasants who were more concerned about land reforms. The national armed forces were in embryonic stage; in January 1919 the Latvian and Lithuanian contingents each numbered about a thousand soldiers and were poorly armed and organized whereas the promised Allied help materialized only in observation delegations and several warships. The Estonian and Latvian

governments had no choice, but to turn for help to better-equipped
White Russian and German forces, which were both fundamentally hostile
to the national independence of the Baltic states. Similarly, the Lithuanian
declaration of independence in December 1917 claimed the 'ethnographic
Lithuanian' lands, including Vilnius, and put the new state on a collision
course with Poland. Threatened by the Soviet offensive, however, the
Lithuanian government was compelled to seek Polish support.[8]

It would be incorrect, however, to ascribe the early successes of the Red
Army merely to fortuitous circumstances. The Soviet-Baltic governments
announced a series of comprehensive social reforms, including the much-
awaited distribution of land-estates, and the formation of the native town
and village councils. The Bolshevik slogans and the transfer of industries to
the workers' councils struck a responsive chord among the Estonian and
Latvian industrial workers, predisposed to socialist ideology since the late
nineteenth century. All these measures won the Bolsheviks substantial
popular backing.[9] In addition, although the memberships of the Estonian,
Latvian, and Lithuanian communist parties were small, they had highly
dedicated members who gained valuable experience as state functionaries
in revolutionary Russia.

However, the rigid application of the Soviet socio-political order heralded
the ultimate defeat of the Bolsheviks, who failed to appreciate the socio-
economic, ethnic, and cultural peculiarities of the borderlands. The Soviet
authorities hastened to set up collective farms, whose productivity was dismal.
What Soviet historians cautiously call 'excesses' (peregiby) also involved the
nationalization of property, forests, and pastures, and food requisitioning.
Middle-size peasant holdings, which according to Bolshevik social criteria
constituted more than 50 per cent of the total in the Baltic region, were
deprived of voting rights guaranteed by the Provisional Government. The
middle class and the intelligentsia were alienated by the Bolsheviks' ban on
political parties and a free press and turned to support the national cause.
Hostility to the Bolsheviks was also generated by the fact that the Soviet
administration, especially in Estonia, was often dominated by ethnic Russians
and resembled the imperial regime, but in a more virulent form.[10]

Meanwhile, foreign aid gradually shifted the balance of power in favour
of the national governments. The Entente leaders increasingly perceived the
Bolsheviks as an ultimate threat to the hard-won peace and were willing to
provide material and financial aid to the new polities. Bolstered by the
arrival of several thousand volunteers from Scandinavia and the support of

the British fleet that had anchored off the coast of Tallinn, the Estonian national army under the able command of the tsarist colonel Johan Laidoner was reorganized into a small but effective force. In addition, Estonia's eastern boundaries were covered by lakes and bogs that made the Red Army's advance difficult. Liberal land reforms, announced by the Estonian and Latvian governments, gradually attracted more peasants to national colours. In January 1919 the Red Army suffered a crippling blow, when the combined Estonian, Baltic-German, and the White Russian troops pushed it out of Estonia.[11]

The defeat in Estonia sealed the outcome of the struggle in Latvia, from where the Red Army had to divert some of its units to the north. Moreover, in December 1918 the Latvian government secured an agreement with the 8th German Army, which still held the front lines in Kurland. The agreement looked promising to both sides. The German command saw it as a godsend opportunity to re-establish its control over the Baltic, whereas the Latvians counted on the might of the well-equipped and experienced German units. The latter were fused into a formation known as the 'Free Corps' (the name may have derived from the notorious mercenary 'free companies' in medieval Italy), whose members felt no connection to the people they came to help and despised equally the 'inferior' Latvians, the Entente, and the Weimar Republic that epitomized to them the loss of the World War.[12]

In February 1919 the 'Free Corps' and the reorganized Latvian forces launched a coordinated offensive that by the end of March brought them to the gates of Riga. Having no help from the Soviet government—it primarily focused on repelling the White Russian armies in southern Russia and Siberia—the Red Army began to falter. It suffered another blow when Lithuanian troops captured Panevėžys and Polish forces occupied Vilnius. In this situation, aghast at the prospect that the Estonians and Latvians would benefit from 'German' victories, in mid-April the Free Corps deposed the Latvian national government and installed a pro-German puppet administration. The coup was followed by a joint German, White Russian, and Latvian attack on Riga that fell on 22 May.[13]

Significantly, the 'miracle on the Daugava River' preceded the famous 'miracle on the Vistula'—the celebrated Polish victory over the Red Army at the gates of Warsaw in 1920—and extinguished Lenin's dream of the Baltic region as a salient for spreading revolution westward. At the same time, it ended German aspirations to dominate the Baltic. After the Bolshevik threat receded the Entente and the Estonian and Latvian governments could afford to dispense with the German military presence in the region. The threat of the Allied economic blockade and a defeat inflicted by the Latvian–Estonian forces on 19-22 June at Césis heralded the end of the Free Corps; in early July it abandoned Riga. The last attempt to rejuvenate the German *Ostpolitik* came in the autumn, when the remnants of the Free Corps joined the White Russian 'Volunteer' Army led by Colonel Pavel Bermondt-Avalov, an adventurer who declared himself supreme ruler of Latvia. In October the 'Volunteer' army advanced towards Riga only to be defeated by the Latvian and Estonian forces.[14] Determined to finish off the last White strongholds in southern Russia, the Soviet government was willing to accept the new status quo. In February, July, and August 1920 it signed peace treaties respectively with Estonia, Lithuania, and Latvia, temporarily renouncing territorial claims in the Baltic.

Making 'Greater Poland'

The road to Poland's independence was equally hazardous. Initially, the decline of the Russian, German, and Austro-Hungarian empires contributed to the rapid mobilization of Polish national identity. When, in accordance with the Brest-Litovsk treaty, the Central Powers allocated some counties of Poland, including the ill-fated Chełm region, to the Ukrainian *Rada* in exchange for food supplies, the two rival camps—the followers of Piłsudski and the *Endeks*—utilized the opportune moment to promote the idea of national sovereignty based on common ethnic and historical foundations. In regard to the future Polish state, Piłsudski envisioned it as a federation of Poles, Lithuanians, Ukrainians, and Byelorussians, capable of withstanding Russian and German aggression, whereas Dmowski promoted the resurrection of the pre-partition Poland as a national state (*państwo narodowe*) that would protect and gradually 'civilize'—Dmowski's euphemism for assimilation—the peoples who had not 'matured' into modern nations. Despite their differences, however, the Polish leaders shared a broad consensus that in either case the ethnic Poles would constitute the ruling elite and that the resurgent Poland would be incomplete without Vilnius and L'viv.

Such plans presaged a conflict with other nationality groups. Simmering during the World War, the Polish–Ukrainian conflict exploded on 16 October 1918, when Emperor Charles issued a manifesto that stipulated the transformation of the Empire into a federal state. While such a solution was acceptable to Ukrainians, who two days later formed a National Council that claimed authority over the Ukrainian ethnic enclaves, it was rejected outright by the Poles. As the disintegration of Austria-Hungary seemed inevitable, on 1 November the Ukrainian National Council declared itself to have assumed power in Galicia. The Council proclaimed Ukrainian statehood in the form of the West Ukrainian National Republic (ZUNR), and guaranteed civil equality and political rights to all national groups. Polish armed formations, however, put up stiff resistance and the conflict soon spread through the province. The ZUNR government counted on the support of the national Ukrainian government, the *Dyrektoriia*, whose troops in December assumed power in Ukraine. However, hard-pressed by the Soviets and the White Russians, the *Dyrektoriia* was fighting for its own survival and could not spare any troops to Galicia. In contrast, the Polish troops received numerous reinforcements and on 21 November captured L'viv.[15]

The Polish cause received a powerful boost in Paris, where the Allied commissions struggled through the ethnic tapestry of the borderlands in order to find solutions that approximated to the principle of self-determination. The Polish diplomatic missions succeed in portraying the ZUNR as a pro-Bolshevik creation and a springboard to Europe, whereas the French government favoured a strong Poland for powerful leverage against Germany. Consequently, it facilitated the transfer of the so-called Blue Army (the Polish units organized and armed by France) to Poland. The renowned pianist and politician Ignacy Paderewski, who acted as a representative of the Polish National Committee in the United States, also won the support of President Wilson.

In spring 1919 the reorganized Polish army launched a two-pronged offensive in Galicia and Volhynia. In May it captured the Boryslav (Boryslaw) oil region, cutting the only economic asset of the ZUNR that was used to buy military hardware in Czechoslovakia. Although the Galician army put up stiff resistance, it eventually gave way under the overwhelming Polish pressure and in mid-July was pushed across the Bug River into Ukraine-proper. In November 1919 the Entente Supreme Council ruled that Poland would receive a twenty-five-year mandate for East Galicia, but the successes of the Bolsheviks against the Whites in Russia forced the Council to table a decision leaving the Polish government a free hand to solidify its position in the conquered territories.

Bolstered by the Allied support, the Polish government was determined to exploit the favourable international situation to reassert Poland's dominant position in Eastern Europe, insisting on the indivisibility of the 'historical' Polish lands. Piłsudski bluntly stated that, whereas territorial acquisitions in the west depended on the good will of the Entente, the east was 'an open door, which opens and closes and it depends who and how wide will open it by force'.[16] Such ambitions contributed to the escalation of fighting on Poland's frontiers, and by January 1919 the Polish forces were engaged in armed conflicts on four fronts: against the Germans in Poznań and Silesia, the Czechs in the Cieszyn (Teshyn) area, the Ukrainians in Galicia, and the Soviets in the borderlands.

In such a situation Piłsudski and Dmowski tried to find a solution to the Polish–Lithuanian conflict, which for the two Polish leaders meant more than just the issue of Vilnius. They entertained the idea of a Polish–Lithuanian union, which would provide a strategic barrier against Soviet Russia and Germany. Understandably, Piłsudski and Dmowski foresaw that within the union Poland would be the senior partner. Such plans were totally unacceptable to the Lithuanian leadership, which insisted that independent Lithuania was impossible without Vilnius and some counties of the Klaipėda region. To counter the Polish pressure, the Lithuanians were willing to turn for help to Poland's arch-enemies, Russia and Germany. The latter, outraged by Polish territorial claims in Poznań and Silesia, was especially eager to lend Lithuania financial and material support.[17]

Lithuanian–Polish relations deteriorated after the joint offensive against the Red Army in April 1919. Although an Entente commission established a demarcation line between the Polish and Lithuanian forces, armed clashes between the two sides escalated in the summer. Piłsudski's suggestion for national plebiscites was rejected out of hand by the Lithuanian foreign minister Augustinas Voldemaras, who declared that the Vilnius area was 'ethnically' Lithuanian regardless of the opinions of its inhabitants. In August the conflict turned into an open war. Since the Lithuanians had also to hold a front line against the Red Army, the Polish troops captured several localities in southern Lithuania. Although in early September the front stabilized, harassment and arrests of prominent citizens behind the front lines continued to spoil relations between the two states. The Polish administration in the Vilnius area began a 'Polonization' campaign that included opening the University of Stefan Batory (a Polish king known for his aggressive foreign policy and military victories in the sixteenth century) and firing civil servants who did not master the Polish language.[18]

Still, aware of potential Allied sanctions, the Polish government acted cautiously towards Lithuania. In contrast, it felt no inhibition in Byelorussia and Volhynia, captured by the Polish army in spring 1919. Although the Polish media praised the democratic foundation of the new Poland, the government disregarded the national aspirations of Byelorussians and in May the Polish *Sejm* declared Byelorussia an inalienable part of the Polish state.[19] Emboldened by diplomatic and military victories Piłsudski was not satisfied, however, with the territorial status quo, which in his opinion did not sufficiently secure Poland's eastern borders. In spring 1920, when the bulk of the Red Army was committed against the White forces in the Crimea, he decided that the time to rectify the eastern boundaries had come. On 25 April the Polish army in alliance with the Ukrainian national forces struck in Byelorussia and Ukraine; on 5 May the Bolsheviks abandoned Kiev. The Polish high command, however, underestimated the Bolsheviks' organizational abilities. The Polish offensive re-ignited Lenin's vision of a European revolution and he ordered the transfer of crack troops from the Southern Front to the Soviet–Polish front. In late May the Red Army mounted a powerful attack in Ukraine and Byelorussia, shattering the Polish defences. The path to Warsaw seemed open when in July the Red Army captured Minsk, Vilnius, and Hrodna; in early August it was closing in on the Polish capital. The possibility of Bolshevik penetration of Europe sent shocks through Europe. '[The Poles] have quarrelled with every one of their neighbours—Germans, Russians, Czechoslovaks, Lithuanians, Romanians, Ukrainians—and they are going to be beaten', grumbled Lloyd George, when the Soviet armies crossed into Poland.[20]

The Soviet advance energized the Lithuanian army, which attacked Polish garrisons along the demarcation lines. On 12 July the Lithuanian government signed a treaty with Soviet Russia, which recognized Lithuania's independence and offered it the Vilnius, Hrodna, and Suwałki regions. Although the Polish government hastened to propose peace terms to Lithuania, in view of the rapid Soviet offensive the latter rejected it. Two days later the Soviet and Lithuanian troops captured Vilnius and to the sounds of the Bolshevik 'International' and the Lithuanian national anthem the Soviets officially transferred the city to Lithuania.[21]

In turn, the Poles marshalled their forces and managed to stop the Red Army at the gates of Warsaw, ending Lenin's plans for a Bolshevik revolution in Europe. By the end of the summer the battered Red Army retreated to Byelorussia. Simultaneously, Lithuanian aspirations to revive the 'historic' Lithuania received a crippling blow as the Polish army advanced towards Vilnius. Although a commission sent by the League of Nations established a new demarcation line that left Vilnius on the Lithuanian side, Piłsudski tacitly approved the so-called March Home by the troops of the Polish general Lucjan Żeligowski, who 'mutinied' and captured the city in October. The Polish–Lithuanian war continued until the end of November, when Żeligowski halted his offensive two miles east of Kaunas. The creation of the so-called Middle Lithuania opened a new page in Polish–Lithuanian relations and would gravely affect the relations between the two states for the following decades.[22]

In 1921 the Soviet–Polish treaty of Riga confirmed the Polish territorial acquisitions in the *Kresy*. Already in possession of East Galicia, Poland received Volhynia and western Byelorussia (the latter included the territories limited by the Dvina River in the north, the Bug River in the west, and the Pripiat'-River in the south) with a population of about 5 million people. In addition, it held the Vilnius region (Map 2). Although the three 'losers' of the frontier wars—the Byelorussians, the Lithuanians, and Ukrainians—found themselves under Polish rule, they did not resign to the military defeat.

Making 'Greater Romania'

Romania emerged as the penultimate beneficiary of the frontier wars. Bolstered by Russian victories in Galicia in 1916, it opportunistically entered the First World War on the side of the Entente. However, a joint German-Bulgarian offensive shattered the Romanian army; in December Bucharest fell and two-thirds of the country was occupied by the enemy. The first chance to make up for the lost territories came in the wake of the Bolshevik coup in Petrograd. In Bessarabia the National Council, *Sfatul Ţării*, advocated autonomy within the Russian Federation. It was, however, challenged by the Ukrainian *Rada* that claimed the province as a Ukrainian territory and by the Soviets who swore allegiance to the government in Petrograd. In late December the Bolshevik forces captured Chişinău and declared

Map 2. The Borderlands, 1920–1939

themselves the sole power in Bessarabia. The Bolshevik revolution invigo-
rated Romania's aspirations to incorporate Bessarabia, held since it had
become an independent state. Having received the consent of the Entente
that was keen on using Romania as a barrier against Soviet Russia, the
Romanian army launched an offensive that by the end of February 1918
pushed the Bolshevik troops behind the Dniester River. Although in
February the *Sfatul Țării* proclaimed itself the government of the independent Moldavian National Republic, it remained a mere pawn in the hands of
the Romanian administration. Romania's territorial acquisition was confirmed by the Bucharest treaty of 5 March 1918 with the Central Powers,
which allowed it to keep Bessarabia in exchange for food supplies and
financial reparations.[23]

The collapse of the Central Powers proved as beneficial for Romania as
the Bolshevik revolution. Since the late nineteenth century Romanian
nationalist writers described Bukovina, the land of ancient Romanian monasteries, as an inseparable part of 'Greater Romania'. Similarly, a Romanian
Refugee Committee from Bukovina that settled in Romania during the war
agitated for the reunification of Romania with its 'lost' territories. In late
October a congress of Romanian politicians in Bukovina established a
National Council. When on 2 November 1918 the Austrian garrison in
Chernivtsi mutinied, the Council appealed to the Romanian government
for help. The Romanian army advanced and quickly occupied the entire
province. On 9 November Romania re-entered the war against the Central
Powers and one month later the *Sfatul Țării* was induced to issue a declaration that stipulated the unification of Bessarabia with 'mother-Romania'. In
February 1919 the Allies assented to the Romanian annexation of Bessarabia
and Bukovina (the latter's occupation by Romanians was seen as a preventive measure against revolutionary turmoil in Hungary).[24]

In spring 1919 Bessarabia became an area of the armed conflict between
Romania and Soviet Russia. Preparing to succour the Soviet Hungarian
Republic, the Red Army pushed the Romanians across the Dniester River.
The military operation was preceded by the formation of a Soviet-'Bessarabian' government that declared Bessarabia a Soviet republic. The further
advance into Bessarabia, however, was thwarted by a large-scale anti-Soviet
rebellion in south Ukraine, which diverted the forces designated for the
operations against Romania. By the end of May the Soviet–Romanian
front stabilized, with the Soviet forces holding positions on the left-bank
Dniester.[25]

The logic of violence

The frontier wars displayed the appalling combination of extreme violence such as pogroms, massacres, the murder of prisoners of war, and collective reprisals. Violence thrived within and without clear ideological foundations and it was committed in the name of ideology as well as base human instincts. Its most disturbing aspect, and arguably its most profound cause, was that in many instances the state structure ceased to exist. In contrast to the clearly demarcated front lines of the First World War, armed confrontations in the frontier wars often had no predictable logic. All sides committed robbery, pillage, and murder regardless of who was winning or losing. Violence was not confined to specific victims, although Jews suffered particularly brutal assaults, nor to political and social distinctions. In the words of a contemporary, the non-combatants experienced an acute sense of uncertainty and helplessness as their homes were invaded by 'all kinds of armies; from one day to the next one didn't know what the political situation would be'.[26]

Unquestionably, such a situation was deeply rooted in the experiences of the First World War. Mass slaughter in the trenches and the cruelties inflicted on civilians by the opposing armies brutalized large segments of the population. The insurgency under the *Ober-Ost* demonstrated the limited ability of the state to stem popular unrest and the February revolution in Russia plunged large territories of the empire into a state of chaos. In fact, the civil war in the countryside began before the Bolshevik revolution. In spring 1917 in Byelorussia and Volhynia armed peasants rejected all authority and divided land among themselves. The return of many soldiers, radicalized by the years of fighting, imported violence and social revolution into the countryside. Although peasant energy was temporarily confined to the land issue, the potential for the spread of violence did not diminish. The traditionally harsh environment in which peasants lived facilitated aggressive patterns towards the state and the city, while the war eliminated any illusions as to the beneficial nature of the Tsarist regime, especially among younger peasant-soldiers, who eagerly absorbed the Bolshevik revolutionary ideology. Conservative peasant societies were also shaken by radical socialist, anarchist, or nationalist ideas, whereas the collapse of the government generated chaos, propensity to anarchy, and the rejection of any official constraints. The revolutionary turmoil even pitted the peasant communities against each other and after the fall of 1917 armed clashes between villages over the disputed land parcels became common. Since many villagers possessed arms and were led by former soldiers, such clashes often acquired the form of formal battles. The Central Powers inherited an extremely volatile situation and when in spring 1918 they and their puppet Ukrainian regime began extracting grain and livestock from the countryside to fulfil the obligations of the Brest-Litovsk treaty, entire districts rose in open revolt. As the peasant war spread with dizzying speed, the German troops responded with punitive expeditions, subjecting rebellious villages to artillery fire and shooting hostages. Soon the situation was out of control and by the summer the Ukrainian countryside was in the hands of the rebels, while the Austro-Germans held towns and cities.[27]

While the Bolsheviks were only too happy to use the opportune moment in the struggle for power, they soon realized that the peasant war could not be easily controlled or channelled into the desirable 'class' course. In Volhynia and Byelorussia bands of armed peasants attacked German garrisons, burned Polish estates, but also refused to recognize the Bolshevik commissars sent to head the resistance. It was an agrarian rebellion against any authority, rooted in Russia's social and political structure. As the traditional life pattern in the villages collapsed under the revolutionary wave, it was replaced by radicalism disseminated by soldiers. The latter, aroused by the Bolshevik slogans of 'peace, bread, and land', became the natural leaders of peasant communities. For centuries fatalistically having accepted their oppressed status, peasants now compensated themselves in a bloody insurgency directed against everybody, including the Polish landlords, the Germans, the Ukrainian nationalist forces, and the Soviet troops. Although the plunder of the landlords' estates did not require deep political motivations, there can be no doubt that the war and the revolutionary chaos inflamed the countryside, which was subjected to confiscations and ravages by all armed formations. Violence became a defensive mechanism to protect the villages and a psychological device to overcome the continuous state of uncertainty. By spring 1919 large areas on both sides of the Polish–Soviet front were controlled by the insurgents. In fact, any determined individual at the head of a group of armed men—plenty of weapons left from the First World War and the dissolution of the Russian imperial army made such endeavours easy—could claim control over entire districts.[28]

Initially most of the opposing forces in the borderlands were small, but they gradually grew in size and displayed different political colours. For the Soviet government the wars became a blueprint for imposing political control over the regions outside Russia-proper, while the native communists in the Baltic, Ukraine, or Byelorussia fought for a utopian society of equals. Conversely, for the anti-Bolshevik Estonians, Latvians, Lithuanians, Poles, and Ukrainians the fight against the Soviets was a national struggle against renewed Russian subjugation. Although many Free Corps members were true mercenaries, others saw themselves as ideological warriors fighting against Bolshevism, the Western democracies, and the hated German republic. A similar crusading ideology held sway among the White Russians, while for the Baltic-Germans the victory of the Bolsheviks or the Baltic national governments was equally portentous since it meant the loss of their privileged status. The frontier wars thus displayed the amalgam of ideological, ethnic, and social polarizations that engendered brutalities by all sides.

The Red Army's ideological warfare crystallized during its first offensive in the winter of 1917–18, when it engaged in random requisitions of food supplies and livestock and its revolutionary tribunals sentenced the droves of 'class enemies'—the intelligentsia, priests, businessmen, students, and officers—to prison terms or executions. In the midst of the 'class'-oriented terror, long-term ethnic animosities also bubbled to the surface as the Red Guards, particularly the Estonians and Latvians who came of age during the upheaval of 1905–7, targeted the Baltic-Germans with particular fury. A Latvian Red Guard wrote to his girlfriend how he and his colleagues murdered her 'former [German] master . . . who begged for his life. I shot him five times and I and my friends took all gold and gold things. My friend pierced the little girl with a dagger like a piglet'.[29]

The Free Corps also left behind a gruesome trail. Inured to violence by trench warfare, the German war veterans lived off the land and treated Latvian and Estonian civilians as enemies, murdering thousands of people suspected of pro-Bolshevik sentiments. After the capture of Riga, the Free Corps ran amok for several days, looting, burning, and killing. In turn, anti-German hatred among the Estonians and Latvians engendered a war of annihilation that shocked even those who had grown immune to human suffering. A Free Corps member Rudolf Höss, who would later become known to the world as a notorious commandant of Auschwitz, recalled that brutalities in the Baltic overshadowed anything he had experienced before as a soldier. Another First World War veteran, Ernst Solomon, remembered that he and his comrades 'killed anything that fell into our hands, burned everything that burned; a great wall of smoke marked our passage'.[30]

The Polish victories in the borderlands were followed by a systematic campaign to 'Polonize' the captured territories and revealed inherent contradictions within Polish ideological and socio-economic objectives. On one hand, the sense of Poland's 'civilizing mission' required the political and social integration of the Ukrainians and Byelorussians as equal citizens of the new state. At the same time, however, the 'civilizing mission' had ominous implications, for similarly to the Russian and German military regimes in the First World War, the Polish administration conceived the process of integration as a nationalization campaign, designed to nationalize first the land and then the people. To this effect, while the war continued and given the history of peasant resistance, the Polish military was bound to treat the populations of the borderlands—known as *Kresy* in Polish parlance—as hostile. The new regime began with the mass dismissal of Ukrainian, Byelorussian, and Jewish civil employees who had not taken the oath of allegiance to the Polish state or those who were considered unreliable. The reduction in Byelorussian and Ukrainian schools and the new agrarian laws, announced by the *Sejm* in July 1919, reflected the Polish government's concerted efforts to redefine the ethnic contours of the regional socio-economic spheres. In contrast to western Poland, where large German estates were parcelled, in Byelorussia and Volhynia the government left intact large-size Polish estates (up to 400 hectares); the redistribution of land predominantly benefited Polish citizens, especially the settlers, who maintained land-holdings of 45 hectares, seven times the maximum limit for the Ukrainians and Byelorussians. Such measures were designed to attract ethnic Poles to the borderlands. Hostility and suspicions towards the native population translated into the brutal conduct of the Polish army, that often behaved as in a foreign country. It requisitioned food and livestock, and subjected to bombardment entire villages that resisted. In consequence, the Bolshevik and the Ukrainian nationalist propaganda gained substantial popular support.[31]

Popular resentments, especially towards Polish landlords, whose position still seemed unassailable, fuelled the peasant resistance. Incited by Bolshevik agitators, peasants seized Polish estates and looted manor houses. After the resumption of the Polish–Soviet war in 1920 in many localities the population enthusiastically welcomed the Red Army with flowers and red banners. Many villagers and town-dwellers participated in the Soviet administration throughout the *Kresy*.[32] As localities changed hands, the Polish and Red armies changed and established new laws, levied taxes, and imposed requisitions and confiscations. Wartime, deteriorating economic conditions, and the rapidly changing political situation had desensitized large segments of the population and reduced moral constraints. The overwhelming sense of chaos and frustration were bound to unleash acts of despoliation and resistance to any authority. The largely peasant Soviet and Polish armies acted in a similar fashion, killing wounded and captured prisoners on the spot. Both sides erected makeshift concentration and prisoner of war camps, where thousands lingered in woefully inadequate conditions; thousands perished from hunger and epidemics (Russian sources claim that as many as 83,500 Red Army personnel died in Polish captivity).[33]

In East Galicia the Polish–Ukrainian war also gradually assumed an extreme character. Initially, the recent comrades in arms in the Austro-Hungarian army accorded military honours to dead enemies, concluded truces to collect the wounded, and released captives upon the word of honour. Although sober minds realized the destructive potential of the conflict and appealed to both sides to stop fighting, the escalating nationalist propaganda prevailed in facilitating mutual resentments. The Polish media disseminated images of the destructive 'Cossack rabble', referring to the brutalities of the Polish–Ukrainian wars of the seventeenth century, and the Polish army refused to recognize Ukrainians as legitimate combatants. Some Polish commanders ordered the execution of Ukrainian civilians caught in possession of arms, and since many ZUNR soldiers did not have proper uniforms, they were considered outside the laws of warfare. After the Ukrainian army was pushed out of Galicia in July 1919, the Polish military launched brutal 'pacifications' of Ukrainian villages and arrested and imprisoned about 100,000 people; thousands died in captivity from hunger and epidemics.[34]

The Ukrainian press, in turn, stressed the centuries-long oppressive rule of the Polish nobility over the Ukrainian peasantry. Although the Ukrainians largely refrained from committing atrocities, Polish sources claimed that about 25,000 Poles were incarcerated in Ukrainian detention camps and prisons. As inflation became rampant, the Ukrainian authorities imposed random taxation to replenish the treasury. Ukrainian commanders carried out confiscations in Polish households and took hostages among prominent citizens. The spiral towards anarchy was exacerbated by masses of refugees, who inundated towns and cities, causing food shortages and epidemics, while army requisitions deprived the population of basic necessities.[35]

By winter 1919 hostage-taking, punitive expeditions, and executions of prisoners intensified and violence became the popular outlet to discharge economic, social, and political frustrations. A key psychological role in facilitating this process, was an ever-present siege mentality atmosphere, whereby the opposing sides often did not know who and where their enemies were. A peasant in daytime could turn into a Polish or Ukrainian guerrilla at night. In response, punitive expeditions were launched against entire villages, where individual positive qualities of the residents were of no consequence.

The Romanian army in Bessarabia and Bukovina behaved like its Polish counterpart in the *Kresy*. Having claimed that Bessarabia and Bukovina were 'lost' Romanian territories, the military administration treated the populations of the provinces as potential enemy-agents. Aiming at eradicating any opposition, the Romanian units robbed villages, confiscated food and cattle, and responded to acts of defiance or resistance by using overwhelming force. In January 1919 such acts caused a popular uprising in the Khotin district in Bessarabia. United by social rather than political or national ties—among the participants were Ukrainians, Russians, Jews, and Moldavians of different political persuasions—the rebels called for the liberation of the province from Romanian aggression and sought help from the Ukrainian national government (*Dyrektoriia*) and the Bolsheviks. By the end of January 1919 the Romanian army had suppressed the uprising, destroying entire villages and murdering thousands of men, women, and children. In the aftermath a speedy 'de-Russification' campaign included a ban on the Russian language and the mandatory use of Romanian. Robbery, beating, confiscation of livestock, and arbitrary mass arrests continued long after the last pockets of resistance were eradicated. As anti-Romanian sentiments grew in intensity, an astute observer mused that in a short period the Romanians managed to achieve a complete Russification of Bessarabia, a feat the Russian government failed to accomplish in one hundred years.[36]

★ ★ ★

One of the most notorious features of the frontier wars was the anti-Jewish pogroms. Although after the Russian retreat in 1915 violence against Jews subsided, they suffered sporadic assaults and indignities until the end of the First World War. Although in the Baltic region a number of Jewish houses and shops were looted in 1917, in general anti-Semitic proclivities in

Estonia, Latvia, and Lithuania were less pronounced, and muted by much stronger anti-German, anti-Russian, or anti-Polish attitudes. In addition, the Estonian, Latvian, and Lithuanian political activists counted on the alleged influence of the Jews in the Allied countries; in Lithuania, where the native middle class was in its infancy, the role of the Jewish middlemen was particularly important while the frontier wars were in progress.

The situation was quite different in the areas that came under Polish domination, where Polish–Jewish relations were characterized by deep ethnic and social polarization. The high density of the Jewish population certainly accounted for the strength of traditional economic and religious anti-Semitism, which also became a part of the Polish national ideology, propagated by the *Endeks*. Conversely, by the end of the First World War many Jews regarded Poland's independence as the least desirable solution. Such attitudes were reflected in the overwhelming support accorded by the Jewish communities to the Germans in the German–Polish contested regions of western Poland and East Prussia. The majority of Jews also favoured an independent Lithuania rather than the Polish-Lithuanian federation; about 5,000 Jews fought in the ranks of the Lithuanian army against the Bolsheviks and the Poles. Similarly, although in East Galicia the bulk of the Jewish political organizations declared neutrality in the Polish–Ukrainian conflict many Jews lent support to or at least sympathized with the ZUNR, especially after the latter recognized Jews as a national minority. A number of Jewish officers from the Austro-Hungarian army joined the Ukrainian officer corps, and Jewish judges, lawyers, doctors, and rail employees took positions in the civil service of the Ukrainian republic.[37]

As a consequence, by the end of 1918 Polish society at large considered Jews as bitter enemies as the Germans, Ukrainians, or the Soviets. Official and popular accusations against the Jews were astonishingly wide-ranged— Jews were blamed for siding with Poland's enemies and for 'subverting' the country from within and from outside. After the Polish troops captured L′viv in November, a large-scale pogrom ensued in the Jewish city-quarters, in which the military units joined the rabble to conduct a punitive expedition. The assailants acted under a premise that the 'punishment' of Jews was sanctioned for treacherous acts committed during the siege, and the pogrom proceeded along the 'Russian' wartime model—the Polish command did not organize the pogrom, but let the troops go on rampage for two days. By the time Polish officer patrols were dispatched to pacify the area the Jewish residential areas were devastated. Up to 150 Jews were murdered (other sources claimed seventy-three fatalities) and many more were wounded. The pogrom became a watershed in Polish–Jewish relations, for the Jewish press abroad accused Polish authorities of complicity in instigating violence, while the Polish media retaliated by blaming Jews for deliberate distortion of facts.[38]

Anti-Jewish violence escalated during the Soviet–Polish war in 1919. Similarly to the Russian military pogroms, attacks on Jews helped reduce the economic cost of combat, for Polish troops were badly fed and clothed and plunder spared the army's limited resources. The rationale of 'punishing' Jews fitted well into the mindset of the Polish rank and file, accustomed to the image of Jews as swindlers and war profiteers. Hence, robbing or beating Jews presented no moral dilemma, while officers indifferently observed the actions of their subordinates or received 'protection' money from the Jewish communities. The pogroms manifested short-term goals—personal enrichment—rather than the physical destruction of Jews, and subsided after several hours. Public humiliation accompanied violent outbreaks, for soldiers amused themselves by forcing Jews to do 'gymnastics', cutting beards, breaking into synagogues during services, and vandalizing religious artefacts. Since neither Germans, nor Lithuanians and Ukrainians, were subjected to similar practices, it stands to reason that humiliating Jews served as a vehicle to separate the repugnant 'others' from a national community.[39]

But perhaps even more dangerous for Jews—from the standpoint of Eastern European ethnic politics—was the widely held notion that they collaborated with and benefited from the Soviet regime. Although many Jewish merchants, peddlers, and traders were pauperized by the Soviet nationalization policies, and the Jewish intelligentsia was persecuted as a socially hostile group, the Polish media stressed that most Jews collaborated with the Bolsheviks. True, as the only ideology that held out the prospect of fundamental social change and ethnic equality Bolshevism attracted many Jews, especially in the former Pale of Settlement where they had traditionally been relegated to second-class citizenship; the 'Polonization' in East Galicia also effectively eliminated the majority of Jewish employees from the civil service. The better educational background of Jews opened up for them positions in the Soviet state apparatus, public service, town and village councils, and managerial offices. The situation was similar to that in the 1905 revolutionary period, when the October Manifesto promised to grant all Russia's citizens full civil rights and the Russian radical right blamed Jews for being the major beneficiaries of the revolution. The prominence of Jews in the Russian and European communist parties lent further credence for such accusations, especially since in a tense political climate ethnicity had become the key indicator of loyalty and patriotism. Consequently, if those Byelorussians, Ukrainians, or Poles, who had collaborated with the Bolsheviks, drew resentment upon themselves as individuals, the image of a Jewish–Soviet official was projected upon all Jews collectively. Charges of collaboration fuelled attacks and reprisals against Jews, especially when the situation at the front seemed critical. In summer 1920 when the Soviet advance on Warsaw seemed unstoppable, the Polish military issued national appeals that barely disguised the incitement to violence. Accordingly, the troops responded with anti-Jewish pogroms in many localities.[40]

★ ★ ★

In the midst of the frontier wars only Bukovina and Transcarpathia remained relatively quiet. In Bukovina relations between the two largest ethnic groups, Ukrainians and Romanians, never reached the point of no return as in East Galicia. Steeped in parliamentarian traditions and accustomed to cooperation, the majority of moderate Ukrainian and Romanian politicians hoped for peaceful power-sharing in the province. Neither side desired armed confrontation, and the Romanian military occupation of the province extinguished any chance for a national rebellion.

The situation in Transcarpathia was a bit more dramatic. In mid-November 1918 Hungary, under the leadership of Count Mihály Károlyi, was proclaimed a republic, claiming jurisdiction over the former lands of the Hungarian kingdom. Centuries of Hungarian rule effectively impeded the emergence of strong national movements, and the leaders of the local ethnic groups looked for different solutions, namely the unification with their ethnic kin in Czechoslovakia, Ukraine, Serbia, or Romania. While most Ukrainians supported a union with Galicia, the Rusyn intelligentsia was divided between the proponents of unification with Hungary, Ukraine, and Czechoslovakia. Given that Galicia was ravaged by the Polish–Ukrainian conflict, the Hungarian option seemed more attractive, especially after December 1918 when the Hungarian government granted Transcarpathia autonomy in education, religion, and national language. The pro-Hungarian faction, however, was opposed by pro-Czechoslovak and pro-Ukrainian groups.[41]

Ultimately, however, the status of Transcarpathia was decided far from Europe—in the United States, where a large émigré Rusyn community from

Transcarpathia grouped around the American National Rusyn Council. The Council's representatives met President Wilson and Tomáš Masaryk, the most prominent Czech statesman, who was on a tour in the United States promoting the independence of Czechoslovakia. Since Wilson was luke-warm to the idea of an independent Transcarpathia, the Rusyn representatives opted for the Czechoslovak solution, as the most promising and viable, especially in the light of Masaryk's democratic credentials and his good rapport with the American president. The plebiscite among the American Rusyns showed that the majority favoured autonomous Transcarpathia with-in democratic Czechoslovakia. The plebiscite was favoured by the Allies, who were concerned at the expansion of Bolshevism to Europe through Galicia and Transcarpathia, and encouraged the occupation of the province by the Czechoslovak troops in December 1918–January 1919. The Hungari-an option was briefly rejuvenated during the Hungarian Soviet Republic that recognized Transcarpathia as an autonomous province with Rusyn as the official language. However, in April the Czechoslovakian and Romanian troops launched a military intervention against Hungary and to spare bloodshed in the province a Rusyn national council decided to support the 'Czechoslovak' solution. In September 1919 by the St Germain peace treaty Transcarpathia officially became a part of the Czechoslovak Republic.[42]

Summary

The First World War and its aftermath were referred to by Tomas Masaryk as a 'laboratory atop a mass graveyard'.[43] Indeed the frontier wars left a profound and disturbing legacy. As an extension of the First World War they ravaged the borderlands, inflicting huge material and human losses. Between 1914 and 1920 Estonia, Latvia, and Lithuania had lost approxi-mately 1.5 million people through combat, evacuations, deportations, and the emigration of Russian, German, and Polish nationals. Latvia alone lost a million residents—its population dwindled from 2.5 million in 1914 to 1.5 million in 1920. Within the same period East Galicia had lost half a million people, including 25,000 direct casualties of the Polish–Ukrainian war and tens of thousands who perished from hunger and epidemics. Many regions of the borderlands were partially or completely ruined. The grain harvest in 1920 reached about 27 per cent of the pre-1914 period. Industry and commerce stagnated completely, and the urban areas were overwhelmed by the multitudes of refugees.[44]

At the same time, the frontier wars facilitated the replacement of the three empires by a string of ethno-national states and temporarily prevented the Bolshevik advance into Europe, contributing to a decisive process of confrontation between the East and West. The wars combined the national and social revolutions and dealt the last crippling blow to the traditional political order. Popular participation in these conflicts was broad, involving all social strata and national groups. The final outcome in the form of the new 'successor-states' that emerged on the ruins of the three empires ultimately depended on whether national aspirations in the borderlands coincided or conflicted with the positions of the three giants, Germany, Russia, and the Entente. The collapse of the Russian empire initially caught the national movements off guard. Trained in political activities within the framework of the imperial order, they were 'catapulted' to power in 1917–18 and gradually and tenuously connected with peasants and workers frustrated by the lack of social reforms.

Wartime witnessed an increasing dependence upon ethnic ties, which became a source of protection and common action. Hence, for many participants the frontier wars were first and foremost a struggle for national independence. The wars glued together the native political institutions and large segments of populations, but also included strong elements of social rebellion, especially in the countryside, where peasant warfare revealed resistance to the intrusion of state power and popular desire for the redistribution of power and wealth. Crucially, since the state-building processes in the borderlands conflated the ideas of ethnicity and 'national' territory, the frontier wars were eventually christened as the 'wars of independence' and helped create a sense of common identity for the new states. At the same time, the outcome of the wars antagonized the Germans and the Soviets, and frustrated Ukrainians, Byelorussians, and Lithuanians. For them the memories of the wars and bloodshed would become a powerful drive to reverse the new order in the borderlands at an opportune time.

4

The Interim, 1920–1939

The revolutionary turmoil of 1917–20 completely transformed the political landscape of the borderlands. After more than a century of Russian imperial rule, the Baltic region was divided between independent Estonia, Latvia, and Lithuania. Western Byelorussia, Western Volhynia, and East Galicia were incorporated into Poland, the Czechoslovak Republic absorbed Transcarpathia, and Bukovina and Bessarabia became the easternmost provinces of the Romanian kingdom. With the exception of Romania, all of the 'successor-states' initially opted for a republican form of government. By 1922 the constituent assemblies in Estonia, Latvia, and Lithuania had passed new constitutions that emulated the Weimar, French, or Swiss models and bestowed major executive powers upon national parliaments; in Poland and Czechoslovakia the president received much more extensive executive powers. The Romanian constitution of 1923 also provided for a strong centralized state that did away with the old Austro-Hungarian autonomies in the newly integrated territories.

The political and economic structure of the 'successor-states' bore a close resemblance to the old imperial order in that they emerged as largely 'incomplete' societies, lacking a stable economic base and split between dominant and dominated groups that shared the same, relatively poor territories. Indeed, examination of the new states' economies would suggest that they had little chance of surviving. After six years of intermittent war, most industries, especially in Latvia, Lithuania, Byelorussia, Volhynia, and Galicia, lay in shambles, trade and agriculture had ground to a standstill, inflation was rampant, and only rudimentary state institutions were functional. The national governments thus faced a truly Sisyphean task of rebuilding viable political infrastructure, restoring and integrating regions of different economic capacities and political experiences into centralized administrative systems.

In the new polities the most profound difference from the old imperial borderlands was constant instability, facilitated by two factors. Since most territorial settlements in the borderlands were decided by force of arms, the 'losers' considered them only temporary. This was especially true in regard to the two revisionist states, Germany and Soviet Russia, which, albeit weakened, assiduously laboured to undermine the peace settlements. Equally challenging was the minority issue that the 'successor-states' inherited from the three empires. A decade after the First World War, despite demographic changes, in East Galicia and Bukovina the minorities made up about 65 per cent of the total populations, in Bessarabia about 40 per cent, and in Estonia, Latvia, and Lithuania minorities constituted about 8, 24, and 18 per cent respectively (see Table 4.1). Accepted into the League of Nations, the 'successor-states' were expected to rule fairly and justly over the diverse domains that had come under their domination.

However, state attempts to superimpose state-national identity on the multiplicity of people, who lacked common political experience and who differed widely in terms of ethnicity, religion, and culture, were bound to backfire. Combined with the threat of the two revisionist powers—Germany and Soviet Russia—the borderland territorial settlement faced a bleak future.

The winners and losers

A prominent historian of Eastern Europe suggested that the post-First World War principle of self-determination, albeit applied imperfectly, nevertheless stimulated the liberation of three times as many people from foreign rule as were subjected to such rule. If the territorial settlement in some regions remained highly unsatisfactory, it was because strategic and economic interests demanded it.[1] True, out of the former imperial domains three (Estonia, Latvia, and Lithuania) turned independent, four (western Byelorussia, Volhynia, East Galicia, and Transcarpathia) were incorporated into the Polish and Czechoslovak republics that claimed democratic credentials, and only two (Bukovina and Bessarabia) became the subjects of monarchical rule.

Hence, the main problem for the interwar stability of the borderlands seemed to be the external threat. In fact, after the termination of the frontier wars the situation on the new Polish–Soviet and the Romanian–Soviet

Table 4.1. The population of the borderlands in the 1930s[a]

| Ethnic group | Estonia | | Latvia | | Lithuania[b] | | Poland | | | | Transcarpathia (within Czechoslovakia) | | Romania | | |
| | | | | | | | Kresy[c] | | East Galicia | | | | Bukovina | | Bessarabia |
	Pop.	%	Pop.	%	Pop.	%	Pop.	%	Pop.	%	Pop.	%	Pop.	%	Pop.	%
Bulgarians															163,000	5.69
Byelorussians			26,800	1.4	4,400	0.2	1,530,400	35.0								
Czechs & Slovaks											35,200	4.9				
Estonians	977,200	92.0	7,000	0.4												
Germans	16,300	1.5	62,100	3.2	90,500	4.2	51,400	1.2	31,000	0.6	13,200	1.8	73,000	7.6	81,000	2.8
Hungarians											108,900	15.0	19,000	1.0		
Jews	4,400	0.4	93,400	4.8	156,200	7.3	251,900	5.7	545,000	10.0	90,500	12.5	102,500	10.6	205,000	7.2
Latvians	4,000	0.4	1,470,600	75.4	9,000	0.4										
Lithuanians					1,776,400	82.0	80,000	1.8								
Moldavians & Romanians													275,000	28.5	1,610,757	56.2
Poles	1,500	0.1	59,300	3.0	55,600	2.6	973,500	20.0	1,353,631	27.7			36,000	3.7	8,000	0.3
Romanians											12,700	1.8				
Russians	46,600	4.4	206,400	10.6	55,500	2.6	45,000	1.0					58,300	6.0	352,000	12.3
Ukrainians							1,419,200	32.6	2,894,339	51.8	447,200	61.7	377,000	39.0	314,000	11.0
Others	12,400	1.2	2,000	0.1	17,500	0.8	45,000	1.0	41,000		17,600	2.4	32,800	3.4	131,000	4.6
Total	1,062,700		1,950,500		2,164,900		4,400,400		4,884,970		672,500		854,800		2,864,757	

[a] Since the interwar statistics vary in different sources, the numbers are approximate.
[b] Including Klaipėda.
[c] Wilno, Polesie, Nowogródek, and Wołyń voivodeship (wojewódstwo).

Sources: Piotr Eberhardt, Ethnic Groups and Population Changes in Twentieth Century Central-Eastern Europe: History, Data, and Analysis (New York: M. E. Sharpe, 2003); The Polish and Non-Polish Populations of Poland: Results of the Population Census of 1931 (Warsaw: Institute for the Study of Minority Problems, n.d.); Mały Rocznik Statystyczny (Warsaw: Ministerstwo ...

frontiers remained extremely fluid, for despite the peace treaties signed by the three states neither side intended to honour the agreements. The Polish and Romanian governments harboured and supported large anti-Soviet formations—more than 40,000 officers and soldiers—that after the Russian civil wars found refuge across the border and until 1922 continuously raided the adjacent Soviet territories, making the imposition of state control extremely difficult. In Byelorussia and Ukraine, these raids evolved into violent assaults on towns and villages, destruction of state property, and the murder of people associated with the Soviet regime. To reduce the threat of insurgency and to establish firmer control over the frontier zones, the Soviet political police deported individuals and families who had relatives across the border, implementing the methods of population management shaped by the civil wars.[2]

In turn, although the Soviet leadership realized its failure to ignite the world revolution, it conceived it merely as a postponement of revolutionary activities until an opportunity presented itself. Publicly accusing its Polish and Romanian counterparts of sustaining the insurgency, the Soviet government doubled its efforts to foment unrest in the Polish and Romanian borderlands and secretly financed and supported communist groups across the border. Special coordinating offices supervised subversive activities in Poland and Romania and in autumn 1923 the Communist International authorized the formation of the communist parties of western Ukraine and western Byelorussia (KPZU and KPZB respectively) within the Polish Communist Party. The parties' political programmes called for the destruction of the Polish and Romanian 'feudal' states and the unification of the Ukrainian and Byelorussian lands with Russia. The party members were actively involved in anti-state propaganda, sabotage acts, and assassinations of police informants and agents-provocateurs.[3] In 1923 the communist-organized uprisings in Hamburg and Bulgaria set a precedent for similar attempts in the borderlands. In September 1924 a revolt organized by the communist underground and Soviet agents in the town of Tatarbunary in Bessarabia was bloodily suppressed by the Romanian army. A month later the Soviet government announced the creation of an autonomous Moldavian republic on the left bank of the Dniester River—a clear indication that the Soviets considered the setbacks in Bessarabia only temporary (a similar entity was established in Karelia to apply pressure on Finland). One more attempt took place on 1 December 1924 in Tallinn, where the communist insurrection was crushed by the Estonian army and security forces.[4]

The outside intervention only highlighted the constant instability in the new states that experienced frequent government changes. The multiplicity of political parties made coordinated government policies extremely difficult. Between 1919 and 1934 there were eighteen cabinets in Latvia and more than twenty in Estonia. Already in May 1926 a coup in Poland demonstrated the growing tendency to an authoritarian model of government. In Lithuania the Christian Democrats, who had been in power since 1920, lost to the leftist National Socialists (*Liaudininkài*), who amnestied political prisoners and restored civil liberties suspended during the frontier wars. These democratic measures, compounded by the signing of the Soviet–Lithuanian non-aggression treaty in September 1926, alarmed the Lithuanian military, the Christian Democrats, and the Nationalist Party (*Tautininkài*), who organized a plot and in December 1926 overthrew the government. The emergency law suspended civil rights and empowered the military to monitor any activities. A new constitution limited the powers of the parliament and provided for independent elections for president.[5]

As if all these problems were not serious enough, the selective application of the much hailed self-determination principle within the borderlands left several key territorial and ethnic issues unresolved. To begin with, long after the frontier wars masses of refugees and expellees were returning home. Between autumn 1920 and late 1921 1,344,400 individuals came back to Poland alone; one-third of this number settled in the eastern borderlands. Since conditions for citizenship included documented proof of habitual residence before 1914, tens of thousands remained stateless.[6]

Territorial disputes were as pressing, and were rarely decided in a mutually satisfactory fashion. The Estonians and Latvians agreed upon dividing up several islands in the Gulf of Riga. Similarly, under British arbitration a Latvian–Lithuanian treaty accorded Lithuania access to the Baltic Sea via Kurland.[7] Such prudence, however, was exceptional, for the frontier wars left an indelible psychological trauma on the collective mentality of the losers, who were constantly reminded of their defeat. Lithuania's loss of Vilnius to Poland became its own Trianon (the harsh peace treaty imposed on Hungary by the victorious Allies) and the most emotional embodiment of grievances against the Riga treaty. This legacy was hardly conducive to establishing normal diplomatic relations between the two states and throughout the interwar period the Lithuanian government continued to insist that 'without Vilnius there can be no Lithuania'. It supported and encouraged anti-Polish protests, demonstrations, and strikes in the Vilnius region; in January 1922 the Lithuanians and Jews in Vilnius boycotted provincial elections. In turn, to demonstrate the Polish character of the city, the Polish government affixed to it some adjacent counties with large Polish populations. In February 1922, with the consent of the Allied observers, the Polish *Sejm* ratified the annexation of Vilnius. Lithuania vehemently objected and the 500-kilometre Polish–Lithuanian border became a 'dead frontier', traversed by empty roads; the postal service, telegraph lines, and communications between the two countries were shut down. Armed skirmishes and acts of sabotage, largely initiated by the Lithuanian side, became a common occurrence. In March 1923 the Allied Conference of the Ambassadors confirmed Poland's eastern acquisitions. Piłsudski's federalist idea was dead.[8]

The Allies further contributed to the proliferation of hot spots in the borderlands by subordinating the principle of self-determination to their own strategic interests. Anxious to create barriers against Russia and Germany, in July 1919 they disregarded the overwhelming victory of the pro-German factions in the national plebiscites in East Prussia and forced Germany to cede the Klaipėda district to international control.[9] Although in June 1922 Lithuania recognized Klaipėda's status in exchange for international recognition, the Allied policies demonstrated to the Lithuanian government that the principle of self-determination could be used as a disguise for territorial expansion. To compensate for the loss of Vilnius, Lithuanian military and political circles prepared a coup. In January 1923 about 1,500 members of the Lithuanian army and paramilitary groups invaded Klaipėda and, after a brief skirmish with the French garrison, captured the city. The Entente, preoccupied with the outcome of the Greek–Turkish war, offered mild protests, while Germany and Russia were only too eager to support the coup, preferring the Lithuanian rather than French or Polish control over Klaipėda.[10]

★ ★ ★

If one applies Lord Acton's dictum 'the civilization of a state is best measured by its respect for minorities',[11] to the interwar borderlands, then the 'civility' of some of the 'successor-states' would raise a lot of questions. It can be argued that the destruction of the peace settlement was already set in motion during the frontier wars. In June 1919 Poland and Romania (also Greece, Czechoslovakia, and Yugoslavia) signed the minority treaties, pledging to guarantee the national minorities equal civil and political rights, religious freedoms, and the right to use native languages in communal life. After the frontier wars in the Baltic, the international recognition of Estonia, Latvia, and Lithuania was also made contingent upon the same guarantees.

Initially, there were encouraging signs of good will and cooperation. Eager to impress upon the world their democratic credentials, the Baltic governments granted their ethnic minorities extensive political and civil rights. The Estonian and Latvian governments seemed to follow the precepts of the minority treaties to the letter. The Germans and other ethnic minorities were guaranteed wide-ranging privileges such as the right to form and run their own corporations, educational facilities, and cultural institutions and use their own languages in official contexts. They also formed small parliamentary factions, actively participating in political debates. In Estonia the minorities were granted the right of cultural autonomy, private and public schooling in the native language, reception of public funds, and limited taxation of their communities. Old grudges seemed temporarily forgotten and in the early 1920s the Baltic-German officers commanded the Latvian and Estonian navies.[12]

Similarly promising was the situation of Jews. At the Versailles Conference the Allies agreed to regard Jews as a religious or ethnic minority entitled to protection and autonomy, and the clauses in the minority treaties promised a considerable amelioration of Jews' civil rights. In the Baltic region the Jews in general supported or at least accepted national independence (though the Jewish upper middle class in Estonia and Latvia probably preferred German dominance); some Jews fought in the ranks of the national armies. Estonia's liberal policies were recognized in 1927 when the Jewish National Fund presented Estonia with a 'Golden Book Certificate'. In 1934 the department of philosophy at Tartu University created its own Chair of Jewish Studies, the only such in Eastern Europe. Similarly, Latvian Jews were guaranteed representation in the National Council and cultural autonomy and some Jewish schools received government subsidies. In Lithuania cultural autonomy provided Jewish communities with self-regulation, imposing its own taxes and supervising religion, education, and cultural matters.[13]

The Estonian, Latvian, and Lithuanian governments also appreciated the role of Jewish merchants, traders, and professionals in economic life. In the early 1920s 48 per cent of Latvian businesses and 27 per cent of industries were owned by Jews. In Lithuania, which had no native middle class, the Jewish economic role was even more impressive—Jews on average owned about 50 per cent of industries and commercial enterprises. In addition, the

Jewish communities—4,434 in Estonia (less than 1 per cent of the total), 94,000 in Latvia (5 per cent), and 157,000 in Lithuania (7 per cent) were too small to make a serious impact on national politics. In July 1925 a short-lived agreement (*ugoda*) was reached between Jewish representatives and the Polish government. The former pledged the loyalty of their constituencies and the latter promised more autonomy for the Jewish communities and aid in maintaining Jewish schools. The government also abolished the Russian imperial discriminatory laws.[14]

However, the hopes of the international community that the minorities and the states in Eastern Europe would come to a mutually beneficial accommodation and subsume their differences in a common collective identity, proved illusionary. After the frontier wars the core-nationality groups perceived themselves as the main proprietors of state politics and assets since otherwise their struggle seemed meaningless. Accordingly, the new governments increasingly opted for the Russian imperial model of ethnic policies, cultivating the predominance of the core-nationality groups and relegating the minorities to the 'minority' status in terms of limited political participation and civil rights.

The first signs of such a trend translated into population management tactics. In Klaipėda the Lithuanian government consistently violated the international convention that provided the district with its own laws, language, administration, and finances. In October 1925, after the Lithuanian parties suffered a crushing defeat in the elections for the district parliament (the German parties received 83.5 per cent of the votes and twenty-seven out of twenty-nine seats), a gradual increase of Lithuanian settlers, whose numbers grew to 30,000 through the interwar period, aimed to alter the district's ethnic profile.[15]

If the Lithuanian government feared that German culture proved more attractive to Klaipėda's Lithuanian residents, the two main Polish political groups associated with Piłsudski and Dmowski were convinced that the Lithuanians, Byelorussians, and Ukrainians would eventually realize and embrace the 'high' Polish culture. The Polish government opposed the minority treaty and yielded its implementation only under the pressure of the Allies, who in the immediate post-war period wielded a considerable influence in Eastern Europe. As early as in December 1919 a British observer in Poland despaired that 'small nations, before they have hardly leaped into the light of freedom, [began] to oppress other races'.[16] Although the Polish establishment publicly acknowledged the necessity of granting territorial autonomy to ethnic minorities, it assumed a highly paternalistic approach to what it viewed as a huge apolitical mass bereft of national self-consciousness. State assimilation seemed to be the most effective solution to the minority issue, especially since the Polish and Romanian governments associated the minorities with the revisionist states that lost territories in the frontier wars. Consequently, in the context of the borderlands' politics any manifestation of non-state political affiliation such as Ukrainian aspirations for autonomy in Galicia or a religious Lithuanian manifestation in Vilnius were viewed as anti-state directed and caused immediate alarm. In the same vein, the administration interpreted the Byelorussians' demands for native schools and for the termination of the Polish settlements in the *Kresy* as social as well as political issues. Also, since the armed forces backed the inception of the Polish state, the government ascribed excessive weight to the use of force at the expense of appreciating the complexity of the political, ethnic, and socio-economic profile of the borderlands.[17]

From 1919 nationality policies in Poland were dominated by the National Democrats, and consequently mirrored Dmowski's vision of the recreated Polish state. Since Dmowski never failed to accentuate the primacy of the Polish majority in politics and the economy, after the frontier wars the Polish administration cast aside all pretences of tolerance and, disregarding the minority treaty obligations, set out to 'Polonize' the borderlands. In 1922 the assassination of President Gabriel Narutowicz, who was elected by a coalition of the Left, the moderate Centre, and the minorities bloc, demonstrated a powerful opposition to any concession to national minorities. The administrative borders were deliberately redrawn to provide the appearance of an increase in the Polish population, and the schools in native languages were consistently reduced. Such policies further alienated the minority groups, particularly the Ukrainians as the largest ethnic minority in Europe which was denied the right to self-determination. In Galicia and Volhynia the numbers of Ukrainian schools dwindled from 1,050 in 1919 to 433 in 1922; by the early 1930s most were made into bilingual Polish–Ukrainian schools. The Ukrainian Chair at the University of L'viv—one of the most prominent legacies of the Austro-Hungarian empire—was closed and Ukrainian attendance was restricted.[18]

The imperial rule in Byelorussia left behind a troubled legacy of a small working class, mostly Polish and Jewish cities, and a largely illiterate peasantry. The economic situation was also aggravated by the Riga treaty assigning to Poland the most rural and backward Byelorussian districts. Initially, poised to eradicate the vestiges of the Russian regime, the administration replaced Russian with Byelorussian in secondary schools. The government also subsidized the Byelorussian press, cultural and educational institutions, and professional associations. The 'Byelorussification' campaign, however, had its limits. In order to demonstrate the Polish predominance in the area, the administration blatantly 'corrected' official censuses by mixing nationality, language, and religion. For example, the 1921 census registered all practitioners of the Roman-Catholic faith as Poles, effectively reducing the numbers of Byelorussians from 3,700,000 to 1,041,760. The campaign against the Orthodox churches in summer 1922 and the distribution of land to the Polish settlers caused protests by the Byelorussian *Sejm* deputies. In turn, the administration began closing Byelorussian schools, which dwindled from 514 in 1920 to 40 in 1924; by 1930 there was none. Byelorussian-language publications and press were shut down, correspondence was confiscated, and the very name 'Byelorussian' disappeared from official use.[19]

All these measures contributed to an upsurge of resistance. In September 1921 the Ukrainians refused to participate in the official census and in October–November 1922 they boycotted the national elections. Organized by former officers of the Ukrainian national armies, an underground Ukrainian Military Organization (UVO) carried out acts of sabotage and assassinations of government officials (in 1921 in L'viv its member attempted to assassinate Piłsudski) and Ukrainians suspected of collaboration with the government. The latter responded by committing troops to restive areas, where 'pacifications' resulted in the arrests and detention of between 15,000 and 20,000 Ukrainians from all walks of life. Many were beaten and tortured to extract confessions.[20] Communist-organized groups also operated across the Polish–Lithuanian–Byelorussian frontier, carrying out anti-Polish propaganda, cutting telegraph wires, and attacking the Polish gendarme and police outposts. Although dispersed by the Polish army and the Border Corps in 1925, the remaining insurgents went underground awaiting an opportune moment, when 'the destruction of the [Polish] bourgeois-landowning state [would be] carried out by an outside force'.[21]

The minorities also responded by expanding the network of educational, cultural, and professional institutions, which simultaneously became centres of political activity. By 1927 the membership of the Byelorussian *Hramada* societies grew to 150,000 members. The Ukrainian educational and literary societies proliferated and sport clubs and athletic associations often combined traditional physical pursuits with paramilitary training. Between 1925 and 1930 the number of agricultural and commercial cooperatives increased from 158,087 to 365,555. Led by the charismatic Andrej Sheptyts'kyi the Uniate Church became the embodiment and the unifying factor of the Ukrainian national identity in Poland. Another element that facilitated the growth of national consciousness among Ukrainians and Byelorussians was the 'indigenization' policies in Soviet Byelorussia and Ukraine, where the government encouraged and supported the expansion of native languages, art, and culture. As a result, by 1928 in Byelorussia alone communist-influenced groups and associations had about 100,000 members, who looked to the USSR as the sole guardian against Polish oppression.[22]

★ ★ ★

If Polish political circles at least entertained the federalist solution for the borderlands, for the Romanian government federalism was a completely alien tradition, and the integration of the new territories was carried out disregarding their political and economic peculiarities. Despite government claims to have liberated Transylvania, Bukovina, and Bessarabia from foreign rule, the populations of these provinces were considered aliens. Such views applied not only to the non-Romanian populations that now accounted to 30 per cent of the new state, but also to the Romanians in Bukovina and Bessarabia who were accustomed to different standards of political activity. The 'Romanization' campaign in Bukovina and Bessarabia began as soon as the new provinces were occupied. Bukovina lost its autonomy and its diet was abolished. In Bessarabia the administration removed the Ukrainian, Moldavian, and Russian employees from the courts, schools, and medical facilities and closed Russian libraries. Concerned that the Habsburg rule in Bukovina 'spoiled' Ukrainians, the administration declared that Ukrainians were in fact 'Romanians who had lost their roots', and proceeded to shut down Ukrainian educational and cultural organizations, compiled lists of potential suspects, mostly teachers and priests, and went as far as confiscating the pictures of the Kaiser that 'awoke inappropriate' memories. The Orthodox Church in Bukovina was integrated into the Romanian Orthodox Church. Between 1918 and 1923 out of thirty-five Ukrainian schools in the Chernivtsi district seventeen were closed, whereas the numbers of Romanian schools rose from 179 to 319. The formerly German-speaking University of Chernivtsi was 'Romanized', its Ukrainian Language Chair was abolished, and the rector became an appointee of the Ministry of Education—rather than elected by the University Senate as under the Habsburgs. Altogether the numbers of Ukrainian university students dropped from 25 per cent in 1914 to 14 per cent ten years later. In summer 1924 the 'Law of the State Elementary Schools' established Romanian as obligatory for the classes of reading, writing, and grammar. Although the 1923 constitution guaranteed equal rights for all Romanian citizens, those who were not born in Bukovina and Bessarabia—especially Jews, Ukrainians, and Russians—were classified as 'foreigners' and they forfeited the right to vote, serve in state institutions, and own land. Corporal punishment for various transgressions was common, strict censorship watched over correspondence, the political press was confiscated, mass gatherings were prohibited, and the security police (*Siguranţa*) monitored all aspects of life. Still, the Romanian government was dissatisfied with the results of 'Romanization' since until 1928 Bukovina was ruled by martial law.[23]

A notable exception to the situation in the borderlands was Transcarpathia, where the Czechoslovak government, which according to an American observer 'seem to have the most ability and common sense', acted according to its promises made at the end of the First World War.[24] Headed by Tomáš Masaryk, who was long sympathetic to the aspirations of the Slavic people, it recognized Transcarpathia as a distinct region, granted the Rusyns the status of state nationality, and guaranteed all minorities full civil rights. It encouraged the growth of the Ukrainian and Rusyn schools, cultural institutions, and professional associations. Although the province did not receive autonomy (the government prevaricated on the ground that the inhabitants 'had not matured' sufficiently to receive autonomous status) in the 1929 national elections the minority groups predominantly voted for pro-government parties—an indication that the government temporarily enjoyed popular support.[25]

Economic crises

Economic stability in the borderlands proved as elusive as political stability, and while economic problems were common for the entire Eastern European region, some were distinctively regional. In addition to war devastation, the old trade and business arrangements were destroyed, since the territorial settlement shut off the borderlands from their traditional

Russian markets. If before 1917 Russia absorbed about 67 per cent of the
borderlands' industrial and more than 80 per cent of agricultural production,
now the Baltic republics and Poland had to compete with much stronger
British, French, and German economies. Such a situation would be extremely difficult for well-developed societies, much more so for predominantly agricultural ones. In the 1920s about 90 per cent of the labour force in
the *Kresy*, Galicia, Bessarabia, and Bukovina were still occupied in agriculture. The industrial labour force constituted less then 2 per cent in Byelorussia and as many were engaged in trade, transport, and public service. Even
in the more advanced Estonia and Latvia the agricultural population made up
approximately 69 per cent of the labour force, while real wages in the
borderlands were on average 4 per cent lower than in the core-areas. The
borderlands' economies were thus too similar to stimulate economic growth.
These problems were compounded by the closed borders between Poland
and Lithuania and the new national tariffs between the 'successor-states'. In
addition, the Polish and Romanian governments were incapable of and
reluctant to invest into the borderlands. For example, whereas by 1925 the
state financial input in the Romanian economy had constituted 40 million *lei*,
Bessarabia received only 1.7 million *lei*. Consequently, in some districts a
single doctor provided medical services to 15,000 people.[26]

The situation in national finances was equally acute. By 1920 the borderlands were flooded by a multitude of different currencies—Russian roubles,
Austrian crowns, and German and Polish marks. Although by the end of the
year Latvia and Poland had succeeded in introducing new currencies, these
rapidly lost their value. Printing more money only caused hyper-inflation.
In November 1918 the Polish government issued 8 million Polish marks; in
December 1923 there were 123,371,000 marks in circulation. Consequently, the rate of exchange rose tremendously—the value of one American
dollar skyrocketed from 8 to more than 6.3 million Polish marks. Inflation
was accompanied by unemployment and total industrial output decreased
by approximately 30 per cent in comparison to 1913.[27]

Crushing poverty amplified these problems. In the *Kresy* the poorest
strata of the peasant population (about 250,000 families) remained landless,
while the overwhelming majority (508,900 families or 68 per cent of the
total) owned between 2 and 10 hectares. At the same time 27,400 Polish
estates owned between 20 and 50 hectares; 7,400 large estates constituted
only 1 per cent of all households, but they owned between 50 and
55 per cent of the entire land surface. A similar problem was prevalent in

western Byelorussia, where much land was covered with forests, meadows, and marshes and even a large peasant household owned a small portion of arable land. Such a situation required effective measures, and in order to build viable economies the new states opted for economic nationalism, emulating the Soviet rather than the Western economic model. A series of reforms in the interwar period were progressively made at the expense of ethnic minorities and reflected less a redistribution of wealth than a 'distribution of poverty'.[28]

Initially, there were positive signs that Estonia and Latvia would begin economic recovery earlier than other borderland states. Using their better-developed economic infrastructure, the Estonians were able to capitalize on the deposits of oil shale between the Gulf of Finland and the Peipsi Lake and increase the output of oil, petrol, and asphalt. Estonian textile and metal industries expanded, making a significant contribution to the national economy. Similarly, Latvia had a strong industrial base—1,430 enterprises that employed 61,000 workers. Since trade with Russia declined, Germany and Britain became Estonia's and Latvia's major trading partners. The two Baltic republics also introduced modern industrial legislation guaranteeing workers an eight-hour working day and establishing strong trade unions.[29]

The situation in agriculture was the most pressing issue in the immediate post-war Eastern Europe and the successor-states tried to alleviate the plight of the peasantry. The most effective and easiest way to achieve this objective seemed the nationalization of land that belonged to the former 'titular' nationality groups. Already in October 1919 the Estonian government announced a land reform that was directed against the Baltic Germans. About 1.8 million hectares or 97 per cent of all the estates were expropriated by the state and distributed to small and mid-size Estonian peasant households. While the law stipulated financial compensation, the government stalled until it reduced the compensation amounts to 3 per cent of the real value of the estates. A similar reform in Latvia in September 1920 resulted in the dispossession of large estate owners, who received no compensation; 3.7 million hectares were distributed to Latvian peasants. As a result of these reforms, about 60 per cent of the Estonian and Latvian households became the owners of the 20–25 hectares of land; war veterans were first to receive new allotments. In Lithuania the land reform of March 1922 targeted the Polish and Russian land estates, reducing large holdings to a maximum of 150 hectares and offering only token compensation. All these reforms seemed to have fulfilled at least two purposes—they undermined the economic power of the 'titular' groups and won the peasantry to the idea of a national state as their main benefactor.[30]

In December 1920 the Polish *Sejm* also announced the distribution of the Russian imperial estates. The reform was run by the Polish military and aimed at colonization of the borderland regions, and by 1922 the army veterans and their families, altogether about 20,000 individuals, had received up to 55,700 hectares and community grazing lands (in the Polish western territories the German estates also lost more than 60 per cent of their holdings). While in the interwar period about 300,000 Poles moved to the countryside and about 100,000 to urban areas in the borderlands, neither Ukrainians nor Byelorussians benefited from the reform. That the reforms were ethnically tainted was attested to by the following statistics: the majority of peasants in East Galicia and Volhynia owned between 2 and 8 hectares and in Byelorussia between 1 and 12 hectares; the peasants could also not increase their holdings without the permission of the district administration. In comparison, 3,400 Polish landlords owned upward of 50 per cent of the privately owned properties, which on average totalled 1,250 acres each. The large estate ownership in the *Kresy* remained one of the highest in the new Poland.[31]

The land reforms in Bessarabia under Romania also aimed to reduce Russian influence in the province. Between 1919 and 1924 the state administration allocated up to 155,000 hectares (half of which had belonged to the Russians) predominantly to military personnel and civil servants from the core-areas. The new settlers received various financial bonuses and special land grants, especially in the largely Ukrainian districts and the areas near the Soviet–Romanian border. In Bukovina, less exposed to potential Soviet aggression by the border configuration, the land reforms benefited the state, for the peasants had to pay off the landowners (the state paid only a half price) for the land and agricultural implements. Once the peasants borrowed money from the banks, high taxation and interest rate soon brought them to ruin, forcing re-sale of the land.[32]

Concomitantly with the measures against the former 'titular' groups, the national governments changed their policies towards the Jews. By the mid-1920s the international situation improved and the Estonian, Latvian, and Lithuanian government no longer needed Jewish support. The growing native middle class demanded the reduction of Jewish participation in national economies and government pressure—in the form of subsidies to native business—contributed to the decline of Jewish monopolies in commerce and trade; Jewish enrolment in the institutions of higher learning also declined. By the mid-1920s all Jewish ministry employees in Lithuania were dismissed or resigned. Similarly, by 1925 out of Latvia's 10,237 civil servants and policemen there were only twenty-two Jews.[33]

The 'de-Judaization' campaign was an inseparable component of the Polish nationalization drive. In Galicia the numbers of Jewish state and civil employees fell from 12,312 in 1912 to 5,186 in 1921 and out of the pre-war 6,000 Jewish rail and postal employees, only 670 retained their posts in 1923. A similar situation prevailed in police, legal professions, and education. Such discriminatory practices achieved their primary objectives, but they simultaneously backfired because more Jews were forced to engage in trade, commerce, and artisanship, aggravating the competition with Poles and Ukrainians.[34]

There were good prospects for successful economic reforms in Transcarpathia. Aiming to utilize its timber and iron ore deposits, the government made substantial investments to build roads, bridges, and a new hydroelectric system. It also subsidized farmers and introduced new agricultural methods of cultivation. To undermine the economic power of the Hungarian nobility, the administration began a land reform, which, however, proceeded slowly—Prague wanted to mitigate tensions with Hungary. In addition, the best land was distributed among the Czech colonists as the most reliable political element in the province.[35]

All in all, the land reforms in the Baltic states and Poland had a positive impact, winning substantial numbers of the peasantry to the idea of a national state and making them less receptive to communist ideology. At the same time, no major reforms were introduced in the cities, where major industries lacked comprehensive social programmes. Combined with the Great Depression, such a situation largely contributed to the receptiveness of industrial workers to Soviet propaganda.

The turn to the right

By the late 1920s the economies of Eastern Europe seemingly stabilized—foreign investment helped increase industrial production in Romania and Czechoslovakia though Poland still lagged behind, not reaching the industrial output levels of 1913. Its eastern borderlands, however, remained on the margins of economic stabilization. But the signs of economic recovery were soon overshadowed by the Great Depression that hit Eastern Europe particularly hard. In Estonia the numbers of industrial workers fell from 44,600 in 1913 to 25,000 in 1930; especially affected were textile and metal industries, where industrial output fell by 50 per cent. In Latvia industrial production dropped by 36 per cent and 43,000 employees lost their jobs. The situation was as dramatic in Bessarabia, where by the mid-1930s 35 per cent of industries were shut down. In Poland between 1928 and 1932 the wage index fell by 61 per cent and industrial output declined by 40 per cent. Still, the borderlands suffered more than the core-areas, and in 1935 the Polish Ministry of the Interior recorded that the 'crisis in the *Kresy* is much more rampant than in the center'.[36]

The second half of the 1930s, therefore, witnessed a steady deterioration of economic conditions in Eastern Europe and of all the borderlands only Estonia and Latvia managed to stabilize their economies by effective currency reforms and reorientation to the Western market. By 1939 the level of unemployment in Estonia and Latvia improved and agricultural output rose by about 60 per cent, largely due to partnership with Germany.[37] By contrast, the Lithuanian, Polish, and Romanian economies stagnated to the pre-First World War level. Since the employment opportunities in the industries during the crisis were greatly reduced, the bulk of the rural population remained on the land, where low income, political oppression, and crushing taxes made it into a potentially explosive force. The crisis also vividly demonstrated the fragility of the predominantly agricultural societies, where in order to compensate for falling prices the peasants increased production. As a result, the prices continued to fall. The Great Depression laid bare not only the fragility of Eastern European economies, but also the vulnerability of the entire post-First World War order in the region.

The political and economic instability and the growing threat of foreign aggression contributed to the shift towards more authoritarian politics, which promised either to protect the status quo against the subversive forces—such as the communists, fascists, or restive minorities—or bring about national regeneration and socio-economic changes. In spring 1934 Estonia and Latvia suspended parliaments, banned political activities, and established authoritarian dictatorships governing by decree—in Estonia Prime Minister Konstantin Päts introduced dictatorial rule on the basis of the constitution and the leader of the Farmers' Party, Karl Ulmanis, did the same in Latvia. A profound political fragmentation in the Baltic states was attested to the fact that the introduction of dictatorial regimes aimed at curbing the activities of the Left and Right political groups. If the Lithuanian coup of 1926 was directed against the leftist National Socialists (the name was purely coincidental to the Nazi Party in Germany), in Estonia it targeted the quasi-fascist Freedom Fighters, who won a majority in the municipal elections in Tallinn and Tartu; the dictatorship in Latvia combated both the Right and the Left. The governments also formed their own militias—in Estonia *Kaitseliit* and in Latvia *Aizsargi* (defence leagues)—which were to function alongside the army.[38]

The changes in political structure did not generate much opposition. While the intelligentsia may have despised the violations of the native constitutions, the middle class and peasants in general were inclined to accept the new regimes for fear of more radical political groups, either the fascists or communists. In addition, the dictatorial governments were mild in comparison to their counterparts in Germany or the USSR and more resembled the conservative regimes in Austria and Hungary. For instance, in contrast to the brutal purges in the Soviet Union that affected hundreds of thousands of people, between 1927 and 1938 about 11,000 individuals suffered persecution in Lithuania by being fined (punished administratively) or imprisoned for political activities. In 1938 the Estonian government amnestied the imprisoned members of the communist parties who were in jail for a long time. The courts remained largely independent, private businesses remained untouched, freedom of religion was guaranteed, and the Baltic governments actively invested in economies, mitigating the effects of the Great Depression.[39]

★ ★ ★

The situation in the Polish borderlands was more complex, as the Great Depression conflated national and social grievances. The deteriorating economy and official minority policies produced a highly combustible atmosphere, which erupted in the early 1930s in a series of peasant rebellions, which targeted large estates. In response, in Byelorussian Polesie and Volhynia the government deployed thousands of policemen and regular army units and introduced martial law in a number of districts. The magnitude of unrest was reflected in the statistics of death sentences in the country, half of which were meted out in western Byelorussia in winter 1931–2. State suppression became increasingly violent as beating and torture in police stations and prisons became routine. The administration closed reading facilities and newspapers, shut down Orthodox churches, and arrested, imprisoned, or exiled individuals suspected of anti-state activities. The 'pacification' campaign culminated in September 1934, when the Polish government unilaterally abrogated the minority treaty. In April 1935 Poland received a new constitution that guaranteed all civil liberties, but provided that these liberties—of religion, speech, and assembly—were subject to considerations of the 'common good, public order, and morals'. Such provisions signalled a new assault on restive minorities and political opponents; in 1935 the Byelorussians lost their last seat in the *Sejm*.[40]

Popular resentment towards what was perceived as the government's deliberate policies to keep the borderlands in economic misery facilitated violent acts to redress the situation. In Galicia and Volhynia the unfulfilled promises of autonomy combined with economic shortages disillusioned many Ukrainians, especially students and the former officers and soldiers, in parliamentary democracy. The UVO became the spearhead of resistance. In 1929 it fused itself with other nationalist groups and formed the Organization of Ukrainian Nationalists (OUN) that aimed at achieving independence through national revolution and opposed the Ukrainian parties which sought a solution by open political participation and through legitimate means. Although initially the OUN ideologists advocated only the removal of the Poles, Jews, and Russians from Ukraine's socio-economic sphere, they increasingly adopted Nazi racial policies as fully corresponding with their aspirations to build an ethnically homogeneous state, which would eventually be ethnically 'purified'. Under the slogan 'with the devil himself, but against Poland' OUN was willing to ally with any power that would help achieve national independence.[41]

In turn, albeit realizing that terror would further antagonize the Ukrainian population, the Polish government preferred strong-arm methods, especially after 1934 when an OUN assassin murdered the Polish Minister of the Interior. In response, the government set up a concentration camp at Bereza near Brest, which became notorious for its brutal regime. By early 1938 the number of inmates increased to about 7,000, including representatives of all ethnic groups and political persuasions, but also women, the elderly, and children. Common suffering did not alleviate differences, as if portending the tragic future. The Polish nationalists were obsessed with the Jewish question and refused to heed Ukrainian aspirations to the *Kresy*, while the Ukrainian inmates associated the brutality of the camp regime with the oppressive nature of Polish society.[42]

The nationalist fever in Poland was fuelled by the political and economic instability, but also by the mass arrests of ethnic Poles in the USSR, which began in August 1937 and engulfed more than a hundred thousand people who were accused of espionage. On 15 November 1938 the law that guaranteed the natives their own schools was repealed, public meetings were prohibited, the Lithuanian cooperatives and cultural organizations in Vilnius were disbanded, and Byelorussian activists were prohibited to participate in municipal elections. In the *Kresy* the administration forbade individuals of Orthodox persuasion to acquire land.[43]

Radicalization in domestic policies was reflected in an upsurge of anti-Semitism. In the late 1920s the growing polarization of the borderland societies (as well as in all Eastern Europe) caused the weakening of democratic and moderate forces and attracted a substantial cross-section of the populations to fascist ideology. Already in the 1920s some right-wing groups such as the *Endeks* were drawn to fascism, which they praised as the expression of 'national sentiments, health, and strength', and were fascinated by ideas of corporatism and national purity. But the real blooming of fascism took place in the aftermath of the Great Depression and the ascent of Hitler. The native fascists admired the Nazi regime, which in contrast to 'feeble' democracies displayed strength, economic growth, and dynamism, and they emulated it, stressing that ethnicity was an immutable biological attribute. By the late 1930s fascism seemed to have offered the answer to all political and economic problems. Consequently, phobic proclivities towards the minority groups, especially the Jews, assumed extremely militant expressions.[44]

The similarity of the Eastern European political and socio-economic patterns was reflected in the resemblance of the fascist groups across the borders. The influx of students into colleges and universities meant that largely agricultural societies could not absorb many graduates, leaving a great number of dissatisfied and bitter youngsters open to radical ideologies. Religion was another prominent factor and the 'Iron Wolf' in Lithuania, the National-Radical Camp (ONR) and the *Falanga* in Poland, and the Legion in Romania perceived Christianity as inseparable from the 'pure' Lithuanian, Polish, and Romanian national identities. Similarly to their Western counterparts, the fascists in the borderlands displayed anti-democratic, anti-liberal, and anti-communist tendencies.

With the exception of Estonia and Latvia, where anti-Jewish sentiments among the fascists were secondary to much stronger anti-German tendencies, anti-Semitism became the ideological cornerstone for fascist ideology in Lithuania, Poland, and Romania. For example, the ONR was uncompromisingly anti-Semitic and promoted the introduction of anti-Jewish laws modelled on the Nazi Nuremberg Laws. The ONR and its sister-organizations terrorized Jewish students, demolished Jewish businesses and shops, and attacked Polish liberal and democratic organizations. Similar tactics were deployed by the *Falanga*, a splinter group from the ONR that won a substantial following among students and advocated the establishment of the totalitarian 'ethnic state'. Although the fascist groups remained on the margins of the Polish political mainstream, after the death of Piłsudski in 1935 the government itself became attracted to German National Socialism as a tool to consolidate the politically fragmented nation. The so-called Colonels (Piłsudski's colleagues in the military) adopted some of the ideological viewpoints of the *Endeks* to gain wider popular support, and encouraged the boycotts of Jewish businesses. Anti-Semitism also became popular among Polish students associated with the *Endeks*. In Vilnius University the radical student groups forced the administration to introduce so-called ghetto benches for Jewish students.[45]

Anti-Semitism was partially fed by the traditional Polish–Jewish economic rivalry that increased dramatically during the Great Depression. Concomitantly, the ghost of 'Jewish communism' that received its momentum during the frontier wars was rejuvenated by the influx of Jews into the communist parties. Although communist elements were marginal for Jewish society, which was dominated largely by the Zionists, the Orthodox, and in the late 1930s by the Bund, communism was certainly attractive for Jews, who saw in it the only ideology that offered fundamental social and political changes. Throughout the interwar period Jews constituted on average 40 per cent of the membership in the KPZU, KPZB, and the Polish communist party. Hence, the association of Jews with communism became one of the most popular political symbols of the Right in interwar Europe.[46]

In late 1930 a wave of anti-Jewish agitation and violence swept through Lithuania, Poland, and Romania. In Lithuania the Business Association called for a boycott of Jewish enterprises, while the 'Iron Wolf' members vandalized Jewish shops.[47] In Poland an economic boycott of Jews was waged under the slogan 'each to his own for his own wares', and physical assaults took place in the Hrodna, Vilnius, L'viv, Brest, Białystok, and Navahrudak (Nowogródek) regions. Between 1935 and 1937 about 2,000 Jews were assaulted or injured and at least two dozen were murdered. Mild sentences for the culprits seemingly attested to state complicity although the administration largely remained inactive. Pogroms were closely connected to the boycott of Jewish businesses—the favourite tool of the *Endeks*—as well as the activities of the Roman-Catholic Church in Poland that throughout the interwar period increasingly targeted Jews as the carriers of communism and economic exploiters. Simultaneously, right-wing Ukrainian organizations called for and practised the boycott of Jewish businesses and anti-Semitic propaganda. In some localities Ukrainian militants forced peasants to set up checkpoints at Jewish shops, smashed Jewish stores, and plundered property.[48]

In Romania anti-Semitism had been a part of intellectual life well before the First World War and was espoused by Romania's most prolific and influential writers so much that 'to be Romanian became synonymous with being an anti-Semite'.[49] The League of National Christian Defence—LANC—led by the leader of the National Democratic Christian Party, Professor Alexandru Cuza, became the vanguard of anti-Semitism. In December 1937 the party formed a new government, which introduced the dismissal of Jewish employees and confiscation of Jewish land. The Yiddish and German-language Jewish press in Chernivtsi was banned, and in Bessarabia and Bukovina universities became hotbeds of anti-Semitism, since college and university graduates perceived their opportunities to be impeded by the Jews. Nationalist students assaulted Jewish students and agitated against the 'preponderance' of Jews in institutions of higher learning under the conniving eyes and support of Romanian officials, including school administrators.[50]

It should, however, be stressed that despite mounting anti-Semitism and discriminatory policies Jewish cultural life flourished throughout the interwar period. In Bessarabia and Bukovina Jewish communities were highly organized and autonomous, and their educational system was efficient and extensive. In Poland the Jewish political parties ran a wide gamut from the Orthodox *Agudat* to the socialist Bund, Zionism, the communist *Kombund*, and assimilators. Despite discriminatory policies, by the late 1930s 72 per cent of lawyers and 50 per cent of doctors in East Galicia were Jews.[51]

Descent to war

By the mid-1930s the national minorities in the borderlands largely perceived themselves as abused, with a deepening sense of injustice, inequity, and dissatisfaction with the government policies. In turn, confronted with mounting symptoms of dissent and disorder, the national governments resorted to repressive measures, which only compounded the hostility and militancy of the aggrieved groups. In the atmosphere of increased international tensions, such a situation made the successor-states more vulnerable to external pressure. Although the three Baltic countries could commit considerable manpower to the field—at least 300,000 military personnel—they failed to establish a unified defence system counting on help from the West (similarly, some form of regional economic union may have helped better sustain the effects of the Great Depression). In 1921 Estonia and Latvia signed a military and political agreement, but were reluctant to invite Lithuania to join them since such a move would automatically place them in the midst of the Lithuanian–Polish conflict. In addition, after Hitler's ascent to power the German government increasingly made clear that sooner or later it would seek the return of Klaipèda. Therefore, an Estonian–Latvian–Lithuanian military alliance could potentially face a confrontation with Germany. Similarly portentous was an alliance with Poland–while for Lithuania it was out of the question until the Vilnius issue was resolved, the Soviet Union and Germany made clear that they would immediately react if the Baltic states entered an alliance with Poland. Hence, when in January 1934 Poland and Germany signed a non-aggression treaty, the Baltic states reacted by contracting a treaty of friendship, which provided for discussions on foreign policies and issues of common interests, but not a military cooperation.[52]

Meanwhile, concerned at the potential gravitation of the Baltic states towards Germany, the Soviet government accused the Baltic states of 'unfriendly policies' towards the USSR. In November 1936 Andrej Zhdanov, the powerful Leningrad oblast´ party boss, publicly threatened the 'small governments' should they engage in any political adventures or let 'fascist' armies pass through their territories. Although Zhdanov's rhetoric was aimed at Finland, it was interpreted in the Baltic capitals with considerable alarm, especially after Soviet planes began frequently violating Estonian airspace. The Soviet border troops also provoked incidents at the Estonian–Soviet frontier.[53]

Hitler's policies in Eastern Europe stirred further commotion among the successor-states. Using the favourable situation created by the German annexation of Austria, the Polish government hastened to reap the benefits from the situation. On 11 March 1938, following an incident, which resulted in the death of a Polish border guard, the Polish military ordered a troop concentration on the Polish–Lithuanian border. Six days later Poland issued a 48-hour ultimatum to Lithuania demanding the restoration of diplomatic relations, a customs convention, and opening of rail and trade communications. Since Berlin and Moscow offered no help, the Lithuanian government was compelled to accept the ultimatum, which in essence implied acceptance of the loss of Vilnius. Although the situation on the Polish–Lithuanian border improved, the precarious situation of Lithuania between Germany, Poland, and the Soviet Union culminated on 23 March 1939, when it was forced to cede the city-port of Klaipėda to Germany. Alarmed by the prospect of German and Soviet aggression in June 1939, Estonia and Latvia signed non-aggression pacts with Germany.[54]

The post-First World War territorial settlement suffered a further blow during the Munich Crisis that reverberated in the borderlands. In early October 1938, hard-pressed by Germany, the Czechoslovak government granted autonomy to Slovakia. Using an opportune moment, the Ukraino-phile and Russophile leaders in Transcarpathia temporarily forsook their differences and demanded the same concession. As the Czechoslovak gov-ernment authorized the formation of an autonomous government in Trans-carpathia, it immediately provoked a violent reaction in Poland and Hungary, which were concerned by a chain reaction among their sizeable Ukrainian minorities. Poised to destroy Czechoslovakia, the Hungarian government secretly supported the bands of irregulars who crossed the border and clashed with the Czech army and border guards. Similarly, keen on 'rectifying' the Cieszyn affair and interested in the common border with Hungary, the Polish government engaged in provocative activities on the Czechoslovak–Polish borders. On 2 November 1938 Hitler awarded Hungary with south-western Transcarpathia.[55]

In March 1939 as the German army invaded Czechoslovakia, the Hun-garian army moved to occupy all of Transcarpathia. It crushed a short-lived but determined resistance by Ukrainian nationalist units (the Ukrainian political factions in Transcarpathia and East Galicia supported the autonomy of the province as the first step to the independence and the unification of all Ukrainian territories). The army and the gendarmerie began 'cleansing' the province from anti-Hungarian elements, primarily communists and politically active Ukrainians. The Hungarian and Polish administration collaborated in eradicating connections between the Ukrainian factions in Transcarpathia and East Galicia. However, since the Hungarian govern-ment considered the province as a model for other Hungarian lands lost after the First World War and restored the province to its rightful owner, it mitigated the repressions by replacing the military administration with a civilian one. The province was renamed *Subcarpathia* and in July 1940 the parliament contemplated an autonomy bill, which included a diet and Rusyn as the province's official language. The bill, however, remained on paper since Hungarian politicians and the military opposed it on the grounds of security—the Soviet occupation of East Galicia and Bukovina in 1939–40 loomed as a constant threat to Hungary's eastern frontiers. To eradicate the vestiges of Czechoslovak rule the government abolished the interwar land reform and, apprehensive of Ukrainian nationalism, the administration moved to shut down all cultural and educational institutions of pro-Ukrainian orientation; on the other hand, it tolerated the Rusyn organizations as the counterbalance to pro-Ukrainian tendencies.[56]

The fate of the borderlands was sealed on 23 August and 28 September 1939 when the German–Soviet agreements divided them into two spheres of influence, whereby the demarcation lines followed the imperial borders of 1795 and the two aggressors promised not to interfere into each other's actions in the occupied territories. The Soviet Union came into possession of the former western provinces of the Russian empire, which included the Baltic region, western Byelorussia, and Volhynia. In addition, the Soviet Union also received East Galicia although it was never a part of the Russian empire. Keen to rectify the 'injustices' of the Riga settlement, Soviet propagandists justified the annexations as the means to 'protect' the Byelorussians and Ukrainians against the ravages of the Polish–German war and to fulfil Russia's historical mission to unify the 'historical Slavic lands' into a single whole. The presence of a large Byelorussian population in the eastern part of the Białystok province was used as a pretext for its integration into Brest oblast´ of the Byelorussian SSR (the western part was annexed to East Prussia). Since no explanation seemed plausible enough in the case of the predominantly Polish Łomża district, inhabited predominantly by ethnic Poles, its annexation was carried out by the right of military conquest. In September–October 1939 the USSR forced Estonia and Latvia to accept Soviet naval and military bases on their territories as defensive measures against potential foreign invasion. The Soviet government cajoled Lithuania into a similar agreement by offering it Vilnius, captured by the Soviet Army during the attack on Poland in September 1939. On 10 October the bulk of the Vilnius district was transferred to Lithuania (several eastern counties were attached to Byelorussia). Molotov explained to the Supreme Soviet that the transfer was done 'not by reason of population', but because the historical past and the aspirations of the Lithuanian nation have been ultimately connected to the city. Consequently, the Soviet government considered it necessary to 'honor these moral factors'.[57]

Further territorial acquisitions followed in June 1940—just as the German offensive in France reached its peak—when the three Baltic states received ultimatums that stipulated the formation of 'friendly' cabinets under Soviet supervision and the stationing of Soviet troops in all strategic centres. Following the ultimatums the Red Army occupied Estonia, Latvia, and Lithuania in clear violation of the non-aggression pacts of 1932. The same month the Soviet government presented Romania with an ultimatum to evacuate Bessarabia and northern Bukovina. Bessarabia was claimed as a formerly Russian territory, while the 'historically Ukrainian' Bukovina was to provide a 'compensation' for Romania's annexation of Bessarabia. By summer 1940 all the territories lost by Russia after the revolution of 1917 were regained.

Summary

Having emerged on the map of Europe the 'successor-states' faced problems of extreme magnitude, overburdened by debts, inflation, and widespread unemployment. They dealt with these problems with a varying degree of success, but in the end, impeded by unstable domestic politics and faltering economies, were bound to give way under external pressure. The shrinking fortunes of the borderlands in the late 1930s and their failure to withstand the pressure of Germany and Russia vividly revealed the economic and geopolitical fragility of the 'Lands Between', squeezed between rapacious powers. One could therefore justifiably argue that 'whether or not they concluded nonaggression pacts with their great neighbors; whether or not they pursued a policy of neutrality; whether or not they treated their ethnic minorities well; whether they banned or allowed Communist parties—all this was of no consequence for the final result'.[58]

The lack of coordination in political and military matters severely undermined the defensive ability of the new states. Whether such alliance could have succeeded against foreign threat is open to debate, but one is inclined to think of the Soviet–Finnish 'Winter War', in which the Finns put up stiff resistance despite the Red Army's overwhelming superiority in man-power and material. Therefore, the combined efforts of the Baltic republics, especially in alliance with Poland, could have severely impeded Soviet aggression. However, the hostility between Poland and Lithuania and the continuous reliance of the successor-states on the strained German–Soviet relations and the help of the West proved fatally flawed.

Constant internal instability played a similarly negative role. The governments of the borderland states were torn apart by different poles of political ideology, from democracy to dictatorship, facilitating the growth of exclusionary nationalism. In sharp contrast to the Austro-Hungarian empire that tolerated multiple loyalties of its subjects, the successor-states failed to produce a supranational ideology that could have united their subjects. Instead, the concept of national identity became based on common ethnicity and religion, conceived as the cultural basis for the legitimacy of the new state, in which the new 'core-nations' perceived themselves as hegemonic elites entitled to collective rewards. In other words, they failed to learn what Alexis de Tocqueville called the 'art of associating together',[59] increasingly acted on the premise of 'natural-national' frontiers, attempting to transform their domains into national states and perceiving the expressions of national consciousness of the ethnic minorities as a threat to state sovereignty. As the state and public institutions became 'nationalized', such policies exasperated minority groups, whose national aspirations were unfulfilled at the end of the First World War and who increasingly considered the replacement of the imperial governments with national ones a poor bargain. As a result, the borderland societies engendered radical ideas and groups that entertained the transformation of their national domains by violent means.

5
Redrawing Ethno-Social Boundaries: Phase I, 1939-1941

We shared the same misfortune: uninvited strangers ruled in our home.[1]

The Second World War marked another watershed (after the First World War) for the history of the borderlands, which experienced three foreign occupations—between 1939 and 1941 by the Soviet Union, from 1941 to 1944 by the Axis Powers, and from 1944 onward again by the Soviet Union. The loss of hard-won independence seemingly heralded a return to the pre-1914 situation, when the borderlands constituted the frontier-areas of the three empires. Here, however, the similarity ended, for the imperial states did not entertain complete social or ethnic re-moulding of their domains. Likewise, although the interwar period witnessed the introduction of laws and regulations that favoured the 'titular' nationality groups, these policies were only partially successful.

In contrast, the two totalitarian states—Nazi Germany and the Soviet Union—aimed at the total altering of their respective domains and turned the borderlands into the testing grounds for massive relocation of population, state-terror on an unprecedented scale, and ferocious internal conflicts. The process began with the Soviet 'social engineering' of the borderlands that involved the elimination of the national elites, continued with Hitler's extermination of the Jews, and was completed after the second Soviet occupation.

These developments deeply traumatized the populations of the borderlands, and the experiences of different communities evoked a wide range of responses, from active resistance to active collaboration in brutal pacifications and genocide. As in other parts of occupied Europe,

Map 3. Territorial Changes, 1939–1941

the overwhelming majority merely tried to adjust to and survive economic hardships, mobilization of hard labour, and violence, as unleashed by the occupying powers, their proxies, and the resistance forces.

This chapter traces the history of the borderlands under Soviet rule from the occupation of eastern Poland to the outbreak of the Soviet–German war. Peacetime Soviet policies towards the borderlands during the interwar period included on one hand the acceptance of diplomatic relations with the national states and on the other hand an unwavering will to alter the territorial status quo at the first opportunity. To pursue this goal, in 1939 the Soviet Union allied itself with Germany and occupied the borderlands, closely following the pattern established during the frontier wars, when military conquest was veiled as 'liberation' and the annexation as the 'fulfilment' of the desires of the oppressed people.

Similarly, between 1939 and 1941 the Soviet government assiduously laboured to recast the borderlands into the 'socialist' mould. To achieve this objective, it used various methods, such as emulating the imperial techniques of co-opting or 'assimilating' the nationality groups, deemed fitting in the new political order. To this effect, the Soviets appealed to the grievances and national sentiments of the groups that suffered discrimination or repression in the national states. Although the efforts of ideological homogeneity were pursued along 'class' lines, in the regions where social status and ethnicity were traditionally interconnected, the latter frequently became a crucial factor in establishing the political credentials of entire communities.

From the Bolshevik revolution onwards a crucial aspect of Soviet internal policies was the clear-cut division between the supporters and opponents of the state, according to Lenin's motto 'those who are not with us, are against us'. Therefore, in planning the invasion of the borderlands, the Soviet authorities had anticipated that individuals and groups outside the ideological mainstream would in all likelihood join the enemies of the USSR. For such eventuality, the state possessed a whole arsenal of repressive methods, from confiscation of property to mass arrests, deportations, and executions. However, the end result of such policies was not the hoped-for formation of a supranational Soviet identity and a socially uniform society, but 'mobilization of ethnicity' and exacerbation of internal conflicts.

The prelude to civil war

In sharp contrast to summer 1914, when the bulk of the populations of the imperial borderlands stood fast by their respective governments, the beginning of the Soviet–Polish war detonated the destructive impulses that had accumulated during the interwar period. Well aware of the boiling popular resentment towards the state and anticipating subversive activities in the borderlands, in the last days of August 1939 the Polish authorities in the *Kresy* launched 'pre-emptive' arrests of Byelorussian and Lithuanian political and civil activists. On 2 September 1939 arrests began also in East Galicia and Volhynia, where the police targeted individuals suspected of ties to the OUN or other Ukrainian nationalist groups as well as those accused of 'defeatism'. Such a vague term was applied randomly to anybody of Ukrainian descent, and according to Ukrainian sources about 15,000 people were incarcerated, including many innocent individuals. The fact that in a number of localities the prisoners were then liberated by the Red Army would play a crucial role in their subsequent behaviour.[2]

What Jan Gross aptly called the 'prelude to civil war' began with the clashes between the Citizens' Guards—the Polish communal self-defence units—and groups of Byelorussians and Ukrainians, who were enticed by Soviet propaganda that called for the annihilation of the 'Polish *szlachta*' and set out to avenge the alleged or real injustices of the interwar period. The attacks on Polish settlements immediately assumed the form of peasant rebellion as the villagers robbed, killed, or denounced their Polish neighbours to the arriving Soviet authorities. Simultaneously, organized by nationalist or communist agitators, the peasants attacked small Polish units and seized power in some villages. The Polish army responded with punitive expeditions, often subjecting villages to artillery bombardment. The reprisals acquired a definite ethnic connotation and were based on the actual behaviour of the culprits as much as on anticipation of their disloyalty. In Volkovyska (Wołkowyska) in the Hrodna district the troops killed six Jews for their alleged hostile behaviour toward Poles. In Trostianets' (Trościaniec) in Volhynia, after the Ukrainian villagers enthusiastically welcomed the Soviet troops (that had lately withdrawn) the Polish army detachment killed ten people and burned the village. In several localities the military shot or hanged Byelorussians and Ukrainians suspected of pro-Soviet sympathies.[3]

The Red Army set the tone for extreme brutality. Egged on by the official propaganda that portrayed Poles as 'fascists' and 'exploiters', the Soviet troops frequently shelled villages and towns, where they anticipated resistance, and in some places massacred Polish civilians. The Soviet administration that had arrived in various localities encouraged 'class' violence and for some time let the population go on the rampage. In Brest oblast´ the Soviet officials supervised the formation of the 'Labour Guard', which comprised workers and peasants who hunted down Polish officers, landowners, and state employees. The communists and individuals released from prisons became the main organizers of armed mobs that descended upon Polish houses and estates. On 18 September 1939 the local communists opened the prison in Hrodna and let out political prisoners and criminals, who engaged in plundering, looting, and rape. After they barricaded themselves in an orthodox church, the Polish gendarmes and policemen had to storm the building in a bloody assault. An actual battle erupted in Vilejka (Wilejka) in Hrodna district, where armed groups of Jews and Byelorussians seized the town before the arrival of the Red Army.[4] In Volhynia and East Galicia the OUN groups were prominent in anti-Polish violence. According to Polish reports, in several localities the OUN units murdered about six hundred Poles; OUN-led peasant mobs attacked police stations, killed Polish officials, and robbed refugees escaping the Red Army.[5]

Violence that spread through the Polish borderlands closely resembled the situation during the frontier wars, when the pent-up resentments in Byelorussia and Volhynia flared up in mass assaults on state institutions and representatives. As in 1918–20 peasants featured most prominently among the perpetrators. The harsh economic environment of the interwar period, the state 'pacifications' and suppression of the Orthodox Church, but also the breakdown of law and order certainly created a psychological atmosphere propitious for most gruesome atrocities. Mobs armed with axes and pitchforks murdered, mutilated, or drowned Polish landowners, settlers, and officials. Since the Soviet courts acquitted those who committed 'revolutionary terror', the opportunity to plunder without adverse consequences blurred the line between political and criminal violence, and many individuals (in some cases also ethnic Poles) participated in robbery and looting.[6]

Contrary to conventional wisdom, the Soviet invasion also sparked a series of anti-Jewish attacks. Although violence against Jews was limited in scope because the Soviets deliberately channelled popular frustrations against ethnic Poles, such instances indicated that the situation could become deadly if the state chose to encourage the assaults. Strong anti-Jewish attitudes, nourished by radical groups such as OUN, were among the driving forces of violence, for the demise of Poland presented a convenient opportunity to continue the intimidation campaign of the late 1930s against Jews as economic rivals. So nationalism and human greed conflated, as in Berezhany (Brzeżany) where the Ukrainian nationalist groups murdered several Jewish families and in several localities in Volhynia peasants converged on towns to loot Jewish apartments.[7]

Although Soviet reports of enthusiastic welcome accorded to the Red Army should be taken with a certain degree of caution, it is unquestionable that in September 1939 many Ukrainians, Jews, and Byelorussians greeted it as liberators. A Ukrainian teacher noted in his diary that the expectations of Poland's defeat filled him and his compatriots with *Schadenfreude*—malicious joy.[8] Such attitudes should not be measured as a genuine love for the new regime, but rather demonstrated that substantial segments of the borderland societies felt out of place in the old Poland and Romania, which remained alien and often repressive powers. For example, the initial reaction among Ukrainians to the Soviet invasion was quite positive. Many hoped that the hated Polish rule was over, while others were swayed by the massive Soviet propaganda that stressed unity and solidarity between the 'Slavic brother-nations'. In many localities, therefore, Ukrainians greeted the Red Army by hoisting national yellow–blue flags and presenting the soldiers with flowers.[9]

The Ukrainians and Byelorussians were ecstatic over the reunification of the borderlands with the Ukrainian and Byelorussian Soviet Republics, while the Lithuanians greeted the return of Vilnius to Lithuania—presented by the Soviets as a 'gift' to the aspirations of the Lithuanian people—as the fulfilment of a national dream, finally accomplished. Such sentiments temporarily overshadowed uneasy feelings about future Soviet plans in the Baltic. A sense of gratitude for the transfer of Vilnius was also reinforced by the relative discipline of the Red Army (in all likelihood the Soviet command issued special guidelines to the troops in this regard). The nationalization of the city began immediately and resembled the Polish 'assimilation' measures of the early 1920s in Byelorussia. Since the Lithuanian population of Vilnius was a demographic minority, to make up for this deficiency, the Lithuanian government attempted to win the Jews and Byelorussians to its cause by channelling state funds to organizing Jewish and Byelorussian institutions under the umbrella of the Lithuanian national organizations. The state also partially financed the Byelorussian schools, cooperatives, and publications; cultural and educational institutions closed by the Polish government were reopened and land distribution—largely at the expense of Polish estates—was partially carried out making Byelorussian peasants a willing tool in the hands of Lithuanian politicians. As in the early 1920s, the Lithuanian government catered to the needs of Jews and even contemplated the idea of Jewish religious autonomy (Jewish secular autonomy existed in Lithuania until 1925). Not surprisingly, Poles in Vilnius complained that the Lithuanian administration used the 'old Galician (Austro-Hungarian)' methods to increase the gap between the Polish and Jewish communities.[10]

Now it was the turn of the Polish population of the Vilnius region to bear the brunt of the 'nationalization' campaign, which was carried out by 20,000 Lithuanian officials. Lithuanian replaced Polish as the state language, Polish co-operatives were liquidated, libraries closed, street and shop signs removed, and associations and institutions, including the University of Vilnius, were shut down. Many Polish civil servants, teachers, lawyers, and doctors were fired or lost their positions and the Lithuanian police arrested some Polish intellectuals and politicians. In March 1940 the Lithuanian government denied the right of citizenship to thousands of Poles who had settled in the Vilnius region in the interwar period. Clashes between Polish students and the Lithuanian police intensified, and individual Poles suffered assaults on the streets and in churches. Not surprisingly as much as poles grieved over the loss of Independence, in the summer of 1940 they greeted the soviet occupation of Lithuania as a 'just' revenge against Lithuanian abuses.[11]

'Social engineering'

In the Bolshevik parlance a social revolution meant the creation of a completely new society, almost a biological process that involved the violent elimination of the old society and the creation of new political and social systems dominated by a totally 'new', ideologically moulded man.[12] Such practices, that included terror, but also the co-optation of as many individuals as possible with the regime, were tested after the Bolshevik revolution and applied in the borderlands. Since 1917 Soviet ideological precepts preached the vitality of the borderlands as the base for the expansion of communism into Europe. Hence, the accretion of the new territories was conceived as a crucial stage in the fulfilment of such objectives. The most pressing task was to strip the borderlands of any features pertaining to the old social and political order. 'Like all people's revolutions', stressed Soviet propaganda, such practices began 'from the destruction of the old state machinery and the creation of the power-structure of the toilers'.[13]

The integration of the borderlands into the Soviet administrative and ideological system began after the military administration was replaced by a civilian one and followed the trajectory established earlier during the anti-nationalism drive of the 1930s. At that time the 'indigenization' campaign of the 1920s, which encouraged the development of national cultures, was reversed, and many national party leaders and the intelligentsia were imprisoned or shot as 'bourgeois nationalists'. Such policies were now transplanted into the new domains and implemented by a plethora of Soviet party and state functionaries. To expedite the process, Stalin dispatched some of his most notorious henchmen—for example, the chief Soviet ideologist Andrej Zhdanov went to Estonia, the chief prosecutor in the show trials of the 1930s Andrej Vyshinsky to Latvia, and the former deputy chief of the security police Vladimir Dekanozov to Lithuania. Since many of the new officials were Russian, for the native populations their actions soon acquired the appearance of the old imperial Russification campaign, especially since similarly to the imperial administration the Soviets considered the annexed territories as 'reunited' rather than occupied. The dismantling of the old system was designed as two-dimensional, aiming at eradicating all social and national vestiges of the interwar period, with the simultaneous involvement of the native populations, especially local communists. According to the 'class' logic, workers and peasants were expected to support the regime.

The first steps of the new administration included the introduction of Russian as the official language that became the supreme medium of the official 'internationalist' ideology. In Bessarabia the reintroduction of Cyrillic script was to highlight the difference between the Moldavian and Romanian cultures (otherwise there were very few grammatical differences between the two languages). In terms of social advancement Soviet policies certainly looked advantageous to several strata of the populations. For many of the intelligentsia, workers, and peasants the expansion of the network of hospitals, clinics, theatres, and libraries seemed highly progressive, especially in contrast to the pre-war Polish and Romanian policies. In the *Kresy* the problem of unemployment was partially alleviated by mass dismissal and deportations of Polish employees and the transfer of thousands of Ukrainians to enterprises and industries in Soviet Ukraine.[14] The expansion of Byelorussian and Ukrainian schools was reflected in impressive statistics: by 1939 there was not a single Byelorussian-language school in Poland, but in 1940 there were already 4,192 schools. In Volhynia and in Drohobych (Drohobycz) oblast´ 907 new Ukrainian-language schools were opened; the numbers of Ukrainian and Jewish teachers rose from 1,207 Ukrainian and 15 Jewish in 1939 to respectively 2,138 and 568 in April 1940 (many replaced Polish teachers who were fired). Open access to education, monthly stipends, and the creation of the departments of Ukrainian language, literature, and history at the L´viv University were also greeted with genuine popular enthusiasm.[15]

In urban areas the distribution of apartments in towns and cities, free medical services, and the 'class' promotion of skilled or talented people, for whom high education or promotion was previously inaccessible, won a large number of individuals to the Soviet cause. Many became mid-level managers in factories, plants, and educational institutions. In the countryside Ukrainians and Byelorussians were appointed as village and town mayors, members of the land distribution committees and of the militia. As such they participated in the disfranchising of the individuals considered 'alien' to the new regime and in dividing up Polish landed estates. Hence, for many Ukrainians and Byelorussians the time of being outcasts—as they perceived themselves in Poland—seemed to be over and the unification of their long-divided lands and people thus complete.

At the same time, the nationalization campaign severely crippled the economic infrastructure of the borderlands. It included the appropriation of industries, businesses, commercial enterprises, banks, and private houses. The owners of small enterprises and businesses that officially were not subjected to nationalization were forced to sell them to the state. By June 1941 the number of small private businesses in Latvia was reduced to 10 per cent. National currencies were devalued. For example, if before the war the Estonian *kroon* was worth 10–15 Russian roubles, it dropped to ten times less, according the state functionaries arriving from Russia unprecedented purchase power. The freeze on banking accounts hit the upper and middle classes especially hard.[16]

The greatest efforts were directed to agriculture as the main economic foundation of the borderlands, where the collectivization campaign closely replicated 'all the processes connected to the preparation and implementation of collectivization in the Soviet Union'.[17] The creation of the first collective farms began in the *Kresy* in autumn 1939, when the Soviets authorized the village committees to chase out the Polish landlords and distribute land among the villagers. By the end of the year the administration had confiscated about 30 per cent of the land and distributed it to needy peasant households— 474,000—in addition to livestock. However, it constituted less than half of the confiscated land, which was retained for state and collective farms. Hence, most peasants were still short of land, and the Soviets probably counted that such a situation would eventually bring them into the state farms. Similar policies were implemented in Byelorussia.[18]

The crash-collectivization resulted in the mushrooming of the collective farms, which were deemed first and foremost a tool of political control, rather than a method of economic productivity. In Byelorussia the pace of collectivization resulted in the formation of 9,169 collective farms by spring 1941. However, many were merely the notorious 'Potiomkin villages' created to make an impression of rapid growth. In Ukraine the process was slower—by April 1940 there were 114 kolkhozes. The Soviet administration justified the slow pace of collectivization by the resistance of the 'kulaks and nationalists' and the 'backwardness' of the population, which in Soviet parlance meant the reluctance of peasants to join. The numbers steadily grew reaching 529 by November 1940 and 2,836 in June 1941. Such numbers, however, concealed the fact that most collective farms were highly inefficient. The 'de-kulakization' campaign that was conceived as a means to speed up the process evolved into settling personal accounts, forcible appropriation of property, and outright robbery of the alleged 'kulaks'. Small numbers of agricultural implements and the lack of enthusiasm among the new members reflected the nature of 'voluntary' membership. Many peasants joined in under coercion, but preferred to work on their private holdings. Others refused to work in the kolkhozes or left them immediately after they signed in.[19] Nevertheless, despite the slow pace of collectivization, private ownership was disappearing.

The results of collectivization in Bukovina and Bessarabia were as meagre. In September 1940 private landownership in the two provinces was limited to 20 hectares per peasant household. Although the amount was certainly larger than in pre-war Romania, without necessary agricultural implements peasants were still struggling to live above subsistence level. The Soviet administration hoped that such a situation would force more individuals to join collective farms. However, although by the end of 1940 there were about 700 kolkhozes, individual households still constituted 88.6 per cent of the total.[20]

In contrast to Byelorussia, Ukraine, and Bessarabia, the Soviet administration in the Baltic took into account the particularities of the region such as the high level of literacy and national consciousness and the efficiency and relative prosperity of peasant households. The preparatory measures began in autumn 1940, when the state nationalized about 2 million hectares of land and pressure was brought upon mid-size households, that were heavily and increasingly taxed. The crash collectivization was planned to begin in spring of the next year.[21]

Another tool for political control and the socio-economic reconstruction of the borderlands was a new border regime. To stem the population movement across the Soviet–German and the old Soviet–Polish border, the government committed large numbers of troops to seal the borders. In one year, between October 1939 and November 1940 the troops apprehended 66,948 people attempting to cross the border. Although such activities were largely motivated by economic considerations, Soviet officials were concerned about any leak of information on problems in the annexed territories. The border troops were therefore ordered to shoot violators of the border regime, and captured individuals were tried for 'counter-revolutionary activities'. Additional measures included introduction of a Soviet passport system in winter 1940. In April–May 1940 a mass resettlement of the population from the immediate vicinity of the Soviet–German border created a five-mile no man's land, from which about 80,000 people were removed.[22]

In addition, in November 1939 Germany and the Soviet Union signed a treaty for population exchange between the two states. The plan fitted well with both German and Soviet visions of the borderlands. Hitler welcomed the opportunity to 'Germanize' the annexed western Polish territories, from which ethnic Poles were removed, while the resettlement fulfilled the Soviet security requirements in eliminating potential troublemakers from the sensitive border areas. The agreement, however, immediately ran into difficulties since many Ukrainians, Poles, and even Jews, horrified by the prospect of living under the Soviets, attempted to pass as Germans. On the other hand, the Soviets were unwilling to accept thousands of Jews escaping the Nazi persecution. Thousands of refugees, therefore, had to endure cold and hunger in several transition camps, where they had to wait for permission to cross the border. The Soviet authorities often broke apart families, allowing only selected members to evacuate or blackmailed others for collaboration in espionage on the other side of the border.[23]

Since mid-July 1940 the Soviets began the resettlement of the Germans from Bukovina and Bessarabia. Altogether about 124,000 Germans as well as those who claimed to be of German background left the Soviet borderlands. Approximately 55,000 individuals left western Ukraine—given that the official statistics maintained there were 40,000 Germans, it means that a sizeable number of non-Germans also left. The resettlement also served an economic objective, for those who left had to abandon their land, livestock, and most agricultural implements (in Bessarabia and Bukovina the Soviets came into possession of 6,000 horses, 16,000 cattle, 147,000 poultry, 60,000 sheep, and 59,000 hectares of land). At the end of December 1939 another German–Soviet agreement provided for the repatriation of Polish refugees; 33,934 left the Soviet zone for German-occupied Poland by June 1940. Another human wave was moving eastward—simultaneously with Soviet deportations, about 48,000 refugees from Poland and unemployed individuals decided to seek employment in the Donbas region, lured by Soviet promises of a better life.[24,25]

★ ★ ★

Historians have traditionally applied the word 'collaboration' to pro-Axis activities among the native populations during the Second World War. Meanwhile, collaboration with the Soviet regime in the borderlands was as widespread, ranging from mere opportunism and desire for social promotion or economic benefits to ideological cooperation and active participation in the terror system. Similarly to the situation under the Germans in Europe, where marginal political groups such as homegrown fascists offered their services to the new regime, in the borderlands it was the local communist parties that surfaced as the collaborationist vanguard. They were instrumental in organizing revolutionary committees and the militia that took control over villages and towns, secured government offices and documentation, and headed the mobs that practised 'revolutionary terror'. However, because the communist parties were too small—excluding Bessarabia, there were approximately 8,000 members (the largest was the Western Ukrainian party that numbered 4,719 members and the smallest was in Estonia with 133 members)[26]—after the establishment of the Soviet regime the local communist groups offered the 'open ticket' to any volunteers and while the membership grew, the professional revolutionaries were sidelined by many fellow travellers. In addition, the Soviet administration was often suspicious of 'nationalist' tendencies among local communists, and delegated to important positions reliable Latvian, Lithuanian, or Ukrainian communists from the USSR.[27]

The regime also counted on a large pool of individuals of socialist, democratic, and liberal orientation, who were either dissatisfied with the national governments or had fled from the German-occupied territories. Certainly, the moderate Polish and Ukrainian intelligentsia preferred the Soviet 'class' politics to the Nazi racial ideology and offered their services to the administration as managers, writers, reporters, and translators, according the regime badly needed support and prestige. The unification of the Byelorussian and Ukrainian lands, the expansion of the native languages, and state-sponsored celebrations of famous Polish and Ukrainian personalities such as Adam Mickiewicz and Ivan Franko played up to national sensibilities and attracted a number of prominent intellectuals to the Soviet cause. For example, the world-renowned Polish poet, writer, and translator Tadeusz Boy-Żeleński became active in the Society of Polish writers in L'viv.[28]

Before the Ukrainians and Byelorussians understood the nature of the Soviet regime, they remembered well the closures of Byelorussian and Ukrainian schools and cultural institutions, the 'pacifications', and the police repression under the Polish Republic. Similarly, virulent anti-Semitism of the late 1930s in Poland alienated many Jews. In contrast, in terms of vertical social mobility the Soviet system initially looked more attractive, and if the political affiliations and loyalties of Poland's minorities may have been divided between nationalism, communism, or fascism, by 1939 they had none 'whatsoever for Poland'.[29] Accordingly, collaborating with the regime presented no moral dilemma. Many OUN members served in the Soviet militia and civil service (later they would be retained by the Germans). Some may have been instructed by their leaders to integrate themselves into the system; others simply joined the winning side.[30] In addition to ideologically driven individuals there were former political prisoners and criminals, who waited for an opportune moment to settle old scores and featured prominently in confiscations and requisitions.[31]

Although popular attitudes towards the Soviets were much cooler in the Baltic, where people deeply resented the loss of national independence, popular reactions to the Soviet regime were not universally hostile. Some representatives of the Lithuanian intelligentsia were critical of the authoritarian policies of the government of Antanas Smetona, and were attracted by Soviet promises of social and economic reforms. The poorer strata of the population approved the nationalization of large and mid-size businesses and enterprises; labour committees, which initially were made responsible for labour issues, were popular among the workers. Similarly, peasants approved the nationalization of large estates over 30 hectares and the church land that was handed over to the land committees. Pronounced anti-Polish policies appealed to Lithuanian peasants who despised Polish landlords. Because the Soviet administration retained low-level administrators and civil servants in their positions, they became staunch supporters of the regime, which guaranteed their employment. Also, alarmed by the prospect of Lithuanian and Ukrainian nationalisms, by spring 1941 the Soviets had relaxed anti-Polish policies. In the Vilnius region the Polish language received equal status with Lithuanian and Russian. The Polish theatres, schools, and journals were reopened, and more Poles found employment in Soviet institutions.[32] Employment opportunities, easy duties, or acquisition of power drew about 10,000 Latvian labourers into the ranks of the so-called Workers' Guards. Similar detachments known as the People's Defence were created in Estonia, which acted as auxiliary law enforcement agencies in the name of the regime.[33]

Conversely, collaboration with the regime further aggravated mutual animosities between nationality groups competing for employment. The de-Polonization of the civil service in Vilnius and the *Kresy* sharpened the rivalry between Byelorussians, Lithuanians, Ukrainians; and Polish refugees to the west blamed their former co-nationals as the main cause for their misfortunes. Much ink has been spilled over the issue of Jewish participation in the Soviet party and state apparatus. The accusations of political opportunism and disloyalty of Jews to the 'host-nations' reached their highest pitch under the Soviet regime, when many Jews became visible in the state apparatus and the communist party. For example, in June 1940 Jews made up 30.6 per cent of the Lithuanian Communist Party and 10 per cent in the Soviet security organ (NKVD). Two of the fifteen Soviet ministers (commissars) in Lithuania were Jews. Out of 1,169 party members in Estonia about 2 per cent were Jewish. In contrast, 414 Jews made up a dominant majority in the West Byelorussian communist party (in addition to seventy-five Poles and ten Byelorussians).[34]

Whether these numbers signify a considerable involvement of a small ethnic group with the regime, or to the contrary show that relatively few Jews—in proportion to the Jewish population—collaborated with the occupier, is open to interpretation. It can be stated for certain that in the context of Soviet occupation these statistics meant more than just a mathematical computation. On one hand there were many definitely positive and attractive features of the Soviet regime. Anti-Semitism was officially outlawed, the hated student quota in colleges and universities was abolished, and the new economic system required workers and as many white-collar jobs, providing opportunities for Jewish engineers, architects, doctors, accountants, teachers, and skilled craftsmen. On the other hand, the Soviet nationalization policies severely undermined the traditional socio-economic and religious infrastructure of the Jews. The state nationalized banks and small credit institutions, Jewish estates, enterprises, and flour and sawmills. The so-called compression of living accommodation, which meant the re-distribution of apartments in cities and towns, affected the Jewish middle class that alongside the Germans constituted the most urban element in the borderlands especially hard. With the introduction of Soviet laws, Jewish lawyers largely lost their living (in comparison, engineers found more opportunities in industries and doctors in hospitals and clinics). The ban on political parties eliminated the activities of the traditional Jewish groups such as the Bund; the Jewish self-government communities (*Kehilah*) were disbanded and their property expropriated, and Jewish religious and educational activities came to a standstill. As a result—and this fact was duly noted by the supreme commander of the Polish underground Stefan Rowecki in his report of July 1941—many Jews who had lost their living sought the existing opportunities in the Soviet apparatus, where they became visible as state functionaries in the regime that destroyed independence of Poland and the Baltic states.[35] Such social reversal, in which the alleged omnipresence of the Jews in the Soviet power apparatus equalled their omnipotence, was especially appalling to nationalistically inclined societies that accepted the image of the *Jew* as the carrier and the major beneficiary of the new regime. Any anti-Semite, therefore, could complain to have suffered from the injustices of the 'Jewish-Bolshevik system'.

It should also be taken into account that among Jews the fear of the Germans was stronger than the fear of the Soviets, especially since thousands of Jewish refugees fled German-occupied Poland, bringing stories of German atrocities. Many Jews were also relieved with the arrival of the

Soviet army especially since the collapse of the Polish state was accompanied by instances of anti-Jewish violence, which subsided after the establishment of the administration. Similarly, many Jews welcomed the Soviets in Bessarabia and Bukovina, where in summer 1940 the retreating Romanian troops staged several brutal pogroms justified as reprisals for the 'Jewish-communist' conspiracies and subversive acts. In addition, the often humiliating experience of the interwar period, especially remembered by young people and professionals, was not forgotten, and they often expressed their sentiments in an arrogant and offensive way. A Jewish contemporary recalled that during the Soviet invasion of Lithuania a group of Jewish communists insulted the Lithuanian policemen and mocked President Smetona.[36]

Interviewed by the Polish government-in-exile information department, the majority of the Polish refugees stressed the 'treacherous' conduct of Jews as the main proxies of the Soviet regime. It should be noted, however, that a number of interviewees named all nationality groups, including Poles, among active collaborators. For example, the refugees from the Jedwabne and Radziłow (Łomża district) regions, which would become the sites of vicious anti-Jewish pogroms in summer 1941, mentioned Jews and Poles (identified as 'communists') who collaborated with the occupiers. Some individuals from Vilnius recalled that Jewish teachers in the Bund-funded schools, who continued teaching the Polish language and expressed solidarity with their Polish colleagues, were weeded out from the education system by the Lithuanian administration.[37]

But by and large the populations of the borderlands refused to see the diversified conduct of Jews, whose alleged and real conduct fitted well with the traditional anti-Semitic prejudices and the more modern ideological images of the 'Judaeo-Commune'. In February 1940 an envoy of the Polish government-in-exile, Jan Karski, reported that the conduct of Jews was similar to that of Byelorussians and Ukrainians and ranged from collaborating with the Soviets to helping persecuted Poles, but the Polish population did not make such distinctions and overwhelmingly waited for the time of 'bloody reckoning'.[38]

The terror campaign

The class-based Soviet doctrine of the irreconcilable differences between the socialist and capitalist worlds predicated the 'social engineering' of the state domain through various methods, among which terror was one of the most prominent and permanent features of the Soviet state-building and efficient deterrent strategy. In the words of a prominent Soviet theoretician, Nicholai Bukharin, 'however paradoxical it sounds, proletarian oppression (*prinuzhdenie*) in all its forms from executions to forced labour, is a method of the separating and forging the communist humankind from the capitalist epoch'.[39]

The Soviet security apparatus meticulously prepared for a campaign in the borderlands. As early as 1925 the secret police began compiling lists of potential enemies who were to be rendered harmless in case of war. Among the prime targets were the members and agents of the Polish, Romanian, and other intelligence services, political police, the 'nationalist counter-revolutionary elements, Ukrainian émigrés, and White émigrés' as the prime targets.[40] Before an attack on Poland, the NKVD formed nine operational groups, whose structure resembled those of the Nazi *Einsatz-gruppen*. Each group numbered between 40 and 70 functionaries, was supported by an infantry battalion, and had multiple tasks: to capture and hold post offices, telegraph, telephone, radio stations, banks and credit unions, publishing facilities, archives, police stations, and military installations. The groups also possessed special lists of individuals who were targeted for 'removal' (*iz'yatie*)—before the transfer of Vilnius to Lithuania, the Soviet secret police obtained documentation on prominent Polish personalities in the city's economic, political, and cultural life. On 8 September 1939, the Commissar of the Interior Lavrentii Beria issued an order of 'executive measures' that were to be implemented in the occupied territories. Within Polish society 195,000 NKVD functionaries and border guards set out to 'remove' entire social groups—landlords, nobles, business-men, political activists, civil servants, and policemen. First mass executions took place in Hrodna, where the NKVD detachments shot its Polish defenders. By early October, advancing behind the Red Army, the five operational groups in western Ukraine arrested 3,914 policemen, gen-darmes, and the representatives of the 'bourgeois' classes. After the cessation of hostilities, the operational groups provided the basis for stationary secret police offices and began creating a widespread network of agents, which encompassed the entire territory of western Ukraine.[41]

The methods of the Soviet repressive apparatus were shaped to perfection in the 1920s and 1930s, and those who survived the Soviet and German occupations conceded that the Soviet security police was much better equipped to deal with the complexities of the borderlands than the dreaded Gestapo. More importantly, in comparison to the Germans, who were largely concerned with political and economic matters, the Soviet authorities were interested in all spheres of life. Accordingly, the entire Soviet system was predicated upon the participation of everybody in state activities and entailed two parallel objectives. On one hand, the required individual participation in various committees, associations, and endless meetings served to integrate the population with the regime, while on the other hand it served as a proof of loyalty. In other words, everyone had to publicly display loyalty or otherwise be tainted as unreliable. Hence, popular participation in political and civil life became a crucial tool for population control.

Mass arrests, launched simultaneously with the military conquest, initially targeted politically engaged individuals such as the members of socialist, liberal, nationalist, and peasant parties. Among the first victims in Byelorussia was Anton Lutskevich, the founder of the short-lived Byelorussian republic during the frontier wars.[42] On 12 July 1940 the arrests in the Baltic region encompassed more than 2,000 civil and political activists, including prominent politicians and their families such as Jaan Tõnisson, the Latvian and Estonian presidents Ulmanis and Päts, and the former Lithuanian Prime-Minister Voldemaras (they all died in Soviet captivity) and many top military personnel. Smetona avoided the same fate by escaping to Germany. Other 'anti-Soviet elements' included officers, priests, policemen, political émigrés, and shopkeepers, but also native communists, socialists, intellectuals, and literati suspected of 'nationalist deviation'.[43] The terror campaign also followed the trajectory of the Soviet purges of the 1930s, assuming an ethnic character, for the diversity of the borderlands impeded rigid ideological application. The targeted groups represented the upper crust of national politics, cultures, education, and religion, that is, the most nationally conscious elements that were considered especially hostile. Altogether by June 1941 in the Kresy and Galicia the NKVD had arrested 41,059 Poles, 20,864 Ukrainians, 7,549 Byelorussians, and up to 12,000 Jews.[44] These represented different political parties and social groups.

Also, the immense experience acquired by the Soviet secret police in two decades translated into the infiltration and destruction of numerous underground cells, whose existence was cut short. Using various methods such as the organization of a fake resistance centre, the police lured real resisters into traps. By spring–summer 1940 NKVD agents in the Kresy and East Galicia had infiltrated the OUN and the Polish underground; in western Byelorussia 3,231 underground members and 5,584 members of various political associations were arrested.[45]

Consequently, prisons and detention places became overcrowded, with dozens of inmates sharing single-man cells. For example, the largest *Kresy* prison in Brest had capacity for 2,680, but by the outbreak of the German–Soviet war it contained 3,807 inmates, who suffered extreme sanitary conditions and poor diet; sick and older people were first to succumb and die. Arrest was followed by hours-long interrogation, mostly conducted at night, and which included psychological intimidation and beating, burning with cigarettes and electrical current, flogging with rubber cables, and hanging by the feet. Such practices resulted in severe internal damage and deep psychological trauma. Admission of guilt or confessions provided the interrogators with new names, which, in turn, were placed on the lists of arrests.[46]

But perhaps the most horrifying experience for the populations of the borderlands was deportations, conceived as the main tool of permanently 'cleansing' the new territories from potentially dangerous elements. The first deportations were carried out in late September 1939 in Vilnius. Anticipating the transfer of the district to Lithuania and certainly planning for the more distant future, the secret police arrested and deported a number of the Byelorussian literati and political activists as a 'prophylactic' measure. From autumn 1939 the deportations spread from the Baltic to Bessarabia in four major waves that affected a whole range of the 'former people' such as state functionaries, officers, priests, intellectuals, landowners, tradesmen, students, and well-to-do peasants. In spring 1940 the secret police began mass executions of the 'inveterate enemies' among captured Poles at Katyn' and other localities (some were executed locally). The last deportations were carried out in May–June 1941; many deportees were sent eastward just a week before the outbreak of the Soviet–German war. Altogether between 1939 and 1941 approximately 350,000 (some sources claim as many as 535,000) individuals were deported from the borderlands. In addition, about 20,000 refugees from Transcarpathia, who in 1939–40 crossed to Galicia, were also deported on charges of espionage.[47]

Although the secret police reported that the deportations were carried out in an organized manner, it admitted that there were 'violations of Soviet legality'—a euphemism to describe the brutal treatment and robberies of the deportees by Soviet functionaries. Since the affected individuals were given limited time to prepare for a long journey, many, particularly those who were deported in winter, collapsed from cold and sickness. It was reported that 'one could hear small babies crying as they were freezing because it was very cold' and Polish women locked in freight cars threw the frozen bodies of their children through the windows at the feet of the guards.[48] The border guards (the old border-lines were initially maintained) frequently confiscated the deportees' possessions, while the Soviet party and state employees often engaged in massive robbery of property and commodities left behind. At the places of exile the local authorities were either unprepared or unwilling to accommodate the masses of arrivals. As a result, by July 1941 12,313 deportees had died in captivity.[49]

Soviet terror, too often totally unrelated to individual guilt, deeply traumatized the borderlands, establishing an atmosphere of fear and uncertainty. As argued by a prominent Russian-American sociologist, the expansion of a totalitarian state in time of emergency is predicated upon diminishing of the integrated system of norm.[50] The Soviet regime indeed deprived people of any integrated system of norms because nobody could be entirely sure whether he or she was guilty or not. Sex, age, political affiliation or the lack of such, and creed seemed irrelevant, for arrests and heavy prison sentences had no visible rhyme or reason. Among the arrested were individuals who had potential connections 'with abroad' such as Esperanto practitioners and stamp collectors, but also dedicated members of the West Ukrainian and West Byelorussian communist parties, which were disbanded by the Comintern in 1938. Despite 'class approach', the security police targeted also people of perfect 'proletarian' background such as workers and peasants. Among the latter were families which owned 2 hectares of land—the limit by which the Soviet authorities identified the poor. Similarly, ethnicity no longer mattered, for in spring 1940 mass arrests began among the Ukrainians, who were previously tolerated at the expense of Poles.[51]

An overwhelming sense of fear and helplessness reigned over the borderlands. The screech of car brakes at night would awake the entire neighbourhood, horrified at the prospect of the arrest, and whole families spent nights in basements to avoid round-ups. Arrests and searches were conducted at night, when barely awake people were totally disoriented and scared. The police used the opportunity to shamelessly rob their victims, taking away valuables, watches, and rags, wantonly destroying what they could not take along, and they left behind desperate, grieving, and enraged relatives of the arrested. Everybody felt equally powerless before the overwhelming apparatus of repression and, as legal rationality and its clear relation to the individual fate evaporated, 'fate itself became so enigmatic as to lose all meaning'.[52]

Deported as a landowner, a woman from Bessarabia recalled that among her fellow-deportees were an

> owner of a pastry shop, a pregnant mother of several half-dressed children whose husband had served in the Romanian army, a cooking instructor, a priest, a priestess, an invalid, a small boy, and the nicely dressed two girls whisked off from a school prom . . . united only by the fact that they did not understand why and what was happening to them.[53]

Enforced and voluntary collaboration was a crucial element in the terror campaign. For example, the process of deportations also involved large numbers of average citizens, who had to publicly approve repressive measures. In October 1939 the National Assemblies of western Byelorussia and western Ukraine that consisted of workers, peasants, and the intelligentsia vehemently attacked the Polish settlers as 'henchmen, spies, and parasites' and appealed to the government to remove them from the borderlands. Such attitudes were generated by a variety of factors. The Soviet authorities deliberately involved as many people as possible into the machinery of suppression, attracting them by the opportunity for social advancement or economic benefits. In the countryside the village councils and the militia compiled the lists of the deportees and split their belongings among themselves.[54] Fear of being labelled an 'enemy of the state' forced some individuals to act conspicuously as political and civil activists, while others hastened to police stations to forestall a potential denunciation by an unfriendly neighbour. Old grudges and offences could easily be settled. In the words of a contemporary, 'everybody could destroy everybody. All [one] needed to do was go to the authorities and make deposition . . . a few accusations and your enemy is lost'.[55]

★ ★ ★

By June 1941 all the borderlands were emotionally overloaded societies. Independence was lost, national sentiments were deeply offended by attacks on religion, language, and independent statehood vilified as the 'fascist dictatorship' or, in the case of Poland, as the 'ugly offspring of the Versailles Treaty' according to Molotov's speech in October 1939. A Polish report in autumn 1940 sadly admitted that the *Kresy* had become a 'large Polish cemetery', implying the destruction of centuries-old history and culture.

Massive anti-church propaganda was accompanied by confiscation of ecclesiastical property and the prohibition of religious publications. In schools and universities the standardized Soviet curriculum was introduced, including the mandatory theory of Marxism, 'unreliable' instructors were purged, and the libraries were cleansed from the sources 'unfavourable' to the Soviet Union. Millions had to adapt to a totally new system of socio-economic relations, traditional political and religious connections were broken and persecuted, forms of personal contacts severed or altered for fear of denunciations; family members were lost to deportations or went into hiding. Against their will, most of the Estonians, Latvians, Lithuanians, and Poles lost their states and against their will became citizens of an alien state, which was not only highly oppressive, but from their standpoint—adding insult to injury—was highly backward. Private life lost its privacy, for in the Soviet state it was considered a part of the public domain.[56]

Popular reactions to the reality varied. Some individuals committed suicide, others hid inside their own rapidly diminishing private world. There was a deep sense of helplessness, despair, and rage and, given the unconvincing official propaganda, most incredible rumours became a primary source of information and were given full credence. Many prayed for the war between Germany and Russia. The breakdown of social and economic order symbolized the destruction of the traditional fabric of society—religion, social relations, law, and self-identity—and escalated distrust, mutual suspicion and fear, and a great number of individuals awaited a time to avenge their suffering, unleashing frustrations against those associated with the Soviets—largely members of other nationality groups. For instance, during the elections to People's Diet in Lithuania some Lithuanian voters dropped anti-Semitic diatribes instead of official ballots, which indicated that in the popular image Jews and Bolshevism were but the same evil.[57]

Concomitantly, resistance grew in strength. The nationalist groups looked to Germany for help, tying themselves to Nazi goals and objectives. Some received training in the German intelligence camps, others operated covertly in the borderlands. In Galicia and Volhynia OUN members carried out sabotage acts, destroyed state property, and spread anti-Soviet propaganda. In Lithuania popular passive resistance included boycotting elections, distributing anti-Soviet leaflets, and ostracizing Soviet instructors in schools and universities. Armed insurgents carried out acts of sabotage, burned forests and oil facilities, and disrupted communications. Thousands participated in various anti-Soviet activities and between July 1940 and May 1941 the Soviet security forces tracked and destroyed seventy-five underground cells.[58]

The majority of Poles also considered the German occupation system preferable to the Soviet one. In comparison to 120,000 people who died in 1939–41 (including 100,000 Jews) in the German-occupied zone, the Polish population in the *Kresy* and East Galicia suffered much higher losses—approximately 200,000 were deported and more than 20,000 Polish prisoners of war were murdered (thousands would perish later during the evacuation of the Soviet prisons in summer 1941). Hence, during the Soviet–German population exchange many Poles literally begged the German authorities for permission to cross over the border. Resistance began in autumn 1939, when the Polish underground cells of different political affiliations collected arms, carried out anti-Soviet propaganda, and fought skirmishes with the Soviet border guards and the security police.[59]

Summary

In 1939–41 the Soviet regime emulated the Bolshevik policies during the frontier wars by attempting to substitute the pluralistic texture of the borderlands with an ideological uniformity. To this effect, all vestiges of the 'old' societies were to be destroyed and replaced with the new classless polity. In comparison to the interwar 'successor-states', Soviet rule was all-inclusive—it aimed at nationalizing the lands and the people and any individual, regardless of his or her ethnicity, could become a state functionary or a deputy to the National Assembly, at the same being equally powerless as the population at large in the face of overwhelming state power.[60]

Jan Gross called the Soviet state a 'spoiler state' that focused entirely on using its power not for having things done, but for preventing anybody getting things done. Therefore, only through association with the state and by sowing mistrust and demoralization could one attain social promotion, at the same time being 'spoiled' by the state.[61] Indeed, large segments of the populations, especially in the former Polish provinces, accommodated themselves to the occupier by 'indirect' or 'direct' collaboration, mostly but not exclusively by becoming low- and middle-level functionaries of the regime. As such they carried responsibilities for the implementation of 'class policies' against alleged enemies of the state. Knowing local conditions and the people well, they became indispensable as an extension of the Soviet power apparatus that eventually forced the borderlands to the 'stress threshold'—a state of mind when self-protection becomes the dominant feature in behaviour, motivates defensive responses, and, if such extreme stress persists, the person ultimately becomes exhausted and suffers a complete breakdown.[62] Such a psychological environment created ideal conditions for a violent eruption during the German invasion.

6

The Holocaust and Local Collaboration 1941–1944

The German invasion of the Soviet Union was predicated upon the conflation of military and ideological objectives—the defeat of the Red Army and the simultaneous annihilation of the Soviet state. Before the war the Nazi elite had entertained several projects in regard to the modes of occupation and governing of the occupied Soviet territories. Hitler dreamed of the large tracts of European Russia being 'cleansed' from the native populations and settled by Germanic colonists. Other Nazi dignitaries such as the chief party ideologist Alfred Rosenberg was in favour of pre-First World War imperial ideas of creating a string of buffer-states on Russia's western and southern frontiers, while the SS and police chief Heinrich Himmler advocated turning the borderlands into a huge dumping ground for Poles and Jews. All these plans visualized the eventual homogeneity of the borderlands, achieved by the removal of the Jews and the gradual elimination of other 'inferior' nationalities, particularly the Slavs.

In the end Hitler decided to create two administrative units, one in the Baltic and Byelorussia and the other in Ukraine, that were to function as temporary entities for the duration of the Soviet–German war. According to the Nazi racial hierarchy, the Estonians and Latvians, traditionally within German political and cultural influence, were allowed to retain a modicum of native administrative structure, whereas the racially 'inferior' Lithuanians, Byelorussians, and Ukrainians were to be ruled directly. Regardless of their status, all the nationality groups in the borderlands were expected to serve as a source of labour and supplies for Germany's economy.

A crucial corollary of the Nazi war against the Soviet Union was the total eradication of 'Jewish Bolshevism'. Ideological precepts that conflated Jews and Bolshevism originated with the inception of the Nazi Party and by 1941 were shared by large segments of the German military, police, and civil service personnel. For the 'political management of the war zone'—a euphemism for the pacification of the conquered territories—Himmler's police and SS apparatus received special plenary powers. To this end, special units—the *Einsatzgruppen*—and police battalions were to follow the German army and to systematically eliminate political and racial opponents, especially Jews. Simultaneously, the Nazi leadership counted on the radicalized elements among the local population who would assist the Germans in the liquidation of the Jews.

Since the mechanisms of the Holocaust in the different regions of the borderlands are discussed in numerous studies, this chapter focuses on the attitudes of the local population towards the situation of Jews. Although it was the German invasion that provided the over-all institutional and psychological framework for the genocide, it was the actions of the willing 'neighbours' that contributed to its totality.[1] Local volunteers constituted a fraction of the populations in which they lived, but their involvement cut across social status, educational level, creed, and age, and entailed a variety of motives. While the political aspirations of the nationalist groups that were particularly active in the initial stages of the war diverged from the Nazi ideological objectives, their interests effectively converged in the elimination of the Jews as ideological enemies or socio-economic rivals.

The 'Jedwabne state'

Operation 'Barbarossa' was launched on 22 June 1941 and its initial successes were astounding. L′viv and Minsk fell on 30 June, Riga on 1 July, and by mid-July the Romanian army had conquered Bessarabia and northern Bukovina. The rapid advance of the Axis forces took the Soviet administration in the borderlands by complete surprise and, panic-stricken, it initiated a scorched-earth policy that entailed the destruction of bridges, roads, plants, and food supplies. Meanwhile, the NKVD speedily concocted contingency plans to evacuate thousands of prisoners. Farther from the front lines prisoners were herded into freight-trains and shipped off eastward. More often, however, the prison administration opted for a more expedient solution and began mass executions several hours after the German invasion. Shortly after the German attack the killings of inmates began in Przemyśl (Peremyshl′) and L′viv; next day about fifty inmates were executed in Tallinn. Mass shootings continued until the complete Soviet withdrawal.[2]

At first, only those convicted for 'counter-revolutionary activities' were shot. Soon, however, selective executions were abandoned in favour of wholesale massacres that were carried out in the most gruesome fashion. In Luts′k (Volhynia) NKVD functionaries and prison guards machine-gunned about 1,500 prisoners, largely Ukrainians. In other places the guards tossed hand grenades into prison cells or set them on fire. Trucks' motors were kept running to muffle the victims' screams and the henchmen burned the corpses or hastily buried them under the cover of darkness. Those who were evacuated eastward fared little better, for they had to endure long 'death marches', during which the weak, sick, and old prisoners died from thirst and exertion or were murdered by the guards. Sometimes the escort commanders ordered the execution of entire transports. Recent estimations suggest that altogether between 20,000 and 30,000 prisoners were murdered in East Galicia and the *Kresy* alone.[3] _velir maght_

Therefore, the invading forces were greeted with genuine enthusiasm, conspicuously similar to one accorded by the non-Polish populations of the *Kresy* to the Red Army in September 1939. Such attitudes stemmed from popular hopes that national independence would be restored, but more profoundly displayed the overwhelming atmosphere of relief after the Soviet retreat. Almost immediately, however, the feelings of joy and elation were shattered by the discoveries of mass graves left behind by the Soviet secret police. When thousands of grieving people converged upon prisons, looking for their relatives and friends, sporadic attacks on Jews soon escalated into large-scale pogroms that swept through the borderlands from Latvia to Bessarabia like a gigantic pendulum, claiming the lives upward of 30,000 Jews. The NKVD massacres certainly triggered the violence as the German and nationalist propaganda identified the 'Jewish Bolsheviks' as the main culprits, thus confirming an image imprinted in the popular psyche during the Soviet occupation.

Popular frustrations were thus channelled towards blaming a specific group and the violence in different locations evolved according to a similar scenario. For example, in L′viv attacks on Jews gained momentum after the Germans opened the city prisons. The Ukrainian militia rounded up Jews, who were forced to run the gauntlet amidst the fury of the mob that savagely beat them; groups of Jewish men were also forced to exhume the bodies of the NKVD victims.[4] In Zolochiv (East Galicia) attacks on Jews were initiated by the personnel of the SS-Division 'Wiking' in reprisal for the death of a regimental commander, who was killed in battle against the Soviet troops. Nevertheless, it was the NKVD headquarters, where bodies of executed inmates had been discovered earlier, which became the main site of the pogrom. Under the supervision of the Germans, the Ukrainian militia and groups of raging youth forced the Jews to exhume corpses. Later, the SS details and the militia murdered the Jewish intelligentsia. In Kremenets' (Volhynia) about 130 Jews, who had unearthed corpses in the town prison, were bludgeoned to death by the Ukrainian militia and the raging mob.[5]

However, although the discovery of the Soviet massacres often served as a signal for anti-Jewish violence, it also erupted in places where there had been no NKVD killings, for example in Kaunas (there were, however, executions in nearby detention camps). On 25 June, under the guidance of *Einsatzgruppe* A, the 'white armbands'—the generic term for the Lithuanian militia—set on fire the synagogues and Jewish houses and dragged Jews into the streets as the crowds cheered. Two days later at the Lietŭkis garage a group of young Lithuanians with iron bars clubbed to death more than fifty Jews.[6] In several instances, the Germans took direct part in the pogroms. In Baranovichi (Byelorussia) German soldiers joined the local population in looting Jewish houses and apartments. On 27 June 1941, under pretext of a 'reprisal' for an alleged shooting, drunken military personnel and policemen staged a pogrom in Białystok, in which about 2,000 Jews were murdered. According to eyewitnesses, the Germans literally ran amok, looting, shooting, and burning. While several firing squads carried out mass executions of captured Jews outside the city, several hundred men, women, and children were locked in a synagogue and burned alive; only a small group escaped owing to the heroic efforts of the synagogue's Polish caretaker, Józef Bartoszka.[7]

If in general the Germans tried to maintain the decorum of being accidental observers, the Romanian troops in Bukovina and Bessarabia led the way in violence. Similarly to the Nazis, the Romanian political and military leadership stressed the ideological character of the 'holy war' against 'Judaeo-Bolshevism'. The dictator Ion Antonescu consistently equated Jews and 'Bolshevik agents', who were to be shot on the spot, while Inspector General of the Gendarmerie Constantin Vasiliu ordered his subordinates to 'cleanse' Bukovina and Bessarabia by annihilating Jews. Accordingly, by mid-July 1941 the Romanian troops engaged in mass murder of Jewish men, women, and children, thus effectively launching the 'Final Solution' ahead of the Germans.[8] Many Romanian officials, who had served in Bukovina and Bessarabia in the interwar period, now returned with the troops and turned for help to individuals or groups. There was no lack of local initiative in inciting anti-Jewish violence. On 27 June 1941 in the village of Ghirovo in Bessarabia some members of the National Christian Party featured prominently as the ringleaders of the pogrom. They organized a civil committee that took over power in the village, established contacts with Romanian troops, and initiated a pogrom against Jews and Soviet activists. A number of villagers joined in plundering Jewish houses. After the Romanian and German troops arrived in the village in early July, the committee members and the villagers participated in the execution of Jewish men, women, and children. In the predominantly Ukrainian counties of northern Bukovina the local OUN activists assisted the Romanians in the robbery and murder of Jewish residents.[9]

All pogroms were marked by extreme brutality. In Radziłów (Łomża district) and Jedwabne the perpetrators drove Jewish men, women, and children into barns and set them on fire. In Tul'chin (Volhynia) a mob murdered about seventy Jews with pitchforks, iron bars, and axes. In the village of Rostoki (northern Bukovina) the native volunteers (mostly members of OUN) savagely beat and shot a group of Jews at a nearby cemetery. The conduct of the assailants was often so violent that in some instances the German and Romanian military personnel were compelled to intervene. Thus, in Rivne and Kovel' (Volhynia) the German commandants prevented the spread of pogroms; in Stăneștii de Jos (northern Bukovina) the pogrom was stopped by a Romanian gendarme officer.[10]

★ ★ ★

The willingness of the local population to merge quickly into the anti-Jewish campaign and extreme brutality of the pogroms raises the crucial question—why did they do it? According to Jan Gross's much celebrated and criticized book about the murder of Jews in the Polish town of Jedwabne in summer 1941, the pogromists were bona fide 'willing executioners', driven by violent anti-Semitism rooted in the centuries-long 'archaic' superstitions and popular convictions that survived well into the twentieth century. A murderer 'could simultaneously endear himself to the new rulers, derive material benefits from his actions, and settle scores for indignities suffered under the Soviet occupation'.[11] Some scholars have also accentuated anti-Semitic prejudices as a crucial element of ethnic discourse in the borderlands that contributed to the predominantly 'native' character of the pogroms, while others have argued that the pogroms were planned and orchestrated as an inseparable component of the Nazi genocidal policies.[12]

It can be argued, however, that the combination of these factors was at the core of the pogroms. Since the annihilation of Jews was inseparable from the Nazi military and ideological preparations for the war, the invasion of the Soviet Union created a particularly murderous environment—aptly named the 'Jedwabne state' by a prominent Polish historian—whereby anti-Semitism and anti-Jewish violence were officially structured and integrated into the emerging pattern of the Holocaust. Where the Germans and Romanians did not partake directly in the pogroms, they acted as organizers and overseers, guiding and encouraging native-driven violence as long as it was directed against the specific target—Jews.[13]

On the other hand, the Axis ideological crusade against 'Judaeo-Bolshevism' fully coalesced with the aspirations of the Latvian, Lithuanian, or Ukrainian nationalist groups that had espoused anti-communism and anti-Semitism as the building blocks of national independence. For example, in the Łomża and Białystok regions, where the most violent pogroms took place in summer 1941, Polish right-wing groups were traditionally strong and vocal in waging vehement anti-Semitic propaganda and promoting an economic boycott of Jewish businesses in the late 1930s. The pre-war anti-Jewish sentiments, however, did not necessarily evolve into violent assaults. For example, in early November 1939, after the Soviets handed over Vilnius to Lithuania, there were several attacks on Jews. Apparently Polish residents, resentful of the rise in bread prices and of the alleged pro-Lithuanian attitudes among the Jews, were the main culprits. Yet there was no pogrom in the city in summer 1941. One could reason that the potential assailants, Poles and Lithuanians, were too engrossed in the wrangle over the city to divert their attention to the Jews.[14]

In Lithuania two rival organizations—organized in 1939–1940 as the Union of Lithuanian Activists (LAS) and the Lithuanian Activist Front (LAF)—advocated militant nationalism, an anti-Soviet alliance with Germany, and removal of 'Jews, parasites, and traitors' (although expulsion rather than murder was conceived as the most appropriate method) as the necessary precondition to a Lithuanian national state. In spring 1941 the LAF stressed in its directives that anti-Jewish and anti-communist actions were necessary 'for the ideological maturity of the Lithuanian people'. Such a formulation implied that the fight against communism was necessarily a fight against the Jews.[15] Although it is conceivable the nationalists hoped that anti-Semitic propaganda would help them curry favour with the Germans, it is no doubt that the anti-Semitism of some LAF and LAS members was genuine.

Similarly, OUN hoped to achieve an independent Ukrainian state with German help. Between 1939 and 1941 in German-occupied West Galicia the Nazi administration tolerated the proliferation of Ukrainian econom-ic, cultural, educational, and paramilitary organizations, providing a startling contrast to the later years of the Polish republic. Consequently, Ukrainian political activists considered this period as the first successful step on the road to independence and were eager to derive as much advantage from cooperation with the Germans as possible. By the late 1930s the OUN ideologists increasingly adopted Nazi racial policies as corresponding to their aspirations to build an ethnically homogeneous Ukraine. On the eve of the Soviet–German war both OUN branches (in April 1940 the OUN split into two rival factions, OUN-B and OUN-M) issued resolutions and statements that identified Jews with communism and 'Moscow imperialism'.[16]

The Nazis fully intended to utilize the anti-communism and anti-Semi-tism of these organizations. In June 1941 the chief of the Reich Main Security Office Reinhardt Heydrich instructed the commanders of his task forces—the *Einsatzgruppen*—to encourage and 'point in the right direction the self-cleansing efforts' of anti-Soviet formations in the Soviet Union, stressing that no trace of German involvement be left. On 1 July he specifically referred to the eastern Polish territories, stressing that Polish anti-communist and anti-Semitic elements should be directed to 'cleansing actions' against Bolsheviks and Jews. By this time the German Security Police and the Security Service (Sipo/SD) had gained valuable experience in such endeavours. During the *Anschluss* (the German annexation of Austria) it organized a mob in Vienna which forced Jews to scrub the pavements on their knees, and 'pointed in the right direction' the right-wing, proto-fascist groups that engaged in anti-Jewish excesses in occupied Warsaw, Paris, and Amsterdam.[17]

By the outbreak of the war the clandestine anti-Soviet organizations in the borderlands had been organized and armed. They carried out the acts of sabotage on Soviet communication lines, served as spotters for the German air-force, and attacked small Soviet detachments and alleged communists.

Simultaneously, they attempted to set up provisional administrative bodies that announced the restoration or establishment of independent statehood. Significantly, a gestation period—most likely used for the division of labour—preceded anti-Jewish violence, which despite its seemingly chaotic nature was nevertheless organized and systematic. In Jedwabne the pogrom began on 10 July, that is, eighteen days after the retreat of the Soviets, under the guidance of a 'supervising' German team. On 23 June 1941 a group associated with the LAF captured the radio station in Kaunas and announced the formation of a national government. Streets were adorned with national flags and the national anthem played on the radio. A day later the city radio warned the population about the 'Jewish shooters' and on 25 June a pogrom began. On 30 June an OUN-B group in L'viv issued a public declaration of the restoration of independent Ukraine. By this time, sporadic attacks on Jews were already in progress, but the violence escalated within hours. In Riga the pogrom began in an atmosphere of national liberation, when the Germans entered the city on 1 July.[18] In other localities such as Boryslav (Borysław) the vigilante groups stepped into the void created by the Soviet retreat, formed a temporary administrative structure, and initiated the pogroms before the arrival of the Germans. Therefore, whether the nationalist groups temporarily controlled the situation, or acted under the Nazi 'supervision', anti-Jewish violence was organized and took place under the spectre of national statehood, giving it the appearance of native initiative.

In turn, the nationalist organizations utilized the pogroms as a psychological remedy to expunge the humiliation of the military defeat and foreign occupation of 1939–41. Indeed, the popular images of the Baltic states just 'rolling over', offering no resistance to the Soviet invasion, left a deep sense of national shame and demoralization. In Lithuania, for example, the Soviet occupation came on the heels of the two other disasters—the acceptance of the Polish ultimatum of 1938, which meant the recognition of Poland's annexation of Vilnius, and giving up Klaipèda to Germany. The Soviet occupation, terror, and deportations left large segments of the population in the borderlands disoriented, traumatized, and craving for psychological reorientation that would help overcome such painful experiences.[19] In such a psychological environment political activists, who initiated anti-Soviet resistance, pointed the way to national emotional recuperation. In turn, Jews became the markers of negative emotions to be erased from memory, for no other group better 'qualified' to fulfil this function. The images of 'Judaeo-Bolshevism' as the ultimate evil fitted well with popular perceptions, nourished in anti-Semitic culture. Blaming Jews for national humiliation and personal grievances entailed a simple and all-encompassing explanation—the nation was stabbed in the back by the perfidious 'aliens' and their homogeneity as a group became a lightning rod for real or displaced frustrations.

National purification, therefore, began with the ritual of violence that heralded the dawn of a new order. After the Soviet retreat large crowds participated in political demonstrations celebrating the end of the 'Jewish Bolshevik' regime. In Kaunas the pogroms were accompanied by a solemn burial of the fallen 'partisans'; in some localities Jews were forced to sing popular Soviet songs, march carrying the portraits of Soviet leaders, or destroy Soviet monuments. In L'viv and other places Jews had to mop streets with toothbrushes, wash pavements with bare hands, and exhume and wash corpses found in prisons.[20] Although one is prone to think of the considerable German 'experience' in such practices, it should be noted that humiliation of Jews was a traditional element of violence during the preceding decades.

In some localities the Germans and their native helpers facilitated the 'cleansing actions' by having appropriately prepared the sites of the NKVD massacres. Many corpses found in prisons were mutilated to an extreme degree, adding to the prevailing atmosphere of shock and grief. Although there is no doubt that the Soviet secret police tortured prisoners to extract confessions, it is questionable whether it could afford to engage in such time-consuming practices when the front lines were moving rapidly. There are indications that at least in some places the Germans and the militiamen deliberately disfigured and defiled corpses before opening the prisons. In winter 1942 an underground Polish group attempted to organize the release of a Polish politician from the Janiv (Janów) labour camp in L'viv. To this end a group emissary approached a Ukrainian police officer named Bilas, who commanded a police detail in the camp. During the talks in Bilas's apartment, the officer got blind drunk and related to his vis-á-vis that in summer 1941, under supervision of an SS officer, the Ukrainian militiamen mutilated corpses in the Łącki prison, where the NKVD had shot its victims. A recuperating German soldier conveyed similar information to a Polish nurse, alleging that he had walked into a L'viv prison and saw the '*Osttruppen*' (native auxiliaries) nailing a corpse to a door. It is also known that Jewish corpses were removed from prisons before the crowds were let in.[21]

Certainly, such 'cosmetic' operations did not cause the pogroms, but facilitated popular inclinations *to believe* that Jews were behind the massacres. A prominent sociologist suggested that 'cognitive categories based on race and ethnicity serve to simplify a highly complex world'.[22] Such a notion definitely makes sense when placed in the context of the ethnically homogeneous Lithuania. However, it falls short in regard to ethnically mixed areas such as Galicia, where Ukrainians and Poles, two long-term rivals, whose antipathies were especially highlighted during the Soviet occupation, joined in anti-Jewish violence. The pogroms signalled a temporary truce, grounded in a convergence of the culture of anti-Semitism, psychological stress, and common economic interests achieved at the expense of Jews. The 'Jedwabne state' environment thus enabled the assailants, regardless of their ethnicity, to act with a modicum of confidence that anti-Jewish actions were sanctioned, while acting in groups reduced any moral or psychological restraints.

Individuals who had suffered under the Soviet regime or whose relatives were imprisoned or deported were among the ringleaders. Among the perpetrators in Jedwabne were escapees from Soviet prisons, whereas the 'Angel of Death'—the young Lithuanian who murdered Jews with an iron bar in the Kaunas garage—had apparently lost his parents to the Soviet terror.[23] A powerful incentive to 'redeem' oneself through violence characterized another group that comprised the former collaborators with the Soviet regime, eager to gain credentials with the Germans or Romanians. After the outbreak of the war many low-level Soviet administration and militia members swelled the ranks of the vigilante and nationalist organizations. Tarnished by collaboration, some individuals turned into zealous anti-communists, such was Victor Arājs, who was to head the most notorious killing unit in Latvia.[24] Some communists and members of the Soviet militia tore off their insignias and participated in the massacres. In fact, the OUN-M leader Andrij Mel´nyk admitted that 'hundreds of thousands' of Ukrainians had served in the communist party and state apparatus. Those, however, who 'retained national consciousness' could be readmitted as full-fledged members of the new Ukrainian community, if they turned against 'Jews, Poles, *Muscovites*, and communists'.[25] Similarly, an appeal issued in March 1941 by the LAF information bureau in Berlin incited Lithuanians to rise against the Soviets and promised pardon for previous 'sins' to those who could prove that they had killed 'at least one Jew'.[26]

While the Germans and the local nationalist groups harnessed popular anti-Semitic sentiments to specific ends, the breakdown of the social order facilitated base instincts such as greed, jealousy, and personal animosities. Hence, many individuals of no political persuasion used the opportunity to enrich themselves at the expense of the most defenceless community. Looting, therefore, consistently accompanied the pogroms. In Kaunas the plunder of Jewish apartments by the 'white armbands' and civilians reached such proportions that on 24 June the city-commandant threatened 'criminal elements' with the death penalty. The majority of the Polish population heeded the government-in-exile and its military arm, the Home Army (AK), which dictated the limits of normative behaviour under German occupation, but despite AK warnings not to take part in the pogroms, anti-Semitic convictions and/or the prospect of looting with immunity were too powerful to resist. Peasants were among the most active participants, arriving at the sites of pogroms in horse-drawn carts into which they loaded the loot from Jewish houses, apartments, and stores. Among the attackers were also people who had borrowed money from Jews and grasped the opportunity to get rid of the lenders.[27]

Participation in the violence also underscored many 'grey zones' between motivations and actions. While the most active culprits acted upon their personal disposition—those who wanted to kill and those who carried out auxiliary functions—ideologically-inclined LAF and OUN activists were as much prone to plunder and robberies as 'ordinary' onlookers. In turn, the latter often mutated into zealous murderers—not necessarily because they were convinced anti-Semites, but because *becoming* anti-Semites accorded unprecedented opportunities for personal enrichment and exercise of power. For example, German photographs of the L'viv pogrom display a number of women and children who took active part in assaulting Jews. At the same time, it is imperative to note that there were attempts to stop violence by those who understood its moral or political implications. A group of Polish intelligentsia and clergymen thus prevented a pogrom in Knyszyn (Białystok province). In Kaunas some members of the Lithuanian Provisional Government tried to dissuade a commander of Lithuanian 'partisans', Algirdas Klimaitis, from instigating pogroms. Similarly, some commanders of the OUN-organized militia forbade their subordinates to take part in the attacks.[28]

The intensity of anti-Jewish violence varied in different regions. Estonia was spared the pogroms owing to the stiff Soviet resistance that prevented German capture of Tallinn until 27 August 1941 and provided the majority of Jews (approximately 4,000 out of 5,000) with precious time to evacuate eastward. By this time, the Germans had terminated the 'self-cleansing actions' and begun the systematic annihilation campaign. In Latvia a large-scale pogrom occurred only in Riga, where after the exhumation of NKVD corpses in the city central prisons on 5 July the Latvian unit led by Victor Arājs set the Choral Synagogue on fire. Still, *Einsatzgruppe* A admitted that the popular mood in Latvia was not 'conducive' to pogroms, ascribing such passivity to the Soviet deportations that had deprived the country of its most active elements.[29] In all likelihood, however, such differences in conduct derived from the character of the country's socio-economic infrastructure. The higher level of industrialization and urbanization contributed to the fact that Latvian Jews were much more acculturated than their co-religionists in Lithuania. In contrast to the predominantly Yiddish-speaking Jews in Lithuania, Galicia, and Volhynia, higher educational standards in Estonia and Latvia compelled more Jews to learn the native languages. Perhaps the Protestant traditions of promoting individualism and economic prosperity, higher living standards, and predominant political orientations on American, French, and British democracies (at least until the mid-1930s) may also have contributed to the mitigation of anti-Semitic attitudes.[30]

Although in Byelorussia the local population took part in plunder and looting of Jewish houses and shops, there were relatively few fatalities. As in Latvia, the Germans ascribed such 'inactivity' of the Byelorussians to the absence of the 'useful non-Bolshevik intelligentsia'. Indeed, Byelorussian nationalism remained the prerogative of a small intelligentsia, for whom anti-Semitism played a marginal role; although several émigré groups were used by the Germans for intelligence-gathering and subversive activities, they never reached an ideological maturity and organizational level comparable to that of the LAF or OUN. In addition, the native middle class in Byelorussia was extremely small and there was no serious economic competition between Jewish and Byelorussian tradesmen, merchants, and artisans like that in East Galicia or Lithuania.[31]

The 'Jedwabne state' revealed that anti-Jewish violence thrived in the psychological and emotional atmosphere poisoned by radical ideologies and by a plethora of motives far remote from ideology and politics but camouflaged as the craving for national liberation.

The 'new order'

While the German occupation provided the overall ideological and administrative framework for governing the borderlands, different political groups
were compelled to adjust their activities to German policies and the changing situation at the front. At the time when the pogrom wave reached its
peak, the indigenous administrations established in the first days of the war
in the Baltic region and in Galicia announced the restoration of independent
statehood, assuming that their services would not go unrewarded. To prove
usefulness to the occupying forces and simultaneously to aspire to more
political power, however, proved extremely difficult, for German willingness to oblige the nationalist groups had severe limits. Already in the summer
of 1941 the Nazi policies laid bare the collision between the interests of the
occupiers and popular aspirations in the borderlands. Although the German
military and the SS were content to utilize the services of the indigenous
administration and the militia, Hitler and the top Nazi leadership envisioned
the borderlands not as 'liberated' territories, but as an important economic
appendage to the Reich. Accordingly, the Latvian, Lithuanian, or Ukrainian
nationalists who had hoped for the Slovak or Croatian puppet-state model
and fully committed themselves to the German cause, outlived their usefulness as organizations capable of independent action. For example, a day
before the attack on the Soviet Union, Heydrich informed the German
High Command and the Foreign Office that Ukrainian political activities
would not be tolerated 'in the present form', since they conflicted with
German interests.[32] On 8 August the short-lived Ukrainian administration
in L'viv was disbanded and the Security Police arrested or executed some
of the most prominent OUN-B members. Three days later the same fate
befell the provisional Lithuanian government. Any last illusions of national
independence were dashed when the Germans divided the borderlands
into two main administrative units: Estonia, Latvia, Lithuania, and half of
Byelorussia west of Minsk became the Reichskommissariat Ostland (RKO).
(The territory east of Minsk remained under the military administration.)
Ideology played a lesser role than administrative expedience in Hitler's
decision to lump together in the RKO the racially 'fair' Estonians and
Latvians and the 'inferior' Lithuanians and Byelorussians. Plans for maximum
exploitation of Ukraine's natural resources and manpower also entailed the

formation of the Reichskommissariat Ukraine (RKU) that included Ukraine west of the Dnieper River, including Volhynia and several southern counties of Byelorussian Polesie. To accommodate Erich Koch, the head of the RKU and the president of East Prussia, a special 'corridor' was created out of the Białystok region, which included the bulk of the Hrodna oblast' in Byelorussia (see Map 4). Contrary to the expectations of Ukrainian nationalists, who had hoped for the unification of all Ukrainian lands under German auspices, East Galicia became a part of the General-Government in Poland, while Romania was awarded northern Bukovina and Bessarabia. The former was made into the governorship 'Bukovina' (it included northern Bukovina and right-bank Bessarabia) and the latter became a part of the governorship of 'Transnistria', comprising left-bank Bessarabia between the Dniester and the Southern Bug rivers.

The only open avenue for the national elites to pursue their goals was to serve in the administrative institutions set up by the occupiers. While the Germans occupied the top positions within the Reichskommissariat administrations, the middle and low ranks were filled with natives. Having at their disposal a large pool of indigenous civil servants, the German administration in Estonia, Latvia, and Lithuania called for the formation of native administrations known as 'Directorates', which were to function as advisory bodies. Similarly, owing to the chronic personnel shortage, the native administrative bodies were retained or created at a lower level in Byelorussia, Volhynia, and Galicia. The militia units that featured so prominently during the pogroms were disbanded and replaced by auxiliary police that became constituents within the German police and SS apparatus. Under German supervision the native administration and police were to maintain order, repair roads and bridges, supervise markets, collect taxes, and from 1942 became fully engaged in anti-partisan warfare. They enjoyed relative freedom of action, especially in the countryside, where they often constituted the only outpost of German power and played an instrumental role in the occupation system. Concurrently, their numbers grew throughout the war. For example, in autumn 1942 the police forces in the RKO consisted of 4,428 German and 56,000 native policemen; 9,000 Estonians, 15,000 Latvians, and 16,000 Lithuanians also served in mobile battalions that carried out anti-partisan operations and participated in the genocide of Jews in the Baltic region, Ukraine, Byelorussia, and Poland. In 1944 the administrative apparatus in Lithuania consisted of 660 German and 20,000 indigenous civil servants.[33]

Map 4. The Borderlands under the Axis Occupation

The harshness or relative forbearance of the occupation in the border-lands depended less on ideological precepts originating in Berlin than on the attitudes of the German military and civil officials in the cities, towns, and villages. For example, Estonia and Latvia were considered potentially 'germanizable' and were eventually to be integrated into the Reich. The German administration also appreciated the relatively high literacy level and the skill of the native administration, while limited economic resources, especially in agriculture, initially generated more careful taxation policies. The members of the Estonian 'Directorate' were paid salaries equal to those received by German functionaries. Former members of the Estonian political police were integrated into the German Security Police and became its major contingent. The Estonians wore German uniforms, held SS ranks, received equal salaries, and were treated according to their rank. Such cooperation became extremely productive since it reduced German manpower to the minimum (while there were 800 Estonians in the Sipo/SD, there were 139 German functionaries.).[34] Schools, libraries, theatres, and museums were allowed to function unhindered and in general the Estonians and Latvians and to a lesser degree Lithuanians were spared the worst abuses common in Byelorussia and Ukraine.

Although the Baltic region received milder treatment, exploitation of all the borderlands constituted the basis of German policies in the east, bound to alienate the population. Economically exhausted during the Soviet occupation, the native population was effectively stripped of money after the German financial reform completely devalued the Soviet rouble. Slated for complete 'Germanization', the city of Riga was made off limits to the Latvian Directorate, and popular expectations of the restoration of private property were dashed when the business and commercial enterprises that had previously been 'nationalized' by the Soviets were taken over by German firms. As the war dragged on, the population in urban areas began experiencing serious food shortages. In Lithuania, which according to the Nazi racial hierarchy was not considered worthy of Germanization, the institutions of higher learning and most of the press were shut down by 1943. In September 1941 the leadership of the LAF complained to Hitler that, despite the considerable help provided to the Germans, the latter disregarded Lithuanian national aspirations, and even confiscated the lands left in private hands during the Soviet rule.[35]

Still, despite economic exploitation and disillusionments over unfulfilled national aspirations, by and large the populations in the Baltic preferred the German regime to the Soviet one. The Germans did not meddle in all aspects of public life, leaving cultural and religious affairs in the hands of the native administration. The rejuvenation of national life reflected in the reopening of the universities in Tallinn, Riga, Kaunas, and Vilnius (the last two were closed again in 1943); theatres and numerous youth organizations functioned throughout the occupation. Since the Nazi terror in Estonia and

Latvia was directed primarily against Jews, it might have been disapproved by some, but in general it was accepted as unpleasant collateral damage. In addition, traditional conservative values such as obedience to law, industriousness, and religiosity contributed to the fact that most Estonians and Latvians associated themselves with German values.[36] Accordingly, some individuals and political groups opted for an unconditional collaboration with the occupiers, hoping that in the long term the Germans would eventually make some political concessions; others simply staked on what seemed to be a winning side.

In Lithuania, after the dissolution of the Provisional Government, the Germans authorized the formation of an advisory council headed by the former Lithuanian chief-of-staff General Petras Kubiliunas. The council was backed up by the Lithuanian Church, which appealed to the population to obey and loyally collaborate with the new regime. The benefits of collaboration with the occupier were especially vivid in the Vilnius district, where the German administration temporarily tolerated the 'second' Lithuanization campaign (the first one was launched after the Soviet transfer of the district in October 1939). Zealous to diminish Polish economic and cultural influence, the Lithuanian administration renamed all localities, prohibited the use of Polish in public, and fired Polish civil employees, teachers, and librarians. Although the Baltic region in general fared better than the other occupied Soviet territories, constant shortages of most immediate commodities—ration cards were introduced in July 1941—turned the Lithuanization drive into a struggle for survival and a fierce ethnic rivalry as Poles and Lithuanians competed for employment.[37]

Hopes for a better future in German-occupied Byelorussia were short-lived. As the German army moved in, the peasants liquidated the hated collective farm system, distributing the livestock and agricultural implements among themselves. The German military, which did not fully comprehend the functions of the kolkhozes, did not impede such practices. At the same time, it allowed the formation of civil committees, which functioned as administrative bodies at town and village levels. However, after the military was replaced by the civil administration, many German officials with little or no administrative experience came to seek opportunities for advancement and personal enrichment. What they lacked in skills, they compensated for by zealotry in implementing ideological precepts of *Lebensraum* and brutal exploitation of the native population. In autumn 1941 the administration in Byelorussia imposed high quota deliveries on agricultural products and livestock, policies that closely resembled the Soviet kolkhoz system. The German garrisons lived off the land, confiscating bread, meat, cattle, and horses, and frequently acted as plundering bands. The peasants were not allowed to sell the products that remained in their hands, for all economic transactions in Byelorussia were regulated by the Central Commercial Company 'East', and any violations entailed high fines, confiscation of cattle, arrest, or incarceration in a concentration camp. The situation of the population in urban areas was even worse, for food supplies were directed to the German garrisons. In some localities the population soon faced starvation and increasingly fell victim to epidemics that ravaged the country, especially in winter.[38]

The German functionaries in general treated the Byelorussians with contempt, stressing the lack of a politically conscious intelligentsia and the disagreements between various émigré groups. Nevertheless, while the *Generalkommissar* Wilhelm Kube considered Byelorussians of a lower racial order, in 1942 the situation at the front forced him to moderate his policies. The Byelorussian youth organizations and scientific societies were expanded and even received some of the previously confiscated property. The nationalist émigrés and local activists were instrumental in organizing the Byelorussian Self-Help that provided educational and social work among the population. In June 1943 Kube eventually allowed the formation of an advisory body, the Byelorussian Regional Council (*Belorusskaia Tsentral' naia Rada*), which was to act in similar capacity as the Baltic Directorates.[39]

One of the most hated features of the German occupation of the borderlands was forced labour. The first calls for volunteers to work in German industries were issued in summer 1941, but already in December Rosenberg ordered a compulsory draft, which was extended to all men and women between 18 and 45. Conscription methods grew harsher with the duration of the war. In autumn 1942 8,000 individuals from Latgalle—the area where Soviet partisans were especially active—were rounded up and sent to Germany. Still, throughout the war the 'Directorates' managed to convince the German administration that mass deportations would disrupt the otherwise smooth functioning of the occupation apparatus. In contrast, there were no comparable institutions to provide such a mitigating influence in Byelorussia and Ukraine, where the recruitment for forced labour mutated into an undisguised manhunt. Ukraine suffered especially brutal treatment, for the head of the RKU, Erich Koch, was known for his hatred of Slavs and referred to its domain as 'German Africa'. Considering terror the most efficient tool to run Ukraine, he authorized an economic policy that effectively stripped the region of agricultural products and brought famine to many localities. The hunt for a labour force was as brutal. By the spring 1942 the police blocked the roads, set checkpoints, and combed through villages to round up able-bodied men and women; the houses of labour dodgers' were burned and their relatives sent to labour camps. In response, many individuals took to the forests, where they waited until the police were gone or joined the partisans. All in all, while 126,000 labourers were sent to Germany from the Baltic region, 2.5 million workers were sent from Byelorussia and Ukraine.[40]

In contrast to the RKU, the German administration in East Galicia pursued 'elastic policies' giving concessions to Ukrainians in economic, cultural, and educational spheres. In March 1942, speaking to the administration of the General-Government, Frank delineated this policy, stressing that Galicia was slated for the future German settlement and as such was to be 'cleansed' of Poles and Ukrainians. However, since during the war such a solution was unattainable and Germany badly needed a massive labour force, the most suitable policy at the time was to play on the animosities between the two peoples. In this regard, Ukrainians were favoured at the expense of the Poles. The administration transferred Polish libraries, museums, and cultural institutions to Ukrainian trustees, the numbers of Ukrainian schools increased from 132 to 3,200, and by 1944 there were 346 Ukrainian admen and town majors, in contrast to six Germans and three Poles. In turn, the Ukrainian National Council in Galicia offered its services to the Germans in hope that Ukrainian participation in the anti-Bolshevik struggle would eventually be recognized and rewarded with their own police and armed forces. Equally forthcoming was the OUN-M, which appealed to Ukrainians to 'assist the Germans in the crusade regardless of difficulties'.[41] At the same time, the quotas on deliveries of grain, vegetables, cattle, sheep, and horses imposed on Galician peasants were rising throughout the occupation. Consequently, although food supply was better than in other parts of the General-Government and in Volhynia, in October 1941 large segments of the population starved.[42]

As much as Hitler insisted that in the east only the Germans carried arms, the situation at the front dictated some modifications to such policies. In fact, the success in the organization of the auxiliary police forces and their efficiency in mass murder convinced the civil administration and the SS that these units could be deployed on the front line. While some

Schutzmannschaft battalions (mobile police units) had already seen action in Byelorussia and Ukraine, where they distinguished themselves for extreme brutality, others were sent as far as Poland and Yugoslavia, where they carried out 'unpleasant tasks of civilian population control'[43]—a euphemism for brutal pacifications. In autumn 1942 Himmler gave an order for the formation of Latvian and Estonian Waffen-SS Legions, which were raised as much through volunteer recruitment as by forcible induction. The impressive combat records of the Estonian and Latvian units in battle against the Soviets compelled the German administration to increase the number of indigenous units. However, in Lithuania the drive to create an SS contingent failed owing to mass resistance, and the Primate Archbishop Juozas Skvireckas refused the requests of German authorities to issue a pastoral letter advocating enlistment. Yet mobilization of a local force—a home guard, created in the light of Soviet successes in February 1944—was successful, as fear of returning Soviets drove thousands of volunteers to recruitment offices.[44]

In contrast, in spring 1943 the Greek Catholic Church in Galicia supported the formation of an SS division, where recruitment offices were flooded with volunteers driven by hatred and fear of the Soviet regime. In 1943 the Estonian and Latvian Legions (in 1944 they were formed into one Estonian and two Latvian SS-divisions) were thrown into action on the Soviet–German front, where they suffered heavy casualties, while the Ukrainian SS-division 'Galicia' was almost obliterated during the Soviet offensive in summer 1944. To replace the losses, these divisions received new contingents, including the policemen who had participated in the Holocaust and in anti-partisan operations, such as a number of the Arājs commando members. In 1943 Kube also allowed the formation of the so-called Byelorussian National Army, which consisted of 24,000 native policemen who took part in the anti-partisan struggle and rearguard actions against the Soviet army.[45]

The 'Romanization' of Bukovina and 'Transnistria' proved a failure from the beginning. The Romanian administrations began their rule by confiscating Jewish property, possessions, and financial assets. The economic aspect of the process, however, failed miserably owing to overwhelming corruption among local officials, who retained most valuables for themselves and auctioned off the bulk of the confiscated goods. The state thus received only a small portion of what had been expected to be a major economic input. In fact, Romanian functionaries referred to Bukovina as 'California', where one could strike it rich without difficulty. Similarly, in Bessarabia those 'who had arrived with a single suitcase, were now in possession of millions'.[46] Also, the deportations of Jews, envisioned as the first stage of the Romanization of the two provinces, eliminated a crucial socio-economic force and contributed to a rapid deterioration of living standards. Throughout the war Bessarabia produced extremely low tax revenue and had to be heavily subsidized from the national budget. Unperturbed, the 'Department of Romanization' contemplated the further 'homogenization' of the provinces by deporting 450,000 'alien' elements—Ukrainians, Russians, and Poles (several thousands of the Gypsies (Roma) were deported from Bessarabia in autumn 1941)—to Galicia and Ukraine. While the Germans objected to such measures, the administration followed the pattern established during the frontier wars. It reduced the number of Ukrainian and Russian schools, forced the 'Romanization' of Slavic names, shut down all political organizations, and the police arrested most prominent Russians and Ukrainians suspected of political activities.[47]

The 'Final Solution'

The establishment of the civil administration in the borderlands corresponded with a transition from 'wild' pogroms to the systematic mass murder of Jews, in which local residents played a crucial role. With the front moving eastward, the offices of the Security and the Order Police commanders oversaw the reorganization of the native police forces that were to be deployed for regular duties, anti-partisan operations, and ultimately for the liquidation of Jews. The first regular auxiliary police units appeared in late June 1941, when the Lithuanian 'white armbands' in Kaunas were disbanded and replaced with the so-called Battalion in Defence of National Labour (TDA). Conceived in March 1941 as the military arm of the LAF, the battalion was initially financed by the Lithuanian administration and commanded by professional officers. Similar developments took place throughout the borderlands, for example in East Galicia, where in August the Ukrainian militia was disbanded and replaced by a regular police force; its officer and NCO ranks were occupied by graduates from the Ukrainian police academies in west Galicia.[48]

The constant shortage of German manpower was but one problem that the native auxiliaries helped resolve. As important was their ability and willingness to carry out the murder of thousands of men, women, and children, at least partially reducing the psychological stress and physical fatigue endured by the German police and security functionaries deployed in carrying out such tasks. Indeed, in any place where the 'Final Solution' was carried out, the role of the native policemen was crucial. They served as guards at ghetto perimeters, hunted down Jews in the cities and the countryside, escorted them to deportation sites, and cordoned off places of mass execution. Their 'auxiliary' functions were also extended to actual killing. To mention only a few instances, in November 1941 Polish and Byelorussian policemen assisted a German infantry company in shooting 1,500 Jews near Baranovichi. During the liquidation of the L'viv ghetto in August 1942, the Ukrainian police reported having helped to round up 8,639 Jews, who were sent to the Bełżec death camp; the policemen shot sixty-one people in the process. In October 1942 the Polish police took part in the liquidation of the ghetto in Brest, where thousands of Jews were shot.[49]

The role of the native policemen mirrored the status of their homelands within the occupied structure. Impressed by the zeal of local vigilantes during the pogroms and the availability of experienced police cadres in the Baltic, the German administration authorized the formation of native security police, a development unprecedented for the borderlands and other Soviet territories. In Lithuania the political police (*Saugumo Policja*) of the interwar period was reinstituted and empowered to arrest and execute Jews, communists, and the members of the Polish underground.[50] Some of the native police details smoothly mutated into proficient and zealous killing squads such as the notorious Arājs commando, which drove through Latvia and murdered at least 26,000 Jews.[51] The role of the special Lithuanian squads was duly appreciated by the commander of the *Einsatzkommando* 3 Karl Jäger, who stressed their contribution to mass executions. About eighty Lithuanians made up the firing detail for the Security Police in Vilnius, murdering thousands of Jews and Poles at Ponary, the former Soviet airbase near the city.[52]

Personal motivations behind the murderous actions of the native policemen were complex. Although some criminal and *Lumpen* elements certainly joined the police, it was not 'a handful of local rabble'[53] that constituted the bulk of the auxiliary formations. Indeed, the social and psychological make-up of the policemen—as can be reconstructed from the Soviet war crime investigation and trials—present cases of ideological and opportunistic modes of behaviour under German occupation. Political activists—individuals who were driven into German service by ideological affiliations—were the most visible though not the most numerous group. Among the first volunteers were members of the pre-war paramilitary and proto-fascist organizations such as the Estonian 'Fighters' League', the Lithuanian 'Iron Wolf', or the Latvian 'Pērconcrust', who filled the officer and NCO ranks.[54]

Recruitment announcements to the volunteers to the Arājs commando invited those 'who would like to actively participate in the cleansing [Latvia] of destructive elements', clearly indicating the future functions of the unit. Some members joined the commando because of hostility to the Soviet regime, others were professional policemen engaged in anti-communist activities before the war. For such individuals the murder of 'destructive elements' was but the first stage of the national revolution embodied in the permanent re-definition of political, socio-economic, and ethnic order. The national revolution entailed the renewal of traditional 'national' values—law and order, peasant-oriented economy, religiosity, and corporatism—as opposed to the 'alien' (read Jewish) atheistic system. Among the most active policemen were also those who were imprisoned under the Soviets or lost relatives in the deportations, or wanted to redeem themselves for collaboration with the Soviets. Arājs himself, a member of a nationalist student fraternity, re-entered a university under the Soviets and studied Marxism, and in spring 1941 received a law degree as a Soviet jurist. Hence, service to the Germans may have served as redemption for his association with the Soviets.[55]

Outside of ideological affiliations, the Holocaust provided an outlet for personal economic improvement and social advancement. Material self-interest, therefore, entailed a powerful affinity with German anti-Jewish measures. Policemen robbed Jews or were rewarded for participation in the murder by sharing among themselves the possessions of the victims. Many policemen were semi-literate; peasants became the predominant element in the police forces in Estonia, Lithuania, Byelorussia, Volhynia, and Galicia. The sense of authority and power, especially for those who had previously occupied low rungs of the social hierarchy, combined with material benefits, were too attractive to resist. Given traditional propensities to socialism among Estonian and Latvian industrial workers, their service with the police can be explained by the desire to avoid labour service in Germany and aspirations for better economic conditions.[56] Although a small number of policemen displayed sadistic inclinations, extreme brutality and a total lack of empathy marked the actions of the majority of the policemen, regardless of social differences and motivations. Having received almost unlimited power over Jews, not only did the policemen carry out their duties with zeal, but they beat and humiliated their victims without German supervision. The 'Ponary shooters' tormented Jews before executions; during the liquidation of the ghetto in Daugavpils the Arājs commando members threw the old and sick Jews through windows and cracked the heads of small children against concrete walls. Still, alcohol, which was consumed in large quantities, suggests the psychological burden upon the killers.[57]

During the liquidation of the ghettos and deportations to death camps, the native police and administration played a conspicuous role in compiling the lists of the deportees, escorting them to collection points, and appropriating Jewish property. The native administration was particularly keen on seizing Jewish property and commodities. Here the interests of the native collaborators, the population at large, and the Germans simultaneously converged and collided. The three groups strove, albeit for different reasons, to redefine the socio-economic space of the borderlands, but since the Germans had priority in getting the most valuable possessions, various native councils complained that Jewish goods were rightfully Estonian, Lithuanian, or Ukrainian and had been 'stolen' by the Jews. On 22 June 1941 the Estonian Liberation Committee specified in its programme the immediate isolation of all Jews in detention camps and confiscation of their property. On 1 August 1941 the Lithuanian Provisional Government issued the 'Statutes on the Situation of the Jews', calling for economic and social isolation of the Jews, although it tried to dissociate itself from the pogroms.[58] In August 1941 the chairman of the Ukrainian Central Committee established before the Soviet–German war in West Galicia, Volodymyr Kubiyovych, appealed to the head of the General-Government Hans Frank that Jewish property, obtained by 'illegal means and exploitation', be distributed among Ukrainians. To receive access to Jewish property and commodities, in some localities in Byelorussia and Volhynia the native administration initiated the ghettoization of Jews.[59]

For ordinary bystanders material self-interests were the main considerations in collaborating with a system that was predicated upon human propensity for violence, greed, and sadism. Since in the borderlands poverty was endemic, some individuals merely used an opportunity to thrive upon the situation of Jews, while others may have perceived the Holocaust as an appalling, but necessary price for the removal of traditional socio-economic competitors. Preoccupied with survival in a situation of economic deprivation and limited employment opportunities, they took part in state-organized robbery. Peasants turned over Jews to the police for reward or used the desperate situation of Jewish refugees in the forests to exchange food or weapons for valuables. The attitudes of the Christian population in Bukovina and Bessarabia were largely informed by the common knowledge that Jews were marked for extermination. During the mass deportations of Jews to 'Transnistria' in September 1941 some Moldavians and Ukrainians alongside the Romanian gendarmes took part in plundering Jewish houses and looting the remaining commodities. In German-occupied areas the population often seized Jewish goods or bought them cheap from Jews about to be ghettoized or deported and the administration ordered the return of the goods under threat of punishment.[60]

The culture of religious and political anti-Semitism was also deeply rooted and affected personal attitudes. In summer 1941 as the first wave of the Holocaust was reaching its peak, in tune with the *Protocols of the Elders of Zion*, a Polish clergyman wrote a letter to the London government-in-exile blaming the Jews for moral corruption and demoralization of Polish society. He praised the genocide as 'a special act of the Almighty because the Polish people, meek and unsystematic, would never have decided to undertake decisive steps necessary in this case'.

> the Germans, outside of many ills they inflicted upon our country, in this singular venue have shown us a good beginning for how to liberate [Polish] society from the Jewish plague, the road upon which, we—although naturally in a less brutal way—must consequently proceed.[61]

That such views were not necessarily the ravings of a religious fanatic was attested to by a report sent to London in September 1941 by the AK commander Stefan Rowecki, who explicitly stated that any positive efforts of the Polish government in regard to the Jewish question 'cause the worst impressions, [for] the country is overwhelming anti-Semitic . . . the differences are only in the methods; there are only a few who advocate emulating the Germans'.[62]

Still, there were groups and individuals who risked their lives saving Jews. For example, among the saviours were the Baptists and the members of the Armenian Church. Under the patronage of the Metropolitan Andrej Sheptyts'kyi the Galician Greek Catholic clergy hid

Jewish children and members of the intelligentsia in monasteries and churches in East Galicia.[63] In Lithuania the Metropolitan Romuald Jałbrzy-kowski appealed against the genocide in his sermons and hid a number of Jews in monasteries. In Vilnius local Poles tried to save their Jewish collea-gues, friends, and acquaintances by providing them with 'Aryan' papers or hiding them.[64] A number of Jews owed their lives to courageous Ukrainians and Poles in Galicia and Volhynia. However, these instances were few and far between, and in general the Jewish escapees from the ghettos and camps found themselves in a deadly trap between the Germans and largely hostile or indifferent native residents.

Summary

The outbreak of the Soviet–German war spelled the demise of the Jewish communities in the borderlands. If by June 1941 approximately 1.3 million Jews lived in the western Soviet borderlands (including thousands of refugees from German-occupied Poland),[65] by 1944 no more than 4 per cent of those living under German occupation survived the war. Out of 80,000 Latvian Jews 4,000 stayed alive. Only 15,000 Jews came out of hiding in East Galicia, the second-largest Jewish enclave in pre-war Europe that before the war numbered half a million people. The Jewish communities in Lithuania, western Volhynia, and western Byelorussia—150,000, 180,000 and 160,000 respectively—were virtually wiped out. Only in Bessarabia and Bukovina was the rate of survivors higher—out of 200,000 about 55,000 Jews returned home from the ghettos in Transnistria.[66]

Although the longer period of German rule in the borderlands (in comparison to the central and eastern regions of the Soviet Union) certainly contributed to such totality of the Holocaust, the role of the native popula-tion proved to be as crucial. The Nazi annihilation campaign coalesced with local national aspirations and created a particular political and psychological environment propitious for 'lateral genocide',[67] whereby the Nazi and Romanian Holocaust mutated into a local heterogeneous form, institutio-nalized existing antagonisms, and divided borderlands societies according to specific ethnic criteria. In turn, many Lithuanian, Polish, or Ukrainian 'neighbours' consciously synchronized anti-Jewish violence with the policies of the occupying forces. Native collaboration in the Holocaust thrived in the psychological and emotional atmosphere poisoned by radical ideologies, but was also driven by motives far remote from ideology and politics. It can be argued that without the active involvement of the 'neighbours' it would have taken the Germans much longer to complete the genocide. Accordingly, given the situation at the Soviet–German front, timing was crucial both for the murderers and the victims, and more Jews could have survived the war.

As harsh as the Axis occupation was, it affected the populations of the borderlands to a lesser degree than the Soviet one. To begin with, the Germans were interested in Germanizing the lands, *not* the people. It mattered, therefore, that as long as one was not a Jew or a member of the resistance, the occupiers largely left one in peace. Political passivity or indifferent attitudes to German or Romanian rule did not constitute criminal activity and until 1944 the direct war losses in the borderlands (with the exception of Byelorussia) were smaller than under the Soviet regime.

It should be noted that Jews were not the sole targets of violence. In summer 1941 the German Security Police began arrests and executions of the Polish intelligentsia, political activists, students, and the clergy. By December in the Vilnius district the Germans and the Lithuanian auxiliaries killed about 1,400 Russians, Poles, and Lithuanians as suspected communists. The Romanian administration arrested and incarcerated the Ukrainians and Moldavians who had previously served in the Soviet administration. Executions in Bukovina and Bessarabia, however, were rare.[68] All in all, in contrast to the Jews who were murdered because they were Jewish, other victims were selected on an individual basis. It was the guerrilla warfare and internal conflicts that would draw much larger segments of the populations of the borderlands into the whirlpool of the war.

Regardless whether anti-Jewish violence was initiated by the invading forces or was 'native-driven', it was appropriated and functionalized to achieve specific goals. The Germans and Romanians tapped local anti-Semitic energies to proceed with the systematic annihilation of the Jews. For the local nationalists anti-Jewish violence constituted a stimulus on the road to national revolution or the nation-building process, in which Jews were singled out as the representatives of the Soviet regime. For 'ordinary' men and women violence became a vehicle to access positions of temporary power and economic resources, a tool to ingratiate themselves with the occupiers, and a way to extinguish fear and rage pent up during Soviet occupation. It can be stated for certain that all the assailants were *volunteers*, whose conduct was generated by a range of motives—the accumulative outcome of the Gentile–Jewish relations in the borderlands, radical political ideologies, desire to avenge alleged ills, and mere greed. Although the numbers of those involved directly in the killing—the 'reliable local residents'—were relatively small, they were 'efficient and thorough'.[69]

7

The Civil Wars, 1941–1944

As in the Soviet period of 1939–41 the political and national divisions in the borderlands served as a vital component of the German 'new order'. While many individuals completely subordinated themselves to serve the occupiers in different capacities, politically engaged groups had to maintain a precarious balance of pursuing national aspirations and catering to German expectations. Conversely, it was the German–Soviet war that provided an essential context for exacerbating further fragmentation of the borderlands into a variety of political and national factions. As the war dragged on, these factions increasingly looked for opportunities to expand their power-base within or outside the occupation system.

If we understand the term 'civil war' as 'combat within the boundaries of a recognized sovereign entity between parties subject to a common authority at the outset of the hostilities',[1] then in 1942 the situation in some regions of the borderlands increasingly looked like a civil war fought between those who served in German-sponsored police formations and the Soviet partisans. At the same time, the brewing Polish–Lithuanian and Polish–Ukrainian conflicts burst into the open. Taken together these conflicts confirm and transcend the conventional definition of civil war. Fought by the citizens or residents of the same sovereign entity (absorbed by foreign aggression), they were also part and parcel of a 'big war' between the two totalitarian regimes that at different periods supported or suppressed the involved groups. It means that the civil wars in the borderlands were multi-sided, involving competing ideologies, ethnicities, and personal interests. Some of these conflicts would continue long after the Second World War.

The single most critical factor that led to the outbreak and escalation of the civil wars in the borderlands were the German and Soviet 'transformative' policies that aimed at redrawing the borderlands' social, political, and ethnic make-up. At the same time, the civil wars were the outcome of specific local conditions and conflicting loyalties and claims that cumulatively escalated the ferocity of these conflicts. The Soviet–German war detonated the brewing 'ethnic un-mixing' of people, whereby the old rivals claimed the contested territories in accordance with often exaggerated claims of ethnic demography and using violence as the most effective homogenizing tool.[2]

This chapter examines the four faces of the civil wars, starting with the guerrilla warfare in which thousands of Lithuanians, Poles, Ukrainians, Byelorussians, and Russians faced each other across the Soviet–German front lines. In the Vilnius region the pre-war Lithuanian–Polish conflict mutated into a 'low-intensity' armed conflict, while the OUN armed formations launched the annihilation of the Polish settlements in Volhynia and East Galicia. Finally, the Soviet–Polish disputes over the borderlands, temporarily settled by the Riga peace treaty, erupted in the late stage of the war, when the Soviet army moved to reoccupy the Polish *Kresy*.

Guerrilla warfare

By autumn 1941 the initial enthusiasm accorded to the Axis armies in the summer was evaporating. The degree of disillusionment, however, was not uniform across the borderlands. If the relatively mild occupation regime in the Baltic region provoked the protests of native administrations, the undisguised robberies and terror tactics in Ukraine and Byelorussia generated armed resistance. The first cells of the anti-German partisan movement were formed by Soviet army stragglers, who during the summer battles in Volhynia and Byelorussia found themselves deep behind the front lines, and by communist functionaries left behind by the NKVD and party organizations. In summer 1941 the first groups of Soviet agents were also parachuted into the forests of Volhynia, where they organized intelligence and sabotage groups. At the beginning of the next year several groups were also parachuted into Lithuania and Byelorussia. Numbers of escapees from prisoner of war camps formed their own groups or swelled the existing partisan units that carried out anti-German propaganda and acts of sabotage. Initially, the main objectives of these units were intelligence gathering and ideological activities, for the Soviet political leadership considered the populations of the borderlands highly unreliable. For example, although

Soviet sources claim that anti-German resistance in the Baltic region consisted of thousands of guerrillas, throughout the war Soviet partisans were
active only in the Vilnius district and in the Latgalle region of Latvia, where
the partisans relied on a large Russian-speaking minority.

In Estonia and Latvia the native-based partisan movement was non-
existent and the population at large, despite frustrations over the unfulfilled
national aspirations, was predominantly anti-Soviet. A similar situation in
Lithuania also prevented the Soviet partisans establishing power-bases,
except in the Vilnius region, where they found support in Byelorussian villages.
Resistance in Transcarpathia comprised a few communist cells, for the
majority of activists escaped to Russia after the Hungarian annexation in
spring 1939. The remaining members tried to carry out anti-Hungarian
propaganda and sabotage activities, but were largely destroyed by the police
and security organs, although passive resistance to the draft into the Hungarian army and labour battalions was common.[3] Similarly ineffective was
the resistance movement in Bessarabia, where Soviet agents, parachuted
into the province, were quickly destroyed by the Romanian security forces.
Although in summer 1943 the Ukrainian Staff of the Partisan Movement
ordered the formation of 'Moldavian' partisan units, it decided that the
situation in the province was not conducive to large-scale activities—a
veiled admission that the population at large was not supportive of the
Soviet regime.[4]

It was, therefore, the *Kresy* where the Soviet partisan command directed
its main efforts. Assuming that the Soviet occupation of 1939-41 left very
few individuals who genuinely sympathized with the Soviet regime, the
Main Department of Partisan Movement in Moscow (which was created to
coordinate the activities of the resistance in all German-occupied territories)
elaborated plans to bolster partisan activities. To this effect, units of saboteurs blew up German facilities or attacked small detachments; German
corpses were mutilated and defiled. The main efforts, however, were
to disrupt the functioning of local administration, destroy warehouses,
grain and lumber storages, and blow up roads, rail tracks, and bridges.
Crucially, the partisans were to act as the representatives of Soviet power,
constantly carrying out propaganda that reminded the population of its
imminent return. Counting on German reprisals as an incentive to join
the resistance, the partisans did not spare their efforts in staging attacks
whenever and wherever it was possible. In turn, the Germans increasingly
launched large-scale operations, in which they routinely burned entire

villages and shot the inhabitants. Fearing terror, the population increasingly took to the forests. Soviet propaganda made full use of such instances and Soviet planes dropped leaflets over the occupied territories, promising a better life after the war. The make-up of the partisans proved that such tactics proved effective. Approximately 10 per cent of the partisans were politically motivated (and the number dwindled with time), 11 per cent were former army personnel, 20 per cent were from the intelligentsia, 17 per cent were workers. Given the predominantly agricultural character of Volhynia and Byelorussia, peasants constituted the largest contingent of the partisan forces—about 40 per cent. Consequently, as the countryside drew upon itself the particular fury of the German punitive expeditions, more and more peasants joined the resistance. In addition, from spring 1942 the German confiscations of livestock and agricultural products and the manhunt for forced labourers generated an increasing flight of villagers to the forests. It was, therefore, German brutalities more than sheer patriotism that fuelled the partisan movement.[5]

The forested and marshy terrain in Byelorussia and Volhynia also provided refuge to the Jewish survivors and ghetto escapees, who formed their own groups that by summer 1942 numbered approximately 11,000 men, women, and children. Searching for food, they often raided the neighbouring villages. The Jewish camps had to be on constant alert for German or native police attacks, but also for the Polish Home Army (AK) units. In addition, Byelorussian Polesie became a home-base for the Ukrainian nationalist formation known as 'Polis'ka Sich'. In summer 1941 it evolved as a Ukrainian militia unit that initially collaborated with the Germans in the liquidation of pockets of Soviet resistance. After the Germans disbanded the 'Sich', some of its members took to the forests and formed guerrilla units hostile to the Germans, the AK, the Soviet partisans, and the Jews. Although different in political affiliations, size, and the social and ethnic make-up, all the guerrillas shared common logistical problems, and their existence depended entirely on ability to obtain food supplies and arms. Hence, they concentrated on raiding warehouses, mills, storage depots, and ultimately villages, more often clashing with each other than fighting the Germans. Struggle for food, therefore, provided one of the building blocks for the civil wars. While some units established cordial relations with peasants, frequently they swept through taking everything by force. Consequently, the partisans became dreaded by the local population, for refusal to provide food could prove fatal. The villagers thus faced a limited choice, to comply or to resist by informing upon the intruders to the German or native police. Such acts, however, entailed reprisals by the partisans. A vicious cycle of violence became a permanent component of life in the countryside.

By spring 1942 the German military command of the rear areas had to commit considerable manpower to fight the resistance. By this time the term 'rules of warfare' was no longer a part of the German military vocabulary, for unrestrained terror against civilians had already become the watchword for the anti-partisan warfare in Poland and Yugoslavia. In September 1941 the German High Command issued an order that specified that any 'bandit war' (*Banditenkrieg*) was communist-inspired and that 100 civilians were to be shot for each German casualty; for each wounded German fifty hostages would be executed. Such 'partisanophobia' reflected the increased anxiety of the German leadership over the outcome of the war. Extreme brutality and the creation of 'dead zones' were to make up for the lack of manpower to combat the resistance.[6] Accordingly, official orders to suppress resistance by any means passed down from Hitler's headquarters to commanding officers and, in combination with prevalent anti-Slavic attitudes, removed any legal or moral constraints on brutalities. Hence, the anti-guerrilla warfare followed a specific logic—the intended destruction of people and buildings would make entire areas unsuitable for the partisans.

Large-scale anti-partisan operations began in earnest in summer 1942. During the 'sweep' in western Belorussia between 21 August and 21 September, the German and auxiliary forces under the command of the SS and Police Leader Friedrich Jeckeln killed 18,363 people, including 389 in combat. In September 1942 partisan activity near the village of Kortelisy (Volhynian Polesie) provoked massive reprisal, which had dwarfed the destruction of Lidiče in Czechoslovakia. In the course of an anti-partisan action, the German and indigenous police units murdered 2,875 people, including 1,624 children; some women were drowned in a pond. Between October 1942 and March 1943 the anti-partisan formations murdered 9,432 'regular' partisans, 12,946 'suspects', 11,000 Jews, and 233 prisoners of war. German losses during the same period were 342 killed and 338 wounded. Ultimately, it was the civilians who died in thousands, their houses burned, and livestock and produce taken away. Survivors were rounded up and sent to forced labour in Germany.[7] To eliminate the power-base of the partisans in Latgalle, in May 1942 and August 1943 the Germans deported 11,500 Russian-speakers suspected of sympathizing with the partisans.[8]

In all anti-partisan operations the native police played a crucial role. After a partisan attack that resulted in the death of several local policemen, on 13 January 1943 the native auxiliaries and a handful of the German gendarmes surrounded the village of Lyadki (the Mir district of Hrodna oblast'). A local informant identified the houses of partisans' relatives, while the policemen who had lost relatives and friends in the partisan attack formed an impromptu death squad. After consuming substantial quantities of alcohol, they moved from house to house killing all residents, including small children. A survivor of the massacre recalled that:

> [One policeman] shot my mother in the back and her chest exploded. They must have been firing explosive cartridges. A shot ripped off my sister's right arm. Another shot ripped off the left arm of my sister's child. Then M. fired at my younger sister and wounded her. Then he turned to the child, who was screaming, and shot him in the head; his brains splattered all over the stove.[9]

The Soviet partisans responded by specifically targeting the native policemen and administration. After the battle of Stalingrad, the commanding staff of the partisan movement ordered raids deep into enemy's territory to prepare the ground for the 're-unification' of the western borderlands. Concurrently, the eradication of 'ideological diversionists' was conceived as an extension of the civil wars that began in 1917 and became a primary task of the partisans.[10] The partisans avoided the confrontation with the large German garrisons and concentrated their attacks on the native officials and police stations. In the area of Slonim (Hrodna oblast') alone between April and November 1942 the partisans killed 1,024 persons, including 111 Germans, 90 auxiliary policemen, 140 members of the civil administration, and 683 local residents. The ideological context of these attacks revealed itself in the social make-up of the targets, who were political activists, teachers, writers, publishers, and members of educational, cultural, and professional organizations that had worked for the Germans.[11]

According to the Byelorussian staff of the partisan movement (which tended to inflate the enemy's losses) in the course of the war, the partisans killed 27,977 and wounded 8,232 native policemen; not infrequently, their family members were killed too. In some cases, the partisans destroyed the entire villages suspected of collaboration with the Germans. In contrast, the German losses did not exceed 15,000 men, while the partisans lost 25,681 men and women. These casualties, however, pale in comparison with the losses suffered by the civilian population. Close to one million people perished in Belorussia alone during Nazi occupation; over 900 localities were totally obliterated.[12]

*   *   *

The guerrilla struggle in the borderlands transcended the ideological Soviet–German boundaries, for its two-dimensional character was further splintered by opposing ethnicities, political affiliations, and opportunities for personal enrichment or joining a winning side. To be sure, in the course of the war many individuals switched their allegiances. For example, some of the native policemen joined the Soviet partisans or the nationalist guerrillas. In some instances the AK units that fought against the Nazis and the Soviets were forced by circumstances to collaborate with both. While many Lithuanians, Byelorussians, or Ukrainians served in the native administration and the police formations, their co-nationals were as active in the ranks of the Soviet army or Soviet partisans. The complexity and tragedy of the guerrilla warfare were further complicated by the fact that the enemies were recent citizens of the same country but fought on opposing sides, but even more so had grown up in the same village, worked together, or served in the same army unit before the war. Such close and personal knowledge of the enemy certainly added to the brutalization of fighting, since many participants knew those they tried to kill.

Although all guerrilla units contained the representatives of different ethnic groups—the Soviet partisans were the most 'international', while the predominantly Polish AK also comprised some Byelorussians and Lithuanians—the opposite sides often identified each other in political and ethnic terms. For example, the Polish and Soviet partisans often referred to the Jewish groups as 'Jews', with whom they competed for food supplies. These Jewish groups found themselves in a particular predicament, facing hostility from other partisans, the Germans, and the auxiliary police. For example, in Volhynia the encounter of Jewish refugees and partisans with the Ukrainian nationalist units was almost certainly fatal. Although on rare occasions the OUN and its armed formations employed Jewish artisans, doctors, and nurses, most definitely none of them survived the war. Nearly as deadly for the Jewish refugee camps were various bands that roamed the forests of Byelorussia and Volhynia.[13] A murderous seesaw warfare escalated as the Jewish partisans raided neighbouring villages for food, the auxiliary police combed forests for the Jewish camps, and the Soviet partisans attacked

Polish and Lithuanian villages suspected of helping the nationalist partisans. The AK often found itself fighting simultaneously the Germans, the Soviet partisans, the Lithuanian police, and the Ukrainian nationalist groups.[14]

The Polish population in the *Kresy* found itself in a predominantly hostile environment. Since the beginning of the Soviet–German war, it had suffered heavy losses at the hands of the Sipo/SD, which targeted the Polish intelligentsia. In Baranovichi alone the Germans and the native auxiliaries murdered over a thousand prominent Poles. However, the shortage of qualified personnel compelled the German administration to retain Polish agricultural experts, employees of railroads, banks, and credit unions, policemen, and managers of agricultural estates—*Liegenschaften*.[15]

Accordingly, Poles employed in the German administration incurred the wrath of the Byelorussian and Ukrainian peasants, who refused to return property or land they acquired during the Soviet retreat. Competition for the positions in the civil service intensified as Poles and Byelorussians appealed to the Germans for intercession, accusing one another of 'Bolshevism.' Similarly to the district governor of East Galicia Otto Wächter, who tolerated Ukrainian national aspirations, the *Generalkommissar* of Byelorussia Wilhelm Kube patronized Byelorussian cultural and educational organizations and associations as a counter-balance against the Poles. Byelorussian clubs and libraries were opened, and theatres staged plays based on literary works prohibited by the Soviet regime. The Byelorussian press advocated complete 'nationalization' of economy and social structure at the expense of Poles and the process seemed under way:[16] by late 1943 about 80 per cent of the personnel in the civil administration in Byelorussia and 60 per cent in the police were of Byelorussian background. As a result, Polish–Byelorussian antagonisms resulted in mutual denunciations and killings. The Byelorussian police participated in the executions of the alleged Polish guerrillas, whereas the Polish police acted in similar fashion in Byelorussian villages. In the Lida district—one of the AK strongholds—the AK attacks on the Byelorussian nationalist émigrés and members of social organizations resulted in the deaths of about 1,200 people. In anticipation for the struggle over the borderlands, some AK units also denounced the members of the communist underground (composed predominantly of ethnic Russians and Byelorussians) to the Germans.[17]

The Polish–Lithuanian conflict over Vilnius that simmered in 1939–41 also erupted anew under German occupation. In the initial stages of the German invasion the Lithuanian 'white armbands' assaulted and murdered a number of Poles, and in the early autumn the Sipo/SD began a systematic campaign against the Polish intelligentsia in the *Kresy*. Since the Lithuanian administration and the police in the Vilnius district played a visible role in this campaign, the Polish population routinely accused Lithuanians of deliberately influencing German policies. Such perceptions were fuelled by the 'second' Lithuanization of the region that included massive layoffs of Polish civil servants, shutting down Polish schools, changing the names of localities to Lithuanian, and a ban on the use of Polish in public places. Although some of these measures were initiated by the Germans, the Poles blamed the Lithuanian administration and the police with whom they had day-to-day contacts. Polish–Lithuanian animosities flared up especially in the countryside around Vilnius and Navahrudak (Nowogródek), where the Germans retained mid-level Polish administrators and estate managers, who dominated the socio-economic sector.[18]

However, despite the efforts to 'de-Polonize' Vilnius, in 1942 the city retained its predominantly Polish character—there were 97,000 Poles in contrast to 33,000 Lithuanians, 30,000 Russians, 7,000 Byelorussians, and 12,000 Jews. Similarly, in the countryside of the Vilnius and Navahrudak districts the Germans retained mid-level Polish administrators and estate managers, responsible for district economies. To even the odds, the Lithuanian administration and the police used the German anti-Polish measures to remove as many prominent Poles as possible from the socio-economic and cultural sphere in the region. During the terror campaign against the Polish intelligentsia, the *Saugumas* actively participated in arrests and investigations. Many Polish politicians, priests, students, and civil employees were shot by the Lithuanian killing squad at Ponary.[19] In spring 1942 the German administration began the forcible resettlement of Poles from south-western Lithuania, which according to the General Plan 'Ost' was to be 'cleansed' to prepare the ground for German settlers. While the Germans supervised the operation, the Lithuanian administration and the police were authorized to prepare proscription lists and they used the opportunity to deport members of Polish educational and cultural organizations, and civil activists. The deportees were sent to resettlement camps, where many died of epidemics, disease, or starvation. The active role of the Lithuanian administration and police in all these measures was so conspicuous that many Poles eventually came to believe that it was not the Germans but Lithuanians who were the main source of their misfortunes. Such attitudes compelled the AK command to issue a statement in its underground newspaper *Niepodległość* (Independence), stressing that the image of a 'third occupier' [besides the Germans and the Soviets] in Vilnius 'confuses [Polish] minds' as to who was the main enemy.[20]

The German defeat at the gates of Moscow forced moderate Lithuanian political groups to contemplate an agreement with the Poles in case the Soviets returned. Through 1942–43 the Polish and Lithuanian representatives held several secret meetings at which the two sides discussed the possibility of common action against the Soviets. Although the Lithuanians promised to take steps to minimize the participation of the Lithuanian police in anti-Polish actions, nevertheless, both sides refused to contemplate any concessions over the Vilnius issue.[21] They seemed to ignore the reality of the situation, which dictated that the issue of Vilnius as well as of all the borderlands would be determined by the Soviet–German conflict. Like the Lithuanians, who insisted on the 'Lithuanian' character of the city, the Polish government-in-exile maintained that Polish borders of 1939 were inviolable and could only grant the other side 'moral concessions' such as joint guardianship over the city historical monuments and landmarks.[22] In addition, the Polish side counted on the tacit support of the Byelorussians, whose national movement was still considered 'immature'. Promises of land reform and a guarantee of cultural development, could, therefore, win them to the Polish cause. Cultural assimilation would follow in due time.[23]

Concurrently with the Polish–Lithuanian talks, the AK propaganda in the Vilnius district maintained a highly hostile tone, portraying the Lithuanians as the 'experts' in the genocide of Jews and even suggested that the Germans 'emulated' Lithuanian methods. In turn, the Lithuanian underground press accused the Polish resistance of provoking German reprisals. Clashes between AK units and the Lithuanian police rapidly escalated and led to reprisals and counter-reprisals, whereby both sides murdered men, women, and children. During the German-organized operations against the Soviet partisans, the Lithuanian police 'pacified' several Polish villages and shot a number of residents. In turn, the AK stepped up its attacks on members of the Lithuanian administration and police. On 19 May 1942, a Soviet partisan group ambushed two German officials and an officer near the village of Święciany. Acting upon the orders of the German military commandant of Vilnius, two days later the Lithuanian police unit—the notorious 'Ponary shooters'—rounded up and shot 400 members of the Polish intelligentsia (some Polish sources claimed the number of victims as high as 1,200).[24]

After the German defeat at Stalingrad, the moderate Lithuanian political groups began organizing an underground movement headed by the Central Lithuanian Committee, which encouraged young men to avoid mobilization to German labour battalions and to wait for an opportune moment to get on the victors' wagon in 1943. Vague contingency plans stipulated to wait for an opportune moment and to take over Vilnius before the Poles. The resistance, however, stalled in summer–fall after the Security Police arrested many of its members.[25]

Meanwhile the low-intensity Polish–Lithuanian conflict broke out into the open, when in winter 1944 the Germans authorized the formation of the Lithuanian Auxiliary Formation (LVR) that was to be deployed against the Polish and Soviet partisans. In spring 1944 about 10,000 LVR members began burning localities suspected of collaboration with the partisans. In several large-scale encounters both the LVR and the AK suffered heavy losses. In March 1944 five AK brigades clashed in a pitched battle with an LVR regiment, which was wiped out. Reprisals and counter-reprisals followed each other in quick succession. After a skirmish with the Polish partisans, a Lithuanian police unit attacked the Polish village of Glitiškês (Glinciszki) and murdered thirty-eight people, including small children. In response, an AK unit attacked the village of Dubingiai (Dubinki) and killed twenty-seven alleged family members of the Lithuanian policemen. The Polish–Lithuanian conflict continued until the Soviet summer offensive of 1944 and ultimately weakened both protagonists, who were unwilling to compromise. The Polish side still evaluated the situation in the *Kresy* according to pre-war political criteria, whereby the small Lithuanian state would be forced to accept some sort of alliance with Poland. In this case, the Vilnius issue would automatically be resolved. The Lithuanians, who counted on German help in winning and 'homogenizing' the disputed territory, by 1944 found themselves without an ally in the impending struggle with the Soviets.[26]

In addition to 'regular' partisan units, the forests of southern Lithuania, Byelorussia, and Volhynia were swarming with various armed gangs who terrorized the population. Also, some partisan units avoided confrontation with the Germans and concentrated entirely on physical survival, hiding deep in the forests and coming out at night to rob the neighbouring villages. A number of Soviet partisan groups became known for loose discipline and for the so-called 'bombardment' operations, when they swept through villages taking food and valuables at gunpoint. Some units evolved into bona fide armed gangs that continuously mistreated and robbed the population. According to official statistics, the partisan courts in Byelorussia executed 2,345 resistance members for treachery, desertion, and petty crimes. All 'regular' and 'irregular' partisans, sometimes dressed in different uniforms to mislead the Germans or to provoke reprisals against the enemy, descended on villages whether in search of food or to induct able-bodied men. The villagers tried to stay alive by accommodating them, the Germans, and the local police, but from mid-1942 the German ability to maintain control over the countryside eroded and the multi-sided civil wars acquired their own dynamics. More often than not the opposing guerrillas considered each other more dangerous than the Germans, especially since the fight over supplies became a matter of survival.[27]

★ ★ ★

Although in 1941–42 the Polish and Soviet guerrilla units occasionally co-operated, especially during the large-scale German anti-partisan operations, in the summer of 1943 the simmering conflict between the two sides erupted into the 'third' Polish–Soviet war. By this time the special NKVD groups were sent to the borderlands to bolster the partisan activities and prepare the ground for the operations against the native political and civic activists, labelled as collaborators. On 22 June 1943, the second anniversary of the German invasion of the Soviet Union, the Central Committee of the Byelorussian Communist Party accepted a resolution of 'military-political measures in the western provinces of Byelorussia' that announced that the region was an 'inseparable' part of the Byelorussian Soviet Republic and only those resistance groups that fought in the interests of the USSR were considered legal. The resolution signified the opening of a stage in the 'reunification' of the borderlands as large partisan formations were sent on raids deep into the enemy's territory. Beside sabotage actions on German communication lines, the partisans were to prepare the ground for the re-establishment of the Soviet regime by 'rendering harmless' potential political opponents.[28]

Accordingly, from midsummer the Soviet partisan units concentrated on attacking the AK groups; battles, in which several hundred men fought on each side, continued until November. In the midst of the Soviet–Polish struggle, the Germans launched a large-scale operation against and inflicted heavy losses on both protagonists in the Naliboki forest (in north-western Byelorussia on the right bank of the Neman River). All villages within a radius of 10 miles were destroyed and 20,000 civilians were captured and sent to forced labour in Germany. Nevertheless, the Soviet offensive against the AK went on unabated. In August the Soviet 'Voroshilov' brigade disarmed an AK unit and executed eighty partisans. The AK retaliated by carrying out 'pacifications' of the Byelorussian villages in Navahrudak district, burning houses and killing residents suspected of collaboration with the Soviets. The AK units also executed Soviet captives, including the prisoners of war who had escaped from German camps.[29]

On 30 November 1943 the chief of staff of the Soviet partisan movement ordered Polish units to be disarmed and sent to detainment camps. Soviet partisan commanders were ordered to begin 'cleansing' the *Kresy* before the arrival of the Soviet army. From this point on, Soviet reports began referring to the Polish partisans as 'White Poles' as a term of the revolutionary phraseology of 1918-20. The offensive was planned by the Soviet government and coincided with Stalin's accusations against the Polish underground as German stooges, uttered during the Teheran Conference. On 1 January 1944, the Political Bureau of the Soviet Communist Party issued a decree that stipulated the restoration of Soviet power in Byelorussia. The decree stressed the importance of liquidating the 'consequences of the German occupation', which by implication connoted the eradication of all non-communist organizations and armed groups operating in the republic.[30] The Polish underground, which had already fought on two fronts against the Germans and the Soviets, faced a daunting task. Therefore, in November–December some Polish commanders contacted the Germans and offered a temporary truce in exchange for German arms supplies. In February 1944 the AK commander of the Vilnius district met the German representatives and agreed to take actions against the Soviets, if the Germans promised to refrain from anti-Polish actions.[31] Having received arms and munitions, in the first half of 1944 a number of Polish units joined the Germans in the fight against the Soviet partisans. The German units, the auxiliary police, and other collaborationist formations such as the Cossacks, who retreated with the German army, joined the fray. The 'everybody against everybody' war was in full swing. Soviet reports referred to hundreds of the 'White Poles, bandits, and nationalists' who were shot, along with the 'bandits' hirelings and helpers'—a euphemism for the civilian population whose houses were burned and livestock confiscated. In May 1944 several hundred Soviet partisans assaulted the AK base in the town of Kamen´ (Vitebsk oblast´) and burned the entire locality. In response, Polish units launched their own 'pacifications' of the villages east of the 1939 Soviet–Polish border, killing individuals suspected of sympathies with the Soviets.[32] The situation was further exacerbated by mass evacuation to the western districts of Byelorussia, inundated by thousands of refugees escaping the Soviet army. Hunger and epidemics decimated the population.

The Polish resistance suffered the heaviest blow in summer 1944, when the AK launched Operation 'Tempest' to liberate Vilnius (alongside Warsaw). Conceived as a measure to supersede the Soviets in establishing the Polish administration in the disputed areas, the AK units in the Vilnius-Navahrudak area fought side-by-side with the Soviet army. However, after Vilnius was liberated, the Soviet command invited senior AK officers to a 'meeting', where they were arrested. Simultaneously, the NKVD launched a large-scale operation to annihilate the AK in Lithuania and Byelorussia.

The Polish–Ukrainian war

Alongside the German anti-partisan warfare in Byelorussia, the Polish–Ukrainian conflict mutated into the most bloody civil war fought in the borderlands. While the roots of the conflict dated back to the Polish–Ukrainian war of 1918–19 in Galicia, mutual hostilities accumulated during the Second Polish Republic erupted under the first Soviet invasion in 1939. Although many Ukrainians fought in the ranks of the Polish army, the subversive activities of the OUN groups and the 'class terror' incited by the Soviets left a powerful imprint in the Polish popular psyche. Rivalry for social advancement during the 'socialist reconstruction' of the borderlands added fuel to mutual grievances, and in some instances the Polish and Ukrainian undergrounds informed upon each other to the Soviet secret police. On the eve of the Soviet–German war Polish reports from the *Kresy* sounded an alarm at the overwhelming hostility of the Ukrainian population.[33]

While the Soviet and German occupations provided the institutional framework for brewing confrontation, the Polish and Ukrainian political objectives demonstrated mutual inflexibility—similar to the Polish–Lithuanian conflict over Vilnius—in regard to the status of the *Kresy*. The Poles hoped that the Allied victory would restore Poland in its 1939 borders, whereas Ukrainian nationalists believed that independent statehood and the unification of all Ukrainian lands was predicated precisely upon the *destruction* of the Polish state. Hence, all means were acceptable to achieve this objective, especially since the Soviet and Nazi population policies demonstrated the value of violence in 'ethnic cleansing'.[34]

In April 1941 the Second Congress of the OUN-B in Krakow outlined immediate objectives for the national revolution. Economic and social life in ethnographic Ukrainian lands was to be purged of 'aliens'—Russians, Poles, and Jews. After the outbreak of the Soviet–German war, the nationalist groups were to take over the administration in Ukraine and present themselves as an irreplaceable equal partner to Germany rather than mere executors of German orders. Similarly, the Congress's resolutions stipulated that if German policies would not coincide with the objectives of the OUN, then the Ukrainian national revolution would enter a 'new stage', with the implication that the eventual collision with Germany was not excluded. During the German attack on the Soviet Union the OUN units ambushed small Soviet detachments and carried out acts of sabotage on communication lines. Simultaneously, OUN propaganda appealed to Ukrainians to partake in the national revolution against the Soviets, Poles, and 'Judaeo-Bolsheviks'. The OUN-organized militia was conspicuously active in anti-Jewish pogroms and also assisted the Germans in the arrest and execution of members of the Polish intelligentsia.[35] In September 1941 a Ukrainian newspaper, *Volyn* predicted that all 'aliens' residing in Ukraine would have to disappear. The first stage of this process was the solution of the Jewish question that was 'currently unfolding'.[36] Such pronouncements portended a gloomy future, and a Polish contemporary lamented that after the Jews 'are done with', Poles certainly would be next.[37]

Ukrainian aspirations for independence under German auspices, however, were short-lived. After, on 30 June 1941, when the OUN-B in L'viv announced the restoration of Ukrainian statehood, the Security Police arrested, executed, or imprisoned a number of leading nationalists. The two Ukrainian national battalions (formed before the war) that crossed the Soviet–German border alongside the German army were disbanded and fused into police units deployed against partisans in Byelorussia. The surviving OUN-B leadership went underground and began planning for a national revolution that was to unfold in several stages. The formation of a national army was to be followed by the cleansing of the Ukrainian territories of 'hostile elements'. In January 1942 an OUN-B instruction stipulated that the Russians, Poles, and Jews actively involved in the anti-Ukrainian struggle were to be eliminated at an appropriate moment to be determined later (to this effect, the instruction suggested a temporary reprieve for Jews useful in national economy), and when in April 1942 the Germans began the liquidation of the Jewish ghettos an OUN declaration stressed that the time was 'not conducive to participate in anti-Jewish actions so that [Ukrainians] did not become a blind weapon in [German] hands'.[38]

By this time the forests of Polesie and north-western districts of Volhynia had become the base of the 'Polis'ka Sich', which changed its name to the Ukrainian Insurgent Army (UPA). Led by its commander Taras Borovets, the UPA carried out small-scale attacks on German grain stores, warehouses, and railroads. In addition to Borovets' units, other Ukrainian nationalist partisans also operated in the same regions. In September 1942 the Soviet partisan units from Byelorussia arrived in the Volhynian forests. Alarmed, the OUN-B command sped up the formation of its own armed groups that were organized territorially and utilized abandoned Soviet military warehouses. In November the Ukrainian guerrillas tested their strength in the first attacks on Polish settlements.[39]

As with attempts at Polish–Lithuanian reconciliation, there were several talks between Polish and Ukrainian representatives. These, however, ran into insurmountable difficulties as the two sides passionately claimed the *Kresy* as the 'historical cradle' of their respective nations. The Polish government-in-exile stressed in its resolutions the 'inviolability' of the Polish eastern borders (such announcements further alienated Ukrainians, but also increasingly irritated Stalin), and in November 1942 the AK commander-in-chief Stefan Rowecki predicted that the restoration of Poland's frontiers was predicated upon armed conflict with the three enemies—the Germans, the Soviets, and the Ukrainians. More radical Polish circles in London considered the possibility of the forcible resettlement of Ukrainians, possibly to Poland's western territories. Similarly, some Ukrainian groups also contemplated an 'ethnic solution'. In March 1942 at the conference of the Ukrainian Regional Committee—a German-sponsored advisory body in East Galicia—its chairman, Professor Volodymyr Kubiyovych, proposed a simultaneous population exchange, whereby all Poles would be resettled to the 'core' Polish territories, while all Ukrainians would move to the 'ethnographically Ukrainian' lands (in 1945–47 the Polish–Soviet 'voluntary' exchange of the population would be carried out precisely according to this formula).[40]

On the other hand, the OUN-B leadership did not want a repetition of the 1920s, when the Allies practically handed over Galicia to Poland, while the latter blatantly violated its international obligations in regard to Galicia's autonomy. Hence, the only efficient way of solving the Polish–Ukrainian conflict was to remove Poles from Volynia and Galicia and create the basis for the homogeneous Ukrainian state, which the victor, whether Germany or more likely the Allies, would have to accept as a *fait accompli*. To this effect, ethnic cleansing rather than genocide would suffice to set the entire Polish population in motion. On 17–23 February 1943, during the Third Conference of OUN near Oles′ki (L′viv district), its most determined members, such as Roman Shukhevych and Dmytro Majivs′kyi took over the leadership. The conference concluded that the German defeat at Stalingrad necessitated an immediate anti-Polish action—especially advocated by Majivs′kyi and Shukhevych—as a crucial component in the struggle for national independence. Such logic was generated by the fear that Poles would eventually ally with the Soviets and the so-called Maiski–Sikorski agreement between Poland and the USSR in July 1941 excluded the creation of an independent Ukraine.[41]

The OUN leadership was also concerned about the Polish underground that had rebuilt its network in the *Kresy*. The OUN, therefore, planned that national revolution, predicated upon the struggle against 'three enemies'— the Soviets, the Poles, and the Germans—would have to start with the elimination of the weakest opponent, the Poles. Such a move would also test the OUN armed forces and the peasant self-defence units that after shedding blood would be irreversibly tied to the national cause. Psychologically, the OUN commanders were prepared to employ the most brutal means to achieve the ultimate objectives. Some of them, such as Shukhevych, Dmytro Grytsai, and Yaroslav Starukh, who were active in the interwar terrorist activities, grew immune to pain and suffering as inmates at the Bereza concentration camp or as the members of the Ukrainian police that participated in anti-partisan operations.[42]

Large-scale attacks began in February and March, when OUN units and peasant self-defence groups murdered 800 Poles in Sarny and Kostopil′ districts (Rivne province). The assailants surrounded Polish villages at night, blocked possible escape routes, and then proceeded from house to house butchering all residents regardless of age and sex. Most of the loot was distributed among peasants; houses were routinely set on fire to prevent any potential return of the Poles. In spring the OUN forces were strengthened by the influx of 6,000 Ukrainian policemen, who deserted en masse to the forests, responding to an OUN propaganda campaign. Since many of them had participated in the murder of Jews, they had developed the necessary experience and insensitivity to inflicting violence. In addition, they most certainly received ideological indoctrination during their training in German police schools, and consequently perceived different ethnic groups in Ukraine along the ethno-ideological divide. In May 1943 the OUN armed units were fused into a single formation, the Ukrainian Insurgent Army (UPA), which comprised between 10,000 to 12,000 armed men ready for action.[43]

The OUN-UPA onslaught took the Germans by surprise and they hastily increased their garrisons. For example, in the town of Kovel'—a crucial rail hub in Volhynia—the German garrison grew from 300 in January to 4,000 in April. Yet the Eastern Front was siphoning off all German resources, and therefore, they managed only to fortify the urban areas, leaving the countryside under OUN-UPA control. Hence, most of the Polish settlements were left undefended and perished in flames. The AK forces in Volhynia lacked manpower and arms to offer organized resistance; only in a few places, such as Perebrody (Przebraże) in Luts'k county, Polish civilians in cooperation with Soviet partisans fought off numerous UPA attacks.[44]

Meanwhile the OUN-UPA assault escalated in April–May 1943. Using superior numbers and organization, nationalist units overran Polish settlements. While some villages were given notice to leave in forty-eight hours, in most cases the attack came without warning. Butchering of all inhabitants was followed by thorough looting and burning, so that after a few hours only charred corpses and smoking ashes bore witness to the Polish presence in the area. The death toll grew dramatically and in two months about 3,000 Poles were murdered in Rivne province; Soviet partisans reported to Moscow that within a radius of 20 kilometres around the town all Polish settlements were gone. To expedite the cleansing, the OUN-UPA units deliberately mutilated corpses. Fear and panic gripped Polish communities, which fled to the cities. The conflict, however, also spilled over to urban areas, where mutual assassinations of prominent Poles and Ukrainians reached its peak in the summer and autumn. According to the diary of a Ukrainian teacher, Victor Petrykevych, every day newspapers reported murders of policemen, scholars, doctors, businessmen, merchants, and teachers.[45]

Alarmed by the situation in the *Kresy*, the underground representation of the Polish government in Poland, the Government Commission (*Delegatura Rządu*), reported to London that the Ukrainians would not accept the pre-war

status quo and proposed several contingency plans that included more intensive integration of Ukrainians into Polish political and social life after the war,
but also a 'voluntary exchange' of Ukrainian and Polish populations. In July
1943 the London government appealed to the Ukrainians to join the struggle
against Germany and promised them equal political and civil rights. The
appeal, nevertheless, stressed that Poland would never accede to giving up its
eastern frontiers 'since the Polish nation has made such an enormous contribution to their civilization and economy'.[46] In March 1944 the Council of
National Unity, a body created to coordinate underground activities of all
Polish groups and organizations, issued a declaration entitled 'What is the
Polish Nation Fighting for?' The declaration appealed to Poland's ethnic
minorities to remain 'loyal and faithful' to the Polish state, which would
respect their political, civil, and cultural rights, though these would be preserved only within the framework of the Polish state. The declaration did not
mention cultural or territorial autonomy, but merely rephrased the pre-war
concept of the national state and clearly indicated that the Polish leadership was
impervious to the realities of the situation and still dreamed of a 'single and
undivided' Poland.[47] Despite profound ideological differences with the 'London Poles', the Union of Polish Communists in the USSR (created under the
auspices of the Soviet government) also issued similar statements that, albeit
passing in silence the future of the eastern frontiers, accentuated that Poland
would become a national state, in which national minorities would enjoy
equal civic rights.[48]

All these pronouncements were made at a time when thousands of Poles
had been murdered and masses of refugees were fleeing for their lives
westward beyond the Zbrucz River. For the OUN the prospect of the
'Ukrainization' of the *Kresy* thus seemed at hand. To stem the spread of
terror and profound disorder, in spring 1943 the Germans began dismissing
Ukrainians from the lower administration in Volhynia and Podolia,
who were suspected of connections with the OUN. At the same time,
OUN propaganda highlighted the activities of Poles who served as estate
managers, foresters, and rail functionaries as the most willing German
collaborators. Hence, attacks on Poles in German service coincided with
the OUN-UPA onslaught. On the other hand, hundreds of Poles
were recruited into the auxiliary police units, which by summer 1943 in
Volhynia numbered up to 2,000 men. Following the desertion of the
Ukrainian auxiliary police *en bloc* in spring 1943, the Germans reconstituted
this force in part from Polish recruits. There were also reinforcements of

Polish policemen sent into Volhynia from other parts of Poland. On 13−14 June the Polish police participated in a punitive expedition against the Czech and Ukrainian villages, where 624 Czechs and 116 Ukrainians were murdered. The ferocity of the Polish police, who often acted in revenge for OUN-UPA attacks, was testified by one member who recalled that 'within a radius of several kilometres [the police] left behind no mill, no church, and no [Orthodox] priest'.[49]

The multi-sided conflict escalated as numerous auxiliary units, both native and transferred from other territories, joined the fray. The Germans used auxiliary units composed of Latvians, Cossacks, Hungarians, and the *Ostruppen*, which ran amok amidst shooting and fires. Criminal bands also ravaged the countryside, attacking estates and plundering villages. Meanwhile the Soviet partisans paralysed German rail communications and became virtual masters in several districts, burning villages suspected of collaborating with OUN-UPA.[50] Petrykevych lamented that the peasants, terrorized by the partisans at night and by the Germans in daytime, 'envied urban dwellers'. His Polish counterpart echoed that 'men became desensitized more quickly and kill as if they knew nothing else. Even those who would otherwise hesitate before killing a fly can quickly forget that they are taking human lives'.[51]

Ethnic cleansing reached its peak in summer 1943. Apparently, the great Soviet offensive at the Kursk salient served as a signal for all-out assault on Polish settlements, for in June the commander of the UPA group 'North', Klym Savur, gave an order for 'total physical liquidation of the Polish population'.[52] Consequently, OUN-UPA terror spread throughout Volhynia. In the last five days of August about 15,000 Poles lost their lives. Reports of Soviet partisans and the recollections of survivors conveyed the horrifying images of almost Dante dimensions of inferno:

> the slaughter and torment defy all words . . . almost all Poles in the villages of the Krzemieniec county have been slaughtered . . . almost all the Polish parishioners from Oleksiniec parish were robbed and killed . . . daily one can see fires; they are burning Polish settlements and murdering in the most bestial manner those who did not escape.[53]

The terror brought a sharp decline of the Polish population, which scared, hungry, and sick, inundated towns and cities and settled in makeshift camps. Others were crossing into neighbouring East Galicia, where Polish relief committees laboured frantically to provide food and clothing. Despite the appeals of the Ukrainian Central Committee and Andrej Shetpys'kyi to Ukrainians to stop massacres, the assaults continued. It is also possible that, once started, the OUN-UPA could not, even if they wished to, stop violence, which assumed dimensions of its own. Fear of Polish retaliation begot 'pre-emptive' strikes. Induced by the opportunity to enrich themselves at the expense of their neighbours, Ukrainian peasants participated in the massacres, although a number of Poles survived owing to the help of their Ukrainian peers. In several instances Jewish survivors and Polish defenders joined forces to stave off UPA attacks. Although in the autumn the scope of the assault subsided, it was only a temporary relief, as the OUN-UPA leadership had to take into consideration the rapid German retreat after the fall of Kiev in November. In addition, in summer 1943 OUN units faced Soviet partisans in pitched battles, where both sides committed large forces and suffered severe casualties. The OUN thus issued several appeals to the population, promising equality to all citizens of the future Ukrainian states. However, in the midst of brutal attacks on Polish settlements in October–November such promises fell on deaf ears.[54]

Impressed by the Soviet progress at the front, the OUN-UPA leadership altered its ideological platform that outwardly included some democratic and socialist principles. In August 1943 the Third Congress of the OUN-B announced that in the future independent Ukraine 'all ethnic' groups would be guaranteed political and civil equality. Given that the majority of Jews had been murdered and the ethnic cleansing in Volhynia was reaching its zenith, the nationalists certainly could afford such statements. In addition, by this time violence had also spilled over into the previously quiet East Galicia. The quick pace of the Soviet offensive and the raid of a large Soviet partisan detachment that in August penetrated into Galicia alarmed both the Germans and the OUN-UPA leadership. Led by an experienced partisan commander, Sydir Kovpak, about 1,500 partisans swept through the southern districts of the province destroying oil refineries, bridges, and warehouses. The German military and SS command were forced to deploy against the partisans 10,000 men, including the multinational *Osttruppen* and the Ukrainian police. The partisans also clashed with the UPA territorial units, which used the opportunity to launch attacks on Polish villages in L'viv and in Tarnopil' provinces. The assault followed the pattern established in Volhynia—villages were given a short notice to leave, but in most cases were attacked without warning. The UPA command also deployed the youth units that were to be baptized by bloodshed. Under the slogan 'a strip of free Ukraine for every dead Pole', Polish houses were looted and burned, all residents were murdered, and corpses were mutilated and defiled. In October OUN-M also attacked Polish villages in Sokal' and Buzsk districts.[55]

The intimidation campaign certainly worked, for thousands of Poles left Galicia for good. The OUN-UPA policies followed the trajectory established two years before in wartime Croatia, where the Ustaše government contemplated the murder of one-third of the Serbian population; one-third was to convert to Catholicism and one-third was expected to leave under duress. Conversion to Greek Catholicism albeit on a smaller scale was also an option contemplated by the OUN leadership. About 800 Poles took such an opportunity in the Ivano-Frankivs'k (Staniswawów) district, but most of the Polish population decided to flee.[56]

In January–February 1944 600 Polish men, women, and children were murdered in Ternopil' (Tarnapol) province; in April 400 perished in Rava and Zhovkva districts. Although some of the OUN leaders considered moderating ethnic policies, especially in view of the impending Soviet occupation, the commanders in the field were determined to carry out the 'removal' of Poles, especially since the terror campaign had gone too far to be terminated.[57] Thousands of Poles rushed to rail stations, where they spent weeks waiting for trains. Others fled on foot, looking over the burning villages and listening to the roar of the Soviet guns in the distance that underscored the prevailing horror and chaos.[58] On the other hand, being subjected to unrelenting terror, the Polish population responded in kind—terror seemed to be the only appropriate and logical response (though emotions more than often overrode logic). Violence generated violence and collective responsibility was applied to all Ukrainians, regardless of political affiliation or age.[59]

Facing the Soviet offensive, the Germans sought accommodation with the UPA. In several instances the German and UPA units carried out pacifications of localities suspected of abetting Polish partisans. In February 1944 the details of the Ukrainian SS 'Galizien' Division, assisted by UPA detachments, obliterated the alleged AK base at the village of Huta Penyat'ska (Huta Peniacka), in Ternopil' province, where upward of 500 Poles were shot or burned alive. In March 1944 the joined German–UPA forces collided with the Soviet partisans near the village of Podkamen'. At the same time, alarmed by the rapidly deteriorating situation in the province, the Germans launched fierce pacifications of Ukrainian villages. Mass round-ups, arrests, and executions of suspected OUN and Polish underground members vividly demonstrated that the 'quiet' East Galicia had become a battleground. In March 1944 in a reprisal for the UPA attack on a group of German functionaries near Rohatyn, the German police murdered 500 Ukrainians. In early July 1944 the German 'pacification' in L'viv district resulted in the murder of approximately 600 Ukrainians. Still, the German representatives indicated to the OUN leadership that they wanted to avoid the 'repetition of the situation in Serbia or Croatia' and were willing to supply the UPA with arms, provided that the nationalists turned exclusively against the Soviets. True to the agreement, the UPA began preparations for the confrontation with the Soviet army and simultaneously continued attacks on Polish settlements.[60]

Summary

With the Soviet offensive in the summer 1944 large parts of the borderlands were liberated from the Germans although the front lines still cut through the Baltic region, where the war would continue until spring 1945. In the meantime, the civil wars that raged under German occupation entered a new stage under the Soviet regime.

While the Soviet–German war desensitized large segments of the population to violence, it was also local initiatives that gave life to the civil wars, for grievances which had incubated during the interwar period exploded under the two occupations into several conflicts fought for the redefinition of political and socio-economic space. Since the aftermath of the frontier wars the winners had perceived themselves as the main proprietors of the new political entities, while the losers felt cheated by the peace settlements. It was no coincidence, therefore, that in 1941–4 the most sanguinary and devastating civil wars transpired in the interwar 'hot spots', East Galicia, Byelorussia, Volhynia, and to a lesser degree in the Vilnius region, informed not only by ideologies or ethnic animosities, but by old grudges, social injustices, and human opportunism. Such a situation forced the opposing factions to fight at one time and collaborate at another with either of the two totalitarian regimes. Threatened by all the belligerents, the population at large faced an even more limited choice of action.

In the end, the major beneficiary of the civil wars was the Soviet Union. The OUN-UPA ethnic cleansing in the *Kresy* claimed approximately 50,000 Polish and 10,000 Ukrainian lives, and the exodus of about

350,000 Poles effectively decimated Polish presence in the region, thus facilitating the re-Sovietization of the region. Crucially, in contrast to the Soviets, who relentlessly pursued their political objectives, the multi-sided conflicts in the Vilnius, Byelorussia, Volhynia, and East Galicia ultimately weakened the national movements, which cracked under the pressure of fighting too many enemies at the same time.[61]

8

Redrawing Ethno-Social Boundaries: Phase II, 1944–1953

The end of the Second World War confirmed the reintegration of the borderlands into the Soviet Union and before the termination of hostilities the Allies decided upon the future borders in Eastern Europe. Stalin was determined to re-establish the frontiers of the Soviet–German Pact of 1939 and the two protagonists—the Polish government-in-exile and the Polish communists—realized that the territories in the East could not be recovered, and expected territorial compensation at the expense of Germany. In October 1943 the Allied foreign ministers in Moscow agreed that Germany would lose East Prussia to Poland and Russia, and in November 1943 at the Teheran conference Stalin, Roosevelt, and Churchill agreed that the eastern Polish territories would be incorporated into the Soviet Union, while Poland would be enlarged by the fusion of eastern Germany. On 27 July 1944, the Polish Committee of National Liberation (PKWN) ceded eastern Poland along the Curzon Line to the Soviet Union; the same agreement provided for the division of East Prussia between Poland and the USSR. In exchange for recognizing the Soviet annexation of East Galicia and the *Kresy*, the PKWN obtained Stalin's concession that west Galicia, the Białystok region, and even some areas east of the San River would be returned to Poland. Although in 1939 the Soviet government justified the annexation of these areas by the presence of large Ukrainian and Byelorussian communities, now Stalin sacrificed the ideology of 'reunification' for political expediency, straightening up the state boundaries for easier administrative management and control. In January 1945 the Soviet–Polish agreement (modified in May 1951) confirmed the border settlement and provided for the 'voluntary exchange' of 1.5 million Poles and 500,000 Ukrainians in the borderlands.[1] The Soviet losses in eastern Poland were compensated for by the acquisition of northern Bukovina and Transcarpathia.

The second Sovietization followed the pattern established in 1939–41, when military conquest was accompanied by socio-economic reconstruction of the borderlands. However, in contrast to that period now the Soviets faced a much more organized and determined resistance of armed factions, which established their presence in the area during the war. The Soviet government was also painfully aware that the bulk of the population in the borderlands did not want to be 'liberated', at least not in the Soviet way. It therefore considered the pacification and integration of the borderlands as the last stage of the frontier wars of 1918–20, which would culminate in the complete destruction of 'counter-revolutionary' forces, whatever form the latter assumed. Simultaneously, the military and police measures would prepare the borderlands for speedy integration into the Soviet economic, ideological, and administrative system.

Insurgency warfare

The Soviet government realized the difficulties that lay ahead. The mentality of the populations in the borderlands certainly made them a difficult material for a 're-educational' process. Less than two years of the Soviet rule in 1939–41 hardly changed popular mentality and, despite all their faults, the Central European rather than Soviet politics and culture were much more attractive to the bulk of the borderlands population.[2] Since the First World War nationalism had acquired powerful potential, erupting in national rebellions during the German invasion and in formation of the guerilla forces that opposed the Soviet regime with arms in hand. Wartime secret reports from western Ukraine clearly indicated that the population was hostile to the Soviet regime and even women and children were sheltering and abetting the nationalist guerrillas. Although official Soviet propaganda did not spare praises for 'enthusiasm' towards the returning Soviet army, even in Byelorussia, ravaged by German pacifications, popular attitudes were, according to Soviet reports, 'directed at private property, against the kolkhoz and against the government'.[3]

As determined as the nationalist guerrillas were, they stood no chance openly confronting the might of the Soviet security and police apparatus. However, while the Soviet government was willing to unleash its destructive potential upon the borderlands, from the ideological point of view it could ill afford to emulate German pacification, wiping out villages and depopulating entire regions. Hence, according to the operational plans devised in Moscow and Kiev, the military conquest was only part of a comprehensive plan that included socio-economic reconstruction and winning, by all means, if not the confidence then at least the submissiveness of the population. Such methods seemed to be effective in Transcarpathia, where the Soviet administration was established without resistance. Although Stalin assured President Eduard Beneš that after the war Transcarpathia would be reunited with Czechoslovakia, after October 1944, when the Soviet troops occupied the province, the Soviet administration in the province gave full support to the communist and pro-Soviet groups. The result of such support culminated on 19 November 1944, when the small communist party of Transcarpathia demanded 'reunification' with Soviet Ukraine as the utmost desire of the toilers and peasants. Popular disaffection with Hungarian rule gave the communist appeal an air of legitimacy, and a week later a national council in Mukacheve (Mucačevo) adopted the same resolution. Although Transcarpathia was never a part of the Russian empire, the Soviet government announced that it was compelled to oblige the 'national will' of the population of the province. In late June 1945 Czechoslovakia officially ceded the province to Soviet Ukraine (in January 1946 Transcarpathia was named the Zakarpattia oblast'). The Soviet Union, consequently, acquired the last of the 'lost' Ukrainian lands and established a stable foothold south of the Carpathian Mountains.[4]

In the Baltic region, Byelorussia, Volhynia, and East Galicia the situation was different. Anticipating the Soviet offensive, the anti-Soviet groups, which represented an array of forces formed under German occupation, organized armed units and set up safe-houses in cities and towns and training camps in forests. In Lithuania several underground groups merged into the Supreme Committee for the Liberation of Lithuania—VLIK—that formulated its political platform on the basis of inviolability of borders that in practice meant the incorporation of all 'historical Lithuanian lands', including Vilnius, into the future Lithuanian state. Similar organizations—the Armed Resistance League (RVL) in Estonia and the Central Committee in Latvia united various political groupings that hoped for the repetition of the post-First World War scenario—the eventual Allied help in establishing national sovereignty.[5]

Although Soviet propaganda consistently portrayed the guerrillas as 'fascist hirelings', 'bourgeois nationalists', and 'bandits', the ideological and social make-up of the resistance was far from uniform. Nevertheless, some guerrillas were trained in German intelligence camps and then were sent behind the Soviet lines, and others were members of the German-sponsored local administration and the auxiliary police, who took part in the genocide of Jews and anti-partisan operations. For example, the UPA commander-in-chief Roman Shukhevych had served as an officer of a police battalion in Byelorussia. Many of the guerrilla commanders in the Baltic region were also former army and police personnel. A substantial part of the resistance cadres was made up of deserters from the German and Soviet armies, especially after the Soviets announced general mobilization for men between 18 to 55 years of age. Undoubtedly, the first Soviet occupation in 1939–41 filled the population with fear, and many students, peasants, and town-dwellers joined the 'forest brothers'. Many were genuine idealists, fighting for national independence against foreign oppression. In addition, by 1942 the initial euphoria over the Soviet–German war had evaporated and German economic policies drove large segments of the population to unarmed resistance, rejecting conscription to forced labour and service in German military units. Such experiences would prove helpful in preparing for the confrontation with the Soviets.[6]

In contrast to the Baltic or Ukrainian resistance movements that had unequivocally declared themselves the inveterate enemies of the Soviet Union, the AK faced a much more complicated situation. Although the Polish government-in-exile was allied to the Western powers (and thus to the Soviet Union), the hostility between the AK and the Soviet partisans flared up in the German-occupied *Kresy*. Low-intensity conflict between the two opponents erupted into an open confrontation in July 1944, when the AK high command launched Operation 'Thunder', aimed at countering the claims of the Polish communists, who under Soviet auspices set up the Polish Committee of National Liberation in Lublin (PKWN). At the same time, the AK high command issued a secret order to the commanders in the field that referred to the Soviet Union both as an ally against Germany and an enemy, particularly in the light of Soviet recognition of the PKWN. However, the situation of the AK became critical because fighting in the open during Operation 'Thunder' effectively facilitated the identification and eventual elimination of its members by the Soviet forces. On 17–18 July near Vilnius under the pretext of consultation the Soviet military arrested almost the entire AK command of the Vilnius and Navahrudek regions. In the following days the NKVD and the Soviet troops disarmed and arrested about 3,500 AK members who were either sent to concentration camps or were forcibly mobilized into the Polish army that functioned under Soviet auspices. Such measures drastically reduced the manpower-base for the resistance.[7]

Facing destruction, in January 1945 the AK high command issued an order that described the situation as an exchange of one occupation for another 'under the façade of the Lublin government, a powerless tool in Russian hands'. The order stipulated the dismemberment of the AK, but stressed that the Soviet victory did not mean the end of the war. Two months later near Warsaw the Soviet security forces lured the AK high command into a trap and in June put them on trial in Moscow for 'collaboration with Germany, terrorism, and diversionist activities'.[8] The same month the Polish resistance suffered another blow as the Allied Powers agreed to the formation of the Provisional Government of National Unity in Poland, which in practice meant the revocation of the sovereignty represented by the Polish government-in-exile in London.

Nevertheless, some AK units decided to continue the struggle, count-ing—as did all the anti-Soviet forces in Eastern Europe—on the impending conflict between the East and the West. These hopes were fuelled by Churchill's 'Iron Curtain' speech and the Berlin Blockade that set the tone for the Cold War. Consequently, reliance on Western democracies necessitated toning down any fascist or xenophobic ideological postulates and accentuating socialist programme with the stress on national independ-ence. Already in August 1943, contemplating Germany's defeat, the OUN Third Extraordinary Congress rejected 'internationalist' and fascist ideology and called for the nationalization of large industries, emancipation of women, and a whole range of liberties such as freedom of religion and expression. Similarly, the political platform of a short-lived Union for the Liberation of Byelorussia (SVB), which planned to become the kernel of the anti-Soviet resistance, included the creation of a social state, the nationali-zation of industries, and political freedoms.[9]

By the time the Soviet army entered the borderlands, the strongest and best-organized guerrilla forces of about 70,000 men operated in Latvia, Lithuania, and western Ukraine; smaller underground groups operated in

Estonia and Byelorussia. Since the OUN concentrated most of its forces in Volhynia and East Galicia, in Bukovina its cells remained small and ineffective. The traditional divisions between the Rusyn and Ukrainian communities and the weakness of nationalism in Transcarpathia contributed to relative tranquillity in the province after the Soviet conquest.

★ ★ ★

Resistance began immediatcly after the advance of the Soviet army into the borderlands. In Volhynia the UPA forces engaged Soviet troops in pitched battles that involved thousands of fighters on both sides. In the Baltic region the guerrillas also concentrated on attacking Soviet detachments. In July 1944 in Vilnius the Polish and Lithuanian undergrounds launched a propaganda campaign, appealing to the population to boycott conscription to the Soviet army. The campaign proved highly effective and only a handful reported to the recruiting stations. Open confrontation with the Soviet army, however, proved costly. Between February and May 1944 the Soviet forces killed 10,619 members of the Ukrainian underground and lost more than a thousand of their own personnel; 8,235 guerrillas were captured.[10]

Facing the much superior Soviet forces, all the underground groups had to abandon large-scale encounters and switched to hit-and-run attacks on local police stations, administrative offices, and (after the beginning of collectivization) collective farms. These tactics, from the Soviet point of view, were the most pernicious aspect of the guerrilla warfare, since they defied the new political order, especially in the countryside. For example, headed by Lieutenant Czesław Zajączkowski ('Ragner'), the largest AK unit in western Byelorussia numbered about 600 men and represented a serious threat to Soviet communication lines and the local administration. Between August 1944 and May 1945 a smaller Byelorussian guerrilla unit in Hrodna oblast′ killed 112 Soviet officials, officers, and soldiers.[11]

At the same time, the guerrilla attacks on native activists, kolkhoz functionaries, and the militia eventually benefited the Soviet regime, which recruited local residents for the entry positions in the administration in the countryside. To deter collaboration with the Soviets, the underground brutally murdered hundreds of Soviet activists and their families, who were garrotted, hacked to pieces, or burned alive. Consequently, a civil war began as the relatives of the murdered officials became avengers, poised to act brutally against the relatives of the underground fighters. Their actions, in turn, generated the reprisals of the guerrillas.[12] The situation of the population, squeezed between the resistance and the Soviet forces, became increasingly desperate. At daytime they were forced to provide the Soviets with information about the resistance and at night the guerrillas came to look for potential traitors or for food and shelter. Tired of fighting, the majority of the population increasingly longed for peace, whichever form it would take.

The war in the countryside gained momentum after the beginning of collectivization. In March 1946 in Vyrumaa district in Estonia the resistance murdered thirteen activists and their families including two children. In one village in Volhynia the guerrillas chopped off the arms of those peasants who supported the creation of the kolkhoz. Such brutalities were not exceptions. Altogether between February 1944 and December 1946 the Ukrainian underground killed about 12,000 Soviet functionaries and wounded 3,914; at least half of the victims were local Ukrainians. In 1946 the Lithuanian guerrillas murdered 6,112 state, party, and kolkhoz functionaries. As a result of the terror campaign, in many villages Soviet power dissipated at night, when the underground reigned unopposed. Death threats to Soviet functionaries and executions of the most active officials contributed to the overwhelming atmosphere of fear and uncertainty.[13]

In addition to military actions, the nationalist underground carried out anti-state propaganda that highlighted the deficiencies of the Soviet economic and political system. During the first elections to the Supreme Council of the USSR in February 1946, the Lithuanian guerrillas called for a boycott of the elections, cut telephone lines, and attacked polling stations. The Ukrainian resistance displayed national blue–yellow colours in public places and disseminated leaflets that mocked the Soviet leadership.[14]

From late 1946 the Ukrainian underground began the demobilization of its fighters, who were ordered to legalize and integrate themselves into the new order, waiting for the signal to reactivate the struggle. The remaining guerrilla units became smaller and more mobile. They hid in camouflaged bunkers, skilfully constructed under houses, barns, and in forests and gardens. In 1945–6 the Soviet military and security apparatus discovered 28,969 such bunkers in western Ukraine.[15] The guerrillas deployed hit-and-run tactics, moving at night, carefully selecting their targets, and disappearing after action.

★ ★ ★

The 'civil war' mentality that had dominated the minds of the Soviet political leadership since the suppression of the resistance in the wake of the Russian Civil Wars and in the campaigns against 'bourgeois nationalism' in the 1930s was now projected upon the borderlands. The Soviet government fully appreciated the danger of a potential Vendèe,[16] which called for extraordinary anti-insurgency measures and required the full force of the state apparatus.[17] These concerns translated into the dispatch of top security officials to the borderlands. In 1944 the NKGB Minister Victor Abakumov and his deputy Sergei Kruglov arrived in Lithuania and the deputy-minister of the NKVD Bogdan Kobulov in Byelorussia to coordinate the anti-insurgency operations. Experienced security functionaries were also sent to Estonia, Latvia, and western Ukraine. At the same time, the Soviet military increased the numbers of troops engaged in the struggle against the guerrillas. In 1946 the Soviet forces in Lithuania numbered 12,000 security personnel and between 40,000 and 60,000 troops. In Volhynia and East Galicia 26,000 troops, 20,000 security personnel, and 18,000 members of the 'destruction battalions' (made up of mobilized native residents) conducted anti-insurgency operations. In contrast to the German security police field offices that on average had about twenty functionaries and dozens of agents in larger localities, in the *Kresy* each district branch of the NKGB-NKVD (in March 1946 the two institutions were renamed MGB and MVD respectively) had at its disposal up to 300 functionaries and hundreds of agents and informants. Coordinated military and police operations grew in frequency and intensity. If between August 1944 and January 1945 the Soviet forces in Lithuania arrested 22,327 individuals, by the end of 1945 they carried out 8,807 anti-guerrilla actions and captured and arrested 58,089 people. By 1947 in Vilnius and Novohradek oblast' the Soviet troops and security units killed 3,000 AK members, arrested 13,000 suspected resisters, and sent approximately 20,000 underground members and their families to concentration camps.[18]

While the troops and security forces carried out 'combings' of forests and the countryside, frequent round-ups of suspects destroyed the underground's economic and manpower base. A constantly expanding network of agents and informants was set up to penetrate the underground. Disguised as guerrillas, groups of security functionaries committed brutalities against the population, including rape and murder, aiming to incite the people against the underground. To cover up the traces of their gruesome activities, these groups often buried their victims in the mass graves left by the German punitive expeditions. From 1946 anti-partisan operations included billeting a company-size unit in every village, checkpoints on roads, and air reconnaissance, while special search-and-destroy groups relentlessly pursued the insurgents, forcing them to disperse into smaller units whose only objective became merely survival. To intimidate the population and identify the insurgents' relatives and friends, the Soviet forces displayed the bodies of the killed guerrillas, who were often stripped to underwear and left in public places. Captured guerrillas were subjected to long inter-rogations, which were conducted frequently at night to weaken the physical and psychological resistance of a suspect, who had to repeat his story over and over again. When 'congenial' methods did not work, threats to one's family members, and then beating and torture were deployed. Consequent-ly, many insurgents preferred suicide rather than surrender and in many instances, when surrounded in bunkers or safe-houses, they shot themselves or blew themselves up.[19]

The offensive against the underground was also maintained on the ideological front. Between 1944 and 1955 the Soviet government an-nounced at least seven amnesties, which partially depleted the resistance ranks as some of the guerrillas laid down arms and surrendered. Official propaganda denounced the guerrillas as wartime collaborators, criminals, and asocial elements. Although it is unclear whether such methods were effective, the fine line between political resistance and petty crime was increasingly difficult to draw as constant economic shortages and political instability contributed to a high crime rate. Armed with abandoned weap-ons, bands with no political affiliation terrorized the population day and night (high crime rate was common for the entire Soviet Union in the first post-war years). In order to obtain money and food the underground used similar methods, robbing banks, credit unions, and stores. The Soviet media made full use of such instances, portraying the guerrillas interchangeably as 'fascist hirelings' and 'bandits and thugs' in an attempt to discredit the resistance.[20]

The engagement of the 'destruction battalions' in anti-insurgency opera-tions added to the ferocity of the post-war struggle in the borderlands. Some individuals volunteered because of ideological affiliations or thirsting for vengeance for the suffering under the Germans; others were impressed into service. By the late 1940s at least a third of the battalion cadres were Estonians, Latvians, or Lithuanians. Despite resentment towards the regime, thousands of Poles took up arms to avenge the OUN-UPA terror and participated in pacifications of Ukrainian villages, where they earned noto-riety for particular brutality. The military usefulness of the 'destruction battalions' was still much less important than their political value, for they demonstrated local support for Soviet power. The Soviet security services also employed a number of Byelorussians, Ukrainians, and Jews, who fought with the Soviet partisans or had suffered from the German occupation. In summer 1944 the Soviet agent network in Baranovichi district alone numbered about 2,000 such individuals. Since the underground specifically targeted the members of the 'destruction battalions' and police agents, their relatives often became spies for the state.[21]

One of the most effective Soviet methods was the creation of pseudo-underground centres that served as baits for real resisters. In fact, only acting in small separate units guaranteed longer existence for the guerrillas, for any attempt to create a large centralized organization was bound to be penetrated by Soviet agents. From spring 1946 Soviet agents infiltrated the highest echelons of the resistance luring its most distinguished commanders into traps. For example, in Lithuania an NKVD agent, Juozas Markulis, who acted as a leader of a fictional intelligence group, managed to become head of an underground organization that served as an umbrella organization for several resistance units. After obtaining the roll-call and photographs of the underground cadres—under pretext of making fake documents—Markulis and other Soviet agents spearheaded the liquidation of resistance groups. In late 1947 the Soviet security organs infiltrated the Estonian RVL and in the next year they destroyed or captured about 500 of its most active cadres.[22]

The combination of different methods gradually sapped the strength of the underground. Military-police operations, accompanied by the collectivization of agriculture and mass deportations (discussed below), finally broke the resistance although some groups continued to operate until the early 1950s. As late as 1953 the Lithuanian underground killed 84 Soviet functionaries and sympathizers. However, the saturation of the borderlands with police agents and informants—in 1951 27,700 security agents operated in Lithuania alone—resulted in the destruction of the last underground cells. The attempts of the Western intelligence services to sponsor the resistance proved unsuccessful as the emissaries from the West almost routinely fell into the hands of the security police.[23]

The death tally of the guerrilla struggle underscores its ferocity. According to Soviet sources, between 1944 and 1956 the underground in Estonia and Latvia murdered 2,953 Soviet functionaries. The civil war aspect in

Lithuania was reflected in the numbers of native victims: out of 25,108 individuals killed by the resistance, 21,259 were Lithuanians, including more than a thousand children. OUN-UPA warfare claimed approximately 30,000 victims (a former NKGB officer estimated as many as 50,000).[24] The Soviet response was overwhelming. By November 1945 the Soviet forces in the borderlands killed 107,166 guerrillas and their helpers (including 98,696 in western Ukraine) and captured 230,217 individuals suspected in anti-state activities. By May 1946 the numbers rose to 110,825 insurgents killed and 250,676 captured.[25] Thousands more were killed as the struggle slowly petered out in the early 1950s.

The 're-moulding' process

While the military-security operations were to guarantee the systematic destruction of the underground, the ideological 're-education' of the population and a total collectivization campaign aimed at irreversibly changing the socio-economic profile of the borderlands and fusing them into the Soviet economic system. Conversely, the new system was expected to create a new society, 'purified' from the 'bourgeois' institutions, individuals, and values. Traditionally, the Soviet leadership perceived its actions against its opponents in Manichaean terms as the struggle between absolute good and absolute evil, a struggle of a new, modern order against the old and decaying one. Hence, the official propaganda consistently presented the reconquest of the borderlands as a 'modernizing' process, achieved by nationalization of the economy, emancipation of the backward population through ideological indoctrination, education, and full integration of the young within the new socialist order. If such arguments sounded plausible in regard to the predominantly agricultural western Ukraine and Byelorussia, they made little sense in the Baltic region, where the degree of literacy and industrialization rate were higher than in some core-areas of Russia. Still, since the official ideology maintained that in 1940 the Baltic republics joined the USSR 'voluntarily', it was sufficient to slate them for socialist modernization.

The economic and cultural assimilation of the borderlands was thus conceived as a multidimensional, comprehensive plan, which began with setting up a new administrative apparatus. In post-war Soviet society, affected by a new wave of vigilantism against alleged wreckers, nationalists,

and enemy agents, the political reliability of native party and state functionaries was deemed highly questionable. Consequently, the ideological and
socio-economic conquest of the borderlands commenced with the dispatch
of thousands of Soviet officials from Russia-proper to the borderlands.
Augmented by ideologically dependable Baltic, Byelorussian, Ukrainian,
and Moldavian officials, the new arrivals became the spearhead of Soviet
power and assured the implementation of 'successful ideological-political
work'.[26]

By autumn 1946 the Russians and Russified Ukrainians occupied key
positions in the party organizations, managerial posts in the economy, and
in the education system in western Ukraine. For example, among 16,129
party and state functionaries in the L'viv district only 2,097 (13 per cent)
were natives. The Sovietization process of 1939–41, spearheaded by functionaries from the administrative power centres, was thus replicated on
a much larger scale. Although in August 1947 out of 17,275 Soviet functionaries in East Galicia about 5,000 were native residents—a sign that the
'indigenization' of the state apparatus was gradually gaining momentum—
the top echelons in the state and party machinery were firmly in the hands of
the newcomers. Even more profound were changes in Byelorussia, where
by the middle of 1946 the bulk of the district party officials and the chairmen
of collective farms were removed from their posts; by 1948 they were all
replaced by Russians.[27]

The situation in the Baltic region revealed a somewhat different pattern.
Although ethnic Russians made up on average 50 per cent in the communist
parties (in 1946 there were 10,987 communists in Latvia, 8,060 in Lithuania,
and 7,139 in Estonia), on the model of the 'triumphal march' of 1918 the
Soviet government exerted its power through the party bureaus headed by
dedicated native communists such as Antanas Sniečkus in Lithuania and
Nikolai Karotamm in Estonia. These bureaus relied on the Estonians and
Latvians who had migrated to Russia in the early twentieth century and were
recruited to fill the top and middle levels of the administration; the Russians
or Russified Ukrainians acted as aides and advisers. In contrast, only a few
such individuals of Lithuanian background were available, and therefore
more Russians and Ukrainians occupied the top and middle positions in the
Lithuanian administration. Outwardly the Estonians, Latvians, and Lithuanians dominated the organs of state power in their respective republics—
during the elections to the Republics' Supreme Councils in 1947 there were
178 Latvian and Estonian deputies against 29 Russian deputies; in Lithuania

the ratio was 152 Lithuanians to 21 Russians. But the Baltic communist parties were still dominated by the non-natives, who by 1949 made up over 50 per cent of the membership.[28]

The Soviet government continually urged the republics' leadership to purge individuals who were considered unreliable. While many village and town council personnel were removed because they could not deliver the assigned agricultural or industrial quotas, Moscow was particularly concerned over the regional 'particular' tendencies developed by the native communist parties during the interwar period. To remind the native communists and the population that they were now fully integrated into the USSR and to eradicate any particularism, the Baltic, Ukrainian, Byelorussian, and Moldavian communist parties removed from their ranks alleged 'fellow travellers' and 'deviationists'. For example, in 1948 the president of the Byelorussian Supreme Soviet, N. Natalevich, was dismissed and the republic's leadership remained predominantly non-Byelorussian. Three years later the Byelorussian government consisted of twenty-two Russians, nine Byelorussians, one Georgian, and one Jew.[29]

The restructuring of the native party and administration cadres was accompanied by a massive 're-education' campaign aimed at the population. Official propaganda in western Ukraine endlessly reiterated that the reunification and progressive development of Ukrainian lands were possible only within the 'brotherly family' of the Soviet people. Large quantities of Russian and Ukrainian textbooks were introduced in Ukrainian schools and Ukrainian and Russian became the state and instruction languages. The Soviet authorities in L′viv emphasized the city's Ukrainian and Soviet character, especially pronounced in view of the rapid decrease of the Polish and Jewish populations; most Polish schools were shut down.[30]

Simultaneously, teachers who had received their diplomas in interwar Poland, Latvia, Romania, or in imperial Russia, were dismissed and replaced by newcomers from Russia-proper. In the course of six months after the Soviet occupation of western Ukraine 44,000 new teachers filled the openings in the education system. Armed with Marxist dogma, their primary task was to indoctrinate the school and university students in communist ideology. Simultaneously, crash courses for reliable native residents began producing thousands of teaching instructors. Such processes immediately affected the level of education, which went down. Undeterred, the Soviet administration maintained pressure on the education system. If in 1945 in

Latgalle there were 68 per cent of teachers who received their certificates in interwar Latvia or abroad, two years later 57.3 per cent of the teaching cadres were the recipients of the Soviet diplomas.[31]

A crucial part of the integration of Galicia and Transcarpathia was an assault on the Greek Catholic Church. In comparison to the 1939–41 period, when the Soviet propaganda labelled religion as the 'opium for the people', after the death of Andrej Sheptyts'kyi in November 1944 attacks became much more vicious and unrelenting. A campaign to eliminate the Greek Catholic Church by subordinating it to the Russian Orthodox Church included the arrests of the Archbishop Josyf Slipyj, all bishops, and many priests, who were accused of anti-state activities. Some Ukrainian historians have estimated that altogether 1,800 priests, monks, and nuns were arrested and 200 were executed. Other clergy were intimidated into becoming members of the so-called 'Initiative Group for the Unification' that advocated the unification of the two rites. In March 1946 under the supervision of the secret police the 'Initiative Group' convened a synod in L'viv (with not a single Greek Catholic bishop present), which voted for breaking with Rome and subordinating themselves to the Moscow Patriarchate. The elimination of the Greek Catholic Church essentially completed the aspirations of the Russian imperial authorities in the Kholm region and in East Galicia in the first two decades of the century. In Transcarpathia, however, the attempt to organize a similar 'initiative group' failed. The Soviet administration then cast off all pretences and moved in to confiscate the Greek Catholic shrine near Mukacheve; the assassination of Bishop Teodor Romsha in November 1947 was followed by the official liquidation of the Greek Catholic Church in Transcarpathia in August 1949, when a group of priests submitted to the pressure and proclaimed their subordination to the Russian Patriarchate. Nevertheless, the influence of the Greek Catholic Church in East Galicia and Transcarpathia continued to concern the Soviet authorities long after its demise. When in 1949 OUN assassins murdered the prominent communist writer Yaroslav Halan, the highly publicized trial of his murderers was turned into a tribune for the prosecution, which lumped together Ukrainian nationalists, the Vatican, and the Greek Catholic Church as the inveterate enemies of the Soviet people. Numerous other trials of OUN members served similar objectives to discredit nationalist resistance under the guise of punishing those who had collaborated with the Nazis.[32]

Collectivization

Although political indoctrination of the population was considered imperative for the successful integration of the borderlands, the Soviet government
deemed it secondary—from the ideological perspective—to the necessity of
eliminating the most conspicuous vestiges of the old order. Only after all
political, socio-economic, and psychological particularities completely disappeared, would the unification of the borderlands with the core-Soviet
area be considered complete.

A crucial feature of this process was the transformation of the agricultural
sector, which became the most blatant example of the doctrinaire application of Stalinist experience. The communist leadership always emphasized
that private landholding was the epitome of the capitalist economic order.
Individual farming made state planning and surveillance impossible, but
most importantly, in the late 1920s Stalin and his cronies decided that the
collectivization of agriculture was imperative for the successful industrialization of the country. At the same time, several other objectives would be
accomplished. Deprived of land and forced into collective farms, peasants
lost the ability to wield any political influence and became merely hired
labourers. Subsequently, the state would acquire a huge pool of surplus
labour and a commanding leverage in population control and economy
management. Finally, by controlling food supplies, the state had at its
disposal a powerful weapon to combat potential resistance, and in the
early 1930s the Soviet government demonstrated its willingness to use this
weapon to starve millions to death.

The collectivization of agriculture and the subjugation of the peasantry in
the borderlands, therefore, were conceived as matters of the highest priority
and even took precedence over the struggle against the nationalist guerrillas.
A comprehensive plan, which involved all means at the state's disposal, was
implemented in several stages. In December 1944, barely had the popular
'will' in Transcarpathia to join the Soviet Union been announced than the
administration began nationalization of banking, transport, communication,
and large and middle-size industries. A year later the land was also
nationalized.[33] Still, the major efforts were directed to the most important
grain-growing regions—Lithuania, Volhynia, East Galicia, and right-bank
Moldavia, where the highly publicized land distribution to the poor

concealed the fact that the state was gradually amassing the bulk of the cultivable land. For example, although by 1948 1,500,000 hectares were nationalized in Lithuania, only half of that was distributed among poor peasants; the state retained the rest.[34]

Congruent with the Russian Civil War model, collectivization began with the official classification of 'kulak' households. Initially, the term applied to households that employed hired labour, owned a mill or dairy used for profit or that could be hired out for transactions, or had a farm exceeding 10 hectares. According to these criteria in East Galicia and Volhynia the de-kulakization process initially affected about 10 per cent of households. But as a result, the distribution of the land belonging to the 'kulaks' did not achieve the expected results, since 354,000 poor families received 513,000 hectares, or about 1.6 hectares per household. Hence, the numbers of the 'kulak' households diminished only slightly and the administration expanded the application of the term to a wider category of peasants. In Lithuania the households that owned 18 hectares were initially designated as 'kulak', but soon the limit was dropped to 5 hectares. Similarly, in Bessarabia the confiscation of land affected the families that owned 5 hectares, making survival of individual households practically impossible. In addition, the local Soviet organs began classifying as 'kulaks' individuals considered socially undesirable such as priests, the relatives of guerrillas, and those peasants who refused to join collective farms. Eventually, anybody who, due to social status or political affiliations, did not fit in the new order was included into the 'kulak' category. In other words, the process of Sovietization in the borderlands acquired biological traits since the targeted groups were considered intractable and intrinsically hostile to Soviet power.[35]

To induce peasants to join collective farms a variety of methods were used: heavy taxes, forced state deliveries, and pressure or coercion by local activists and party officials. Relatively prosperous households were considered the potential socio-economic base of the underground and subjected to special taxation that included up to 70 per cent income tax, crushing quotas on agricultural product-deliveries that by far surpassed those imposed on 'poor' peasant households (at times by 50 per cent), and confiscation of draught animals, grain, and finally the farms. For example, in Moldavia the taxation on the alleged 'kulaks' increased 230 per cent between 1947 and 1948. The 'kulaks' were also forced to buy state bonds and 'donate' for the military-industrial complex in addition to regular taxes. Consequently, the numbers of individual households were diminishing and many were speed-ily brought to ruination. Thousands of individual landowners applied to sell their land to the state; but since it involved a reimbursement, local autho-rities as a rule rejected such applications, preferring that the privately owned implements, livestock, and agricultural products be squandered. As a direct result, state deliveries fell short and state planning went awry, but the Soviet authorities blamed the underground and 'hostile elements' for these failures.[36]

By late 1947 the farms over 10 hectares in western Ukraine completely disappeared and the administration could claim that the socio-economic base of the underground was destroyed. At the same time, however, many ruined peasants joined the collective farms, which were notoriously unpro-ductive. Still, the escalation of the Cold War made the pacification and integration of the borderlands imperative and the Soviet government con-stantly urged its representatives to complete collectivization in the shortest possible terms. The local authorities interpreted such instructions as a green light to use any means and official reports grudgingly admitted numerous 'deviations', which in official Soviet parlance meant power abuse, forcible induction into a kolkhoz, and falsification of delivery quotas.[37]

In 1946 a terrible famine hit eastern Ukraine and resulted in a huge reduction of livestock and rampant shortages of grain. The influx of many people from the east to western Ukraine in search of food hardly made a positive impact upon the mentality of the local population and the attrac-tiveness of the kolkhoz system. In March 1947 Khrushchev, who since 1938 had held the post of the first secretary of the Ukrainian communist party, was dismissed and replaced by Lazar Kaganovich, one of the most zealous and brutal of Stalin's henchmen. Kaganovich, who had distinguished himself in combating 'nationalist deviations' in pre-war years, forced the increase of collective farms in western Ukraine from 274 by the end of 1946 to over 1,400 in January 1948. Still, all collective farms had low productivity, for they lacked the necessary buildings and implements—despite constant financial infusions by the party and state finances. Frequently, kolkhoz members received a small portion of grain in lieu of their wages. Hence, many displayed extreme reluctance to work—in 1949 in Hrodna oblast' 38 per cent of the kolkhoz members did not fulfil their minimal quotas, while 15 per cent did not show up for work.[38]

Similarly dismal was the situation in Moldavia. In 1946–7 it suffered a horrific drought that resulted in the deaths of more than 17,000 people (some scholars estimated that at least 70,000–80,000 people died). Starvation and a high death rate, especially among children, caused unrest and civil disobedience. In 1947 alone 70 per cent of kolkhoz members did not fulfil their obligations; some did not work in the kolkhoz a single day. Murder over most necessary commodities became common; some individuals attempted to cross the Soviet–Romanian border.[39] Still, the administration routinely ascribed the failure of the kolkhoz system and economic problems to the 'nationalist heritage' left by Romanians. Although armed resistance in Moldavia was rare, there were numerous acts of sabotage and anti-Soviet agitation. In July–August 1946 the Soviet security organs reported that they had liquidated twenty-four 'bandit groups' of seventy-five members and confiscated many firearms. Since official phraseology did not differentiate between the politically motivated resistance and criminal activities, it is unclear whether the liquidated groups were members of the underground or petty criminals. Nevertheless, out of 10,545 individuals charged with criminal activities in 1946 more than 50 per cent were poor peasants, a clear sign that the state was at war with the people, including the same social group whose interests the government claimed to be protecting.[40]

Despite all state efforts the collectivization campaign was proceeding slowly. By early 1949 between 17 and 24 per cent of peasant households in East Galicia and Volhynia, 4 per cent in Lithuania, 6 per cent in Estonia, and 8 per cent in Latvia were collectivized, and apparent consequences were the pauperization and alienation of the peasantry.[41] Moscow's dissatisfaction translated into several resolutions to expedite the process and in December 1948 and in January–February 1949 the communist parties of Ukraine, Byelorussia, the Baltic Republics, and Moldavia were instructed to speed up collectivization.

Accompanied by mass deportations (see below) the crash collectivization was carried out at a breakneck tempo. In 1950 the numbers of collective farms in Moldavia rose to 1,763 (85 per cent) and in January 1951 the collectivization in the republic was complete. In Estonia the number of collective farms increased from five in 1947 to 455 by the end of 1948; in 1952 the Soviet authorities reported that practically all peasant households were collectivized. In western Byelorussia the numbers of collective farms more than doubled between January and October 1949—from 1,158 to 3,995. By mid-1951 only about 10 per cent of households in the republic remained privately owned.[42]

In western Ukraine the process of collectivization was as swift. In 1947 Khrushchev was reinstated in power and began his reign by creating clusters of collective farms in specifically designated areas—in contrast to Kaganovich's methods of forming kolkhozes in large areas simultaneously. Khrushchev's method seemed to work since new collective farms, especially in the localities with large troop details, had more chances to survive economic hardship and the attacks of the underground. The results seemed impressive—if in January 1947 there were 72 collective farms in Ternopil oblast´, there were 511 in November. Similarly, in Ivano-Frankivs´k oblast (Stanislaviv) between January 1949 and the end of 1950 the number of collectivized kolkhozes rose from 16.7 to 97 per cent. The ruination of individual peasant households, however, caused severe economic problems and between 1950 and 1955 the borderlands experienced a drastic decrease in agricultural output. In comparison to 1940 grain production in Latvia dropped 50 per cent and in Lithuania the numbers of dairy cattle dropped from 848,000 in 1939 to 504,000 in 1951. Still, the Soviet authorities refused to recognize the shortcomings of the system and blamed 'hostile elements' that allegedly had penetrated the kolkhoz system.[43]

Deportations

Mass population replacement was integral to the process of Sovietization and organically linked to socio-economic reconstruction and political consolidation of the borderlands. It followed the same rationale, established in 1939-41, namely the intention to eject potentially troublesome groups, whose economic and financial assets were used for the benefit of the state. While officially the elimination of these groups was to facilitate the restructuring of the borderlands, it eventually acquired national aspects, affecting specific communities. To begin with, from the Soviet point of view the ethno-cultural diversity and different political traditions of the borderlands represented a significant problem and proof of the existence of potential enemies. Since social class and ethnic category in the borderlands were traditionally intertwined, class definition, broadly defined, and applied in the deportation process, embraced in one sweep objective and subjective guilt of the targets. Importantly, mass deportations directly contributed to the pace of collectivization and the destruction of the underground, depriving it of popular support. In other words, the maxim of 'draining water to kill the fish' became the strategic recipe for counter-insurgency warfare. Such a process was already unfolding during the war, when the Soviet offensive generated a huge mass of refugees escaping to the west (including Jewish survivors) and mass arrests took place across the territories liberated from the Germans.[44]

Since the experience of 1939–41 had convinced the Soviet leadership that the cohesive Polish community was incapable and, more importantly, unwilling to integrate into the new order, its resettlement was conceived as imperative for the political homogenization of the borderlands. Already in summer–fall 1944 the de-Polonization of the Kresy had begun: Polish symbols were removed and the NKVD launched mass arrests within Polish society. The first targets were the Polish intelligentsia—in early January 1945 the Soviet secret police arrested 772 individuals, including professors, doctors, engineers, actors, students, and priests, all accused of being active members of the nationalist movement. Many peasants and workers were also placed on target lists; those who had been arrested and released in 1939–41 were arrested again.[45]

If in 1940 the Soviets somewhat mitigated their anti-Polish drive, from 1944 there would be no let-up in arrests and deportations. Pressure on the Polish communities was unrelenting, and consequently many opted to resettle in Poland. The Soviet–Polish agreement of 9 September 1944 expedited the process by stipulating 'voluntary' population exchange between the two countries. In June 1945 a similar agreement was signed between the Soviet Union and Romania. As a result, by early 1945 the number of Poles leaving Ukraine reached 117,114; by May 264,937 people had registered for evacuation from Byelorussia. The repatriates headed to the Poznań province, where the Soviet army had already laid the land waste. By September 1946 more than half a million Poles (and Jews) had left the borderlands and by November 1949 approximately 83,000 Romanians, Ukrainians, and Jews from Bukovina and Bessarabia migrated westward.[46]

The decisions for mass deportation were taken at the highest echelons of the Soviet government, and its scale increased with the political consolidations of the borderlands. In western Ukraine the first deportations began in March 1944 and aimed at the alleged kulaks and the families of the guerrillas. The make-up of the arrested and deportees, however, showed that the 'class' approach to the repressions was ineffectual. Out of 416 court sentences in a single district imposed on resistance members and their families, the courts classified only twenty-eight individuals as kulaks.[47] As the struggle against the underground intensified, class differentiation was often abandoned and deportations affected anybody suspected of connections to the resistance. If in early September 1945 about 23,000 individuals were deported from western Ukraine, in October 1947 77,791 people were deported. Entire villages whose residents had provided food or shelter to the insurgents—quite often at gunpoint—were placed on deportation lists. In this fashion, on 20–21 October 1947 the Soviet administration, the military, and the NKVD carried out the largest deportation to date, sending eastward from Volhynia about half a million people.[48]

Similarly, in the Baltic region the Soviet administration used deportations as the means to annihilate the resistance and expedite collectivization. Between summer 1945 and winter 1947 142,543 individuals were deported.[49] Since the collectivization pace was still considered unsatisfactory, the Central Committee of the communist party and the Council of Ministers reached a decision to remove from the region 'unreliable' elements, who avoided earlier deportations. On 28 February 1949 Operation 'Tide' was set in motion, targeting 30,000 families. Disguised as a military exercise, the operation involved large contingents of the MGB and MVD, including the elite units from military academies—an indication of its high priority: altogether 76,212 military and police personnel. However, it was local activists—communists, state functionaries, and the members of the 'destruction battalions'—who constituted about 60 per cent of the personnel involved in the operation. It lasted until late March and affected 94,779 individuals, of whom almost 68,000 were women and young children. The deportees were given a short time to pack and those who tried to escape were shot or hunted down by trained dogs. In August–September 1949 the Soviet government rewarded more than a hundred participants in the deportations for the 'successful execution of the special task of the Soviet government'.[50] Indeed, the deportations partially fulfilled the expectations of the government, since thousands of peasants hastened to join the kolkhozes as the only way to avoid being deported. Consequently, between March and April 1949 the pace of collectivization in Latvia jumped from 11 to 50 per cent and in Estonia from 8 to 64 per cent; by the end of the year 62 per cent of farms were collectivized in Lithuania.[51]

The deportations in the Baltic were emulated in Moldavia, where the republic's government blamed the slow pace of collectivization on subversive elements. On 17 March 1949 the Central Committee of the Moldavian Communist Party appealed to Moscow with a request to deport all 'anti-Soviet elements' and their families—altogether 39,000 individuals. On 6 April Moscow ordered to begin Operation 'South', which involved mass deportations from Moldavia (and the Black Sea coast and the Crimea), for which 12,000 MGB-MVD personnel and 22,560 party and state functionaries were mobilized. In early July 11,000 families from Moldavia—35,050 men, women, and children—were deported and their houses, horses, cattle, and agricultural implements were sold to collective farms.[52]

As the deportations evolved, the atmosphere of fear and desperation became overwhelming. Nobody could be sure of tomorrow because those who were driven like a herd into the freight cars, scarcely looked like kulaks or 'bourgeois elements'. Many deportees were so poor that they 'did not have even a cat…and wherever [one] looks, everywhere is misery and sorrow; last night they picked up sixty families and we're waiting for our turn'.[53] At their destination the situation of the deportees did not improve. Most arrivals lived in appalling sanitary conditions in cold barracks or dugouts, and suffered harsh climate, epidemics, and hunger. As a result, by December 1950 4,123 Estonians, Latvians, and Lithuanians who were deported in March 1949 died in exile.[54]

Summary

The Second World War and its aftermath brought about tremendous human losses and material destruction to the borderlands. According to a number of sources the combat and civilian casualties amounted to about 1.2 million people between 1939 and 1953; Jews constituted approximately 60 per cent of that number. More than 3 million people were subjected to forcible relocation. The scale of destruction varied from region to region. The swift Soviet advance left northern Bukovina relatively unscathed and Transcarpathia, which remained deep behind the front lines, remained quiet throughout the war. The Baltic region and East Galicia were largely spared destruction until they became battlefields in summer 1944, while the war wrought heavy damage in Volhynia and utterly devastated Byelorussia.

Further destruction and suffering accompanied the second Sovietization campaign of 1944-53, which entailed a complete transformation of the borderlands' socio-economic fabric and the elimination of entire communities associated with the old order. Initially, the armed resistance to the

Soviets enjoyed considerable popular support and presented a serious problem for the local authorities, disrupting the functioning of the administration and collective farms. The fighting was most intense between 1944 and
1947, and inflicted considerable losses upon the underground, the Soviet
administration, and the population.

Military operations against the resistance were accompanied by thorough
ideological and socio-economic measures that were integral to the re-
establishment of Soviet power. Land reform became the focal point of the
struggle for power between the Soviet government and its opponents. The
collectivization process, patterned after the kolkhoz system in Russia-proper, aimed to deprive the resistance of its power-base and to incorporate the
borderlands into the Soviet economic structure. As important were the
reforms in administrative, educational, and cultural institutions that replaced
old specialists with politically reliable individuals. Mass deportations of
allegedly unreliable or intractable groups were carried out within the
framework of the Soviet official dogma of 'class struggle'. Often, however,
it was sidelined by ethnic criteria or religion, which served as catalysts for
measuring one's attitude to the state.[55] After the 'Final Solution' reduced
the Jewish population to a minimum, the anti-Polish drive, camouflaged as
the 'voluntary' population exchange, effectively eliminated one of the most
influential socio-economic communities from the area.

Although the Soviets never commanded the genuine support of
a demographic minority, the population at large, exhausted by the ravages
of fighting, collectivization, and deportations, had perforce to accept and
submit to the Soviet rule.

9

From the Union to Independence

B y the early 1950s the borderlands were pacified and fully incorporated into the Soviet political, administrative, and socio-economic system. Accompanied by a massive influx of ethnic Russians and Ukrainians, the incorporation process altered the old socio-economic structures and the ethnic composition of the new republics, making any prospects for achieving national independence as remote as ever. Beneath complete political domination, however, the Soviet government faced problems similar to those experienced by its predecessors. Cultural and linguistic differences facilitated the chasm between the newcomers and the native populations and underscored the socio-economic and political conflicts that characterized the relations between the 'titular' and 'subject' nationalities under the empires and the nationalizing states. At the same time, deeply rooted identities of locality, language, ethnicity, and religion militated against the 'internationalist' Soviet ideology, making it impossible for the state to impose a supra-national identity upon its subjects.

On the other hand, the population of the borderlands realized that Soviet rule would last longer than the occupation of 1939–41. Although many people were never reconciled to the regime, the post-war years taught them of its potential for enforcing the new laws. Therefore, the impulses to resist the Soviets gradually gave way to a tendency to adjust to the situation and gain as much personal benefit as possible by operating within the framework of the new system.[1]

This chapter discusses the Soviet socio-economic and nationality policies in the borderlands between the death of Stalin and the breakup of the Soviet Union. As in the borderlands under the Russian empire, these policies could be termed 'defensive-reactive', oscillating from relative liberalization to repressive measures. Although the co-optation of the population and the socio-economic elites for some time seemed effective, the Soviet government always appreciated the danger of nationalism, especially since official policies unwittingly stimulated its existence. Indeed, the administrative divisions of the country into national republics and autonomous regions, each assigned to a particular nationality group and governed by native bureaucracies, facilitated the affirmation of national identities, fixed permanently by the passport system. Such population control methods effectively institutionalized nationalist sentiments, which erupted when the Soviet government's grip on power weakened in the late 1980s.

Liberalization and repressions

The incorporation of the borderlands into the Soviet Union eliminated a crucial pillar of the 'fatal triangle' of conflicting nationalisms, particularly pronounced during the interwar period: the nationalizing states (Poland or Romania), the ethnic minorities, and the 'external homelands' (the Soviet Union or Lithuania) that claimed the adjacent territories and professed to be the protectors of their ethnic kin across the border. With the nationalizing states no longer in the picture, the Soviet nationality policies eventually followed the pattern established by the Austro-Hungarian and the Russian empires. As the monarchies tried to impose some sort of common identity upon their diverse subjects—based upon trans-national loyalty to the crown—they simultaneously allowed the proliferation of national cultures. Likewise, the Soviet 'affirmative action' state attempted to impose a common ideological identity—the Soviet *man* or the Soviet people—and encouraged and cultivated different national cultures. Another similarity to the Austro-Hungarian and Russian policies was the Soviet confirmation of the privileged status of the 'state' and 'titular' nationalities: ethnic Russians on the top and the Estonians, Latvians, Lithuanians, or Ukrainians in auxiliary positions within the state and party hierarchy. Hence, though never a nation-state as a whole, the Soviet Union was a conglomerate of the territorial units that defined people, cultures, and languages in national terms.[2]

Such an approach to the nationality question revealed itself almost immediately after the death of Stalin, when the power-struggle that ensued in the Kremlin forced the Soviet policy-makers to make significant concessions to the republics. Already in June 1953, on the pattern of the 'indige-nization' policies of the 1920s, the Soviet government issued a resolution that called to 'end distortions in nationality policy'. The resolution stipu-lated the elevation of the ideologically reliable native elite to key positions in the Republics' state and party apparatus and the use of native languages in official correspondence.[3] The 'indigenization' resulted in an increase of native communists into the Republics' leadership, which was to carry out Moscow's guidelines in encouraging ethnic diversity and simultaneously upholding the parameters of the Soviet ideological system. Such methods resulted in the replacement of thousands of state and party functionaries (mostly associated with the hardliners in Moscow) with reliable native cadres in the Baltic region and Ukraine. This reverse-process—in contrast to the immediate post-war period—seemed especially important since from Moscow's point of view the communist parties in the borderlands were small and suffered from lack of active participation by the native population. Egged on by the centre, the republics' communist parties began intensive recruitment and steadily increased their membership. From 1953 to 1961 membership in the Estonian communist party rose from 44 to 49 per cent; in the 1960s it reached 50 per cent and would remain so until the early 1980s; the numbers of Lithuanians in the Central Committee of the Lithuanian communist party also grew from 56 per cent in 1952 to 77 per cent in 1976. By the mid-1960s the native communist cadres in the Baltic republics made up about 50 per cent of the communist parties.[4]

The changes affected even the party top echelons. In spring 1953 the First Secretary of the Ukrainian communist party, L. Mel'nikov, was blamed for 'deviations from the Leninist-Stalinist policies' by promoting non-Ukrai-nians to key positions in western Ukraine and removed from his post. Political changes were accompanied by expressions of cultural revival such as the utilization of native languages, literature, folklore, and upward social mobility. Naturally, all liberalization policies were contingent upon the two crucial features of Soviet nationality policies—ideological reliability and the mastery of the Russian language, which was to serve as a unifying vehicle for multilingual populations. In contrast to the Sovietization period of 1939–41, when the top cadres of the party and state apparatus were ethnic Russians or the Estonians, Latvians, or Ukrainians who had arrived from Russia, by the 1970s they were the true natives, steeped in native traditions and simulta-neously thoroughly Sovietized functionaries. Similar accommodation took place in the social sphere. Although popular resentment towards the Soviet

Union remained strong, life dictated adjustment to the system and many local residents applied for employment in Soviet institutions.[5]

Such conversions certainly resembled the co-optation of the native elites by the Russian imperial government. In addition, the relatively high living standards in the Baltic region and East Galicia (until the early 1950s), where small private enterprises were temporarily allowed to function, contributed to the mitigation of radical sentiments. The Soviet government also demonstrated its willingness to mollify national sensibilities by issuing in 1958 an education law that guaranteed the right to choose the language of education for children. The native literati were authorized to write history in native languages as long as they praised the 'progressive importance' of the Soviet annexations. Khrushchev's 'Thaw' in the cultural field entailed the gradual sidelining of the socialist realism dogmas by the promotion of national cultures and opened a flood of the publications that had previously been banned, including those by the exiles and deportees and the translations of Western literary works. In December 1956 an autobiographic poem 'Unfinished Song' by a former Latvian prisoner Harijs Heislers caused a sensation by addressing the painful theme of the Soviet concentration camp system, anticipating Alexander Solzhenitsyn's *One Day in the Life of Ivan Denisovich* by six years.[6]

The republics' administration also encouraged theatrical performances and publications in native languages, and sponsored cultural and folk festivals that became an open forum for expressions of national patriotism and attracted thousands of visitors. In 1965 a festival in Estonia drew 120,000 people—one-eighth of the nation—who sang 'My homeland is my love', the unofficial anthem of the Estonian people. Liberalization policies went so far in the late 1950s that the Estonian athletic teams appeared in the uniforms brandishing the name 'Estonia' instead of the mandatory 'Estonian SSR'. Some national markers and symbols were integrated into the official Soviet symbolic. In 1958 the Latvian administration authorized the transfer of the graves of the Soviet soldiers and partisans to the Brethren Cemetery in Riga, where the heroes and victims of the frontier wars of 1918–20 were buried. Such an act effectively legitimized the cemetery as a national shrine. Cultural youth associations and student groups in Lithuania organized ethnographic expeditions to villages, where they recorded local traditions and expressions of folklore. The spirit of new times culminated in 1966 with the release of a celebrated film-drama *None Wanted to Die* by the Lithuanian producer Vytautas Žalakevičius. Although maintained within the official ideological parameters, the film skilfully fused the Soviet 'socialist-realist' style with the brutal realities of the civil war that raged in the Baltic in the aftermath of the Second World War.[7]

The indigenization processes in Lithuania and Ukraine were so prevalent because the republics' bosses—Antanas Sniečkus and Petro Shelest—were the main patrons of national economy and culture. Shelest in particular was instrumental in changing the ethnic composition of the party—by the early 1970s its top leadership was predominantly Ukrainian—and laboured to keep most of the republic's funds in Ukraine, contrary to the established priority of Moscow in such matters.[8]

Other measures, especially after Khrushchev assumed power in 1956, included the relative decentralization of administrative structures as the republics were allowed to formulate their own civil and criminal codes. In the economic field, liberalization of the system resonated in the more fair distribution of state capital investments and the withdrawal of some industries from Moscow's control and their subordination to the republics' economic councils. Outwardly, this move was justified by more efficient economic management, but in reality it was to accord the republics' leadership more power, as Khrushchev hoped that they would support him in his struggle with his opponents in Moscow. The new economic policies also channelled more state funds into the consumer sector, especially the medical field, education, and housing, which improved by the mid-1960s. Since the Soviet government made efforts to make the Baltic republics into the showcase for the Western world, they received preference in supplies of consumer goods, fuel, grain, and raw materials. Expanded access to the education system contributed to the growth of educated youth that would eventually constitute the backbone of the national elite. For example, between 1959 and 1970 the numbers of school students in Estonia and Latvia were among the highest in the Soviet Union, slightly below the Georgians, Armenians, and Russians. Concurrently, between 1960 and 1989 the number of professionals in the Baltic region increased by 350,000. The changes in social structures were mirrored by the urbanization level—the urban population in Lithuania rose from 28 per cent in 1939 to 68 in 1990.[9]

In contrast to the Baltic republics, the situation in western Ukraine and western Byelorussia was more complicated since these regions were parts of larger administrative units and were subordinated to two power-centres— the republics' capitals and Moscow. On the one hand, such subordination resulted in the possibility of the regional leadership to manoeuvre between the two forces, while on the other hand it subjected them to double pressure. Similarly to its imperial predecessor, the Soviet government refused to recognize the Byelorussians and Ukrainians as two distinct nationalities in their own right, but considered them as branches of their 'big' brother—the Russians. From the mid-1950s the Byelorussian intelligentsia and literati cautiously criticized Moscow's language policies as yet another drive for Russification (although the term was not used). In 1957 the Central Committee of the Byelorussian communist party also complained that in primary and secondary schools all subjects, except the Byelorussian language and literature, were taught in Russian. Although such criticism was well within the parameters of indigenization policies, the fact that Moscow considered Byelorussian merely a dialect of the Russian language generated stiff resistance to the expansion of the national language. In January 1959 during the celebration of the fortieth anniversary of the Byelorussian party in Minsk, the First Secretary of the party, Kiril Mazurov, delivered his speech in Byelorussian. Khrushchev, the honorary guest at the proceedings, was so angered that he grumbled that the 'sooner we start speaking Russian, the faster we'll build communism'. The Soviet leader's reaction put into words Moscow's expectations that the linguistic and cultural proximity of Byelorussians and Russians would expedite the successful fusion of the two people (at the expense of the former) into the new historic-national community—the Soviet people.[10]

Official propaganda in western Ukraine also consistently emphasized the common roots of the local inhabitants and their connection to Russia-Ukraine, 'interrupted' by Austro-Hungarian, Polish, and Romanian rule. The entire academic apparatus was directed to rewrite history, accentuating the historical links between the populations of western and eastern Ukraine. Nevertheless, given the strength of Ukrainian nationalism, and the size and economic importance of Ukraine, the Soviet government was willing to allow the republic's leadership more latitude than in Byelorussia. The Ukrainian language became official, on a par with Russian, and the new Soviet-Ukrainian identity of the population was consistently propagated through television, radio, and variety of publications. The opening of new hospitals, schools, and cultural facilities was to highlight the benefits of the Soviet era. For example, the media never failed to stress that the previously Polish- and Yiddish-speaking L'viv was effectively turned into a predominantly Russian- and Ukrainian-speaking city. In 1968 in Transcarpathia, which alongside Bukovina was the poorest of the

Ukrainian provinces, the increase of medical personnel—one doctor per 554 and one nurse per 164 individuals—and better diet contributed to demographic growth in the province, the most impressive in Ukraine. Between 1950 and 1970 the population of the province rose from 797,900 to 1,056,800. The numbers of Ukrainian schools increased from 445 in 1944 to 852 in 1950/1 and 743 in the 1970s, while the opening of the Uzhhorod State University—first in the history of the province—indicated the Soviet government's efforts to 'elevate' the province to the level of the republic. As a result, by the early 1970s the majority of the younger generation in the province identified themselves as Ukrainians.[11]

The Soviet economy in the 1950s–1960s also showed signs of stability and relative growth. After the collectivization campaign devastated agriculture, the borderlands followed the all-Union model towards the reduction in the numbers of kolkhozes, which were sidelined by more productive state-run farms (*sovkhozes*). A relatively well-developed industrial base, especially in the Baltic, improved rail network, skilled labour force, and education level, all contributed to rising living standards, on average higher than in the pre-war period and in Russia-proper. The Baltic republics became dominant in the food, electric equipment, and footwear industries and surpassed other republics in per capita national income. The growth of the industrial labour force—between 1955 and 1975, the numbers of industrial workers in Estonia rose from 104,675 to 186,500—was accompanied by a reduction of the agricultural sector. By the mid-1970s those engaged in agriculture in Estonia, Latvia, and Lithuania dropped to approximately 22 per cent of the entire labour force. Such processes, in turn, accelerated the urbanization rate: by the late 1970s Riga had a population of 835,000, Vilnius 481,000, and Tallinn 430,000.[12]

Simultaneously, however, the integration of the borderlands into the Soviet economic system showed troubling signs indicative of the socialist central planning. Although the socio-economic profile of the western provinces gradually changed, the government retained their profile from the pre-First World War period, assigning them specific roles in the Union's economy. Since Estonia and Latvia were among the most industrialized regions of the Soviet Union, the Soviet government capitalized on this factor by expanding their industrial sector. On the other hand, agricultural regions such as Lithuania, East Galicia, and Volhynia were expected to supply the country with grain and foodstuffs. Forty per cent of Lithuania's agricultural production was exported to other republics of the Soviet

Union, which in turn exported to Lithuania cotton, cars, and agricultural machinery. Although between 1966 and 1985 western Ukraine increased its industrial output from 62 to 78 per cent, along with western Byelorussia it remained a predominantly agricultural region and its industrial base was limited to the food-producing factories and the manufacture of agricultural implements. Similarly, Moldavia supplied the USSR with 12 per cent of corn production and remained one of the most important regions of food-producing industries and the largest wine-production administrative unit in the country. Crucially, the elimination of private property and collectivization campaign in the 1940s wrought irreparable damage on agriculture and drastically lowered supply and service standards in the consumer sector. Hence, already in the mid-1950s life standards in western Ukraine and Byelorussia deteriorated. Shortages of basic commodities such as bread, sugar, meat, and flour were accompanied by a rise of prices. Unrest in cities and long lines of shoppers after basic commodities became a common occurrence. A slow decline in economic standards prevailed in Estonia, although the improvement in crop productivity maintained relative prosperity in food supplies until the mid-1970s.[13]

At the same time as the Soviet government made strenuous efforts to defuse nationalist sentiments, it exacerbated nationality conflicts by population policies. To capitalize on the economic potential of the borderlands and tighten up political control, it encouraged and sponsored massive immigration of Russians and Ukrainians. Between 1944 and 1959 200,000 and 300,000 Russians and Ukrainians moved into Moldavia; by 1970 about 300,000 immigrants settled in Estonia, 400,000 in Latvia, and up to 270,000 in Lithuania. In western Ukraine 327,000 Russians arrived (247,000 going to East Galicia, 51,000 to northern Bukovina, and 29,000 to Transcarpathia). Since the newcomers settled predominantly in the urban areas, such processes led to a dramatic alteration in the borderlands' ethnic and social make-up (see Table 9.1). In Latvia and Estonia the Russian-speaking immigrants came to constitute 27 and 20 per cent respectively of the urban populations. In 1989 the native population in Estonia dropped to 68 per cent in contrast to 92 per cent in 1934.[14] Since the majority of the Russians and Ukrainians never learned the native languages and became a predominant industrial force, Russian replaced Estonian, Latvian, Lithuanian, or Moldavian in the republics' political and economic system. As a result, the Russian-speaking immigrants enjoyed a higher upward

Table 9.1. Ethnic structure of the borderlands within the Soviet Union

Ethnic group	Estonia				Latvia				Lithuania			
	Pop. 1959	%	Pop. 1989	%	Pop. 1959	%	Pop. 1989	%	Pop. 1959	%	Pop. 1989	%
Byelorussians	10,900	0.9	27,700	1.4	61,600	2.9	119,700	4.5	30,300	1.1	63,200	1.7
Estonians	892,700	74.6	963,300	68.2	4,600	0.2	3,300	0.1				
Finns	16,700	1.4	16,600	1.4								
Germans	700	0.1	3,500	0.6								
Jews	5,400	0.5	4,600	0.4	36,600	1.7	22,900	0.9	24,700	0.9	12,300	0.3
Latvians	2,900	0.2	3,100	0.2	1,297,900	62	1,387,800	52	6,300	0.2	5,100	0.1
Lithuanians									2,150,800	79.3	2,924,300	79.6
Poles	2,300	0.2	3,000	0.2	59,800	2.9	60,400	2.3	230,100	8.5	258,400	7
Russians	240,000	20.1	474,800	24.7	556,400	26.6	905,500	34	231,000	8.5	344,500	9.4
Ukrainians	15,800	1.3	48,300	2.1	29,400	1.4	92,100	3.5	17,700	0.7	44,800	1.2
Other	9,200	0.7	20,800	0.8	14,800	0.8	40,400	1.4	20,500	0.8	22,600	0.7
TOTAL	1,196,800		1,565,700		2,093,500		2,666,600		2,711,400		3,674,800	

Ethnic group	Western Byelorussia[a]				Western Ukraine[b]				Moldavia			
	Pop. 1959	%	Pop. 1989	%	Pop. 1970[c]	%	Pop. 1989	%	Pop. 1959	%	Pop. 1989	%
Byelorussians	1,681,214	77.5	1,901,500	72.8					6,000	0.2	19,600	0.5
Bulgarians									62,000	2.1	88,400	2.0
Gagauz									96,000	3.3	153,400	3.5
Germans									3,800	0.1	7,300	0.2
Gypsies (Roma)					151,900	1.7	155,700	1.6	7,300	0.3	11,600	0.3
Hungarians												
Jews	17,493	0.8	5,500	0.2	82,200	0.9	30,700	0.3	95,000	3.3	65,700	1.5
Moldavians					78,400	0.9	84,500	0.9	1,887,000	65.4	2,794,700	64.5
Poles	289,475	13.35	332,500	12.7	71,700	0.8	26,900	0.3	4,800	0.2	4,700	0.1
Romanians					108,300	1.3	129,800	0.3				
Russians	179,691	8.3	270,200	10.3	445,700	5.1	491,800	5.1	293,000	10.2	562,100	13.0
Ukrainians	n/a		84,100	3.3	7,721,900	88.2	8,663,800	89.2	421,000	14.6	600,400	13.8
Others	n/a		18,600	0.7	94,600	1.1	130,400	1.3	8,100	0.3	27,500	0.6
TOTAL	2,167,837		2,612,400		8,754,700		9,713,600		2,884,000		4,335,400	

[a] Hrodna and Brest oblast' without the western counties of the Vitebsk oblast'.

[b] Volhynia, Rivne, L'viv, Ivano Frankivs'k, Ternopil', Chernivtsi, and Transcarpathia oblast'.

[c] The author was unable to obtain information for 1959.

Sources: Piotr Eberhardt, *Ethnic Groups and Population Changes in Twentieth Century Central-Eastern Europe: History, Data, and Analysis* (New York: M. E. Sharpe, 2003). Some numbers were calculated by the author on the basis of the Soviet censuses (electronic versions).

social mobility, prompting ethnic tensions. If continued unabated, such tendencies led to a situation in which the native populations in Estonia and Latvia could have potentially been relegated to second-class minorities in their own homelands. The lower level of industrialization in Lithuania (in comparison to Estonia and Latvia) attracted fewer Russian settlers, while a high birth rate and the almost complete elimination of the Jewish and Polish minorities were conducive to more thorough 'Lithuaniazation' of the country.[15]

★ ★ ★

By the late 1950s active resistance to the Soviet rule was deemed impossible. The dominant majority of the borderland populations adapted to the situation by functioning within the system, which provided stability and employment. However, although from the official point of view such a situation seemed satisfactory, the Soviet government found it increasingly difficult to encourage 'indigenization' and simultaneously to monitor nationalist expressions that time and again bubbled up in the borderlands. Concerns over dormant nationalism materialized in autumn 1956 when the unrest in Poland and particularly the Hungarian revolution reverberated in the Soviet Union. The potential of the 'harmful' influences from abroad was considered all the more dangerous since they originated from the Soviet satellite-states and coincided with the massive influx of former Gulag prisoners into the borderlands, amnestied by the Khrushchev government. Already in 1954–5 about 91,000 prisoners returned to the Baltic republics, Byelorussia, western Ukraine, and Moldavia. Since many returnees were former members of the nationalist resistance, including several hundred Greek-Catholic (Uniate) priests, the local administration were duly alarmed, especially since individual die-hard guerrillas were still hiding in the forests. Hence, an odd situation ensued as on one hand numerous decrees resulted in the release of thousands of prisoners, while on the other hand the local Soviet officials increasingly objected to such processes. In 1959 the release of the film *Ivanna* in Ukraine signalled a spurt of vicious campaigning against Ukrainian 'bourgeois' nationalism and the Uniate Church, accused of collaborating with the Nazis during the war. For the same purpose numerous trials of individuals charged with collaboration and war crimes were staged throughout the Baltic republics and western Ukraine in the 1960s. The disagreements between Moscow and the governments of the republics over nationality policies reflected the chasm between the old Soviet cadres and the new native functionaries elevated to their positions by the 'indigenization' policies.[16]

Although the unrest in Poland and the revolution in Hungary were suppressed, the proximity to the 'socialist camp' generated a flow of information from the West. The Polish and Hungarian radio broadcasts were easily accessible in East Galicia and Transcarpathia, whereas the Western cultural forms such as the hippie movement became popular in Lithuania in spite of official prohibition. Such ideological 'leaks' the Soviet government had assiduously laboured to prevent since its inception in 1917. Also, according to the Soviet–Polish and Soviet–Hungarian agreements, the residents of the border-zones received special permits to visit their relatives across the border. Such access to potential harmful influence, particularly during the Polish and Hungarian crisis was a grave concern to the Soviet administration, since the exposure of the borderlands to Western culture, films, and music attracted large numbers of young travellers from Russia-proper. For example, by 1968 about a million visitors from Russia had visited Lithuania. The potential ideological contamination of the young Russians became a priority to the Soviet institutions responsible for watching over the ideological 'health' of the population.[17]

The higher cultural and living standards in the Baltic republics and the memories of the Soviet terror never reconciled the majority of the Estonians, Latvians, and Lithuanians, who preserved a strong sense of self-identity. For example, the monument to Latvia's independence, built in 1933, and left intact by the administration, remained a powerful symbol of the country's independent past. Another such symbol was religion. In general, the Soviet political establishment treated religion as 'opium for the people' and at the same time tried to use the Roman Catholic and Protestant churches on the pattern established with the Orthodox Church—making them into expedient tools of population control. While tolerating the activities of the Roman Catholic Church in Lithuania, Soviet officials fully realized that it served as a symbol of the national self-identity and resistance to Soviet rule. Indeed, official suppression, which included transforming the Vilnius Cathedral into a storehouse and an art gallery, was popularly perceived as an attack on Lithuanian culture.[18]

The population at large considered the Russian settlers as the stooges of the regime, and non-violent resistance transpired in various forms. In the early 1950s some university students in Latvia refused to attend lectures on Marxism-Leninism or disseminated anti-Soviet leaflets, while the return of many prisoners and exiles after the amnesty of 1956 created a new pool of politically engaged individuals.[19] The potential collusion of native nationalism and influences from abroad was not, therefore, a product of inflated imagination among Soviet officials. In October 1956, as the Hungarian events were reaching a climax, anti-Soviet (and anti-Semitic) agitation gained momentum in Transcarpathia. In Volhynia peasants did not hide their hostility towards the kolkhoz system and in the Vilnius region Poles flatly refused to work on collective farms. In Vilnius student demonstrations broke out and the tradition of lighting candles in the cemeteries in Lithuania and Latvia turned into mass demonstrations.[20]

Although Khrushchev's 'secret speech' in February 1956 has been praised as the beginning of the 'Thaw', the Soviet leader criticized the methods of the terror, but not its contents. While mass repressions were no longer an option, the system possessed a whole variety of repressive tools. Although the population of the concentration camps was gradually reduced, special commissions were set up in the western provinces to decide what categories of prisoners were to be released. In November 1956 the Ukrainian government issued decrees that effectively prohibited political prisoners and prominent underground members to return home. In January and October 1957 the Supreme Councils of the Baltic republics followed suit. As a result, by 1958 145,968 individuals were still inhabiting special settlements in the remote corners of Russia without the right to leave.[21]

Besides shattering the seeming tranquillity of the borderlands, the Hungarian crisis also completed a process of ethnic 'un-mixing' that began in the 1940s. From January 1957 according to the Soviet–Polish agreements thousands of individuals, predominantly Poles and Jews who claimed Polish citizenship, were repatriated to Poland; more than 100,000 left by the end of the year. By the end of the 1950s the Soviet government could claim that the 'class war' in the borderlands was finally over.

That liberalization had its limits was also vividly demonstrated in Latvia, where by the late 1950s native Latvians became a leading force in the high echelons of the state apparatus and the party. The new leadership laboured to expand the network of hospitals and housing, increased pensions for retirees, and concentrated on the production of consumer goods. All these measures alone would not have caused negative reactions from Moscow, but when high-placed Latvian communists, including the members of the Central Committee of the Latvian Communist Party, E. Berklavs and V. Krůmiņš, and the Director of the Institute of Economics of the Latvian

Academy of Sciences spoke against the influx of Russian immigrants into the country, the Soviet government was stirred into action. By this time Khrushchev had eliminated his main rivals and had no intention of pushing liberalization further. In 1959 a purge of the Latvian communist party ensued that affected all administrative levels. The Estonian and Lithuanian communist elites avoided the purges by acting more cautiously and playing up to Moscow's sensibilities. They were duly rewarded, when after the fall of Khrushchev they largely retained their positions.[22]

The Soviet–Romanian dispute over Bessarabia revealed that not all border disputes disappeared with time. It began in April 1964 when the Romanian communist party directly challenged Moscow's dominance in Eastern Europe by insisting it be able to make independent decisions. Simultaneously, Romanian propaganda broadcasts to Moldavia unequivocally stressed that 'Bessarabia' was a historically Romanian territory. Such actions greatly alarmed the Soviet government, particularly since Romanian aspirations were voiced at the time when Soviet–Chinese tensions were reaching their zenith. The chasm in the socialist camp burst open when the Romanian leader Nicolae Ceauşescu openly criticized the Soviet invasion in August 1968 of Czechoslovakia, where a democratization process was unfolding under the communist party leader Alexander Dubček. In fact, the Prague Spring created a climate similar to the situation in 1956. The revival of Ukrainian national life in eastern Slovakia released a flood of publications critical of the Soviet system and the activities of the Uniate Church, suppressed in Soviet Ukraine, as but two symbols of potential 'harmful influences' across the border (border control in Romania, Poland, and Czechoslovakia was much more lax than in the Soviet zone). Public demonstrations and protests against the Soviet intervention in Czechoslovakia erupted in the Baltic, where it was popularly compared to the Soviet occupation in 1940. Letters from Czechoslovak workers and students stirred public opinion and several self-immolations that took place after the 'Prague Spring' traumatized both the population and the administration.[23]

★ ★ ★

The suppression of the Czechoslovak revolution could be considered the end of a particular period in the history of the Soviet Union. Within fifteen years of Stalin's death the Soviet system experienced dramatic changes, mutating from a revolutionary regime, poised to impose radical ideas upon the world, to a stable totalitarian system, bent on preservation of the status quo. Indeed, by the early 1970s the country was governed by a predominantly aged leadership, alarmed by Khrushchev's experiments and determined to reimpose stricter party control over all aspects of life.

In the cultural and nationality fields such policies aimed at the gradual fusion of national cultures into a single Soviet culture and an emphasis on vigilantism against the manifestations of 'bourgeois-nationalism'. The return of the socialist-realist style translated into the glorification of Soviet patriotism and attacks on the literati and artists who did not abide by the official ideological precepts; those, who did not 'recant' were dismissed from the All-Union of Writers. In Byelorussia a number of university students who petitioned the authorities to introduce Byelorussian into the curriculum were accused of nationalism. Similarly, individuals who agitated for the official use of Byelorussian were dubbed 'nationalists', fired from work, and blacklisted.[24]

A renewed campaign to promote Russian as the second 'native' language of the country was a reaction to demographic changes—by the mid-1970s the birth rate among ethnic Russians fell below those in the national republics (especially in Central Asia) and slightly more than a half of the country's population was non-Russian. To balance the process, the Russification or rather Sovietization of the national elites seemed the most effective tool. The Russian language programmes in schools were expanded, starting with the first grade; radio broadcasting and television programmes in Russian were also increased. In the Baltic, however, such attempts ran into difficulties, as most parents continued to send their children to national rather than bilingual schools. In 1967 in Latvia out of 1,500 schools only 240 were made bilingual (in the rest Latvian was the language of instruction); similarly, a limited number of bilingual schools existed in Estonia, where mastery of Russian fell from 29 per cent in 1970 to 24 per cent in 1979.[25]

The resistance to what seemed a renewed 'Russification' campaign was expressed in various forms, such as refusal to speak Russian, placing flowers at national landmarks and the graves of the national heroes, and cheering against the Russian athletic teams. The underground *samizdat* press became the vocal tool for expressing public opinion. For example, the Lithuanian *Aušra*, named after the first Lithuanian newspaper in the Russian empire, emphasized spiritual and national values. In May 1972 Lithuanian society was shocked by the self-immolation of a student, Romas Kalanta, who set himself on fire in protest against the Soviet occupation. Kalanta's death generated mass riots and within a few days three other self-immolations took place in the republic. The Lithuanian Roman Catholic Church continued to be the heart of Lithuanian national culture and identity, while its underground bulletin published in the West reported on violations of human rights in the USSR. In 1974 a small group of activists formed a National Popular Front that demanded the use of Lithuanian as the primary language. More dangerous, however, from Moscow's point of view, was the Front's protests against 'colonial practices'—clearly implying Soviet policies—and demands for human rights. In 1972 two dissident groups in Estonia—the Democratic Movement and the National Front—which demanded the restoration of Estonia's independence were arrested and sentenced to harsh prison terms. Some scientists voiced national aspirations through ecological issues such as careless oil-shale and phosphate mining; a joint appeal by the Estonian, Latvian, and Lithuanian scientists, made on the anniversary of the Molotov–Ribbentrop pact of 1939, called for the Baltic region as a nuclear-free zone. The government responded by putting on trial a number of dissidents. In Ukraine the increasing activities of dissidents, whose publications in Czechoslovakia and the West caused embarrassment for Soviet authorities, led to a wave of repression. To combat the dangers of 'bourgeois nationalism' a series of trials of the former OUN members, wartime collaborators, and dissidents swept through the republic. The Ukrainian communist party was also subjected to purges, which eventually reached the top brass. The boss of Ukraine, Shelest, found himself under attack after a book entitled *Ukraine: Our Soviet Country* was published under his name. The Soviet ideologists accused the book (and the author) of promoting nationalism, and Shelest was forced to resign.[26]

Struggle against nationalism particularly resonated in regard to the 'Jewish question', which continued to be a sore issue for the Soviet government. As in the Russian empire, the Jews remained the most visible minority in the western regions of the USSR, despite a drastic reduction of the Jewish population. On one hand, Jews in the borderlands were still among the most educated and urbanized elements, engaged in the white-collar sector. Largely the representatives of the middle class, their socio-economic status often incurred jealousy of their neighbors. In addition, while in the Baltic republics they tended to be more acclimatized to the national languages, many, especially those who migrated after the war, preferred the Russian language and appeared to be the bearers of Russian culture. On the other hand, official anti-Semitism that had gained momentum since the late 1940s was reflected in various secret restrictions that limited the access of Jews to educational and professional spheres. Conversely, the growing self-affirmation of Jews as a nationality reflected itself in increasing emigration to Israel that deeply disturbed the Soviet government. The Suez Canal crisis of 1956 corresponded with the Polish and Hungarian revolts and heightened the suspicions of the Soviet government about the 'Zionist' proclivities among Soviet Jews. A vicious propaganda campaign, initiated by the top echelons of the Soviet political establishment, combined anti-Jewish and anti-Israel elements. In 1961–3 a series of show trials, in which the majority of the defendants were Jews employed in the consumer sector, were conducted in L'viv, Ivano-Frankivs'k, Chernivtsi, Kiev, Kharkiv, Odessa, and other cities. The charges against the defendants, some of whom were sentenced to death, were thinly veiled propaganda that highlighted the corrupting role of Jews in the Soviet economy. At the same time, an anti-Jewish campaign in the late 1960s, heightened by the visibility of several Jews in the Czechoslovak revolution, led the party leadership and the KGB to blame 'Zionists' for undermining the socialist system. In 1971 and 1972 the Central Committee of the communist party issued two resolutions, which called for vigilance against pro-Zionist sympathies among Soviet Jews, imperative as Jewish emigration to Israel and elsewhere intensified. Besides Odessa and Kiev, the largest share of immigrants came from cities in the western provinces such as Chernivtsi, Chişinău, and Riga. In 1978 out of 12,500 Jews who left Ukraine, 10,500 immigrants were the residents of L'viv, Chernivtsi, and Transcarpathia. These processes roused official concern that the population of the borderlands, in particular Jews, still cherished cultural proclivities to the West.[27]

By the mid-1970s a new generation in the borderlands, for whom independence was a distant history, grew up under the Soviet regime. Although many became completely reliable Soviet functionaries, they were mostly interested in career-making, trying to derive as many benefits from the system as possible (such attitudes were common for the bulk of the country's population). At the same time, this generation's subculture—admiration for Western music, literature, and fashion—provided the ground for dissent, and although the age of consumerism helped the regime to maintain its grip on the society, at the same time it weakened the ideological foundations of the system.

The revolutionary era

The deaths of several Soviet leaders in the early 1980s, including Brezhnev and the chief ideologist Mikhail Suslov, ushered in a new and the final stage in the history of the Soviet Union. The succession of political leadership coincided with the rapid economic decline, as was noted by some highly placed communist authorities. The system's main problem was its centralized planning, the emphasis on heavy industries, and the consequent neglect of the consumer sector. Despite official protestations that the country was reaching the stage of 'advanced socialism', the gross national product in the last years of Leonid Brezhnev's tenure barely reached 55 per cent of its American counterpart. Already in October 1980 economic shortages produced unrest in several cities, including Tallinn and Tartu, and coincided with unrest in Poland, portending a gloomy beginning of the new decade.[28]

The launching of Gorbachev's 'glasnost' and 'perestroika' resembled the period between the two Russian revolutions of 1917 in that it was initially welcomed by the bulk of the population, which hoped for improvement of economic standards and relaxation of the political regime. While the new era began with unprecedented liberties such as freedom of expression, press, and assembly, Gorbachev was determined to pursue the modernization of the Soviet economy and administrative system for a singular reason of preserving the hegemony of the communist party. Also, as in the revolutionary period in spring 1917, the national intelligentsia in the borderlands did not aspire to independence, but instead focused on achieving autonomy in economic, cultural, and administrative matters. In this regard, what had previously been voiced by small groups of nationalist dissenters was now taken to the public forum by the intelligentsia and public organizations. Historians began rewriting national history with major emphasis on the Soviet system of terror of the 1940s. The Estonian Heritage Society played a major role in restoring historical landmarks and monuments (by August 1990 under its guidance more than a half of the independence-era monuments were restored). In June 1987 the Latvian Writers' Union appealed to Moscow, demanding rights similar to those of Ukraine and Byelorussia—sovereignty (within the USSR) and a seat in the United Nations—but also self-management of the economy and its own armed forces, with Latvian as

the language of command. In September 1987 a group of Estonian intellectuals called for the creation of an autonomous Estonian ecological zone.
Since Moscow did not allocate any resources for its implementation, it was a
clear sign that any major changes within the framework of the USSR were
unlikely.[29]

The Lithuanian activist groups publicly commemorated the anniversary
of independence in February 1988. While such initiatives were certainly
unpleasant for Moscow, it was even more infuriated by the conduct of
communist functionaries, who increasingly joined the national movements.
Moscow's suspicions that exposure to the West made the borderlands a
breeding ground for disloyalty and dissident movements seemed to have
come true. By the end of the year the activist groups in the Baltic were fused
into loosely joined organizations called Popular Fronts that appeared as
representatives of the Estonian, Latvian, and Lithuanian nations and became
the main public forum for national aspirations that combined issues of
history, language, and ecology. The Estonian Popular Front protested
against extensive phosphate mining, while its Lithuanian counterpart demonstrated against expanding chemical industries. Cultural societies
connected to the Popular Fronts celebrated national holidays, previously
prohibited under the Soviets, such as independence days. In June 1989 the
Latvian 'Helsinki group' (signed by the Soviet Union in 1975, the Helsinki
Accords guaranteed the state-observance of human and civil rights) called
for a public commemoration of the deportations of 1941. Staged as a
popular tribute to the victims of Stalinism rather than of the Soviet
Union, the demonstration fitted within the parameters of the 'glasnost'
and therefore did not provoke a violent reaction from Moscow.[30]

On the contrary, such activities seemed to have the full support of
Gorbachev. Concerned over the hardliners, who increasingly criticized
his reforms, and seeking support outside of the capital, in August 1988
Gorbachev dispatched to the Baltic his close associate Alexander Yakovlev,
who met the leaders of the national movements. His visit was followed by
the dismissal of several communist hardliners and the formation of the
Lithuanian *Sajudis* (movement), which united most activist groups under
its umbrella. A year later the Supreme Soviet admitted the existence of
the secret protocols of the Molotov–Ribbentrop Pact of 1939, effectively
acknowledging the illegitimacy of Soviet rule in the Baltic.[31]

On 23 August 1989 the Popular Fronts in the Baltic proved that they had
reached maturity by organizing a colossal human bridge of two million

people, who formed a living chain from Tallinn to Vilnius in commemoration of the fiftieth anniversary of the Pact. Such public condemnation of the
illegality of the Soviet occupation was again engendered by the lack of
response from Gorbachev, who realized that violence would badly damage
his reputation as a liberal in the West. Importantly, the Baltic republics'
'western' outlook—in terms of education and mentality—helped them to
receive increasing official and public support from the West. Hence, when
in March 1990 the Supreme Soviet in Lithuania, headed by the *Sajudis*
majority, declared independence, Moscow hesitated before using force.
Indeed, the image and the reputation of the Baltic Republics as the most
'European' regions of the Soviet Union became abundantly clear, when the
Soviet assault on the radio station in Vilnius in January 1991 caused the
death of thirteen people. Although the numbers of casualties were small (by
Soviet standards), the attack caused more outrage and protests in the West
than the far more violent conduct of Soviet troops during the suppression of
peaceful demonstrations in Tbilisi and Baku in 1990.[32]

* * *

A relatively strong national movement emerged in Moldavia, where in May
1989 several democratic organizations patterned themselves after the Baltic
Popular Fronts and demanded socio-economic and political reforms. As in the
Baltic region, their activities were bolstered by communist authorities, who
felt that they were deserted by the central government—concerned about the
situation in the Baltic and Ukraine, Moscow seemed to ignore the situation
in Moldavia—and they supported the Popular Front, which displayed
Romanian national colours, demanding the introduction of Romanian on a
par with Russian, and commemorated the Soviet–German Pact of 1939.[33]

The first attempts at cultural autonomy in Byelorussia were made at the
end of 1986 by a group of the Byelorussian literati and intelligentsia, who
wrote the 'Letter of the Twenty-Eight'. The letter connected the existence
of the Byelorussian nation with the national language and protested against
the systematic Russification campaign that began in the 1950s. The demands
for language reform corresponded with the nuclear fallout of Chornobyl'
and became the platform of the national movement, which was spurred into
existence by the discovery of the mass graves of the Stalinist victims in
the forest of Kuropaty near Minsk in summer 1988. The lack of experience
in independence in Byelorussia revealed itself during the constituent conference of the Popular Front that referred to the sovereignty of the

Byelorussian nation as starting in spring 1918 under the Germans (the Byelorussian Democratic Republic) and under the Soviet Socialist Republic created in January 1919. The Byelorussian party and state leadership, initially opposed to political reforms, were compelled to collaborate with the Popular Front only after they realized that Moscow would not provide any help. Still, the declaration of sovereignty in July 1990 merely emulated a similar announcement in Kiev and reflected the traditional weakness of nationalism in Byelorussia.[34]

The Ukrainian equivalent of a Popular Front *Rukh* (movement) was founded in September 1988. It defended the rights of the minorities, making a special effort to downplay the negative images associated with anti-Semitism in Ukraine. It participated in the March 1990 elections and advocated the sovereignty of Ukraine, the creation of a market economy, and freedom of worship, including the registration of the Uniate Church— a crucial development for East Galicia and Transcarpathia, where it was granted free activities in December 1989.[35] *Rukh*'s potential for success, however, was arrested by the multitude of political parties in Ukraine, but most importantly the communist party was still in full control of the state apparatus, the army, and the police.

Despite the successes of the national movements, however, their longevity still depended upon the reaction of Moscow and thus necessitated caution in dealing with the Soviet government. Although the appearance of more radical political groups that advocated full independence, eventually forced the Popular Fronts to assume the same course, this would have been impossible had it not been 'forced' upon the borderlands.[36] The major role in this process was played by the president of the Russian Federation Boris Yeltsin, who was poised to replace Gorbachev and encouraged the separatists. In July 1990 Yeltsin, then the chairman of the Supreme Council of the Russian Federation, arrived in Latvia and signed the first agreement between Russia and the Baltic states, indicating his support for the national movements. In January 1991 when the Baltic republics announced their sovereignty, Yeltsin ordered the Soviet armed forces in the region to remain in their barracks.[37] Finally, it was Yeltsin's agreement with the presidents of Ukraine and Byelorussia in December 1991 that spelled the end for the Soviet Union and released the borderlands from bondage.

A peaceful breakaway of the Baltic Republics, Ukraine, and Byelorussia was thus conditioned by several factors, the most crucial being that the Russian president himself was bent on the destruction of the USSR against

Map 5. The Borderlands in 1992

the will of the majority of the Soviet people and the state leadership (with the exception of Estonia, Latvia, and Lithuania, the other Soviet republics initially desired to stay within the Union). The fact that the communist elements in the breakaway republics joined the national movements, the disintegration of the country and ethnic conflicts and unrest in the Caucasus and Central Asia demonstrated that Moscow no longer possessed the political will to maintain the grip on the borderlands. Also, in comparison to the downfall of the Russian empire and the frontier wars of 1918–20, the political situation in 1991 was strikingly different. The disintegration of the USSR transpired in peacetime and there was no intervention of a major state-power such as Germany or Poland. Concerned with upholding his 'democratic' image in the West and groomed in the political stables of Brezhnev and his successor Yuri Andropov, Gorbachev was certainly not a man to begin a full-scale civil war and risk his reputation as a moderate. The ethno-political forces that were so visible in the Baltic region, Bye-lorussia, and Ukraine during the frontier wars—the Germans, the Poles, and the Russians—and could have challenged the secessionist movements were gone or ineffective as a political force. On the other hand, the Baltic and Ukrainian émigré communities in the West provided their co-nationals in the USSR with financial and political support, while the age of information exposed the situation in the borderlands to the world public opinion.[38]

The Moldavian civil war

In the light of the peaceful disintegration of the Soviet Union in the western borderlands, Moldavia stands out as the sole exception, the only province that experienced a brief civil war. Outwardly, Moldavia followed a com-mon pattern of socio-economic and political development of the border-lands in the post-Stalinist period. The liberalization period witnessed a sizeable state investment into the republic's economy, the literati were encouraged to write about the historical past in the Moldavian language, and the government tolerated an increased volume of publications and subscriptions from Romania to Moldavia. The expansion of the education system also drastically reduced the level of illiteracy. However, in the context of the Soviet–Romanian dispute in the 1960s, the overwhelming enthusiasm accorded by the Moldavian population to visiting Romanian artistic groups, hoisting the Romanian national colours, and anti-Russian graffiti were interpreted as dangerous nationalist activities. Accordingly, the volume of the publications in Moldavian was limited, travel between Moldavia and Romania was curtailed, and the central government continu-ally reminded the administration of the republic to be politically vigilant.[39]

At the same time, several features set Moldavia apart from the other borderlands. In comparison to Estonia, Byelorussia, or Ukraine the ethnic composition of the Moldavian communist party reflected the predominance of the Russians and Ukrainians. In the 1970s out of 67,706 party members there were approximately 14,200 Moldavians (21 per cent), while the Political Bureau of the Central Committee of the Communist Party comprised eight Russians and Ukrainians and only one Moldavian. The Soviet linguistic policies also succeeded in Moldavia to a much higher degree than in the Baltic republics. Since attaining social advancement was impossible without the mastery of Russian, it became customary for the Moldavian socio-economic elite to send their children to Russian-language schools. For example, by 1989 75 per cent of all Moldavians in the republic's capital Chişinău were fluent in Russian and only 44 per cent were fluent in Romanian.[40]

Another aspect of Moldavia's particular situation was a compact Russian-Ukrainian enclave on the left bank of the Dniester River. Created in 1924 as a counter-measure to the Romanian occupation of Bessarabia, the so-called Transdniestria (the official name was the Moldavian Autonomous Soviet Socialist Republic) has not been a part of Romania and remained Russian in terms of socio-economic dominance, language, and culture. Whereas Moldavia had the lowest level of industrial productivity and income per capita among the western republics, the Russians and Ukrainians, largely employed in industries, on average enjoyed higher life standards. For example, seventy-five Russians and Ukrainians per thousands owned a car—in comparison to the forty-eight per thousand among the Moldavians. Traditionally, the Russians and Ukrainians (largely Russified), who in 1989 made up about 27 per cent of the total population of the Republic, were contemptuous of the Moldavians as backward, corrupt, and inferior 'country bumpkins'. In the context of the disintegration of the Soviet Union in the late 1980s, for the Russian-Ukrainian population Moldavia's independence presented a dangerous potential to terminate their privileged status.[41]

Finally, in contrast to the Baltic region, the communist leadership of Moldavia remained highly conservative and hostile to any expressions of pro-Romanian sentiments among the population. In March 1983 the first secretary of the Moldavian communist party, Simion Grossu, called upon the state and party functionaries to combat 'any manifestations of national narrow-mindedness', implying the accentuation of ethnic and linguistic ties between Moldavians and Romanians. In December 1986, at a conference of professors and lecturers in social sciences, the party ideologists urged the gathering to highlight the role of the Russian language as the main factor 'in strengthening the international unity of the Soviet people'.[42] In November

1988 the Central Committee of the Moldavian communist party, the Presidium of the Supreme Soviet, and the republic's Council of Ministers issued a 'Thesis' that reconfirmed the similarity of the Moldavian and Romanian languages, but simultaneously stressed that the Cyrillic alphabet 'corresponded' with the phonetic nature of the Moldavian language. The 'Thesis' generated a wave of protests that transformed into demonstrations against Moscow's nationality policies. Politically engaged groups in Moldavia, however, were split. Those who promoted a union of Moldavia with Romania argued that there was no separate 'Moldavian' identity, but a Romanian identity 'spoiled' by Russian influence; a total renunciation of the Russian language would ensure the dominance of the Romanian identity. Others advocated the maintaining of a separate 'Moldavian' identity, but were opposed to the union with Romania. Still, in 1989 the formation of the Popular Front and demonstrations and protests against the Soviet annexation of Bessarabia seemingly indicated that Moldavia was moving in the same direction as the Baltic states.[43]

In October 1989, on the pattern established in other borderland republics, the ruling Moldavian leadership made Romanian (Moldavian) the state language, restored the Latin script, and introduced the Romanian national anthem and flag. The Popular Front received a legitimate status and in November the communist party boss, the conservative Simion Grossu, was replaced by Petru Lucinski, a more moderate functionary from Central Asia. At the same time, language became a primary issue that alarmed the Russian minority, which conceived it as the first step on the way to separation from Russia and union with Romania. Such fears were exacerbated as the pro-Romanian militants harassed individuals who conversed in Russian and desecrated Russian monuments bringing back memories of the Romanian occupation during the Second World War and facilitating popular support for the separatist leaders in Transdniestria who advocated a break with Moldavia. First violent clashes occurred in November 1989, when an attempt of pro-Romanian groups to seize the building of the Ministry of Internal Affairs resulted in injuries to 200 people.[44]

By this time Moscow's ability to control the situation in the borderlands was slipping away. One of the last attempts to hold the country together came in April 1990, when the Soviet government introduced a new law that stipulated the use of Russian on all territories of the USSR as a means of 'interethnic communication for the purpose of union among the republics'. In response the Moldavian parliament replaced the Soviet flag with

the Romanian national colours and in May the extreme nationalist leader
of the Popular Front Mircea Druc, who advocated a break with Russia.
became prime minister. These developments spurred to action the Russian-
Ukrainian leadership in Transdniestria. Counting on Moscow's support, in
September it proclaimed in Tiraspol' (the capital of Transdniestria) the
formation of the Transdniestria-Moldavian Soviet Socialist Republic. Clashes
between the Popular Front-organized demonstrations and the Russian-
Ukrainian crowds erupted in several localities and in October the volunteers from the two sides intervened in the Gagauz districts in southern
Moldavia, where an autonomy referendum was taking place. At the
referendum in March 1991 the population in Transdniestria almost unan-
imously voted for maintaining allegiance to the Soviet Union (the Moldavians boycotted the referendum). The Moldavian Popular Front
responded on 23 May 1991 by changing the name of the Soviet Socialist
Republic of Moldavia to the Republic of Moldova. In August, prompted
by the coup in Moscow, the Moldavian parliament passed a declaration of
independence.[45]

Although the Interior Troops subordinated to Moscow managed to keep
the two warring factions apart, the August 1991 coup in Moscow served as
the signal for an open confrontation, which escalated in the autumn. During
the first election for Moldavia's president in December 1991, the government in Tiraspol' ordered the KGB and Cossack volunteers to use force to
prevent the voters reaching the polling stations. As a result, about 3,000
Moldavians—mostly the faculty and students from Tiraspol' State University, crossed over the river and became political refugees.[46]

Crucially, the secessionists received help from the Russian Fourteenth
Army stationed in Moldavia. It transferred large quantities of arms to the
paramilitary groups, while its commander assumed the post of defence
minister of the Transdniestria Republic. Some Russian units—under the
conniving eyes of the commanders or under direct orders—went over to
join the rebels. Armed clashes became more frequent in March 1992 and
Tiraspol' turned to Russia for help. Since Yeltsin considered Transdniestria
an intrinsically Russian territory, he unequivocally warned the Moldavian
government that if the conflict continued Moldavia would lose more
territories. Similarly Russian officials such as Vice-President Alexander
Rutskoi openly supported the secessionist republic. In June the units of
the Fourteenth Army, stationed in Transdniestria, openly joined the fighting and helped the rebels push the Moldavian troops from Bender (Tigh-

ina). The war claimed about a thousand casualties and 30,000 refugees. In July Yeltsin and the Moldavian president Mirca Snegur agreed to a ceasefire and concurred that should Moldova unite with Romania, Transdniestria was to decide its own fate. Since that time the status of the breakaway region has remained ambiguous.[47]

★ ★ ★

The war in Moldavia was generated and driven by several forces. Since the incorporation into the Russian empire, the Russian-Ukrainian enclave in Transdniestria was heavily 'Slavic' in terms of ethnic composition, socio-economic profile, and culture. Consequently, in the late 1980s it possessed several constituents necessary for autonomy or independence: a bounded geographic area, a government, and an ethnically or culturally homogeneous population, which behaved markedly differently from its co-nationals in the Baltic republics. Although the relatively compact Russian community in Latgalle had the potential to turn into the Latvia's 'Transdniestria', the higher living standards in the Baltic region, especially in the light of deteriorating economic conditions in Russia-proper, and the respect for the 'high' cultures of the Estonians and Latvians among the Russian minority promoted a more moderate approach to the breakaway tendencies than in the economically backward Moldavia. Socio-economic priorities, therefore took precedence over ideology and political rights. In fact, the Russians, Ukrainians, and Byelorussians in general considered the Baltic people, especially Estonians and Latvians, the most 'cultured' and advanced nationality groups in the entire Soviet Union (the proximity to the West certainly contributed to such views). Most Russians, therefore, accepted the independence of the Baltic republics, especially since the younger generation was steeped in Soviet rather than Russian culture and was therefore less inclined to respond to the appeals of nationalism. Crucially, the Russians in the Baltic received no encouragement from Moscow, which was unable and unwilling to commit the army to stifle the independence movements.

In sharp contrast, the traditional contempt among the Russians and Ukrainians towards the Moldavian 'peasant' nation played into the hands of the Transdniestria separatists. The October 1989 language law compelled young Russians and Ukrainians who wanted to continue their education to move to Transdniestria, where they joined the Soviet-educated intelligentsia and managerial and technical elite. For these groups the separation and the potential reunification of Moldavia with Romania meant relegation to second-class citizenship. On the other side, whereas the Moldavians realized their kinship with the Romanians, many considered themselves to be members of a culturally different group. Consequently, less than 50 per cent supported the breakaway from the Soviet Union. Another ethnic group, the Gagauz, also opposed Moldavia's secession, since their status in the new republic would be questionable and entailed the obligation to learn one more language—in addition to Russian. Consequently, the Moldavian national movement faced too many adversities to handle successfully the situation in Transdniestria, particularly since the active intervention of the Russian army and Moscow sharply differed from a more cautionary approach to the situation in the Baltic.[48]

Summary

After the death of Stalin the Soviet regime changed its policies from radical revolutionary expansion to preservation of the former imperial possessions. For two decades the regime demonstrated its willingness to improve living standards, individual security, and relative economic well-being, and guaranteed the development of national cultures. It can be said, therefore, that similarly to Russian imperial nationalism, the Soviet policies in the borderlands were predominantly defensive in character and were committed to maintain the status quo in the domain built by the Tsars. Although the regime retained its repressive apparatus and demonstrated its will to use coercion and force, the political and cultural changes since the mid-1950s gave hopes for a better future. The population at large reciprocated by grudgingly accepting the Soviet rule and such mutual accommodation seemed to lay the ground for cooperation between the state and the people.

The modernization process in the 1950s–1960s also transformed the borderlands into regions that boasted a high educational level, a sizeable middle class, nationally conscious intelligentsia, and large urban sites. At the same time, the socio-economic changes made it easier for the Soviet regime to control and monitor its subjects, by imposing its norms of behaviour and weakening the traditional cultural and religious ties of the borderland societies. From Moscow's point of view, such an evolution would eventually 'de-nationalize' the borderlands and convert them into thoroughly Soviet enclaves.

The economic decline and the political stagnation of Soviet power in the 1970s–1980s gave strength to the national movements, which promoted autonomy and, eventually, independence. However, it was only the implosion of the Soviet Union that singularly contributed to the breakdown of the country and the sovereignty of the republics. As in the revolutionary period of 1917–20, the disintegration of the country generated 'ethnic mobilization', whereby competition for economic and social privileges became ethnically relevant. In the borderlands, the 'state' nationality group—the Russians—were relegated to the status of ethnic minorities ruled by the formerly dominated nationality groups.[49]

Still, in contrast to the Caucasus and Central Asia the breakaway processes in the western borderlands produced a single violent conflict in Moldavia. Different socio-economic and cultural context in the discourse between the Russian minorities and the nationality groups elevated to 'state' status contributed to the peaceful resolution of the potential conflict in the Baltic region, Ukraine, and Byelorussia. In Moldavia the combination of Russia's intervention, deep hostility to the independence movement among the Russian population, and geographical boundaries that favoured the secessionist movement laid the ground for the civil war.

The downfall of the Soviet Union facilitated the re-formation of the nationalizing states in the borderlands. As in the interwar period, the new political elites promoted the 'ownership' of their respective domains and pursued a variety of methods to alter the socio-economic pattern established in the Soviet period. In this way, the post-Soviet borderlands came again to face a dilemma of the traditional 'fatal triangle'—the strained relations between the host nations and the Russian minorities backed up by the new Russian state. The door for potential conflict, therefore, remains open.

Conclusion

This study has attempted to examine the processes that transpired in the borderlands during the transition from the multinational imperial domains into the nationalizing, racial, and socialist states. Such transformation involved the overlapping of geographical spaces and political ideas between the empires and the newly mapped nations, the relationship between the state and the population at large, and the efforts of different ethnic and nationality groups to accommodate themselves to the changing political climate.

The frontier-zones between the three empires represented the 'classic' borderlands subjected to multiple influences. Situated between more powerful neighbours, they had complicated histories, being the testing grounds for the relations of these neighbours, and moved from one authority-zone to another. Such processes could not but affect the national identities and political affiliations of the population of the borderlands. Although vastly different linguistically, religiously, and culturally, the borderlands shared a 'classic' East European feature—they lagged behind in terms of socio-economic and political development, thus forming a clearly different territorial pattern from Western Europe. Such a weighty heritage revealed itself during the modernization period in the second half of the nineteenth century, when the borderlands (and the Austro-Hungarian and Russian empires in general) experienced great difficulties fitting into the European economic system. This situation created a propitious environment for negative emotions, which entailed conflicts between various ethnic groups competing for the socio-economic space.

A common reaction to this situation was the emergence of nationalist ideology, which was heavily influenced and at the same time profoundly differed from its Western European counterpart. If in the latter nationalism contributed to the formation of powerful and generally prosperous nation-states, where state-sovereignty exercised supranational authority, in Eastern Europe it consolidated ethno-communal identities, which were in conflict with each other. The East European nationalists in general believed that only the national state, with the 'core'-nationality group as its major proprietor, would eliminate poverty and bring stability to the territories they claimed as the historical cradles of their constituencies. Before the First World War the nationalist groups became visible in the political processes in the borderlands, but in general failed to generate mass support since their ideologies found little response in the predominantly agricultural societies.

Nevertheless, the combination of economic backwardness and the geopolitical vulnerability of the borderlands made the imperial authorities constantly concerned about the loyalties of their multicultural subjects. The issues of nationality and religion, therefore, became inseparable from matters of security and internal stability. Of special concern for the imperial authorities were ethnic groups living on all sides of the demarcation lines, such as Poles, Ukrainians, or Germans, and whose loyalties were not necessarily confined by state borders. Russian Jews, who traditionally practised different cultures, values, and beliefs from those of their host nations featured prominently on the lists of potential enemies.

To keep their diverse subjects in check, Austro-Hungarian and Russian statesmen tried several approaches. Having accepted the multinational fabric of their domains, they attempted to create—the former certainly more successfully than the latter—a brand of ideology that allowed multiple loyalties of its subjects. In Galicia one could be a Ukrainian nationalist and at the same time an ardent Austrian patriot; to some degree the same can be said about the Baltic Germans in the Russian empire. Therefore, while the imperial past was certainly not idyllic, the fact remains that in comparison to what would come later it was a period of a relatively long albeit enforced coexistence in the borderlands.

This period ended in summer 1914 and from that point on the borderlands experienced frequent and brutal manifestations of state-sanctioned and inter-communal repression and violence. Some of these manifestations developed into sustained and deadly assaults on specific groups and have come to symbolize the 'Age of Extremes'. It was in the Eastern front-zone of the First World War, where the Russian military conceived the remoulding of the borderlands into a more homogeneous enclave and practised forcible population transfer for economic and security reasons. The war also provided cover and justification for other forms of violence, some inherent in the nature of warfare, others rooted in the particular socio-economic and ethnic fabric of a specific region.

Throughout the war the populations of the borderlands were forced to reorganize and adjust to the changing front lines and political climate, while the opposing armies were keen on utilizing dormant pre-war social grievances and ethnic animosities. To this effect, the imperial governments used the slogan of self-determination, unwittingly unleashing the forces of nationalism. Conversely, the nationalist groups, initially small and inefficient, grew in strength; they articulated political and socio-economic demands in national phraseology, compensating for the lack of national history or national statehood by appealing to their constituencies' common suffering. At the end of the First World War, the nationalists achieved what they could not have dreamed before, for the combination of the military defeat and revolution generated the dissolution of the empires and entailed the formation of new successor-states.

The imperial collapse, however, did not usher in an era of peace, but a crescendo of revolutionary upheaval and a series of frontier wars on the peripheries of the imperial domains. These wars prolonged the old and engendered the new conflicts, causing further destruction and extensive social dislocation, and the dissolution and restructuring of political and social identities and affiliations. Ultimately, in the collision between the Bolshevik and nationalist ideologies the latter proved more attractive, for the combination of national independence, social equality, and the redistribution of economic wealth.

In the aftermath of the First World War the situation in the borderlands seemed to be improving, since the discriminatory imperial practices were over and changes in the political structure promised better inter-communal relations. The new states guaranteed the equality of all citizens and the right of the minorities to practise their culture and religion. It was certainly possible that the democratic principles upon which the successor-states (with the exception of Romania) were built would convince ethnic minorities to accept the status quo and eventually assimilate into the cultures of the major nationality group. However, the new political boundaries did not coincide with the deeply rooted identities of locality, language, ethnicity, and religion, and conflicted with the successor-states' objectives to create homogeneous national identities delimited by state borders. Gradually, the winners of the frontier wars presented themselves in a similar way to the imperial states: they assumed the role of the pre-1914 'titular' groups and strove to dominate national politics and economies. Accordingly, the assignment of privileges based upon ethnic criteria became predominant, while discriminatory legislations, falsified censuses, and police suppression were deployed to deal with the minority issues.

As a result, the relations between the state and the minorities, especially in Poland and Romania, became strained to the limit. Compounded by the aggressive policies of Germany and the Soviet Union, rampant economic crises, and imbalances in regional development, the situation in the borderlands became precarious. Internal conflicts were detonated immediately by the outbreak of the Second World War, in which the two totalitarian states attempted to redefine the occupied territories according to their respective ideological outlooks. Driven by the vision of socialist progress, the Soviet administration considered the borderlands in dire need of cultural and economic elevation, and the methods of 'improvement' included both socio-economic reforms and the elimination of groups considered intractable. In comparison, the Nazi regime envisioned the utilization of the borderlands as a source of food supplies and labour manpower, and eventual homogenization of the population through brutal ethnic policies. The implementation of these policies began with the annihilation of the Jews, which was nearly completed with the active help of local volunteers. The Soviet–German war generated a series of smaller, but often as vicious conflicts, for the Soviet and German methods convinced the radical elements in the borderlands that contest over disputed territories could successfully be resolved by the 'final solutions'.

The second Sovietization began in 1944 and went further in a complete political and socio-economic restructuring of the borderlands, using well-tested methods—universal education, new social opportunities, and mass terror, leaving not a single individual outside of the state's reach. The drive to achieve ideological homogeneity involved the elimination of the resistance as well as entire nationality groups such as Poles, who did not fit into the new order and the destruction of all capitalist vestiges, particularly the traditional agrarian order. The Soviet government partially succeeded in altering the borderlands' political, socio-economic, and cultural outlook. By the late 1940s the Polish *Kresy*, East Galicia, Bukovina, and Bessarabia became more ethnically homogeneous—due to the mass population losses—while the collectivization campaign changed the traditional profile of the countryside.

Although the Soviet state was willing to suppress any dissent by force, it strove to impress its legitimacy upon the majority of the population. From the mid-1950s the regime introduced a series of reforms that aimed to win this popular support and stabilized the situation in the borderlands. The government integrated all Byelorussian and Ukrainian lands, eliminating one bloc of conflicting nationalisms, so rampant in the interwar period, when the revisionist states claimed to be the protectors of their kin across the border. The most 'troublesome' ethnic groups, the Germans, Poles, and Jews, were eliminated as political and economic forces, although at the price of mass deportations, ethnic cleansing, or outright genocide and redrawn political boundaries. The liberalization policies in the late 1950s and the early 1960s helped the state to cultivate a sort of supranational identity—somewhat similar to the Austro-Hungarian 'live and let live' principle. As long as an individual remained a loyal citizen, he or she was spared arbitrary police abuse and could practise native language, religion, and culture.

At the same time, the stratification of people into distinct cultural-linguistic groups, confining them to specific places of residence, and the passport system, which clearly indicated the ethnicity of the bearer, made the construction of such a supranational identity a difficult pursuit. In fact, the Soviet industrialization drive and the expansion of the education system produced a highly educated and nationally conscious population that in the late 1980s challenged the state monopoly on power.

* * *

All in all, it can be stated that the conflict period of 1914–53 was not rooted in the borderlands' particular propensity to violence. Rather it was specific circumstances that created a specific environment in which the culture of conflict became acceptable for the state and, to a certain degree, for the population at large. Although the major powers initiated the World Wars, introducing a prolonged period of violence and instability, the population of the borderlands was not an amorphous mass governed without opposition. Violence during this period was so destructive precisely because of its dual character—launched by the state, and exacerbated by popular participation. It is imperative to note that initially many individuals accorded an enthusiastic reception to the Soviets in 1939–40 and to the German troops in 1941, and although such attitudes were eventually dissipated by the two regimes' brutality, collaboration (and internal conflicts) provided a crucial foundation for the maintenance of Soviet and German power.

State violence inflamed political radicalization and ethnic tensions in the borderlands, specifically because it gave a clear signal that assaults on certain groups were officially encouraged. At the same time, encouraging popular participation, the state gradually lost its monopoly on violence. Its use became customary and pursued for a variety of goals, from ideology to social advancement and personal enrichment. Such a mixture of motives became especially apparent during the persecution of the Jews, a landmark of the borderlands' history during the two World Wars. Jews became a metaphor of evil and an ideal scapegoat in the regions where anti-Semitism was traditionally strong and where the Jewish communities were the largest. From 1917 the images of 'Judaeo-Bolshevism' amalgamated anti-Semitism, anti-communism with traditional socio-economic rivalries and social rivalries and religious animosities towards the Jews.

★ ★ ★

If traditionally the borderlands remained emotionally overloaded spatial domains periodically claimed by the neighbouring states, the territorial equilibrium between the national and 'natural' frontiers was achieved after the Second World War and consolidated after the collapse of the USSR. Today the borderlands seem no longer the fateful crossroads in the East European political landscape. The border new settlements diminished the possibility of conflicts, with the exception of one 'hot spot'—Transdniestria—where the possibility of conflagration remains.

Still, close scrutiny reveals that the post-Soviet states have inherited at least two old legacies. First of all, they have attempted to define themselves in terms of territory, ethnicity, and citizenship, thus in many ways resembling their antecedents in the post-First World War period. Second, the most palpable reality of the imperial times—the borderlands' vulnerability to forces beyond their borders—did not disappear altogether, and the situation in the Baltic republics, Byelorussia, and Moldavia largely depends on the relations of these states with Russia. The republics have done much in maintaining internal stability by introducing liberal constitutions and the groups that promote intolerance and ethnic hatred remain on the margins of the political spectrum. The economic situation from the Black to the Baltic Sea, however, remains precarious and the dependence on Russia's economic support and natural resources translates into the political field. In such situation the issue of large Russian minorities has acquired a special importance and Moscow has already demonstrated its willingness to use this issue as a political lever. The integration of the Baltic states into the European Union on one hand fortified the prestige of Estonia, Latvia, and Lithuania, but on the other hand placed them in an unenviable position at the mercy of international financial organizations and Russia's gas and oil policies. Much, therefore, depends on a visionary and enlightened leadership, which would be able and willing to pursue a precarious balance between political reforms and economic development, and at the same time would tolerate and attempt to forge different cultures into a single national identity based on inclusion and tolerance.

Notes

INTRODUCTION

1. Andrzej Stasiuk and Iurii Andrukhovych, *Moia Evropa: dva esei pro naidyvnishu chastynu svitu* (L'viv: Klasyka, 2005), 100–1.

2. I have appropriated the term from Alan Warwick Palmer's *The Lands Between: A History of East-Central Europe since the Congress of Vienna* (New York: Macmillan, 1970).

3. Alfred J. Rieber, 'Changing Concepts and Constructions of Frontiers: A Comparative Historical Approach', *Ab Imperio* 1 (2003), 23, 32–3.

4. Terry Martin, *The Affirmative Action Empire: Nations and Nationalism in the Soviet Union, 1923–1939* (Ithaca, NY: Cornell University Press, 2001).

5. For example, Robert Bideleux and Ian Jeffries, *A History of Eastern Europe: Crisis and Change* (London: Routledge, 1998); Joseph Rothschild, *East Central Europe between the Two World Wars* (Seattle: University of Washington Press, 1974), Ivan T. Berend, *Decades of Crisis: Central and Eastern Europe before World War II* (Berkeley and Los Angeles: University of California Press, 1998).

6. Dietrich Beyrau, *Schlachtfeld der Diktatoren: Osteuropa im Schatten von Hitler und Stalin* (Göttingen: Vandenhoeck & Ruprecht, 2000); Eric Hobsbawm, *The Age of Extremes: A History of the World* (New York: Vintage, 1996).

7. Kate Brown, *A Biography of No Place: From Ethnic Borderlands to Soviet Heartland* (Cambridge, Mass.: Harvard University Press, 2004); Timothy Snyder, *The Reconstruction of Nations: Poland, Ukraine, Lithuania, Belarus, 1969–1999* (New Haven and London: Yale University Press, 2003).

8. Edward D. Wynot, *Caldron of Conflict: Eastern Europe, 1918–1945* (Wheeling, Ill.: Harlan Davidson, 1999), 3.

9. Donald L. Horowitz, *Ethnic Groups in Conflict* (Berkeley: University of California Press, 1985), 145–7; Jonathan Fletcher, *Violence and Civilization: An Introduction to the Work of Norbert Elias* (Cambridge: Polity Press, 1997), 57–8; Rogers Brubaker and David D. Laitin, 'Ethnic and Nationalist Violence', *Annual Review of Sociology* 24 (1998), 437–8.

10. Miroslav Hroch, 'Real and Constructed: The Nature of the Nation', in John A. Hall, ed., *The State of the Nation: Ernest Gellner and the Theory of Nationalism* (Cambridge: Cambridge University Press, 1998), 96.

CHAPTER I

1. Henning Bauer, Andreas Kappeler, and Brigitte Roth, eds, *Die Nationalitäten des Russischen Reiches in der Volkszählung von 1897* (Stuttgart: Franz Steiner, 1991), ii. 34; Piotr Eberhardt, *Ethnic Groups and Population Changes in Twentieth Century Central-Eastern Europe: History, Data, and Analysis* (New York: M. E. Sharpe, 2003), 28, 31, 92.

2. Eberhardt, *Ethnic Groups*, ii. 92–3, 190–1.

3. T. Karjahärm, Ia. Krastyn, and A. Tila, *Revolutsiia 1905–1907 godov v Pribaltike* (Tallin: Akademia Nauk Estonskoi SSR, 1981), 13–14; Dominic Lieven, *Empire: The Russian Empire and its Rivals* (New Haven: Yale University Press, 2000), 215–16.

4. Andreas Kappeler, *The Russian Empire: A Multiethnic History* (London and New York: Pearson Education, 2001), 221.

5. Paul Robert Magosci, *A History of Ukraine* (Toronto: University of Toronto Press, 1996), 425, 429; S. S. Kostyshyn et al., *Bukovyna: istorychnyi narys* (Chernivtsi: Chernivets'kyi derzhavnyi universytet im. Iu. Fed'kovycha, 1998), 118.

6. Karjahärm, *Revolutsiia*, 9-10; Derek H. Aldcroft, *Europe's Third World: The European Periphery in the Interwar Years* (Aldershot: Ashgate, 2006), 94; Kappeler, *Empire*, 307.

7. V. M. Fainshtein, *Stanovlenie kapitalizma kak razreshenie protivorechii tovarnogo feodal' nogo proizvodstva (na materialakh pribaltiiskikh gubernii Rossii)* (Tallin: Eesti raamat, 1987), ii. 178-80; Kostyshyn, *Bukovyna*, 84–5, 94–5, 118.

8. Bauer, *Nationalitäten*, i. 526, 528; ii. 40; V. Kopchak, 'O nekotorykh strukturnykh izmeneniiakh naseleniia Zakarpat'ya za sto let (1869-1970)', *Ekonomika Sovetskoi Ukrainy* 14/6 (1972), 69; A. M. Lazarev, *Moldavskaia Sovetskaia gosudarstvennost' i bessarabskii vopros* (Chişinău: Kartia Moldoveniaske, 1974), 283; Michael F. Hamm, 'Kishinev: The Character and Development of a Tsarist Frontier Town', *Nationalities Papers* 26/1 (1998), 24.

9. Miroslav Hroch, *Social Preconditions of National Revival in Europe: A Comparative Analysis of the Social Composition of Patriotic Groups among the Smaller European Nations* (Cambridge: Cambridge University Press, 1985).

10. Paul Robert Magosci, *The Shaping of National Identity: Subcarpathian Rus', 1848–1948* (Cambridge, Mass.: Harvard University Press, 1978), 56–61, 63–5, 68.

11. Aviel Roshwald, *Ethnic Nationalism and the Fall of Empires: Central Europe, Russia and the Middle East, 1914–1923* (London: Routledge, 2000), 15; Paul Robert Magocsi, *The Roots of Ukrainian Nationalism: Galicia as Ukraine's Piedmont* (Toronto and London: University of Toronto Press, 2002), 73-82.

12. Mariana Hausleitner, *Die Rumänisierung der Bukowina: Die Durchsetzung des Nationalstaatlichen Anspruchs Grossrumäniens 1918–1944* (Munich: Oldenburg, 2001), 56–9, 61–4; Kostyshyn, *Bukovyna*, 166–73, 178–81, 184, 188–90, 195–6.

13. Alexander Victor Prusin, *Nationalizing a Borderland: War, Ethnicity, and Anti-Jewish Violence in East Galicia, 1914–1920* (Tuscaloosa: University of Alabama Press, 2005), 2–3; Teresa Andlauer, *Die jüdische Bevölkerung im Modernisierungsprozess Galiziens (1867–1914)* (Frankfurt am Main and Berlin: Peter Lang, 2001), 87.

14. Magosci, *Ukraine*, 456–7.

15. The military general-governments also ruled the Caucasus, Central Asia, and east Siberia.

16. Lieven, *Empire*, 220.

17. Magocsi, *Ukraine*, 456; Kappeler, *Empire*, 101, 265; Hamm, 'Kishinev', 26–7, 30–31; Iu. I. Semenov, ed., *Natsional'naia politika v imperatorskoi Rossii. Tsivilizovannye okrainy (Finlandiia, Pol'sha, Pribaltika, Bessarabia, Ukraina, Zakavkaz'ye, Sredniaia Aziia)* (Moscow: Staryi sad, 1997), 83–4.

18. Theodore R. Weeks, *Nation and State in Late Imperial Russia: Nationalism and Russification on the Western Frontier, 1863–1914* (DeKalb: Northern Illinois University Press, 1996), 112–13; Kappeler, *Empire*, 218–19.

19. G.A. Yevreinov, *Natsional'nye voprosy na inorodcheskikh orkainakh Rossii. Skhema politicheskoi programmy* (St Petersburg: Tipographiia A. Benke, 1908), 8–9, 11–12, 14–15, 35–9; Weeks, *Nation*, 31–4, 37, 55–8, 64–7, 77, 98–100.

20. Lieven, *Empire*, 275; S. M. Sambuk, *Politika tsarisma v Belorussii vo vtoroi polovinie XIX veka* (Minsk: Nauka i Tekhnika, 1980), 25–6, 32, 36–8, 41, 43, 145; Weeks, *Nation*, 98–100.

21. Fainshtein, *Stanovlenie*, 178–80; Tönu Parming, 'Population and Ethnicity as Intervening Variables in the 1905/1917 Revolutions in the Russian Baltic Provinces', in Andrew Ezergailis and Gert Pistohlkors, eds., *Die Baltischen Provinzen Russlands zwischen de Revolutionen von 1905 und 1917* (Cologne: Böhlau Verlag, 1982), 3–4; Toivo U. Raun, 'Estonian Social and Political Thought, 1905–February 1917', ibid. 59–60.

22. In Berend, *Crisis*, 38–9.

23. V. Merkis, *Razvitie promyshlennosti i formirovanie proletariata Litvy v XIXv.* (Vilnius: Mintis, 1969), 361–2, 369–70; Hamm, 'Kishinev', 28–9.

24. M. Dolbilov and A. Miller, eds., *Zapadnye okrainy Rossiiskoi Imperii* (Moscow: Novoe Literaturnoe obozrenie, 2006), 322; Lieven, *Empire*, 221.

25. Darius Staliūnas, 'Anti-Jewish Disturbances in the North-Western Provinces in the Early 1880s', *East European Jewish Affairs* 342 (2004), 119–38.

26. Edward H. Judge, *Easter in Kishinev: Anatomy of a Pogrom* (New York: New York University Press, 1992), 26, 30–1, 49–61.

27. Brian Porter, *When Nationalism Began to Hate: Imagining Modern Politics in Nineteenth-Century Poland* (New York: Oxford University Press, 2000), 158; William Hagen, *Germans, Poles, and Jews: The Nationality Conflict in the Prussian East, 1772–1914* (Chicago: University of Chicago Press, 1980), 231–2, 245.

28. George Urbaniak, 'Lithomania versus Panpolonism: The Roots of the Polish-Lithuanian Conflict before 1914', *Canadian Slavonic Papers* 31/2 (1989), 115–25; Weeks, *Nation*, 53, 67–8, 121–2.

29. Louis Roman, 'The Population of Bessarabia during the 19th Century: The National Structure', *Romanian Civilization* 3/2 (1994), 55.

30. Kappeler, *Empire*, 330.

31. James D. White, 'The 1905 Revolution in Russia's Baltic Provinces', in Jonathan D. Smele and Anthony Heywood, eds., *The Russian Revolution: Centenary Perspectives* (London and New York: Routledge, 2005), 61; Uldis Ģērmanis, *Oberst Vācietis und die lettischen Schützen im Weltkrieg und in der Oktoberrevolution* (Stockholm: Almqvist & Wiksell, 1974), 54; Georg Rauch, *The Baltic States: The Years of Independence. Estonia, Latvia, Lithuania, 1917–1940* (Berkeley: University of California Press, 1974), 11–12.

32. Karjahärm, *Revolutsiia*, 20–1; 58–9; Iu. Kirsh, *Agrarnaia revolutsiia v Pribaltike* (Moscow: Mezhdunarodnyi agrarnyi institute, 1931), 19–20; Abraham Ascher, *The Revolution of 1905: Russia in Disarray* (Stanford, Calif: Stanford University Press, 1988), 135, 160.

33. Raun, 'Thought', 63–4; Karjahärm, *Revolutsiia*, 53–8; 'Pribaltiiskii krai v 1905 godu', *Krasnyi arkhiv: istoricheskii zhurnal* 11–12 (1925), 263–4.

34. Ascher, *Disarray*, 196; Wiktor Sukiennicki, *East Central Europe during World War I: from Foreign Domination to National Independence* (Boulder, Colo.: East European Monographs, 1984), i. 38; Romuald J. Misiunas and Rein Taagera, *The Baltic States: Years of Dependence, 1940–1990* (Berkeley, University of California Press, 1983), 7–8.

35. Karjahärm, *Revolutsiia*, 61–2, 73–5, 80–1; Kirsh, *Revolutsiia*, 47–8, 52–3; Rauch, *Baltic States*, 21–3; 'Pribaltiiskii krai', 265, 270, 272, 280.

36. Nicholas P. Vakar, *Belorussia: The Making of a Nation* (Cambridge, Mass.: Harvard University Press, 1956), 85–9; Hamm, 'Kishinev', 29–32.

37. Shlomo Lambroza, 'The Pogroms of 1903–1906', in John Klier and Shlomo Lambroza, eds., *Pogroms: Anti-Jewish Violence in Modern Russian History* (Cambridge: Cambridge University Press, 1992), 237; Ascher, *Disarray* 133–4; *Die Judenpogrome in Russland* (Cologne and Leipzig: Jüdischer Verlag, 1910), i. 212–13; ii. 91–5, 97–102.

38. Karjahärm, *Revolutsiia*, 53–4.

39. Lazarev, *Gosudarstvennost'*, 296.

40. Peter Holquist, 'To Count, to Extract, and to Exterminate: Population Statistics and Population Politics in Late Imperial and Soviet Russia', in Ronald Grigor Suny and Terry Martin, eds., *A State of Nations: Empire and Nation-Making in the Age of Lenin and Stalin* (New York: Oxford University Press, 2001), 111–9.

41. Peter Gatrell, *A Whole Empire is Walking: Refugees in Russia during World War I* (Bloomington: Indiana University Press, 1999), 16; Semen Goldin, 'Deportation of Jews by the Russian Military Command, 1914–1915', *Jews in Eastern Europe* 1 (2000), 45–6.

42. Ivan G. Sobolev, *Bor'ba s 'nemetskim zasil'yem' v Rossii v gody pervoi mirovoi voiny* (St Petersburg: Izdatel'stvo 'Rossiiskaia natsional'naia biblioteka', 2004), 18–19; N. S. Andreyeva '"Ostzeiskii vopros" i Pervaia mirovaia voina', in A. O. Chubar'yan, et al., *Rossiia i Baltiia* (Moscow: Institut vseobshchei istorii RAN, 2002), ii. 33–4; William C. Fuller, *The Foe Within: Fantasies of Treason and the End of Imperial Russia* (Ithaca, NY, and London: Cornell University Press, 2006), 18–20.

43. A. Iu. Bakhturina, *Politika Rossiiskoi imperii v vostochnoi Galitsii v gody pervoi mirovoi voiny* (Moscow: AIRO-XX, 2000), 47–50, 54, 73; Kostyshyn, *Bukovyna*, 171, 174; Magosci, *Identity*, 68.

44. Dolbilov, *Okrainy*, 372–7; Weeks, *Nation*, 173–92.

45. Magosci, *Identity*, 44–5; P. N. Yefremov, *Vneshniaia politika Rossii, 1907–1914* (Moscow: izdatel'stvo Instituta Mezhdunarodnykh Otnoshenii, 1961), 236–8; Prusin, *Borderland*, 15.

46. Berend, *Crisis*, 40.

47. Lieven, *Empire*, 191.

48. Urbaniak, 'Lithomania', 124–5.

CHAPTER 2

1. Peter Holquist, 'Forms of Violence in the First (1914–1915) and Second (1916–1917) Russian Occupations of Galicia', unpublished paper, 20. I am grateful to the author for his generous permission to use this paper.

2. Mark von Hagen, 'The Russian Empire', in Karen Barkey and Mark von Hagen, eds., *After Empire: Multiethnic Societies and Nation-Building: The Soviet Union and the Russian, Ottoman, and Habsburg Empires* (Boulder, Colo.: Westview Press, 1997), 64–5.

3. Volodymyr Zapolovs'kyi, *Bukovyna v ostannii viini Avstro–Uhorshchyny 1914–1918* (Chernivtsi: Zoloti lytavry, 2003), 38–40; M. Altshuler, 'Russia and her Jews: The Impact of the 1914 War', *Wiener Library Bulletin* 27, 30–1 (1973–4), 12.

4. John Horne and Alan Kramer, *German Atrocities, 1914: A History of Denial* (New Haven: Yale University Press, 2001), 114.

5. Peter S. Hardy, ed., *Voennye prestupleniia Gabsburgskoi monarkhii: Galitskaia Golgofa* (Trumbull, Conn.: Hardy Lane, 1964), i. 125–6.

6. Hans Hautmann, 'Kriegsgesetze und Militärjustiz in der österreichischen Reichshälfte', in Erika Weinzierl and Karl R. Stadler, eds., *Justiz und Zeitgeschichte* (Vienna: J. H. Pospisil, 1977), 103–4.

7. Zapolovs'kyi, *Bukovyna*, 183; Christoph Führ, *Das k.u.k. Armeeoberkommando und die Innenpolitik in Österreich 1914–1917* (Graz and Vienna: Böhlau, 1968), 6 ff.

8. Hautmann, 'Kriegsgesetze', 104–5, 108, 113; Zapolovs'kyi, *Bukovyna*, 94–5, 184–5, 187; Magosci, *Identity*, 72–3; Hannes Leidinger, 'Der Einzug des Galgens und des Mordes: die parlamentarischen Stellungnahmen polnischer und

ruthenischer Reichsratsabgeordneter zu den Massenhinrichtungen in Galizien 1914–1915', *Zeitgeschichte* 533 (2006), 245.

9. Russian spy–mania culminated in spring 1915, when Colonel Sergei Miasoedov, an intelligence officer, was arrested on the charge of espionage. The affair magnified the rumours of a widespread German spy network among the government, the military, and even within the court. Fuller, *Foe*, 142–4, 162.

10. I. I. Rostunov, *Russkii front pervoii mirovoii voiny* (Moscow: izdatel'stvo Nauka, 1976), 113–14; Goldin, 'Deportation', 47–8.

11. Mark von Hagen, *War in a European Borderland: Occupations and Occupation Plans in Galicia and Ukraine, 1914–1918* (Seattle and London: University of Washington Press, 2007), 29.

12. Fritz Gause, *Die Russen in Ostpreussen 1914/15. Im Auftrage des Landeshauptmanns der Provinz Ostpreussen* (Kaliningrad: Cräfe und Unzer Verlag, 1931), 35; T. Hunt Tooley, 'World War I and the Emergence of Ethnic Cleansing in Europe', in Steven Béla Vardy and T. Hunt Tooley, eds., *Ethnic Cleansing in Twentieth–Century Europe* (New York: Columbia University Press, 2003), 77.

13. Horne, *Atrocities*, 79–81; Gause, *Russen*, 122–3; A. Altenberg, 'Die Besetzung Memels durch die Russen (18.–21.März 1915)', *Ostpreussische Kriegshefte* 3 (1916), 26–8, 30.

14. Mark Grimsley and Clifford J. Rogers, 'Introduction', in Mark Grimsley and Clifford J. Rogers, eds., *Civilians in the Path of War* (Lincoln: University of Nebraska Press, 2002), p. xv.

15. Zapolovs'kyi, *Bukovyna*, 29.

16. S. G. Nelipovich, 'Repressii protiv poddanykh "Tsentral'nykh Derzhav": deportatsii v Rossii, 1914–1918 gg', *Voenno–istoricheskii zhurnal* 6 (1996), 32–5; Fuller, *Foe*, 132, 165–6; Hoover Institution on War, Revolution and Peace (HI), 'Zhurnal voennykh dieistvii', 3, 8, 10, 17.

17. Holquist, 'Violence', 29–30.

18. Piotr Wróbel, 'Barucha Milcha galicyjskie wspomnienia wojenne, 1914–1920', *Biuletyn Żydowskiego Instytutu Historycznego* 2/158 (1991), 92; S. Ansky, *The Enemy at his Pleasure: A Journey through the Jewish Pale of Settlement during World War I* (New York: Metropolitan Books, 2002), 272–3.

19. Prusin, *Borderland*, 30.

20. A. Iu. Bakhturina, *Okrainy Rossiiskoi imperii: gosudarstvennoe upravlenie i natsional'naia politika v gody pervoi mirovoi voiny (1914–1917 gg.)* (Moscow: Rosspen, 2004), 88–91, 93–4; Sobolev, *Bor'ba*, 18, 24–5; Eric Lohr, *Nationalizing the Russian Empire: The Campaign against Enemy Aliens during World War I* (Cambridge, Mass.: Harvard University Press, 2003), 96–7.

21. Lohr, *Empire*, 64; Ģērmanis, *Vācietis*, 64–5; Andreyeva, '"Ostzeiskii vopros"' (Ch. 1 n. 42 above), 28–31, 35; Bakhturina, *Okrainy*, 86–90, 99–101; Sobolev, *Bor'ba*, 25–6, 29–32, 77.

22. Bakhturina, *Okrainy*, 24; Prusin, *Borderland*, 29.

23. Bakhturina, *Politika*, 74–5; Sukiennicki, *Europe*, i. 97–8; V. N. Savchenko, 'Vostochnaia Galitsiia v 1914–1915 godakh (etnosotsial'nye osobennosti i problema prisoyedineniia k Rossii', *Voprosy istorii* 11–12 (1996), 99.

24. Ivan Petrovych, *Halychyna pid chas rosiis 'koi okupatsii, serpen' 1914–cherven' 1915* (L'viv: Politychna Biblioteka, 1915), 71–83, 104; Bakhturina, *Politika*, 66–7; Prusin, *Borderland*, 36.

25. Petrovych, *Halychyna*, 115; Zapolovs'kyi, *Bukovyna*, 44–5, 48–9.

26. Lohr, *Empire*, 96–7; Bakhturina, *Politika*, 64–6; Savchenko, 'Galitsiia', 103–4; 265–6.

27. Jacob Schall, *Żydostwo galicyjskie w czasie inwazji rosyjskiej w latach 1914–1916* (L'viv: nakładem Księgarni I. Madfesa, 1936), 9–10; Ansky, *Enemy*, 122–3; Ivan Bazhans'kyi, *Viina: shchodennyk–khronika bukovyns'koho pedahoha ta pys'mennyka/Vashkivtsi, 31.8.1914–12.1918/22* (Chernivtsi: Zelena Bukovyna, 2006), 99.

28. Joshua A. Sanborn, 'Unsettling the Empire: Violent Migrations and Social Disaster in Russia during World War I', *Journal of Modern History* 77 (2005), 307; Leidinger, 'Einzug', 242.

29. Mark Levene, *The Rise of the West and the Coming of Genocide* (London and New York: I. B. Tauris, 2005), 298–9; Goldin, 'Deportation', 42–3, 47–8; Bakhturina, *Politika*, 72.

30. Goldin, 'Deportation', 41ff., 52–4, 57; Gause, *Russen*, 236–46; Aba Strażas, 'Die Tätigkeit des Dezernats für Jüdische Angelegenheiten in der "Deutschen Militärverwaltung Ober Ost" ' in *Baltischen Provinzen*, 315–16.

31. Nelipovich, 'Repressii', 32–3; Bazhans'kyi, *Viina*, 57ff; Lohr, *Empire*, 97–8, 125, 129–33.

32. Lohr, *Empire*, 136; Luba Vital', ed., *Bezhanstva 1915 hoda* (Białystok: Prahram-naia rada tydnëvika 'Niva', 2000), 29, 32, 43, 63; Mariusz Korzeniowski, 'Polacy wobec Rosji i Rosjan w latach I wojny światowej', in Ryszard Kołod-ziejczyk, ed., *Społeczeństwo polskie w dobie pierwszej wojny światowej i wojny polsko–bolszewickiej 1920 roku* (Kielce: Kieleckie Towarzystwo Naukowe, 2001), 53.

33. Sukiennicki, *Europe*, i. 116–17; Gatrell, *Empire*, 21; Goldin, 'Deportation', 58; G. Z. Ioffe, 'Vyselenie evreev iz prifrontovoi polosy v 1915 godu', *Voprosy Istorii* 9 (2001), 85; Andreyeva, 'Ostzeiskii vopros', 32–3.

34. Lohr, *Empire*, 98–9; Friedrich Rink, 'Expulsion of the German Colonists from Wolhynia, 1915–1916', *Heritage Review* 25/1 (1995), 21; Bakhturina, *Politika*, 193–4.

35. Prusin, *Borderland*, 55; Eric Lohr, 'The Russian Army and the Jews: Mass Deportation, Hostages, and Violence during World War I', *Russian Review* 60 (2001) 406–7, 416; John Klier, 'Kazaki i pogromy: chem otlichalis' 'voennye' pogromy?', in O. V. Budnitskii et al., *Mirovoi krisis 1914–1920 godov i sud'ba vostochnoevropeiskogo evreistva* (Moscow: Rosspen, 2005), 60–1.

36. Goldin, 'Deportation', 55; Fuller, *Foe*, 178; Lohr, 'Army', 411.

37. Valentina Utgof, 'In Search of National Support: Belarussian Refugees in World War One and the People's Republic of Belarus', in Nick Baron and Peter Gatrell, eds., *Homelands: War, Population and Statehood in Eastern Europe and Russia, 1918–1924* (London: Anthem Press, 2004), 53; L. I. Lubny-Gertsyk, *Dvizhenie naseleniia na territorii SSSR za vremia mirovoi voiny i revolutsii* (Moscow: Izdatel'stvo Planovoe khoziaistvo, 1926), 23; Goldin, 'Deportation', 44.

38. Vakar, *Belorussia*, 96; Sukiennicki, *Europe*, i. 107–10; Gatrell, *Empire*, 158–62; Piotr Łossowski, *Konflikt polsko–litewski 1918–1920* (Warsaw: Wydawnictwo Książka i Wiedza, 1996), 18.

39. Józef Buszko, 'Dezintegrujące i integrujące czynniki w kształtowaniu polskiej tożsamości narodowej w latach 1914–1920', in *Społeczeństwo polskie*, 23–4; Rauch, *Baltic States*, 26; Ģērmanis, *Vācietis*, 63–4; T. Karjahärm, 'Popytki reform mestnogo upravleniia v Pribaltike v 1914–1916 gg.', in Chubar'yan et al., *Rossiia i Baltiia*, ii. 48–9, 53–4.

40. Peter Graf Kielmansegg, *Deutschland und der Erste Weltkrieg* (Frankfurt am Main: Akademische Verlagsgesellschaft Athenaion, 1968), 279–80, 288; Sukiennicki, *Europe*, i. 138–47; Vejas Gabriel Liulevicius, *War Land on the Eastern Front: Culture, National Identity and German Occupation in World War I* (Cambridge, Mass.: Cambridge University Press, 2000), 61–2.

41. Liulevicius, *War Land*, 22–3, 26–7, 39, 46–7.

42. Roshwald, *Nationalism*, 118–19.

43. Liulevicius, *War Land*, 64–8, 72–3, 181–2; A. Strazhas, *Deutsche Ostpolitik im Ersten Weltkrieg: Der Fall Ober Ost 1915–1917* (Wiesbaden: Harrassowitz Verlag, 1993), 29–30.

44. Robert Lewis Koehl, 'A Prelude to Hitler's Greater Germany', *American Historical Review* 59/1 (1953), 54; *Lietuvos Valstybės Istorijos Archivas* (LVIA), 641/1/53, pp. 97–9, 133–4. I am grateful to Jürgen Matthäus for this source. Also, Liulevicius, *War Land*, 70–1, 75, 105; Werner Basler, *Deutschlands Annexionspolitik in Polen und im Baltikum 1914–1918* (Berlin: Rütten & Loening, 1962), 282–3.

45. LVIA, 641/1/53, pp. 146–7; Jürgen Matthäus, 'German Judenpolitik in Lithuania during the First World War', *Leo Baeck Institute Yearbook* 43 (1998), 158; Liulevicius, *War Land*, 78–9, 93; Strazhas, *Ostpolitik*, 17–19, 36–7, 53–4, 215–19.

46. Hagen, *War*, 60.

47. Roshwald, *Nationalism*, 118–20; Vakar, *Belorussia*, 96–7; Utgof, 'Search', 54, 59.

48. Sukiennicki, *Europe*, i. 128–30, 148–9, 151–4; Vakar, *Belorussia*, 93–6; Zenowiusz Ponarski, 'Konferederacja Wielkiego Księstwa Litewskiego 1915–1916: pytania i odpowiedzi', manuscript, 10–12; Strazhas, *Ostpolitik*, 136; Zygmunt Jundziłł, 'Z dziejów polskiej myśli politycznej na Litwie historycznej', *Niepodległość* 6 (1958), 69.

49. Michael Garleff, 'Die Deutschbalten als nationale Minderheit in den unabhängigen Staaten Estland und Lettland', in Gert Pistohlkors, ed., *Baltische Länder* (Berlin: Siedler Verlag, 1994), 457.

50. Roshwald, *Nationalism*, 70.

51. Sukiennicki, *Europe*, i. 88–90; Snyder, *Reconstruction*, 58–9.

52. Oleh S. Fedyshyn, *Germany's Drive to the East and the Ukrainian Revolution, 1917–1918* (New Brunswick, NJ: Rutgers University Press, 1971), 15, 31–2; Włodzimierz Mędrzecki, *Niemiecka interwencja militarna na Ukrainie w 1918 roku* (Warsaw: Wydawnictwo DiG, 2000), 19; Zapolovs´kyi, *Bukovyna*, 38–40.

53. S. A. Makarchuk, *Ukrains´ka Respublika Halychan: narysy pro ZUNR* (L´viv: Svit, 1997), 26–40; Hagen, *War*, 59–63.

54. Leon Grossfeld, *Polityka państw centralnych wobec sprawy polskiej w latach pierwszej wojny światowej, 1914–1918* (Warsaw: Państwowe Wydawnictwo Naukowe, 1962), 187.

55. Roshwald, *Nationalism*, 122–4; Stražas, 'Tätigkeit', 317–18; Matthäus, 'Juden-politik', 164; Prusin, *Borderland*, 69–70.

56. Vakar, *Belorussia*, 96–7; Tomas Balkelis, 'In Search of a Native Realm: The Return of World War One Refugees to Lithuania, 1918–1924', in *Homelands*, 76–7; Stražas, *Ostpolitik*, 81–3, 159.

57. A. T. Bugayev et al., *Bor´ba trudiashchikhsia Volyni za Vlast' Sovetov (mart 1917 g.–dekarbr´ 1920 g.): sbornik dokumentov i materialov* (Zhytomyr: Zhitomirskoe oblastnoe izdatel´stvo, 1957), 22–5, 70.

58. A. V. Antosiak, 'Revolutsiia i kontrrevolutsiia v Bessarabii v 1917–1918 godakh', *Voprosy istorii* 12 (1988), 48–9; Hamm, 'Kishinev', 32.

59. Sukiennicki, *Europe*, 1. 307–8; Rauch, *Baltic States*, 27; Karl Aun, 'The 1917 Revolutions and the Idea of the State in Estonia', in *Baltischen Provinzen*, 289; Olavi Arens, 'The Estonian *Maapäev* during 1917', in Stanley V. Vardys, and Romuald J. Misiunas, eds., *The Baltic States in Peace and War, 1917–1945* (University Park: Pennsylvania State University Press, 1978) 20–1.

60. Kirsh, *Revolutsiia*, 73–4, 82; Rauch, *Baltic States, 33–4*, 36; Aun, 'Revolutions', 290–1; Arens, '*Maapäev*', 29–30.

61. Gatrell, *Empire*, 181–2; Ģērmanis, *Vācietis*, 147, 152, 164, 197; Aija Priedite, 'Latvian Refugees and the Latvian Nation State during and after World War One', in *Homelands*, 36–8.

CHAPTER 3

1. Norman Davies, *White Eagle, Red Star: The Polish–Soviet War, 1919–1920* (New York: St Martin's Press, 1972), 21.

2. Olavi Arens, 'Soviets in Estonia, 1917/18', in *Baltischen Provinzen* 313–14; I. I. Mints et al., *Bor´ba za Sovetskuiu vlast´ v Pribaltike* (Moscow: Nauka, 1967), 142–3, 174–5, 188; Rauch, *Baltic States*, 45, 59; Oskar Angelus, 'Die ersten bolschewistischen Deportationen aus Estland', *Baltische Hefte* 91 (1962), 2–13.

3. Parming, 'Population', 8; Andrew Ezergailis, 'The Causes of the Bolshevik Revolution in Latvia', in *Baltischen Provinzen*, 267–70; Rauch, *Baltic States*, 40, 42.

4. Sukiennicki, *Europe*, i. 171–2; Stražas, 'Tätigkeit', 318–19.

5. Liulevicius, *War Land*, 200–1; Strazhas, *Ostpolitik*, 223–5; Vakar, *Belorussia*, 101–2, 104–5; V. Sīpols, *Die ausländische Intervention in Lettland 1918–1920* (Berlin: Rütten & Loening, 1961), 28–30; Basler, *Annexionspolitik*, 244–5.

6. Sukiennicki, *Europe*, ii. 874; Adam B. Ulam, *Expansion and Coexistence: The History of Soviet Foreign Policy, 1917–1967* (New York and Washington: Frederick A. Praeger, 1968), 93.

7. Rauch, *Baltic States*, 50–1; Mints et al., *Bor′ba*, 215; Łossowski, *Konflikt*, 32–4.

8. National Archives and Records Administration (NARA), RG–256, M820, roll 503, vol. 477, frame 0029; Łossowski, *Konflikt*, 19.

9. NARA, RG–256, roll 508, vol. 482, frames 0240–1.

10. E. N. Shkliar, *Bor′ba trudiashchikhsia Litovsko–Belorusskoi SSR s inostrannymi interventami i vnutrenniei kontrrevolutsiyei (1919–1920 gg)* (Minsk: Gosudarstven-noe izdatel′stvo BSSR, 1962), 50–1, 70–1, 84–5, 92; A. Matsko, *Revolitsionnaia bor′ba trudiashchikhsia Pol′shi i Zapadnoi Belorussii protiv gneta burzhuazii i pomeshchikov, 1918–1939 gg.* (Minsk: Izdatel′stvo 'Belarus', 1972), 36; Parming, 'Population', 13–14.

11. Karsten Brűggemann, 'Defending National Sovereignty against Two Russias: Estonia in the Russian Civil War, 1918–1920', *Journal of Baltic Studies* 341 (2003), 25–6; Rauch, *Baltic States*, 50; Mints et al., *Bor′ba*, 225–6.

12. Robert G. L. Waite, *Vanguard of Nazism: The Free Corps Movement in Postwar Germany 1918–1923* (Cambridge, Mass.: Harvard University Press, 1952), 98–100, 104–5, 107–8; Sīpols, *Intervention*, 83; Mints, *Bor′ba*, 529–31.

13. Brűggemann, 'Sovereignty', 30–1; Waite, *Vanguard*, 112–14; Rauch, *Baltic States*, 61–2.

14. NARA, RG–256, M820, roll 503, vol. 477, frames 0221–2, 0246; Vasilii Gorn, *Grazhdanskaia voina na severo–zapade Rossii* (Berlin: Izdatel′stvo Gamaiun, 1923), 273–4.

15. Maciej Kozłowski, *Zapomniana wojna: walki o Lwów i Galicję Wschodnią, 1918–1919* (Bydgoszcz: Instytut Wydawniczy Świadectwo, 1999), 167.

16. Janusz Pajewski, *Budowa Drugiej Rzeczypospolitej, 1918–1926* (Krakow: nakładem Polskiej Akademii Umiejętności, 1995), 97.

17. Łossowski, *Konflikt*, 29–30, 35–8; Snyder, *Reconstruction*, 62; Karl–Heinz Ruffmann, 'Deutsche und litauische Memelpolitik in der Zwischenkriegszeit: ein Vergleich', *Nordost–Archiv* 2/2 (1993), 223.

18. K. Navitskas, *Litva i Antanta (1918–1920 gg.)* (Vilnius: Izdatel′stvo Mintis, 1970), 63; Łossowski, *Konflikt*, 46–8, 62–3, 67–8, 106; Snyder, *Reconstruction*, 62–3; Shkliar, *Bor′ba*, 126.

19. Vakar, *Byelorussia*, 110–11.

20. Margaret MacMillan, *Peacemakers: Six Months that Changed the World* (London: John Murray, 2002), 238.

21. Łossowski, *Konflikt*, 114–15, 121–3, 126–31, 155; Jürgen Pagel, 'Der polnisch–litauische Streit um Wilna und die Haltung der Sowjetunion, 1918–1938', *Jahrbücher für Geschichte Osteuropa* 40/1 (1992), 57.

22. Łossowski, *Konflikt*, 151, 179–90.

23. Mikhail Mel′tiukhov, *Osvoboditel′nyi pokhod Stalina: Bessarabskii vopros v sovetsko-rumynskikh otnosheniiakh (1917–1940 gg.* (Moscow: Iauza–Eksmo, 2006), 28; Antosiak, 'Revolutsiia', 52–3, 56–7; Hamm, 'Kishinev', 33.

24. Hausleitner, *Rumänisierung*, 90–2, 95–6, 98–100; Erich Prokopovych, *Kinets′ avstriis′koho panuvannia v Bukovyni* (Chernivtsi: Zoloti lytavry, 2004), 18, 39–40, 46; MacMillan, *Peacemakers*, 136–7; Mel′tiukhov, *Pokhod*, 71–3.

25. Mel′tiukhov, *Pokhod*, 79–80, 85–6, 92–3, 95–6; Lazarev, *Gosudarstvennost′*, 179–82.

26. Dov Levin, 'Jewish Autonomy in Inter-war Lithuania: An Interview with Yudl Mark', *Polin: Studies in Polish Jewry* 14 (2001), 197.

27. B. V. Malinovskii, 'Avstro–Vengriia i agrarnaia reforma v Ukrainie, 1918 r.', *Voprosy germanskoi istorii: sbornik nauchnykh trudov* (2003), 197; Bugayev, *Bor′ba trudiashchikhsia Volyni*, 96, 110–11, 125, 127–8, 136–7, 140; Piotr Wróbel, 'The Seeds of Violence: The Brutalization of an East European Region, 1917–1921', *Journal of Modern European History* 1 (2002), 133–4.

28. Wróbel, 'Seeds', 133–4; Mędrzecki, *Interwencja*, 241, 243.

29. Erich Köhrer, ed., *Das wahre Gesicht des Bolschewismus! Tatsachen—Berichte— Bilder aus den baltischen Provinzen, November 1918–Februar 1919* (Berlin: Verlag für Sozialwissenschaft, n.d.), 10–12, 18–19; Rauch, *Baltic States*, 59; George Popoff, *The Red Plague: Soviet Rule in a Baltic Town* (New York: E. P. Dutton & Co., 1932), 320–1.

30. Waite, *Vanguard*, 118–19; Mints, *Bor′ba*, 229–30, 435–6; Sīpols, *Intervention*, 65–6, 122–3; *Wspomnienia Rudolfa Hoessa, komendanta obozu Oświęcimskiego* (Warsaw: Wydawnictwo prawnicze, 1956), 38; Ernst Salomon, *The Outlaws* (London: Jonathan Cape, 1931), 131.

31. Shkliar, *Bor′ba*, 126; Stephen M. Horak, 'Belorussian and Ukrainian Peasants in Poland, 1919–1939: A Case Study in Peasantry under Foreign Rule', in Ivan Volgyes, ed., *The Peasantry of Eastern Europe* (New York: Pergamon Press, 1979), i. 137–8; Nina Zielińska, 'Postawy mieszkańców Wołynia w czasie wojny polsko–bolszewickiej (na podstawie raportów Towarzystwa Straży Kresowej)', in *Społeczeństwo polskie*, 275.

32. Witold Stankiewicz, *Konflikty społeczne na wsi polskiej, 1918–1920* (Warsaw: Państwowe Wydawnictwo Naukowe, 1963), 288–91, 303–07.

33. I. I. Kostiushko, ed., *Pol′sko–sovetskaia voina 1919–1920 gg. Ranee nie opubliko- vannye dokumenty i materialy* (Moscow: Izdatel′stvo Instituta slavianovedeniia i balkanistiki RAN, 1994), i. 165, 179; M. V. Filimoshin, 'Desiatkami strelial liudei tol′ko za to, chto... vygliadeli kak bol′sheviki', *Voenno–Istoricheskii Zhurnal* 2 (2001), 45–7.

34. Kozłowski, *Wojna*, 200–5, 225; Wróbel, 'Seeds', 138.

35. Kozłowski, *Wojna*, 206–8; Michał Adamczyk, 'Zachodnioukraińska Republika Ludowa, 1918–1919', in Zygmunt Mańkowski, ed., *Niepodlegść Polski w 1918 roku a procesy państwowotwórcze w Europie środkowo–wshodniej* (Lublin: wydawnictwo Uniwersytetu Marii Curie–Skłodowskiej, 1996), 193–4.

36. HI, 'A. N. Krupenskii', box 2, ii. 5–6; Mel´tiukhov, *Pokhod*, 50–1, 55–7, 73–5, 79–80; Lazarev, *Gosudarstvennost'*, 172–5, 254.

37. Levin, 'Autonomy', 207; Prusin, *Borderland*, 97–100.

38. Prusin, *Borderland*, 141–59; Jerzy Tomaszewski, 'Lwów, 22 listopada 1918 roku', *Przegląd Historyczny* 75/2 (1984), 284.

39. Alexander V. Prusin, 'The "Stimulus Qualities" of a Scapegoat: The Etiology of Anti-Jewish Violence in Eastern Poland, 1918–1920', *Simon Dubnow Institute Yearbook* 4 (2005), 237–56.

40. Pajewski, *Budowa*, 175–80; Prusin, *Borderland*, 111.

41. Andrei Pushkash, *Tsivilizatsiia ili varvarstvo: Zakarpat´ye 1918–1945* (Moscow: Izdatel´stvo Evropa, 2006), 29, 31–2; Magosci, *Identity*, 86–7.

42. Mykhailo Boldyzhar, *Zakarpattia mizh svitovymy viinamy: fakty, podii, liudy, otsinky* (Uzhhorod, 2001), 14–22, 24–5, 33–6; Magosci, *Identity*, 84–5, 88–95.

43. Nick Baron and Peter Gatrell, 'Introduction', in *Homelands*, 3.

44. Rauch, *Baltic States*, 81; Kopchak, 'O strukturnykh izmeneniiakh', 67; Kirsh, *Revolutsiia*, 64–5.

CHAPTER 4

1. Rothschild, *Europe*, 4.

2. Vakar, *Byelorussia*, 115–16; Nina Stużinska, 'Białoruski ruch antybolszewicki (1917–1925)', in Małgorzata Giżejewska and Tomasz Strzembosz, eds., *Społeczeństwo białoruskie, litewskie i polskie na ziemiach północno–wschodnich II Rzeczypospolitej (Białoruś zachodnia i Litwa wschodnia) w latach 1939–1941* (Warsaw: Instytut Studiów Politycznej Polskiej Akademii Nauk, 1995), 363.

3. Tsentral´nyi derzhavnyi arkhiv hromads´kykh orhanizatsii Ukrainy (TsDAHOU), 57/2/337b, pp. 108–30; 6/1/323; 1/20/428, pp. 3–4; Alexander J. Motyl, 'The Rural Origins of the Communist and Nationalist Movements in Wołyń Województwo, 1921–1939', *Slavic Review* 37 (1978), 415; Aleksandra Bergman, *Sprawy białoruskie w II Rzeczypospolitej* (Warsaw: Państwowe Wydawnictwo Naukowe, 1984), 25.

4. V. G. Lysenko, 'Utvorennia i rozvytok Moldavs´koi ASSR u skladi USSR (1920–1940)', *Ukrains´kyi Istorychnyi Zhurnal* 9 (1974), 47–8, 51; Mel´tiukhov, *Pokhod*, 113–14; Rauch, *Baltic States*, 111–14.

5. V. Stanley Vardys, 'The Rise of Authoritarian Rule in the Baltic States', in *Baltic States in Peace and War*, 67–9; Manfred Hellmann, 'Der Staatsstreich von 1926 in Litauen: Verlauf und Hintergrűnde', *Jahrbűcher fűr Geschichte Osteuropas* 28/2 (1980), 221–2, 224, 226, 234–5.

6. Werner Benecke, *Die Ostgebiete der Zweiten Polnischen Republik: Staatsmacht und öffentliche Ordnung in einer Minderheitenregion 1918–1939* (Cologne and Weimar: Böhlau, 1999), 34, 44–8, 53.

7. Rauch, *Baltic States*, 99–100.

8. Instytut Polski i Muzeum im. generała Sikorskiego (IMPS), file 'MSZ', syg. A.12.P8/1, pp. 76–7; Isabel Rőskau–Rydel, 'Polnisch–litauische Beziehungen zwischen 1918 und 1939', *Jahrbűcher fűr Geschichte Osteuropas* 35/4 (1987), 564–5; Pagel, 'Streit', 41–2.

9. Ruffmann, 'Memelpolitik', 222.

10. Alfred E. Senn, 'Die Besetzung Memels in Januar 1923', *Forschungen zur Osteuropäischen Geschichte* 10 (1965), 335–43, 351–2; Ruffmann, 'Memelpolitik', 220–1, 223–4, 227–8; Pagel, 'Streit', 58.

11. Rauch, *Baltic States*, 237.

12. Ibid. 135–41.

13. Tönu Parming, 'The Jewish Community and Inter–Ethnic Relations in Estonia, 1918–1940', *Journal of Baltic Studies* 10/3 (1979), 246, 251–2; Ezra Mendelsohn, *The Jews of East Central Europe between the World Wars* (Bloomington: Indiana University Press, 1983), 247; Zofia Waszkiewicz, 'Żydzi łotewscy', in Zenon Hubert Nowak and Zbiegniew Karpus, eds., *Studia i szkice z dziejów Żydów w regionie Bałtyku* (Toruń: wydawnictwo Uniwersytetu Mikołaja Kopernika, 1998), 141–2.

14. Parming, 'Community', 242–3, 251, 256; Waszkiewicz, 'Żydzi', 141; Mendelsohn, *Jews*, 217–18, 244.

15. Ruffmann, 'Memelpolitik', 227–8; Senn, 'Besetzung', 351–2; Ernst–Albrecht Plieg, *Das Memelland 1920–1939: deutsche Autonomiebestrebungen im litauischen Gesamtstaat* (Wűrzburg: Holzer Verlag, 1962), 27–8, 35, 52–3.

16. MacMillan, *Peacemakers*, 236.

17. Studium Polski Podziemnej (SPP), ms. B.II.633, Maurycy Szeptycki, 'Kwestia ukraińska i polska myśl polityczna, 1939–1944', lists 1–3; Gabriele Simoncini, 'The Polyethnic State: National Minorities in Interbellum Poland', *Nationalities Papers* 22, supplement 1 (1994), 8; Snyder, *Reconstruction*, 65.

18. John–Paul Himka, 'Western Ukraine in the Interwar Period', *Nationalities Papers* 20/2 (1994), 348–49.

19. Siergiej A. Jackiewicz, 'Oświata narodowa na Białorusi Zachodniej w latach 1939–1941', in *Społeczeństwo białoruskie*, 161; Benecke, *Ostgebiete*, 16–18, 21–2; Simoncini, 'State', 13.

20. Mykhailo Shvahuliak, 'Patsyfikatsiia': pol´s´ka represyvna aktsiia u Halychyni 1930 r. i ukrains´ka suspil´nist' (L´viv: Akademiia Nauk Ukrainy—Instytut Ukrainoznavstva, 1993), 8.

21. Siargej Tokc´, 'Barac´ba za belaruskuju dziarzhaunasc´ na absharach Garadzenskaj (Bershtauskaj) pushchy u 1920–kh gadakh', *Belaruski gistarychny zbornik* 15 (2001), 136–7; S. A. Vaupshasov, *Na trevozhnykh perekrestkakh: zapiski chekista* (Moscow: Izdatel´stvo politicheskoi literatury, 1974), 108–9, 112–17, 136–9.

22. Vakar, *Belorussia*, 125–7; Tokc', 'Barac'ba', 138–9; Motyl, 'Origins' (n. 3 above), 412–20; Himka, 'Ukraine', 357–8.

23. Himka, 'Ukraine', 354–55; Irina Livezeanu, *Cultural Politics in Greater Romania: Regionalism, Nation Building, and Ethnic Struggle, 1918–1930* (Ithaca, NY: Cornell University Press, 1995), 64–5, 66, 70–2, 77, 99, 109–10, 116–17; Hausleitner, *Rumänisierung*, 139–42, 149, 160–3, 178; David Sha'ari, 'The Jewish Community of Cernăuți between the Two World Wars', *Shvut: Studies in Russian and East European Jewish History and Culture* 7/23 (1998), 112–13.

24. MacMillan, *Peacemakers*, 241, 245.

25. Magocsi, *Ukraine*, 603–7; Magosci, *Identity*, 209; Himka, 'Ukraine', 354–5.

26. O. H. Mykhailiuk, ed., *Istoriia Volyni z naidavnishykh chasiv do nashykh dniv* (L'viv: Vyshcha shkola, 1988), 89–90; Lazarev, *Gosudarstvennost'*, 284, 286–7, 323, 335.

27. Kirsh, *Revolutsiia*, 100; Berend, *Crisis*, 226; Zbigniew Landau and Jerzy Tomaszewski, *W dobie inflacji* (Warsaw: Książka i Wiedza, 1967), 101–3, 279–80, 320.

28. Rauch, *Baltic States*, 80, 89; Landau and Tomaszewski, *W dobie*, 47, 54, 147–9; Vakar, *Belorussia*, 119; Mykhailiuk, *Istoriia Volyni*, 89–90; Rothschild, *Europe*, 15.

29. Rauch, *Baltic States*, 124–7; Aldcroft, *World*, 97–8.

30. Rauch, *Baltic States*, 88–91; Aldcroft, *World*, 96–7, 101; Kirsh, *Revolutsiia*, 109–10, 114–16, 127.

31. Landau, *W dobie*, 164–7; Motyl, 'Origins', 417; Mykhailiuk, *Istoriia Volyni*, 91; Vakar, *Belorussia*, 132; Jan Zaprudnik, *Belarus: At a Crossroads in History* (Boulder, Colo.: Westview Press, 1993), 83.

32. Lazarev, *Gosudarstvennost'*, 252–53, 286; HI, 'A. N. Krupenskii', box 2, MS 'Dva mesiatsa v Bessarabii', 4; Hausleitner, *Rumänisierung*, 151, 157–8.

33. Levin, 'Autonomy', 193–4, 203–4, 206–8; Waszkiewicz, 'Żydzi', 139–40, 144–5.

34. Schiper, *Dzieje*, 593. Ignacy Schiper, *Dzieje handlu żydowskiego na ziemiach polskich* (Warsaw: nakładem Centrali Związków Kupców, 1937), 593.

35. Magocsi, *Ukraine*, 605; Himka, 'Ukraine', 363 ff.; Pushkash, *Tsivilizatsiia*, 86–9.

36. Rauch, *Baltic States*, 123–7; Lazarev, *Gosudarstvennost'*, 286–7; Mykhailiuk, *Istoriia Volyni*, 89–91; Matsko, *Bor'ba*, 195–202; I. V. Poluian, *Zapadnaia Belorussiia v period ekonomicheskogo krizisa 1929–1933 gg.* (Minsk: Navuka i tekhnika, 1991), 58–9.

37. Rauch, *Baltic States*, 124–6, 148, 160–1; Aldcroft, *World*, 103.

38. Vardys, 'Rise', (n. 5 above) 73–6; Piotr Łossowski, 'Rządy dyktatorskie w państwach bałtyckich, 1926–1934–1940: studium porównawcze', *Studia na faszyzmem i zbrodniami hitlerowskimi* 8 (1982), 14–15.

39. Rauch, *Baltic States*, 157; V. Sherstobitov et al., *Istoriia natsional'no-gosudarstvennogo stroitel'stva v SSSR, 1917–1978* (Moscow: Mysl', 1979), ii. 49; Łossowski, 'Rządy', 14–17; Vardys, 'Rule', 75–8.

40. Mykhailiuk, *Istoriia Volyni*, 100–2; Matsko, *Bor'ba*, 203, 228–9; Vakar, *Belorussia*, 127–8; Poluian, *Belorussiia*, 91–3, 110–11.

41. Frank Golczewski, 'Die Kollaboration in der Ukraine', in Christoph Dieck-mann, Babette Quinkert, and Tatjana Tönsmeyer, eds., *Kooperation und Ver-brechen: Formen der 'Kollaboration' im östlichen Europa 1939–1945* (Göttingen: Wallstein Verlag, 2003), 152–3.

42. Benedykt Heydenkorn, 'Ukraińska polemika o Berezie Kartuzskiej', *Zeszyty Historyczne* 62 (1982), 206–8; V.N., 'Ukraińskie wspomnienia z Berezy', *Kultura* 9/12 (1955), 78–81, 82–4.

43. Roman Dąbrowski, 'Die social–wirtschaftliche Tätigkeit der litauischen Minderheit in der Zweiten Republik (1918–1939)', *Studia Historiae Oeconomicae* 21 (1994), 105–6; Vakar, *Belorussia*, 130–1; Zaprudnik, *Belarus*, 85–6.

44. Roman Wapiński, 'Kształtowanie się w Polsce w latach 1922–1939 poglądów na ruchy faszystowskie w Europie,' *Studia nad faszyzmem i zbrodniami hitlerows-kimi* 9 (1985), 95, 98; Alexander J. Motyl, *The Turn to the Right: The Ideological Origins and Development of Ukrainian Nationalism 1919–1929* (New York: Columbia University Press, 1980), 68–72.

45. Tadeusz Dumin, 'Nacjonalizm i antysemityzm w programie Obozu Naro-dowo–Radykalnego', *Studia na faszyzmem i zbrodniami hitlerowskimi* 3 (1977), 338–9, 343–8; Szymon Rudnicki, *Obóz Narodowo Radykalny: geneza i działal-ność* (Warsaw: Czytelnik, 1985), 180–2, 223–4, 285–6, 299, 303–5, 313–16; Michał Musielak, 'Narodowy socjalizm w myśli sanacyjnej', *Studia na faszyz-mem i zbrodniami hitlerowskimi* 20 (1997), 29, 35.

46. Maksym Gon, *Iz kryvdoiu na samoti: ukrains' ko-yevreis' ki vzayemyny na zakhid-noukrains' kykh zemliakh u skladi Pol' shchi (1935–1939)* (Rivne: Volyns' ki ober-ehy, 2005), 97–103.

47. Solomonas Atamukas, 'The Hard Long Road toward the Truth: On the Sixtieth Anniversary of the Holocaust in Lithuania', *Lituanus* 47/4 (2001), 19–21.

48. Wojciech Śleczyński, *Zajścia antyżydowskie w Brześciu nad Bugiem 13 maja 1937 roku* (Białystok: Archiwum Państwowe w Białymstoku, 2004), 14–15, 20; Jolanta Żyndul, 'Zajścia antyżydowskie w Polsce w latach 1935–1937— geografia i formy', *Biuletyn Żydowskiego Instytutu Historycznego* 159 (1991), 59, 61–3, 70; Gon, *Iz kryvdoiu*, 71, 77–9.

49. Quoted in Livezeanu, *Politics*, 12.

50. Sha'ari, 'Cernăuţi', 111, 139; Livezeanu, *Politics*, 79–87, 124–5, 291; Hausleit-ner, *Rumänisierung*, 209–11, 295.

51. Aharon Weiss, 'Some Economic and Social Problems of the Jews of Eastern Galicia in the Period of Soviet Rule (1939–1941)', in Norman Davies and Antony Polonsky, eds., *Jews in Eastern Poland and the USSR, 1939–1946* (New York: St Martin's Press, 1991), 80.

52. Rauch, *Baltic States*, 181–5; Edgar Anderson, 'The Baltic Entente: Phantom or Reality?' in *Baltic States in Peace and War*, 127–9.

53. Rauch, *Baltic States*, 191, 194; Alexander Dallin, 'The Baltic States between Nazi Germany and Soviet Russia', in Vardys and Misiunas, *Baltic States in Peace and War*, 99.

54. Marian Zgórniak, 'Polskie ultimatum do Litwy w 1938 roku', *Annales Universitatis Mariae Curie–Skłodowska* 14 (1996), 163–5, 169–70; Pagel, 'Streit', 55–6, 72–5; Dallin, 'Baltic States', 100, 102–3.

55. Magosci, *Identity*, 237–9; Boldyzhar, *Zakarpattia*, 42–3.

56. Boldyzhar, *Zakarpattia*, 46–49, 55–8; Oleksandr Baran, 'Uhors'ka administratsiia na okupovanomu Zakarpatti (1939–1944)', *Ukrains'kyi istoryk* 35/1–4 (1998), 172–3; Magosci, *Identity*, 239–49.

57. Zaprudnik, *Belarus*, 89.

58. In Dallin, 'Baltic States', 107.

59. Samuel P. Huntington, *Political Order in Changing Societies* (New Haven: Yale University Press, 1968), 4.

CHAPTER 5

1. Quoted in Vakar, *Belorussia*, 169.

2. Mirosław Sycz, 'Pierwsze dni II wojny światowej na Kresach Wschodnich RP', *Dzieje Najnowsze* 26/1 (1994), 121–5; Ryszard Torzecki, *Polacy i ukraińcy: sprawa ukraińska w czasie II wojny światowej na terenie II Rzeczy Pospolitej* (Warsaw: Wydawnictwo Naukowe PWN, 1993), 26.

3. Michał Gnatowski, 'Radziecka polityka okupacyjna na Białostocczyźnie w latach 1939–1941: Zarys tematu i problemy badawcze', in *Społeczeństwo białoruskie*, 108; Jan T. Gross, *Revolution from Abroad: The Soviet Conquest of Poland's Western Ukraine and Western Belorussia* (Princeton: Princeton University Press, 1988), 18–21.

4. Wiktor Krzysztof Cygan, *Kresy w ogniu: wojna polsko–sowiecka 1939* (Warsaw: Warszawska Oficyna Wydawnicza, 1990), 42–3; Marek Wierzbicki, 'Stosunki polsko–żydowskie na Zachodniej Białorusi w latach 1939–1941', in Paweł Machcewicz and Krzysztof Persak, eds., *Wokół Jedwabnego* (Warsaw: Instytut Pamięci Narodowej–Komisja Ścigania Zbrodni Przeciwko Narodowi Polskiemu, 2002), i. 137.

5. *Archiwum Akt Nowych* (AAN), file 'Delegatura Rządu na Kraj,' syg. 202/III–134, lists 9–11; Grzegorz Motyka, 'Postawy wobec konfliktu polsko–ukraińskiego w latach 1939–1953 w zależności etnicznej, państwowej i religijnej', in Krzysztof Jasiewicz, ed., *Tygiel narodów: stosunki społeczne i etniczne na dawnych ziemiach wschodnich Rzeczypospolitej, 1939–1953* (Warsaw: ISP PAN, 2002), 286.

6. Marek Wierzbicki, 'Niektóre aspekty stosunków polsko–białoruskich w czasie pierwszych miesięcy okupacji sowieckiej (1939–1940)', in *Społeczeństwo polskie*, 239–40; S. G. Filipov, 'Deiatel'nost' organov VKP(b) v zapadnykh oblastiakh Ukrainy i Belorussii v 1939–1941 gg.', in L. S. Eremina et al., *Repressii protiv*

polakov i pol'skikh grazhdan (Moscow: Zven'ia, 1997), 49; Gross, *Revolution*, 35–45.

7. Stanisław Ciesielski, Grzegorz Hryciuk, and Aleksander Srebrakowski, *Masowe deportacje radzieckie w okresie II wojny światowej* (Wrocław: Instytut Historyczny Uniwersytetu Wrocławskiego, Wrocławskie Towarzystwo Miłośników Historii, 1994), 34 ff; Shmuel Spector, *The Holocaust of Volhynian Jews, 1941–1944* (Jerusalem: Yad Vashem, 1990), 23 ff.

8. Sofia Gracheva, ed., 'Shchodennyk Viktora Petrykevycha (1883–1956)— Stanislaviv 1939–40, Buchach 1941–1944, Drohobych 1944, Kolomyja 1944–1956', electronic version.

9. Gross, *Revolution*, 20–1, 24; Ryszard Torzecki, 'Die Rolle der Zusammenarbeit mit der deutschen Bezatsungsmacht in der Ukraine für deren Okkupationspolitik 1941–1944', in Werner Röhr, ed., *Okkupation und Kollaboration (1938–1945). Beiträge zu Konzepten und Praxis der Kollaboration in der deutschen Okkupationspolitik* (Berlin: Hüthig Verlagsgemeinschaft, 1994), 241.

10. IPMS, file 'PRM', syg. 9, pp. 11, 15, 74.

11. Ibid., syg. 9, pp. 7, 9, 17–19, 78–9; file 'MSW', syg. A.9.V/3, p. 9; SPP, file A6–4.7, pp. 1–2, 4–6; Liekis Sarunas, 'The Transfer of Vilna District into Lithuania, 1939', *Polin* 14 (2001), 213, 216, 221; Mieczysław Krzepkowski, 'Wspomnienia dzienikarza z czasów okupacji (Wilno 1939–1941)', *Zeszyty Historyczne* 45 (1978), 158–9, 162; Stanisława Lewandowska, *Życie codzienne Wilna w latach II wojny światowej* (Warsaw: Neriton, 1997), 28–9, 32, 73–4.

12. Amir Weiner, 'Introduction: Landscaping the Human Garden', in Amir Weiner, ed., *Landscaping the Human Garden: Twentieth–Century Population Management in a Comparative Framework* (Stanford, Calif.: Stanford University Press, 2003), 11.

13. A. D. Pedosov et al., *Postroenie sotsializma v Sovetskoi Pribaltike: istoricheskii opyt kompartii Litvy, Latvii, Estonii* (Riga: Avots, 1982), 162.

14. David R. Marples, *Stalinism in Ukraine in the 1940s* (New York: St Martin's Press, 1992), 26.

15. Filipov, 'Deiatel'nost', 67; Czesław Grzelak, 'Działania Armii Czerwonej na Białorusi we wrześniu 1939 roku', in *Społeczeństwo białoruskie*, 114 ff.; Oksana W. Pietrowska, 'Polityka w dziedzinie oświaty i kultury na obrzarze Polesia Brzeskiego w latach 1939–1941', ibid. 174; O. S. Rubliov and Iu.A. Cherchenko, *Stalinshchyna i dolia zakhidnoukrains'koi intelihentsii, 20–50–ti roky XX st.* (Kiev: Naukova Dumka, 1994), 194–5.

16. Włodzimierz Bonusiak, 'Przemiany ekonomiczne w Małopolsce Wschodniej w latach 1939–1941', in Piotr Chmielowiec, ed., *Okupacja sowiecka ziem polskich 1939–1941* (Warsaw and Rzeszów: Instytut Pamięci Narodowej—Komisja Ścigania Zbrodni przeciwko Narodowi Polskiemu, 2005), 94–5; V. Stanley Vardys, 'The Baltic States under Stalin: The First Experiences, 1940–1941', in Keith Sword, ed., *The Soviet Takeover of the Polish Eastern Provinces, 1939–1941* (New York: St Martin's Press, 1991), 282.

17. V. I. Pasat, ed., *Trudnye stranitsy istorii Moldovy, 1940–1950–e gody* (Moscow: 'Terra', 1995), 10–11.

18. Marples, *Stalinism*, 28–32.

19. Bonusiak, 'Przemiany', 102–3; Gross, *Revolution*, 64–6; David R. Marples, 'The Ukrainians in Eastern Poland under Soviet Occupation, 1939–1941: A Study in Soviet Rural Policy', in Sword, *Takeover*, 247; Filipov, 'Deiatel'nost', 63–5.

20. Pasat, *Stranitsy*, 229; Lysenko, 'Utvorennia', 54; Lazarev, *Gosudarstvennost*, 674.

21. *Postroenie Sotzializma*, 215–19, 285–6.

22. V.M. Danylenko, "Likvidatsiia pol'skoi derzhavy ta vstanovlennia radians' koho rezhymu v Zakhidnii Ukraini," *Ukrains'kyi Istorychnyi Zhurnal* 3/468 (2006), 114–116, 118–119, 121; Vassyl Cholodnytckyj and Sergij Osatchuk, "Zur Geschichte der Umsiedlung und Deportation der Bevölkerung der Nordbukowina in den Jahren 1940/1941," in Cécile Cordon und Helmut Kusdat, eds., *An der Zeiten Ränder. Czernowitz und die Bukowina: Geschichte, Literatur, Verfolgung, Exil* (Vienna: Theodor Kramer Gesellschaft, 2002), 182; Grzegorz Gryciuk, "Przemiany demograficzne w Galicji Wschodniej w latach 1939–1941," in *Okupacja sowiecka*, 118–119.

23. T. S. Ilarionova, 'Obmen naseleniem mezhdu SSSR i Germaniei nakanune i v nachale vtoroi mirovoi voiny', *Otechestvennaia istoriia* 4 (2004), 56–8.

24. Pasat, *Stranitsy*, 71, 123–5, 131; Lazarev, *Gosudarstvennost'*, 795–7; Cholodnytckyj, 'Umsiedlung', 174, 178–9; Gryciuk, 'Przemiany', 115–18.

25. Danylenko, 'Likvidatsiia' 114–16, 118–19, 121; Cholodnytckyj 182; Gryciuk, 'Przemiany' 118–19.

26. Mykhailiuk, *Istoriia Volyni*, 102, 107; Vardys, 'Rise' (Ch. 4 n. 5 above) 67; Krzysztof Jasiewicz, *Pierwsi po diable. Elity sowieckie w okupowanej Polsce 1939–1941 (Białostocczyzna, Nowogródczyzna, Polesie, Wileńszczyzna)* (Warsaw: Instytut Studiów Politycznych PAN and Oficyna Wydawnicza Rytm, 2002), 1151.

27. Pedosov, *Postroenie sotzializma*, 50, 52–3, 58–9; Grzelak, 'Działania', 110.

28. Bogdan Czaykowski, 'Soviet Policies in the Literary Sphere: Their Effects and Implications', in Sword, *Takeover*, 107–8; Mieczysław Inglot, 'The Socio-Political Role of the Polish Literary Tradition in the Cultural Life of Lwów: The Example of Adam Mickiewicz's Work', ibid. 133–7.

29. Vakar, *Belorussia*, 125.

30. HI, 'Reports of Polish Deportees', box 209, interviews 7317, 1339; box 217, interviews 8870, 9876; IPMS, 'MSW', syg. A.9.III.2a/19, lists 5–7, 9–10, 70.

31. Jasiewicz, *Pierwsi*, 1205, 1208–10, 1215; HI, 'Reports of Polish Deportees', box 230, interviews 1108, 11059, 3375.

32. IPMS, 'PRM', syg. 9, pp. 16, 36, 45, 58, 89; File, 'MSW', syg. A.9.V/3, lists 8–9; Lewandowska, Życie, 209–10.

33. Pedosov, Postroenie sotzializma, 164–5.

34. Ibid., 62–3; Michael MacQueen, 'The Context of Mass Destruction: Agents and Prerequisites of the Holocaust in Lithuania', Holocaust and Genocide Studies 12/1 (1998), 33; Anton Weiss–Wendt, Murder without Hatred: The Estonians and the Holocaust (Syracuse, NY: Syracuse University Press, 2009), 53; Wierzbicki, 'Stosunki polsko–żydowskie' (n. 4 above) i. 141–2.

35. Machcewicz and Persak, Wokół Jedwabnego, ii. 133.

36. Harry Gordon, The Shadow of Death: The Holocaust in Lithuania (Lexington: University Press of Kentucky, 1992), 11; Yad Vashem Archive (YVA), file 03/2468, p. 4.

37. HI, 'Reports of Polish Deportees', box 230, interview 3526, 4755, 10274, 3728, 10179, 10842, 5550; Machcewicz and Persak, Wokół Jedwabnego, ii. 96–7, 99–100, 109–11; Jasiewicz, Pierwsi, 102–3.

38. Machcewicz and Persak, Wokół Jedwabnego, ii. 127–8.

39. Peter Holquist, 'State Violence as Technique: The Logic of Violence in Soviet Totalitarianism', in Weiner, Landscaping, 19–45; Pasat, Stranitsy, 12.

40. Danylenko 'Likvidatsiia', 123.

41. Ihor Iljuszyn and Grzegorz Mazur, 'Utworzenie i działalność czekistowskich grup operacyjnych NKWD w zachodnich obwodach Ukrainy w latach 1939–1940 (na podstawie materiałów Państwowego Archiwum Służby Bezpieczeństwa Ukrainy)', Zeszyty Historyczne 135 (2001), 49–52, 58, 60–4; Grzelak, 'Działania', 74.

42. Snyder, Reconstruction, 80–1.

43. Rauch, Baltic States, 226; Ciesielski, Deportacje, 165–6; Rubliov, Stalinshchyna, 188–9.

44. O. A. Gorlanov and A. B. Roginskii, 'Ob arestakh v zapadnykh oblastiakh Belorussii i Ukrainy v 1939–1941 gg.', in Eremini, Repressii, 88.

45. Iljuszyn and Mazur, 'Utworzenie', 67–70; Albin Głowacki, 'Organizacja i funkcjonowanie więziennictwa NKWD na Kresach Wschodnich II Rzeczypospolitej w latach 1939–1941', in Janina Mikoda, ed., Zbrodnicza ewakuacja więzień i aresztów NKWD na Kresach Wschodnich II Rzeczypospolitej w czerwcu–lipcu 1941 roku (Warsaw: Główna Komisja Badania Zbrodni przeciwko Narodowi Polskiemu, 1997), 21; Gross, Revolution, 164–8, 172–3.

46. Głowacki, 'Organizacja', 23–7, 30; Sławomir Kowalczyk, 'Ewakuacja więzienia w Berezweczu w 1941 r. jako przykład zbrodniczej działalności sowieckiego aparatu terroru', in Mikoda, Zbrodnicza ewakuacja, 85–6; Waldemar Monkiewicz, 'Czerwiec 1941 roku na Białostocczźnie i Polesiu', ibid. 106.

47. Aleksander Chackiewicz, 'Aresztowania i deportacje społeczeństwa zachodnich obwodów Białorusi (1939–1941)', in Giżejewska and Strzembosz, *Społeczeństwo białoruskie*, 121; Pasat, *Stranitsy*, 147; Ciesielski et al., *Deportacje*, 68, 167; Magosci, *Identity*, 252.

48. Ciesielski, *Deportacje*, 66; Pasat, *Stranitsy*, 147, 159–60, 167; Chackiewicz, 'Aresztowania i deportacje' 135; Vakar, *Belorussia*, 160; Gross, *Revolution*, 216.

49. Ludwik Karakulko, 'Więzienia i lagry', in Lucja Jakubowska et al, *Nieświeskie wspomnienia* (Warsaw: Łośgraf, 2001), 261; Ciesielski, *Deportacje*, 35–6; N. F. Bugai, *Narody Ukrainy v 'Osoboi papke Stalina'* (Moscow: Nauka, 2006), 73.

50. Pitirim A. Sorokin, *Man and Society in Calamity: The Effects of War, Revolution, Famine, and Pestilence upon Human Mind, Behavior, Social Organization and Cultural Life* (New York: E. P. Dutton, 1943), 230.

51. Ciesielski, *Deportacje*, 37, 165–6, 186; Vakar, *Belorussia*, 165; Zaprudnik, *Belarus*, 91.

52. Głowacki, 'Organizacja', 19; Leo Lowenthal, 'Terror's Atomization of Man', *Commentary* 1/3 (1946), 2–3.

53. Pasat, *Stranitsy*, 25–6.

54. HI, 'Reports of Polish Deportees', box 209, interview 5310, 3817; Zbigniew K. Wójcik, 'Okupacja i konspiracja w rejonie przemyskim (1939–1941). Studium porównawcze', in *Okupacja sowiecka*, 63.

55. Gross, *Revolution*, 146; Leon Weliczker Wells, *The Janowska Road* (New York: Macmillan, 1963), 28–9; Jan Malanowski, 'Sociological Aspects of the Annexation of Poland's Eastern Provinces to the USSR in 1939–1941', in Sword, *Takeover*, 78.

56. IPMS, File, 'MSW', syg. A.9.III 1/1, list 184; Malanowski, 'Aspects', 72–6.

57. Mykhailiuk, *Istoriia Volyni*, 110, 114; Siegfried Gasparaitis, ' "Verrätern wird nur dann vergeben, wenn sie wirklich beweisen, dass sie mindestens einen Juden liquidiert haben": die 'Front Litauischer Aktivisten' (LAF) und die antisowjetischen Aufstände 1941', *Zeitschrift für Geschichtswissenschaft* 49/10 (2001), 889–90; A. Vitkovskii and V. Iampol'skii, eds., 'Vchera eto bylo sekretom (dokumenty o litovskikh sobytiiakh 40–50–kh gg.', *Izvestiia TsK KPSS*, 10 (1990), 131–2, 134.

58. Mykhailiuk, *Istoriia Volyni*, 110, 114; vitkovskii, "Vchera", 134.

59. Ilarionova, 'Obmen', 58; Gross, *Revolution*, 226–9; Rafal Wnuk, 'Polska konspiracja antysowiecka na Kresach Wschodnich II RP w latach 1939–1941 i 1944–1952', in *Tygiel*, 176–9.

60. Gross, *Revolution*, 230–1.

61. Ibid. 234–5.

62. Russell G. Geen, *Personality: The Skein of Behavior* (St Louis: C. V. Mosby Company, 1976), 73–4.

CHAPTER 6

1. Jan T. Gross, *Neighbors: The Destruction of the Jewish Community in Jedwabne, Poland* (New York: Penguin Books, 2001).

2. Piotr Chmielowiec, 'Ostatnie tygodnie sowieckiej okupacji Przemyśla (maj–czerwiec 1941 r.)', in, *Okupacja sowiecka*, 231–2; Gross, *Revolution*, 179–81; Weiss–Wendt, *Murder*, 42.

3. Krzysztof Popiński, 'Ewakuacja więzień kresowych w czerwcu 1941 r. na podstawie dokumentacji 'Memoriału' i Archiwum Wschodniego', in Mikoda, *Zbrodnicza ewakuacja*, 75–7; Sławomir Abramowicz, 'Więzienia NKWD w Dubnie i Łucku w czerwcu 1941 r.', ibid. 115–20.

4. Tadeusz Tomaszewski, *Lwów 1940–1944: Pejzaż psychologiczny* (Warsaw: UNI–DRUK, 1996), 62–3; Bogdan Musial, '*Kontrrevolutionäre Elemente sind zu erschiessen': Die Brutalisierung des deutsch–sowjetischen Krieges im Sommer 1941* (Berlin: Propyläen Verlag, 2000), 252–3.

5. Samuel Lipa Tennenbaum, *Zloczow Memoir* (New York: Shengold Publishers, 1986), 169, 177; Spector, *Holocaust*, 68.

6. Helmut Krausnick and Hans–Heinrich Wilhelm, *Die Truppe des Weltanschauungskrieges: Die Einsatzgruppen der Sicherheitspolizei und des SD 1938–1942* (Stuttgart: Deutsche Verlags–Anstalt, 1981), 205–6; Avraham Tory, *Surviving the Holocaust: The Kovno Ghetto Diary* (Cambridge, Mass.: Harvard University Press, 1990), 8–9.

7. Christian Gerlach, *Kalkulierte Morde: Die deutsche Wirtschafts- und Vernichtungspolitik in Weißrußland 1941 bis 1944* (Hamburg: Hamburger Edition, 1999), 536–8, 542–3; Yad Vashem Archives (YVA), file M–49/1465, lists 1–2; M–49/1466, list 1; Edmund Dmitrów, 'Oddziały operacyjne niemieckiej Policji Bezpieczeństwa i Służby Bezpieczeństwa a początek zagłady Żydów w Łomżyńskiem i na Białostocczyźnie latem 1941 roku', in *Wokół Jedwabnego*, i. 310–11, 313.

8. *Final Report* (Bucharest: International Commission on the Holocaust in Romania, 2004), 127–8; Vladimir Solonari, 'Patterns of Violence: The Local Population and the Mass Murder of Jews in Bessarabia and Northern Bukovina, July–August 1941', *Kritika: Explorations in Russian and Eurasian History* 8/4 (2007), 755–9.

9. Solonari, 'Violence', 763, 765–6, 768.

10. Spector, *Holocaust*, 64–6, 68–70; YVA, file 03/1218, list 2; file 03/2468, lists 4–5, 7–8.

11. Gross, *Neighbors*, 14, 79–81.

12. Alexander Rossino, 'Polish "Neigbors" and German Invaders: Anti–Jewish Violence in the Bialystok District during the Opening Weeks of Operation Barbarossa', *Polin: Studies of Polish Jewry* 16 (2003), 431–52; Klaus–Peter Friedrich, 'Spontane 'Volkspogrome' oder Auswűchse der NS–Vernichtungspolitik? Zur Kontroverse um die Radikalisierung der antijűdischen Gewalt im Sommer 1941', *Kwartalnik Historii Żydów* 4 / *Jewish History Quarterly* 212 (2004), 587–611.

13. Dariusz Stola, 'A Monument of Words', *Yad Vashem Studies* 30 (2002), 46–7.

14. Krzepkowski, 'Wspomnienia', 147.

15. MacQueen, 'Context', 38; Kārlis Kangeris, 'Kollaboration vor der Kollabora-tion? Die baltische Emigranten und ihre 'Befreiungskomitees' in Deutschland 1940/1941', in Rohr, *Okkupation und Kollaboration*, 171–4, 182; Algirdas Martin Budreckis, *The Lithuanian National Revolt of 1941* (Boston: Lithuania Encyclo-pedia Press, 1968), 21–2, 121–4.

16. Dieter Pohl, *Nationalsozialistische Judenverfolgung in Ostgalizien, 1941–1944: Organisation und Durchführung eines staatlichen Massenverbrechens* (Munich: R. Oldenbourg Verlag, 1997), 57; Frank Golczewski, 'Die Kollaboration in der Ukraine', in *Kooperation und Verbrechen*, 159–61.

17. Dmitrów, 'Odzialy', 294; Tomasz Szarota, *U progu zagłady: zajścia antyżydows-kie i pogromy w okupowanej Europie: Warszawa, Paryż, Amsterdam, Antwerpia, Kowno* (Warsaw: Wydawnictwo Sic!, 2000), parts I, II, and III.

18. Szarota, *U progu*, 296–300; Andrew Ezergailis, *The Holocaust in Latvia, 1941–1944: The Missing Center* (Riga: Historical Institute of Latvia, 1996), 213–16; Dmitrów, 'Oddziały', i. 345.

19. Atamukas, Hard Road, 19–21.

20. Szarota, *U progu*, 305, 307, 308; Machcewicz and Persak, '*Wokół Jedwabnego*', i. 46.

21. SPP, MS B.II.715, Zygmunt Asłan, 'Endlösung der Judenfrage in Lemberg', pp. 23–5; Musial, *Elemente*, 273; Andrzej Żbikowski, 'Inny pogrom', *Karta* 6 (1991), 132–3; Alfred Jasiński, 'Borysławska apokalipsa', *Karta* 4 (1991), 112.

22. Roger D. Petersen, *Understanding Ethnic Violence: Fear, Hatred, and Resentment in Twentieth-Century Eastern Europe* (Cambridge: Cambridge University Press, 2002), 46.

23. YVA, file M–49/4163, pp. 2–3; YVA, file 03/2468, p. 8; Jasiewicz, *Pierwsi*, 58.

24. Margers Vestermanis, 'Die lettische Anteil an der "Endlösung" ': Versuch einer Antwort', in Uwe Backes, Eckhard Jesse, and Reiner Zitelmann, eds., *Die Schatten der Vergangenheit: Impulse zur Historisierung des Nationalsozialismus* (Frankfurt am Main: Ullstein, 1990), 443; Ezergailis, *Holocaust*, 182–3.

25. USHMM, syg. 229/1, 'Teka Lwowska', p. 144; IPMS, 'MSW', syg. A.9. III.2a/19, pp. 5–7, 9–10, 70; A.9.III.2c/44, list 15; Tomaszewski, *Lwów*, 63.

26. Gasparaitis, 'Verrätern', 893–4; Szarota, *U progu*, 254–6, 304–5.

27. USHMM, syg. 229/19, 'Teka Lwowska', pp. 153–4; Szarota, *U progu*, 304; Gasparaitis, 'Verrätern', 900–1; Jasiewicz, *Pierwsi*, 37; Machcewicz and Persak, *Wokół Jedwabnego*, ii. 276; Dmitrów, 'Oddziały', i. 295; Spector, *Holocaust*, 64–6.

28. Szarota, *U progu*, 232–3; Knut Stang, *Kollaboration und Massenmord: Die litauische Hilfspolizei, das Rollkommando Hamann und die Ermordung der litauischen Juden* (Frankfurt am Main: Peter Lang, 1996), 115; Pohl, *Judenverfolgung*, 58.

29. Weiss–Wendt, *Murder*, 125–6, 132–5; Hans–Heinrich Wilhelm, *Die Einsatz-gruppe A der Sicherheitspolizei und des SD 1941/42* (Frankfurt am Main: Peter Lang, 1996), 105–6.

30. Wilhelm, *Einsatzgruppe A*, 107–11.

31. Bernhard Chiari, *Alltag hinter der Front: Besatzung, Kollaboration und Widerstand in Weißrußland 1941–1944* (Düsseldorf: Droste Verlag, 1998), 96; Jerzy Turonek, *Białoruś pod okupacją niemiecką* (Warsaw: Książka i Wiedza, 1993), 41–5; Vital Luba, ed., *U novai aichyne: shtodzënnae zhytstsë belarusau Belastochchyny u mizhvaenny peryiad* (Białystok: Prahramnaia rada Tydnëvika Niva, 2001), 186–7, 190–2.

32. Czesław Madajczyk, *Faszyzm i okupacje, 1938–1945: wykonywanie okupacji przez państwa Osi w Europie* (Poznań: Wydawnictwo Poznańskie, 1983), i. 621.

33. Robert G. Waite, '"Reliable Local Residents": Collaboration in Latvia, 1941–1945', in Andris Caune, Daina Kļaviņa, and Inesis Feldmanis, eds., *Latvia in World War II: Materials of an International Conference, 14–15 June 1999, Riga* (Riga: Latvijas vēstures instytūta apgāds, 2000), 225–6; Seppo Myllyniemi, *Die Neuordnung der baltischen Länder 1941–1944: Zum nationalsozialistischen Inhalt der deutschen Besatzungspolitik* (Helsinki: Vammalan Kirjapaino, 1973), 228; Eric Haberer, 'The German Police and Genocide in Belorussia, 1941–1944', *Journal of Genocide Research* 3/1 (2001), 18–19.

34. Weiss–Wendt, *Murder*, 61; Ruth Bettina Birn, 'Collaboration with Nazi Germany in Eastern Europe: The Case of the Estonian Security Police', *Contemporary European History* 10/2 (2001), 185–7.

35. IPMS, 'MSW', syg. A.9.III.2d/9, pp. 1–2, 4–5; *Misiunas, Baltic States*, 51–2; Myllyniemi, *Neuordnung*, 97–8, 102.

36. Misiunas, *Baltic States*, 51–2; Birn, 'Collaboration', 197.

37. IMPS, 'MSW', syg. A.9.III 2c/44, p. 206; Maria Wardzyńska, *Sytuacja ludności polskiej w Generalnym Komisariacie Litwy, czerwiec 1941 –lipiec 1944* (Warsaw: Agencja Wydawnicza MAKO, 1993), 31–2, 49–53; Lewandowska, *Życie*, 89–91, 93.

38. Gerlach, *Morde*, 245–9, 266–8, 290–1.

39. A. K. Solov'yev, *Belorusskaia Tsentral'naia Rada: sozdanie, deiatel'nost', krakh* (Minsk: Navuka i tekhnika, 1995), 11–13, 32–3; Turonek, *Białoruś*, 63–4, 138,143–4.

40. Misiunas, *Baltic States*, 53–4; Karel C. Berkhoff, *Harvest of Despair: Life and Death in Ukraine under Nazi Rule* (Cambridge, Mass.: Belknap Press of Harvard University Press, 2004), 266–7.

41. Wlodzimierz Bonusiak, *Małopolska Wschodnia pod rządami Trzeciej Rzeszy* (Rzeszów: Wydanie Wyższej Szkoły Pedagogicznej w Rzeszowie, 1990), 10–12; Golczewski, 'Kollaboration', (n. 16 above) 164–5.

42. Bonusiak, *Małopolska*, 64–5, 92–4.

43. Misiunas, *Baltic States*, 55.

44. Saulius Sužiedėlis, 'The Military Mobilization Campaigns of 1943 and 1944 in German-Occupied Lithuania: Contrasts in Resistance and Collaboration', *Journal of Baltic Studies* 21/1 (1990), 36–8, 43.

45. IMPS, 'MSW', A.9E/62, p. 2; SPP, A3–1–1–12, p. 3; Misiunas, *Baltic States*, 56–9; Vakar, *Belorussia*, 202–3; Turonek, *Białoruś*, 200–1.

46. Hausleitner, *Rumänisierung*, 399; S. Ia. Afteniuk et al., *Moldavskaia SSR v Velikoi Otechestvennoi voine Sovetskogo Soiuza 1941–1945: Sbornik dokumentov i materialov v dvukh tomakh* (Chişinău: Shtiintsa, 1976), ii. 102.

47. Afteniuk, *Moldavskaia SSR*, ii. 114–15; Hausleitner, *Rumänisierung*, 422–3; Vladimir Solonari, '"Model Province": Explaining the Holocaust of Bessarabian and Bukovinian Jewry', *Nationalities Papers* 34/4 (2006), 487–90.

48. Stang, *Kollaboration*, 155–69; Gabriel N. Finder and Alexander V. Prusin, 'Collaboration in Eastern Galicia: The Ukrainian Police and the Holocaust', *East European Jewish Affairs* 34/2 (2004), 103–4.

49. Arūnas Bubnys, 'The Holocaust in the Lithuanian Province in 1941: The Kaunas District', David Gaunt, Paul A. Levine, and Larvz Palosuo, eds., *Collaboration and Resistance during the Holocaust: Belarus, Estonia, Latvia, Lithuania* (Bern: Peter Lang, 2004), 288–9; Finder and Prusin, 'Collaboration', 107–8; Martin Dean, 'Poles in the German Local Police in Eastern Poland and their Role in the Holocaust', *Polin: Studies in Polish Jewry* 18 (2005), 356; Gerlach, *Morde*, 717.

50. MacQueen, 'Context', 38–9; Jarosław Wołkonowski, 'Penetracja polskiego podziemia na Wileńszczyźnie przez litewską policję bezpieczeństwa (listopad 1939–lipiec 1940)', in *Społeczeństwo bialivuskic*, 344.

51. Ezergailis, *Holocaust*, 173, 249–61; Vestermanis, 'Anteil', (n. 24 above), 403–25.

52. Aya Ben-Naftali, 'Collaboration and Resistance: The Ninth Fort as a Test Case', in Gaunt, *Collaboration and Resistance*, 365; Stang, *Kollaboration*, 103–4, 155–69; Bubnys, 'The Holocaust in the Lithuanian Province', 295–6; Wardzyńska, *Sytuacja*, 32–3.

53. Misiunas, *Baltic States*, 60.

54. Ruth Bettina Birn, 'Collaboration' (n. 34 above), 183; Stang, *Kollaboration*, 114, 175–6, 179; Saulius Sužiedėlis, 'The Burden of 1941', *Lituanus*, 47/4 (2001), 56.

55. USHMM, RG–06.027, case 702; case 1623, microfiche 1, 2, 3; Ezergailis, *Holocaust*, 177, 182–3.

56. Rudīte Vīksne, 'Members of the Arājs Commando in Soviet Court Files: Social Position, Education, Reasons for Volunteering, Penalty', in Andris Caune et al., *The Hidden and Forbidden History of Latvia under Soviet and Nazi Occupations 1940–1991: Selected Research of the Commission of the Historians of Latvia* (Riga: Institute of the History of Latvia, 2005), 194–200.

57. Geoffrey Swain, *Between Stalin and Hitler: Class War and Race War on the Dvina, 1940–1946* (New York: RoutledgeCurzon, 2004), 88; Kazimierz Sakowicz, *Ponary Diary, July 1941–November 1943: A Bystander's Account of a Mass Murder* (New Haven: Yale University Press, 2005), 11–13, 16–17, 28, 35–36; Spector, *Holocaust*, 177–8, 181–3, 240.

58. Andres Kasekamp, 'The Ideological Roots of Estonian Collaboration during the Nazi Occupation', in Anu Mai Kõll, ed., *The Baltic Countries under Occupation: Soviet and Nazi Rule, 1939–1991* (Stockholm: Acta Universitatis Stockholmiensis,

2003), 87; Kangeris, 'Kollaboration?', (n. 15 above), 182–3; Finder and Prusin, 'Collaboration', 101–2; Sužiedēlis, 'Burden', 54–5.

59. Martin C. Dean, 'Seizure, Registration, Rental and Sale: The Strange Case of the German Administration of Jewish Moveable Property in Latvia (1941–1944)', in Caune, *Latvia in World War II*, 375–6; Finder, 'Collaboration', 101; Jean Ancel, 'The Romanian Way of Solving the "Jewish Problem" in Bessarabia and Bukovina, June–July 1941', *Yad Vashem Studies* 19 (1988), 194; Weiss-Wendt, *Murder*, 139–40.

60. Spector, *Holocaust*, 119–20, 239–41 ff.; Tomaszewski, *Lwów*, 67.

61. In Jasiewicz, *Pierwsi*, 42–3.

62. Machcewicz and Persau, *Wokół Jedwabnego*, ii. 141.

63. Bonusiak, *Małopolska*, 134.

64. Wardzyńska, *Sytuacja*, 41.

65. Mordechai Altshuler, *Soviet Jewry on the Eve of the Holocaust: A Social and Demographic Profile* (Jerusalem: Centre for Research of East European Jewry), 329–31; Frank Golczewski, 'Polen', in Wolfgang Benz, ed., *Dimension des Völkermords: Die Zahl der judischen Opfer des Nationalsozialismus* (Munich: Dtv, 1996), 442–3.

66. Waszkiewicz, 'Żydzi' (Ch.4 n. 13 above), 137; Pohl, *Judenverfolgung*, 385.

67. Mark Levene, 'Frontiers of Genocide: Jews in the Eastern War Zones, 1914–1920 and 1941', in Panikos Panayi, ed., *Minorities in Wartime: National and Racial Groupings in Europe, North America and Australia during the Two World Wars* (Oxford: Berg, 1993), 86–7.

68. Tomaszewski, *Lwów*, 77–9; Wardzyńska, *Sytuacja*, 29–30, 37, 38, 46, 48–9; MacQueen, 'Context', 41ff.; Solonari, 'Violence', 775–76.

69. Waite, 'Residents', 133.

CHAPTER 7

1. Stathis N. Kalyvas, *The Logic of Violence in Civil War* (Cambridge and New York: Cambridge University Press, 2006), 17.

2. Rogers Brubaker, 'Aftermaths of Empire and the Unmixing of Peoples', in Barkay and Hagen, *After Empire*, 158.

3. Hausleitner, *Rumänisierung*, 424–5; Magosci, *Identity*, 248–9; B. I. Spivak, *Narysy istorii revoliutsiinoi borot' by trudiashchykh Zakarpatttiia v 1930–1945 rokakh.* L'viv: vydavnytstvo L'vivs'koho universytetu, 1963), 308–11, 332–33.

4. Afteniuk, et al, *Moldavskaia SSR, ii. 305–6, 471–2, 477–8.*

5. Zygmunt Boradyn, *Niemen—Rzeka niezgody: Polsko-sowiecka wojna partyzancka na Nowogródczyźnie, 1943–1944* (Warsaw: Oficyna Wydawnicza Rytm, 1999), 62; Vakar, *Belorussia*, 194–8; Gerlach, *Morde*, 862.

6. Philip W. Blood, *Hitler's Bandit Hunters: The SS and the Nazi Occupation of Europe* (Washington: Potomac Books, 2006), 63–4.

7. Turonek, *Białoruś*, 152–4; Mykhailiuk, *Istoriia Volyni*, 123–5; Aliaksei Litvin, *Akupatsyia Belarusi (1941–1944): pytanni supratsivu i kalabaratsyi* (Minsk: 'Belaruski knigazbor', 2000), 234–7; Gerlach, *Morde*, 869, 899, 901, 931, 938; Swain, *Class War*, 107, 215.

8. Pedosov, *Postroenie sotsializma*, 179; S. Kuznetsov and B. Netrebskii, eds., 'Pod maskoi nezavisimosti (dokumenty o vooruzhennom natsionalisticheskom podpol'ye v Latvii v 40–50–kh gg.', *Izvestiia TsK KPSS*, 11 (1990), 118; SPP, file A3–1–113–3, p. 13; Swain, *Class War*, 107, 215.

9. Martin Dean, 'Microcosm; Collaboration and Resistance during the Holocaust in the Mir Rayan of Belarus, 1941–1944', in Gaunt, *Collaboration and Resistance*, 248–52.

10. Alfred J. Rieber, 'Civil Wars in the Soviet Union', *Kritika: Explorations in Russian and Eurasian History* 4/1 (2003), 139–40, 152.

11. Turonek, *Białoruś*, 117–18; Boradyn, *Niemen*, 105, 214; K. I. Kozak, 'Germanskie okkupatsionnye voennye i grazhdanskie organy v Belarusi 1941–1944 gg.: analiz i itogi poter', in V. F. Balakira and K. I. Kozak, *Pershaia i drugaia sysvetnyia voiny: akupatsyia i iaye nastupstvy na Belarusi* (Minsk: Gistarychnaia maisternia Minsku, 2006), 122, 125–6.

12. Kozak, 'Organy', 139, 153; Gerlach, *Morde*, 866.

13. Spector, *Holocaust*, 270–2; Evgenij Rosenblat, 'Belarus: Specific Features of the Region's Jewish Collaboration and Resistance', in Gaunt, *Collaboration and Resistance*, 277–8; Chiari, *Alltag*, 283–4; Wardzyńska, *Sytuacja*, 75–6.

14. Spector, *Holocaust*, 302–303; TsDAVO, 3833/1/126, pp. 23, 35.

15. SPP, file A3–1–1–13–1A–C, p. 3; Grzegorz Motyka, 'Postawy wobec konfliktu polsko–ukraińskiego w latach 1939–1953 w zależności od przynależności etnicznej, państwowej i religijnej', in *Tygiel*, 289; Litvin, *Akupatsyia*, 121; Boradyn, *Niemen*, 28.

16. Zaprudnik, *Belarus*, 98.

17. Chiari, *Alltag*, 273–4, 278; Turonek, *Białoruś*, 65–6, 73, 137–8, 185–7; Boradyn, *Niemen*, 32–3; IMPS, 'MSW', syg. A.9E/62, p. 2; 'MSZ', syg. A.9E/113, p. 10.

18. IPMS, 'MSW', syg. A.9.III 2c/44, p. 206; Lewandowska, *Życie*, 212; Wincenty Borodziewicz, 'Rozmowy polsko–litewskie w Wilnie 1942–1944', *Przegląd Historyczny* 80/2 (1982), 317; Wardzyńska, *Sytuacja*, 48–53.

19. Wardzyńska, *Sytuacja*, 57–8, 60–1, 64.

20. SPP, file A3–1–113–3, p. 8; Wardzyńska, *Sytuacja*, 18 ff., 102–7.

21. Borodziewicz, 'Rozmowy', 319–21; MPS, 'MSW', A.9E/62, no page; SPP, file A3–1–113–3, pp. 15, 18.

22. IPMS, 'PRM', syg. 6/6–6/7, pp. 56a; 'MSW', syg. A.9.III 2c/44, p. 103.

23. IPMS, 'MSZ', syg. A.9E/113, p. 10; A.11. 85/c/1, p. 3; A.9.III 2c/44, p. 208.

24. IPMS, 'MSW', syg. A.9E/62, p. 1; Wardzyńska, *Sytuacja*, 73–4, 77, 81–2; IPMS, 'PRM', sig. 56, no page.

25. SPP, file A3–1–113–3, pp. 5–6, 12; IPMS, 'MSW', A.9.V/13, no page.

26. Wardzyńska, *Sytuacja*, 83–6; Borodziewicz, 'Rozmowy', 334–5.

27. Kozak, 'Organy', 140; Boradyn, *Niemen*, 47–8, 62, 82–5; YVA, 03/1286, p. 30.

28. Chiari Litvin; Piotr Kołakowski, *NKWD i GRU na ziemiach polskich 1939–1945* (Warsaw: Dom Wydawniczy Bellona, 2002), 213, 219–220.

29. Kozak, 'Organy', 143; Boradyn, *Niemen*, 126–7, 131, 148–9; Chiari, *Alltag*, 284–5.

30. SPP, file A3–1–1–13–1A–C, p. 5; Boradyn, *Niemen*, 157–60; Rieber, 'Civil Wars', 156–7.

31. Litvin, *Akupatsyia*, 139–51.

32. SPP, file A3–1–1–12, pp. 9–10, 13, 88, 100; Boradyn, *Niemen*, 178–80, 188, 203–9; Turonek, *Białoruś*, 203–6; Chiari, *Alltag*, 285–6, 294; Kozak, 'Organy', 144.

33. IPMS, syg. 'MSW', A.9.III 2c/44, p. 208; Rafal Wnuk, 'Polska konspiracja antysowiecki na Kresach Wschodnich II RP w latach 1939–1941 i 1944–1952', in *Tygiel*, 179.

34. Timothy Snyder, 'The Causes of Ukrainian–Polish Ethnic Cleansing 1943', *Past & Present* 179 (2003), 200, 204.

35. Alexander V. Prusin, 'Revolution and Ethnic Cleansing in Western Ukraine: The OUN–UPA Assault Against Polish Settlements in Volhynia and East Galicia, 1943–1944', in Tooley, *Ethnic Cleansing*, 517–35; Józef Anczarski, *Kronikarske zapisy z lat cierpień i grozy w Małopolsce Wschodnie* (Krakow: J. Anczarski, 1998), 180, 186.

36. Spector, *Holocaust*, 239.

37. Anczarski, *Kronikarske zapisy*, 186.

38. A. Vais, 'Otnoshenie nekotorykh krugov ukrainskogo natsional'nogo dvizheniia k evreiam v period Vtoroi mirovoi voiny', *Vestnik evreiskogo universiteta v Moskve* 2/9 (1995): 108. TsDAVO, 3833/1/74, p. 24; 3833/1/70, pp. 12, 15; 3833/1/69, p. 37.

39. Prusin, 'Revolution', 524; Mykhailiuk, *Istoriia Volyni*, 126.

40. Bonusiak, *Małopolska*, 114, 151; Krystyna Kersten, 'The Polish–Ukrainian Conflict under Communist Rule', *Acta Poloniae Historica* 73 (1996), 136–7.

41. SPP, Szeptycki, 'Kwestia ukraińska', p. 6.

42. Snyder, 'Causes', 210–12; SPP, file A3–1–1–13–1A–C, k. 13.

43. AAN, syg. 202/III/13, pp. 74–5; 202/III/134, p. 1. 242; *Rossiiskii gosudarstvennyi arkhiv sotsializma no-politicheskoi istorii* RGASPI, 69/1/563, p. 110; 69/1/1032, pp. 75–6, 69/1/1033, p. 5; 45 Snyder, *Reconstruction*, 158–62; Finder, 'Collaboration', 106–8.

44. TsDAHOU, 1/23/523, pp. 44–46; RGASPI, 69/1/25, p. 200.

45. TsDAHOU, 1/23/530, p. 12; 1/23/527, p. 6; RGASPI, 69/1/708, pp. 94, 118; 69/1/709, pp. 27, 66; Anczarski, *Kronikarskie zapisy*, 307; Gracheva, 'Shchodennyk Viktora Petrykevycha'.

46. AAN, 202/III–203, pp. 14–15; Kersten, 'Conflict', 137; Bonusiak, *Małopolska*, 156–7; SPP, Szeptycki, 'Kwestia ukraińska', 7.

47. Kersten, 'Conflict', 136.
48. Ibid. 139.
49. Motyka, 'Postawy', 296; AAN, syg. 202/III/121, pp. 130–2.
50. TsDAVO, 3833/1/161, pp. 8–15, 18, 22–3, 25, 36, 40; 3833/1/121, pp. 13–14, 19–20; AAN, syg. 202/III–203, p. 13; syg. 202/III/122, p. 30; syg. 202/III–197, p. 22; SPP, A3–1–1–12, p. 100; Motyka, 'Postawy', 387–8; Mykhailiuk, *Istoriia Volyni*, 126–7.
51. Gracheva, 'Shchodennyk Viktora Petrykevycha'; in Kalyvas, *Logic*, 56.
52. Motyka, 'Postawy', 329.
53. Tadeusz Piotrowski, *Poland's Holocaust: Ethnic Strife, Collaboration with Occupying Forces and Genocide in the Second Republic, 1918–1947* (Jefferson, NC: McFarland & Co., 1998), 243–4.
54. TsDAHOU, 1/23/523, p. 190; 1/23/530, p. 12; AAN, 202/III/131, p. 72; Mykhailiuk, *Istoriia Volyni*, 128; Spector, *Holocaust*, 267.
55. Anczarski, *Kronikarske zapisy*, 293–4; AAN, 202/1–41, p. 21; 202/III/128, p. 2; 202/III/1–35, p. 108; 202/III/129, p. 75; TsDAHOU, 57/4/338, pp. 413, 455–457, 462; TsDAVO, 3833/1/126, p. 2.
56. Motyka, 'Postawy', 301.
57. TsDAVO, 3833/1/89, p. 93; 3833/1/126, pp. 6, 37–8; TsDAHO, 57/4/338, p. 423.
58. AAN, syg. 202/III–134, pp. 10–11; 202/III–196, pp. 2–5; TsDAVO, 3833/1/126, p. 79; TsDAHO, 1/23/927, p. 6; 1/23/892, pp. 6–7; 3833/1/74, pp. 84–85; Anczarski, *Kronikarske zapisy*, 321–2.
59. Motyka, 'Postawy', 298, 302.
60. AAN, syg. 202/III–134, pp. 12, 21, 25; TsDAHO, 57/4/338, pp. 170–173, 184–5, 254–5; Bonusiak, *Małopolska*, 221; Motyka, 'Postawy', 375.
61. Prusin, 'Ethnic Cleansing', 534.

CHAPTER 8

1. Vakar, *Belorussia*, 207–8.
2. Magosci, *Ukraine*, 648.
3. RGASPI, 69/1/1033, list 1; Gerhard Simon, *Nationalism and Policy toward the Nationalities in the Soviet Union: From Totalitarian Dictatorship to Post–Stalinist Society* (Boulder, Colo.: Westview Press, 1991), 210.
4. Boldyzhar, *Zakarpattia*, 92–5; Spivak, *Narysy*, 365–7, 370–1; Magosci, *Identity*, 253–5.
5. Vitkovskii, 'Vchera', 138; Dalia Kuodytė, 'Zarys polityczny i ideologiczny zbrojnego ruchu oporu antykomunistycznego na terytorium Litwy', in Piotr Niwiński, ed., *Aparat represji a opór społeczeństwa wobec systemu komunistycznego w Polsce i na Litwie w latach 1944–1956* (Warsaw: Instytut Pamięci Narodowej-Komisja Ścigania Zbrodni przeciwko Narodowi Polskiemu, 2005), 33; Myllyniemi, *Neuordnung*, 264–5.

6. Juozas Daumantas, *Fighters for Freedom: Lithuanian Partisans versus the USSR, 1944–1947* (New York: Manyland Books, 1975), 20–1; Jeffrey Burds, *Sovetskaia agentura:ocherki istorii SSSR v poslevoyennye gody (1944–1948* (Moscow and New York: Sovremennaia Istoriia, 2006), 97 ff.

7. I. A. Valakhnovich, *Antisovetskoe podpol' ye na territorii Belarusi v 1944–1953 gg.* (Minsk: BGU, 2002), 73; Kołakowski, *NKWD*, 75, 226–7; Henryk Piskuno-wicz, 'Zwalczanie polskiego podziemia przez NKWD i NKGB na kresach północno–wschodnich II Rzeczypospolitej', in Andrzej Ajnenkiel, ed., *Wojna domowa czy nowa okupacja? Polska po roku 1944* (Wrocław: Wydawnictwo Zak-ładu Narodowego im. Ossolińskich, 1998), 64; Kozak, 'Organy', 146.

8. Rafał Wnuk, 'Polityczne i ideowe oblicze podziemia antykomunistycznego w Polsce', in Niwiński, *Aparat represji*, 14–15; Kołakowski, *NKWD*, 267–8.

9. Valakhnovich, *Antisovetskoe podpol' ye*, 20, 34–5.

10. Bugai, *Narody Ukrainy*, 131.

11. Valakhnovich, *Antisovetskoe podpol' ye*, 20, 34–5, 38–9; Wnuk, 'Polska konspiracja', in *Tygiel*, 232; *Osvobozhdennaia Belarus': dokumenty i materialy, ianvar'–dekabr' 1945* (Minsk: Natsional'nyi Arkhiv Respubliki Belarus'), ii.: 65–6, 68, 73, 179; Andrzej Krzysztof Kunert, 'Rozbicie Polskiego Państwa Podziemnego', in Ajnenkiel, *Wojna domowa*, 40–1; Kozak, 'Germanskie or-gany', 144.

12. Gracheva, 'Shchodennyk Viktora Petrykevycha';Wierzbicki, 'Zmiany spo-łeczne', 134; Christoph Mick, 'Die Ethnisierung des Stalinismus: Zur Wirk-samkeit ethnischer Kategorien bei der Sowjetisierung der Westukraine 1944–1948', in Jörg Baberowski, ed., *Moderne Zeiten? Krieg, Revolution and Gewalt im 20. Jahrhundert* (Göttingen: Vandenhoeck & Ruprecht, 2006), 152; Burds, *Sovetskaia agentura*, 67–9, 71–2.

13. *Osvobozhdennaia Belarus'*, 2: 178–9; *Pedosov Postroenie sotsializma*, 291; Mart Laar, *War in the Woods: Estonia's Struggle for Survival, 1946–1956* (Washington: Compass Press, 1992), 182; Marples, *Stalinism*, 123; Vitkovskii and Iampol'skii, 'Vchera', 139.

14. Nijolė Gaškaite–Žemaitienė, 'The Partisan War in Lithuania from 1944 to 1953', in Arvydas Anušauskas, ed., *The Anti–Soviet Resistance in the Baltic States* (Vilnius: DuKa, 1999), 27, 30; Misiunas, *Baltic States*, 87.

15. Burds, *Sovetskaia agentura*, 49–50.

16. A province of western France, where in 1793–6 a powerful insurgency move-ment fought the French revolutionary government.

17. Rieber, 'Civil Wars', 130; M. K. Ivasiuta, *Narysy istorii kolkhospnoho budivnytstva v zakhidnykh oblastiakh Ukrains'koi RSR* (Kiev: vydavnytsvo Akademii Nauk Ukrains'koi SSR, 1962), 85; Vaupshasov, *Na perekrestkakh*, 474.

18. Juozas Starkauskas, 'The NKVD–MVD–MGB Army', in Anušauskas, *Anti–Soviet Resistance*, 54; Bugai, *Narody*, 56, 132–3; Piotr Kołakowski, 'NKWD–NKGB a podziemie polskie: Kresy Wschodnie 1944–1945', *Zeszyty Historyczne*

136 (2001), 83; Piskunowicz, 'Zwalczanie', in Ajnenkiel, *Wojna domowa*, 67, 77, 81, 84.

19. Burds, *Sovetskaia agentura*, 18–9, 27–8, 73–4; Daumantas, *Fighters*, 125; Kołakowski, 'NKWD–NKGB', 76–7; Kołakowski, *NKWD*, 263, 275.

20. Laar, *War*, 24; Heinrihs Strods, 'The Latvian Partisan War between 1944 and 1956', in Anušauskas, *Anti–Soviet Resistance*, 150; Daumantas, *Fighters*, 68; Vaupshasov, *Na perekrestkakh*, 473; Mick, 'Ethnisierung', 150.

21. Starkauskas, 'NKVD', 61; Heinrihs Strods and Matthew Kott, 'The File on Operation "Priboi": A Re–Assessment of the Mass Deportations of 1949', *Journal of Baltic Studies* 33, 1 (2002), 24–6; Kołakowski, *NKWD*, 214.

22. Daumantas, *Fighters*, 259–61; Laar, *War*, 120–5; Gaškaite–Žemaitienė, 'Partisan War', and 'Jonas Zemaitis', in Anušauskas, *Anti–Soviet Resistance*, 32 and 73–4.

23. Gaškaite–Žemaitienė, 'Partisan War', 36; Vitkovskii, 'Vchera', 139; Gaškaitė–Zemaitiene, 'Jonas Zemaitis', 75.

24. Pedosov, *Postroenie sotsializma*, 440; Kuznetsov, 'Pod maskoi', 120–1; S. Kuznetsov et al, 'Vooruzhennoe natsionalisticheskoe podpol'ye v Estonii v 40–50–kh godakh', *Izvestiia TsK KPSS*, 8 (1990), 176; Georgii Sannikov, *Bol'shaia okhota: razgrom vooruzhennogo podpol'ya v Zapadnoi Ukraine* (Moscow: 'Olma–Press', 2002), 10–11.

25. Kołakowski, 'NKWD–NKGB', 73–4; Bugai, *Narody*, 132; Burds, *Sovetskaia agentura*, 54.

26. Simon, *Nationalism*, 210.

27. Mick, 'Ethnisierung', 162; Marples, *Stalinism*, 78; Simon, *Nationalism*, 210–11; Vakar, *Belorussia*, 215; Zaprudnik, *Belarus*, 104.

28. *Postroenie sotsializma*, 90; Misiunas, *Baltic States*, 76–7; Sherstobitov et al., *Istoriia*, ii. 87.

29. Misiunas, *Baltic States*, 79; Vakar, *Belorussia*, 213–15.

30. Mick, 'Ethnisierung', 158–9; Hausleitner, *Rumänisierung*, 428.

31. Mick, 'Ethnisierung', 152; Swain, *Class War*, 205.

32. Magosci, Ukraine, 650; Amir Weiner, 'The Empires Pay a Visit: Gulag Returnees, East European Rebellions, and Soviet Frontier Politics', *Journal of Modern History* 78 2 (2006), 366.

33. Boldyzhar, *Zakarpattia*, 92–5; Spivak, *Narysy*, 365–7, 370–1; Magosci, *Shaping*, 253–5.

34. Sherstobitov, *Istoriia*, ii.: 90.

35. Gaškaite–Žemaitienė, 'Partisan War', 33; Marples, *Stalinism*, 99, 102; Misiunas, *Baltic States*, 97.

36. Marples, *Stalinism*, 105; Mihai Gribincea, *Agricultural Collectivization in Moldavia: Basavabia during Statinism 1944–1950* (Boulder, Colo: East European Monographs, 1996) 67; Daina Bleiere, 'Repressions against Farmers in Latvia in 1944–1953', in Caune et al., *Hidden and Forbidden History*, 244–5.

37. Ivasiuta, *Narysy*, 107–8; Gribincea, *Collectivization*, 62.

38. Marples, *Stalinism*, 87.

39. Gribincea, *Collectivization*, 82, 96; Pasat, *Trudnye stranitsy*, 226–8, 242–6, 298–9.

40. Pasat, *Trudnye stranitsy*, 221–5, 231, 235.

41. Marples, *Stalinism*, 105; Misiunas, *Baltic States*, 93–4, 96.

42. Gribincea, *Collectivization*, 102; Pedosov, *Postroenie sotsializma*, 310–12, 321; Marek Wierzbicki, 'Zmiany społeczne i gospodarcze we wsi kresowej w latach 1939–1953', in *Tygiel*, 136–9.

43. Wierzbicki, 'Zmiany społeczne', 129–30; Ivasiuta, *Narysy*, 122; Mykhailiuk, *Istoriia Volyni*, 144–5; Marples, *Stalinism*, 87–8, 121; Misiunas, *Baltic States*, 103.

44. Hausleitner, *Rumänisierung*, 428.

45. 'Polacy znad Wilii, Niemna, Narwi i Bugu w Łagrach sowieckich w latach 1944–1947 (praca anonimowa)', *Zeszyty Historyczne* 67 (1984): 155–62; TsDAVO, 3833/1/126, pp. 94, 97, 99; Kołakowski, 'NKWD–NKGB', 83–4.

46. Mick, 'Ethnisierung', 150–1; Motyka, 'Postawy', 308–9; *Osvobozhdennaia Belarus'*, 2: 111–14, 162; Jan Czerniakiewicz, *Repatriacja ludności polskiej z ZSRR, 1944–1948* (Warsaw: Państwowe Wydawnictwo Naukowe, 1987), 133–4, 154; Hausleitner, *Rumänisierung*, 428.

47. Mick, 'Ethnisierung', 153.

48. Bugai, *Narody Ukrainy*, 130–1, 134; Marples, *Stalinism*, 106.

49. Gaškaite–Žemaitienė, 'Partisan War', (n. 14 above), 37; V. N. Zemskov, 'Prinuditel'nye migratsii iz Pribaltiki v 1940–1950 gg'., *Otechestvennye arkhivy* 1 (1993), 4–5; Vitkovskii, 'Vchera', 139.

50. Strods and Kott, 'Operation "Priboi"', 11, 18; H. P. Strods, 'Deportatsiia naseleniia Pribaltiiskikh stran v 1949 godu', *Voprosy Istorii* 9 (1999), 130–5; Laar, *War*, 175–9.

51. Misiunas, *Baltic States*, 99; Gaškaite–Žemaitienė, 'Partisan War', 37.

52. Pasat, *Stranitsy*, 375–6, 393, 455, 485; Gribincea, *Collectivization*, 125.

53. Pasat, *Stranitsy*, 498–9.

54. Strods, 'Operation "Priboi"', 23.

55. In 1951–2 the Jehovah Witnesses were classified as 'class enemies' and deported from Moldavia. Pasat, *Stranitsy*, 552, 555, 557.

CHAPTER 9

1. Misiunas, *Baltic States*, 129.

2. Rogers Brubaker, *Nationalism, Reframed: Nationhood and the National Question in the New Europe* (Cambridge, England: Cambridge University Press, 1996) 5, 28–9.

3. Simon, *Nationalism*, 228–9, Toivo U. Raun, *Estonia and Estonians* (Stanford, Calif.: Hoover Institution Press, 1991), 190–1.

4. Raun, *Estonia*, 190–191; Simon, *Nationalism*, 275.

5. Weiner, Empires, 374.

6. Misiunas, *Baltic States*, 152–3.

7. Ibid, 135, 178; Simon, *Nationalism*, 282; Egidija Ramanauskaitė, 'Lithuanian Youth Culture versus Soviet Culture: On the Path of Cultural Liberalization toward Post Modernism', in *Baltic Countries under Occupation*, 325–6.

8. Lieven, *Empire*, 290–1; Simon, *Nationalism*, 283.

9. Simon, *Nationalism*, 267, 281–2; Sara Ginaite, 'The Legacy of Lithuania's Former Economic System and Its Transition to a Market Economy: Reflections and Considerations', in Eberhard Demm, Roger Noël, and William Urban, eds., *The Independence of the Baltic States: Origins, Causes, and Consequences. A Comparison of the Crucial Years 1918–1919 and 1990–1991* (Chicago: Lithuanian Research and Study Center, 1996), 105.

10. Zaprudnik, *Belarus*, 106–7.

11. Marples, *Stalinism*, 78; Simon, *Nationalism*, 237; Kopchak, 'O strukturnykh izmeneniiakh', 67, 69; Magosci, *Identity*, 259, 266–7.

12. Raun, *Estonia*, 199; Misiunas, *Baltic States*, 184–6, 192, 217; Thomas Remeikis, 'The Impact of Industrialization on the Ethnic Demography of the Baltic Countries', *Lituanus*, 13, 1 (1967), 36.

13. Ginaite, 'Legacy', 102–4; Magosci, *Ukraine*, 656; Gracheva, 'Shchodennyk Victon Petrytevyche'; Nicholas Dima, *Moldova and the Transdnestr Republic* (Boulder,: East European Monographs, 2001), 63–4, 67–8; Raun, *Estonia*, 202–3.

14. Eberhardt, *Ethnic Groups*, 35, 51–2.

15. Remeikis, 'Impact,' 33–5; Magosci, *Ukraine*, 651; Dima, *Moldova*, 74; Ken Ward, 'The Baltic States', in Seamus Dunn and T. G. Fraser, eds., *Europe and Ethnicity: The First World War and Contemporary Ethnic Conflict* (London: Routledge, 1996), 153; Rauch, *Baltic States*, 232.

16. Weiner, 'Empires', 337–43; Heinrihs Strods, 'The Nonviolent Resistance Movement in Latvia (1944–1958)', in Anušauskas, *Anti–Soviet Resistance*, 172.

17. Misiunas, *Baltic States*, 172; Amir Weiner, 'Déjà Vu All Over Again: Prague Spring, Romanian Summer and Soviet Autumn on the Soviet Western Frontier', *Contemporary European History* 15/2 (2006), 163.

18. Nadia Diuk and Adrian Karatnycky, *The Hidden Nations: The People Challenge the Soviet Union* (New York: William Morrow and Co., 1990), 123; Lieven, *Empire*, 290–1.

19. Strods, 'Nonviolent Resistance', 172–3; Diuk, *Hidden Nations*, 119.

20. Weiner, 'Empires', 353–6; Misiunas, *Baltic States*, 136.

21. Weiner, 'Empires', 362; Zemskov, 'Prinuditel'nye migratsii,' 11–13.

22. Strods, 'Nonviolent Resistance', 172; Misiunas, *Baltic States*, 142–7.

23. Weiner, 'Déjà Vu', 166–70, 174–5, 181–2, 185, 190.

24. Zaprudnik, *Belarus*, 110.

25. Simon, *Nationalism*, 320–3; Misiunas, *Baltic States*, 196–7, 211–13.

26. Misiunas, *Baltic States*, 252–3, 259–60; Raun, *Estonia*, 196; Lieven, *Empire*, 293; Simon, *Nationalism*, 283; Magosci, *Ukraine*, 662.

27. Weiner, 'Déjà Vu', 180–1; M. Mitsel, 'Yevrei Ukrainy u 1950–1990–kh rokakh XX st.', in Leonid Finberg and Volodymyr Liubchenko, eds., *Narysy z istorii ta kul' tury yevreiv Ukrainy* (Kiev: Dukh i Litera, 2005), 220–1, 226; Nora Levin, *The Jews in the Soviet Union since 1917: Paradox of Survival* (New York: New York University Press, 1990), ii: 726.

28. Marshall I. Goldman, *USSR in Crisis: The Failure of an Economic System* (New York: Norton, 1983), 35–41; Misiunas, *Baltic States*, 253–4.

29. Raun, *Estonia*, 233, 236–7.

30. Ward, 'Baltic States', 154–5; Diuk, *Hidden Nations*, 108–9; Lieven, *The Baltic Revolution: Estonia, Latvia, Lithuania and the Path to Independence* (New Haven: Yale University Press, 1993), 221.

31. Lieven, *Baltic Revolution*, 220–3.

32. Lieven, *Empire*, 333–4; Ward, 'Baltic States', 155.

33. Dima, *Moldova*, 144.

34. Zaprudnik, *Belarus*, 125–7, 131–3, 149–54; Snyder, *Reconstruction*, 248.

35. Magosci, *Ukraine*, 670.

36. Soren Rinder Bollerup and Christian Dons Christensen, *Nationalism in Eastern Europe: Causes and Consequences of the National Revivals and Conflicts in Late–Twentieth Century Eastern Europe* (New York: St. Martin's Press, 1997), 60–1.

37. Arturs Puga, 'Relations between the Baltic States and Russia during the Collapse of the Soviet Empire', in Demm, *Comparison of the Crucial Years*, 151–2; Brubaker, *Nationalism*, 42.

38. Alfred Erich Senn, 'Comparing the Circumstances of Lithuanian Independence, 1918–1922 and 1988–1992', in Demm, *Independence of Baltic States*, 17–18; Lieven, *Empire*, 379–80.

39. Dima, *Moldova*, 52–54.

40. Ibid. 87–8; Alla Skvortsova, 'The Cultural and Social Makeup of Moldova: A Bipolar or Dispersed Society?' in in Pål Kolstø, ed., *National Integration and Violent Conflict in Post–Soviet Societies: The Case of Estonia and Moldova* (Lanham, and Md. Rowman & Littlefield, 2002), 171.

41. Bollerup, *Nationalism*, 87, 91–2.

42. Michael Bruchis, *The Republic of Moldavia: From the Collapse of the Soviet Empire to the Restoration of the Russian Empire* (Boulder: Colo. East European Monographs, 1996), 32.

43. Skvortsova, 'Makeup', 167; Stuart J. Kaufman, *Modern Hatreds: The Symbolic Politics of Ethnic War* (Ithacany, Ny Cornell University Press, 2001), 139; Bruchis, *Moldavia*, 32–3.

44. Bollerup, *Nationalism*, 61; Dima, *Moldavia*, 144–5; Skvortsova, 'Makeup', 184; Kaufman, *Modern Hatreds*, 140–1.

45. Bollerup, *Nationalism*, 82; Bruchis, *Moldavia*, 44, 170.

46. Igor Munteanu, 'Social Multipolarity and Political Violence', in Kolstø, *National Integration*, 215.

47. Ibid. 216–17; Jeff Chinn and Steven D. Roper, 'Ethnic Mobilization and Reactive Nationalism: The Case of Moldova,' *Nationalities Papers* 23, 2 (1995), 307–9; Bollerup, *Nationalism*, 82.

48. Pål Kolstø and Hans Olav Melberg, 'Integration, Alienation, and Conflict in Estonia and Moldova at the Societal Level: A Comparison', in Kolstø, *National Integration*, 34–5, 56–68; Chinn, 'Ethnic Mobilization', 293–6, 299, 311; Bollerup, *Nationalism*, 62–3, 65.

49. Miroslav Hroch, 'Nationalism and National Movements: Comparing the Past and the Present of Central and Eastern Europe', *Nations and Nationalism* 2/1 (1996), 41–2.

Select Bibliography

ARCHIVAL SOURCES

Archiwum Akt Nowych (AAN), Warsaw, Poland.

File 'Delegatura Rządu na Kraj'.

Hoover Institution on War, Revolution and Peace (HI), Stanford, California.

'A. N. Krupenskii'.

'Poland. Ministerstwo Informacji i Dokumentacji [Reports of Polish Deportees]'.

'Zhurnal voennykh dieistvii'.

Instytut Polski i Muzeum im. generała Sikorskiego (IPMS), London, Great Britain.

File 'Posiedzenia Rady Ministrów' (PRM).

File 'Ministerstwo Spraw Wewnętrznych' (MSW).

File 'Ministerstwo Spraw Zagranichnych' (MSZ).

Lietuvos Valstybės Istorijos Archivas (LVIA), Vilnius, Lithuania.

Fond 641 'Lietuvos Katinės Administracijos Viršininkas (Chief of the military administration of Lithuania).

National Archives and Records Administration (NARA), Washington, DC.

Record Group-242 'Foreign Records Seized Collection'.

Record Group-256 'General Records of the American Commission to Negotiate Peace, 1918–1931'.

Rossiiskii gosudarstvennyi arkhiv sotsial'no-politicheskoi istorii (RGASPI), Moscow.

Fond 69: 'Tsentral'nyi Shtab Partisanskogo Dvizheniia'.

Studium Polski Podziemnej (SPP), London, Great Britain.

Files A3-1-1-13-3, A3-1-1-13-1A-C, A3-1-1-12, A6-4.7.

MS B.II.633, Maurycy Szeptycki, 'Kwestia ukraińska i polska myśl polityczna, 1939–1944'.

MS B.II.715, Zygmunt Asłan, 'Endlősung der Judenfrage in Lemberg'.

Tsentral≪nyi derzhavnyi arkhiv hromads≪kykh orhanizatsii Ukrainy (TsDAHOU), Kiev, Ukraine.

Fond 1: 'Tsentral'nyi komitet komunistychnoi partii Ukrainy'.

Tsentral'nyi derzhavnyi arkhiv vyshchykh orhaniv vlady ta upravlinnia Ukrainy (TsDAVO), Kiev, Ukraine.

Fond 3833 'Krayovyi Provid Orhanizatsii Ukrains'kykh Natsionalistiv (OUN) na Zakhidno-Ukrain'kykh zemliakh'.

United States Holocaust Memorial Museum (USHMM), Washington, DC.

RG-15.069M, accession 1996.A.0228, 'Teka Lwowska = Lwow files, 1898–1979'.

RG-06.027, 'Latvian State Archives of the Former Latvian KGB (State Security Committee) records from Fond 1986 relating to war crimes investigations and trials in Latvia, 1941–1995 (bulk 1944–1966)'.

Yad Vashem Archive (YVA), Jerusalem, Israel.

Files 03/1218, 03/1286, 03/2468, 05/80, M-49/1465, M-49/1466, M-49/4163.

PUBLISHED DOCUMENTS

Afteniuk, S. Ia., D. D. Yelin, A. A. Korenev, I. E. Levit, and I. I. Terekhina, eds. *Moldavskaia SSR v Velikoi Otechestvennoi voine Sovetskogo Soiuza 1941–1945: Sbornik dokumentov i materialov v dvukh tomakh.* 2 vols. Chişinău: 'Shtiintsa', 1976.

Ajnenkiel, Andrzej. *Wojna domowa czy nowa okupacja?: Polska po roku 1944.* Warsaw: Światowy Związek Żołnierzy Armii Krajowej-Oficyna Wydawnicza RYTM, 2001.

Bugai, N. F. *Narody Ukrainy v 'Osoboi papke Stalina'.* Moscow: Nauka, 2006.

Bugayev, A. T., A. N. Gayevskii, S. D. Pil′kevich, and D. V. Shmin, eds. *Bor′ba trudiashchikhsia Volyni za Vlast′ Sovetov (mart 1917 g.–dekarbr′ 1920 g.): sbornik dokumentov i materialov.* Zhitomir: Zhitomirskoe oblastnoe izdatel′stvo, 1957.

Kostiushko, I. I., ed. *Pol′sko–sovetskaia voina 1919–1920 gg. Ranee nie opublikovannye dokumenty i materialy.* 2 parts. Moscow: Izdatel′stvo Instituta slavianovedeniia i balkanistiki RAN, 1994.

Osvobozhdennaia Belarus′: dokumenty i materialy, ianvar′–dekabr′ 1945. Minsk: Natsional′nyi Arkhiv Respubliki Belarus′, 1975.

Pasat, V. I., ed. *Trudnye stranitsy istorii Moldovy, 1940–1950–e gody.* Moscow: Terra, 1995.

SECONDARY LITERATURE

Books

Aldcroft, Derek H. *Europe's Third World: The European Periphery in the Interwar Years.* Aldershot: Ashgate, 2006.

Altshuler, Mordechai. *Soviet Jewry on the Eve of the Holocaust: A Social and Demographic Profile.* Jerusalem: Centre for Research of East European Jewry, 1998.

Anczarski, Józef. *Kronikarske zapisy z lat cierpień i grozy w Małopolsce Wschodnie.* Krakow: J. Anczarski, 1998.

Andlauer, Teresa. *Die jüdische Bevölkerung im Modernisierungsprozess Galiziens (1867–1914).* Frankfurt am Main and Berlin: Peter Lang, 2001.

Ansky, S. *The Enemy at his Pleasure: A Journey through the Jewish Pale of Settlement during World War I*. New York: Metropolitan Books, 2002.

Anušauskas, Arvydas, ed. *The Anti-Soviet Resistance in the Baltic States*. Vilnius: DuKa, 1999.

Ascher, Abraham. *The Revolution of 1905: Russia in Disarray*. Stanford: Stanford University Press, 1988.

Baberowski, Jörg, ed. *Moderne Zeiten? Krieg, Revolution und Gewalt im 20. Jahrhundert*. Göttingen: Vandenhoeck & Ruprecht, 2006.

Backes, Uwe, Eckhard Jesse, and Reiner Zitelmann, eds. *Die Schatten der Vergangenheit: Impulse zur Historisierung des Nationalsozialismus*. Frankfurt am Main: Ullstein, 1990.

Bakhturina, A. Iu. *Politika Rossiiskoi imperii v vostochnoi Galitsii v gody pervoi mirovoi voiny*. Moscow: 'AIRO-XX', 2000.

—— *Okrainy Rossiiskoi imperii: gosudarstvennoe upravlenie i natsional'naia politika v gody pervoi mirovoi voiny (1914–1917 gg.)*. Moscow: Rosspen, 2004.

Balakira V. F., and K. I. Kozak. *Pershaia i drugaia sysvetnyia voiny: akupatsyia i iaye nastupstvy na Belarusi*. Minsk: Gistarychnaia maisternia' Minsku, 2006.

Barkey, Karen, and Mark von Hagen, eds. *After Empire. Multiethnic Societies and Nation-Building: The Soviet Union and the Russian, Ottoman, and Habsburg Empires*. Boulder, Colo.: Westview Press, 1997.

Baron, Nick, and Peter Gatrell, eds. *Homelands: War, Population and Statehood in Eastern Europe and Russia, 1918–1924*. London: Anthem Press, 2004.

Basler, Werner. *Deutschlands Annexionspolitik in Polen und im Baltikum 1914–1918*. Berlin: Rütten & Loening, 1962.

Bauer, Henning, Andreas Kappeler, and Brigitte Roth, eds. *Die Nationalitäten des Russischen Reiches in der Volkszählung von 1897*. 2 vols. Stuttgart: F. Steiner, 1991.

Bazhans'kyi, Ivan. *Viina: shchodennyk-khronika bukovyns'koho pedahoha ta pys'mennyka/Vashkivtsi, 31.8.1914-12.1918/22*. Chernivtsi: Zelena Bukovyna, 2006.

Benecke, Werner. *Die Ostgebiete der Zweiten Polnischen Republik: Staatsmacht und öffentliche Ordnung in einer Minderheitenregion 1918–1939*. Cologne, Weimar, and Vienna: Böhlau, 1999.

Benz, Wolfgang, ed. *Dimension des Völkermords. Die Zahl der judischen Opfer des Nationalsozialismus*. Munich: Dtv, 1996.

Berend, Ivan T. *Decades of Crisis: Central and Eastern Europe before World War II*. Berkeley and Los Angeles: University of California Press, 1998.

Bergman, Aleksandra. *Sprawy białoruskie w II Rzeczypospolitej*. Warsaw: Państwowe Wydawnictwo Naukowe, 1984.

Berkhoff, Karel C. *Harvest of Despair: Life and Death in Ukraine under Nazi Rule*. Cambridge, Mass.: Belknap Press of Harvard University Press, 2004.

Beyrau, Dietrich. *Schlachtfeld der Diktatoren: Osteuropa im Schatten von Hitler und Stalin*. Göttingen: Vandenhoeck & Ruprecht, 2000.

Bideleux, Robert, and Ian Jeffries. *A History of Eastern Europe: Crisis and Change.* London: Routledge, 1998.

Blood, Philip W. *Hitler's Bandit Hunters: The SS and the Nazi Occupation of Europe.* Washington, D.C.: Potomac Books, 2006.

Boldyzhar, Mykhailo. *Zakarpattia mizh svitovymy viinamy: fakty, podii, liudy, otsinky.* Uzhhorod: n.p., 2001.

Bollerup, Soren Rinder, and Christian Dons Christensen. *Nationalism in Eastern Europe: Causes and Consequences of the National Revivals and Conflicts in Late-Twentieth Century Eastern Europe.* New York: St Martin's Press, 1997.

Bonusiak, Włodzimierz. *Małopolska Wschodnia pod rządami Trzeciej Rzeszy.* Rzeszów: Wydawnictwo Wyższej Szkoły Pedagogicznej w Rzeszowie, 1990.

Boradyn, Zygmunt. *Niemen–Rzeka niezgody: Polsko-sowiecka wojna partyzancka na Nowogródczyźnie, 1943–1944.* Warszawa: Oficyna Wydawnicza Rytm, 1999.

Brown, Kate. *A Biography of No Place: From Ethnic Borderlands to Soviet Heartland.* Cambridge, Mass.: Harvard University Press, 2004.

Brubaker, Rogers. *Nationalism Reframed: Nationhood and the National Question in the New Europe.* Cambridge: Cambridge University Press, 1996.

Bruchis, Michael. *The Republic of Moldavia: From the Collapse of the Soviet Empire to the Restoration of the Russian Empire.* Boulder, Colo. East European Monographs, 1996.

Budnitskii, O. V., O. V. Belova, V. E. Kel'ner, and V. V. Mochalova, eds. *Mirovoi krisis 1914–1920 godov i sud'ba vostochnoevropeiskogo evreistva.* Moscow: Rosspen, 2005.

Budreckis, Algirdas Martin. *The Lithuanian National Revolt of 1941.* Boston: Lithuania Encyclopedia Press, 1968.

Burds, Jeffrey. *Sovetskaia agentura: ocherki istorii SSSR v poslevoyennye gody (1944–1948).* Moscow and New York: Sovremennaia Istoriias, 2006.

Caune, Andris, Daina Kļaviņa, and Inesis Feldmanis, eds. *Latvia in World War II: Materials of an International Conference, 14–15 June 1999, Riga.* Riga: Latvijas vēstures institūta apgāds, 2000.

Caune, Andris, et al. *The Hidden and Forbidden History of Latvia under Soviet and Nazi Occupations 1940–1991: Selected Research of the Commission of the Historians of Latvia.* Riga: Institute of the History of Latvia, 2005.

Chiari, Bernhard. *Alltag hinter der Front: Besatzung, Kollaboration und Widerstand in Weißrußland 1941–1944.* Düsseldorf: Droste Verlag, 1998.

Chmielowiec, Piotr, ed. *Okupacja sowiecka ziem polskich 1939–1941.* Warsaw-Rzeszów: Instytut Pamięci Narodowej—Komisja Ścigania Zbrodni przeciwko Narodowi Polskiemu, 2005.

Chubar'yan, A. O., A. A. Komarov, M. L. Korobochkin, and E. L. Nazarova, eds. *Rossiia i Baltiia, i. Narody i strany: vtoraia polovina XIX—30-e gg. XX v.; ii. Epokha peremen (1914–1924)* Moscow: Institut vseobshchei istorii, RAN, 2000, 2002.

Ciesielski, Stanisław, Grzegorz Hryciuk, and Aleksander Srebrakowski. *Masowe deportacje radzieckie w okresie II wojny światowej.* Wrocław: Instytut Historyczny

Uniwersytetu Wrocławskiego, Wrocławskie Towarzystwo Miłośników Historii, 1994.

Cordon, Cécile, and Helmut Kusdat, eds. *An der Zeiten Ränder. Czernowitz und die Bukowina: Geschichte, Literatur, Verfolgung, Exil*. Vienna: Theodor Kramer Gesellschaft, 2002.

Cygan, Wiktor Krzysztof. *Kresy w ogniu: wojna polsko-sowiecka 1939*. Warsaw: Warszawska Oficyna Wydawnicza, 1990.

Czerniakiewicz, Jan. *Repatriacja ludności polskiej z ZSRR, 1944–1948*. Warsaw: Państwowe Wydawnictwo Naukowe, 1987.

Daumantas, Juozas. *Fighters for Freedom: Lithuanian Partisans versus the USSR, 1944–1947*. New York: Manyland Books, 1975.

Davies, Norman. *White Eagle, Red Star: The Polish–Soviet War, 1919–1920*. New York: St. Martin's Press, 1972.

—— and Antony Polonsky, eds. *Jews in Eastern Poland and the USSR, 1939–1946*. New York: St. Martin's Press, 1991.

Demm, Eberhard, Roger Noël, and William Urban, eds. *The Independence of the Baltic States: Origins, Causes, and Consequences. A Comparison of the Crucial Years 1918–1919 and 1990–1991*. Chicago: Lithuanian Research and Study Center, 1996.

Dieckmann, Christoph, Babette Quinkert, and Tatjana Tönsmeyer, eds. *Kooperation und Verbrechen: Formen der 'Kollaboration' im östlichen Europa 1939–1945*. Göttingen: Wallstein Verlag, 2003.

Dima, Nicholas. *Moldova and the Transdnestr Republic*. Boulder, Colo.: East European Monographs, 2001.

Diuk, Nadia, and Adrian Karatnycky. *The Hidden Nations: The People Challenge the Soviet Union*. New York: William Morrow and Co., 1990.

Dolbilov, M., and A. Miller, eds. *Zapadnye okrainy Rossiiskoi Imperii*. Moscow: Novoe Literaturnoe obozrenie, 2006.

Dunn, Seamus, and T. G. Fraser, eds. *Europe and Ethnicity: The First World War and Contemporary Ethnic Conflict*. London: Routledge, 1996.

Eberhardt, Piotr. *Ethnic Groups and Population Changes in Twentieth Century Central-Eastern Europe: History, Data, and Analysis*. New York: M. E. Sharpe, 2003.

Eremina, L. S. et al., *Repressii protiv polakov i pol'skikh grazhdan*. Moscow: Zven'ia, 1997.

Ezergailis, Andrew. *The Holocaust in Latvia, 1941–1944: The Missing Center*. Riga: Historical Institute of Latvia, 1996.

—— and Gert Pistohlkors, eds. *Die Baltischen Provinzen Russlands zwischen den Revolutionen von 1905 und 1917*. Cologne: Böhlau Verlag, 1982.

Fainshtein, V. M. *Stanovlenie kapitalizma kak razreshenie protivorechii tovarnogo feodal'nogo proizvodstva (na' materialakh pribaltiiskikh gubernii Rossii)*. 2 vols. Tallin: Eesti raamat, 1987.

Fedyshyn, Oleh S. *Germany's Drive to the East and the Ukrainian Revolution, 1917–1918*. New Brunswick, NJ: Rutgers University Press, 1971.

Final Report. Bucharest: International Commission on the Holocaust in Romania, 2004.

Finberg, Leonid, and Volodymyr Liubchenko, eds. *Narysy z istorii ta kul'tury yevreiv Ukrainy*. Kiev: Dukh i Litera, 2005.

Fletcher, Jonathan. *Violence and Civilization: An Introduction to the Work of Norbert Elias*. Cambridge: Polity Press, 1997.

Fűhr, Christoph. *Das k.u.k. Armeekommando und die Innepolitik in Österreich*. Graz and Vienna: Böhlau, 1968.

Fuller, William C. *The Foe Within: Fantasies of Treason and the End of Imperial Russia*. Ithaca, NY, and London: Cornell University Press, 2006.

Gatrell, Peter. *A Whole Empire Is Walking: Refugees in Russia during World War I*. Bloomington: Indiana University Press, 1999.

Gaunt, David, Paul A. Levine, and Laura Palosuo, eds. *Collaboration and Resistance during the Holocaust: Belarus, Estonia, Latvia, Lithuania*. Bern: Peter Lang, 2004.

Gause, Fritz. *Die Russen in Ostpreussen 1914/15. Im Auftrage des Landeshauptmanns der Provinz Ostpreussen*. Kaliningrad: Cräfe und Unzer Verlag, 1931.

Geen, Russell G. *Personality: The Skein of Behavior*. St Louis: C. V. Mosby Company, 1976.

Gerlach, Christian. *Kalkulierte Morde: Die deutsche Wirtschafts- und Vernichtungspolitik in Weißrußland 1941 bis 1944*. Hamburg: Hamburger Edition, 1999.

Ģērmanis, Uldis. *Oberst Vācietis und die lettischen Schützen im Weltkrieg und in der Oktoberrevolution*. Stockholm: Almqvist & Wiksell, 1974.

Giżejewska, Małgorzata, and Tomasz Strzembosz, eds. *Społeczeństwo białoruskie, litewskie i polskie na ziemiach północno-wschodnich II Rzeczypospolitej (Białoruś zachodnia i Litwa wschodnia) w latach 1939–1941*. Warsaw: Instytut Studiów Politycznej Polskiej Akademii Nauk, 1995.

Goldman, Marshall I. *USSR in Crisis: The Failure of an Economic System*. New York: Norton, 1983.

Gon, Maksym. *Iz kryvdoiu na samoti: ukrains'ko-yevreis'ki vzayemyny na zakhidnoukrains' kykh zemliakh u skladi Pol'shchi (1935–1939)*. Rivne: Volyns'ki oberehy, 2005.

Gordon, Harry. *The Shadow of Death: The Holocaust in Lithuania*. Lexington: University Press of Kentucky, 1992.

Gorn, Vasilii. *Grazhdanskaia voina na severo-zapade Rossii*. Berlin: Izdatel'stvo Gamaiun, 1923.

Gribincea, Mihai. *Agricultural Collectivization in Moldavia: Basarabia during Stalinism, 1944–1950*. Boulder, Colo.: East European Monographs, 1996.

Grimsley, Mark, and Clifford J. Rogers, eds. *Civilians in the Path of War*. Lincoln: University of Nebraska Press, 2002.

Gross, Jan T. *Revolution from Abroad: The Soviet Conquest of Poland's Western Ukraine and Western Belorussia*. Princeton: Princeton University Press, 1988.

——— *Neighbors: The Destruction of the Jewish Community in Jedwabne, Poland*. New York: Penguin Books, 2001.

Grossfeld, Leon. *Polityka państw centralnych wobec sprawy polskiej w latach pierwszej wojny światowej, 1914–1918*. Warsaw: Państwowe Wydawnictwo Naukowe, 1962.

Hagen, Mark von. *War in a European Borderland: Occupations and Occupation Plans in Galicia and Ukraine, 1914–1918*. Seattle and London: University of Washington Press, 2007.

Hagen, William. *Germans, Poles, and Jews: The Nationality Conflict in the Prussian East, 1772–1914*. Chicago: University of Chicago Press, 1980.

Hall, John A., ed. *The State of the Nation: Ernest Gellner and the Theory of Nationalism*. Cambridge: Cambridge University Press, 1998.

Hardy, Peter S., ed. *Voennye prestupleniia Gabsburgskoi monarkhii: Galitskaia Golgofa*. Trumbull, Conn.: Hardy Lane, 1964.

Hausleitner, Mariana. *Die Rumänisierung der Bukowina: Die Durchsetzung des Nationalstaatlichen Anspruchs Grossrumäniens 1918–1944*. Munich: Oldenburg, 2001.

Hobsbawm, Eric. *The Age of Extremes: A History of the World*. New York: Vintage, 1996.

Horne, John, and Alan Kramer. *German Atrocities, 1914: A History of Denial*. New Haven: Yale University Press, 2001.

Horowitz, Donald L. *Ethnic Groups in Conflict*. Berkeley: University of California Press, 1985.

Hroch, Miroslav. *Social Preconditions of National Revival in Europe: A Comparative Analysis of the Social Composition of Patriotic Groups among the Smaller European Nations*. Cambridge: Cambridge University Press, 1985.

Huntington, Samuel. *Political Order in Changing Societies*. New Haven and London: Yale University Press, 1968.

Ivasiuta, M. K. *Narysy istorii kolkhospnoho budivnytstva v zakhidnykh oblastiakh Ukrains'koi RSR*. Kiev: vydavnytsvo Akademii Nauk Ukrains'koi SSR, 1962.

Jakubowska, Lucja, et al. *Nieświeskie wspomnienia*. Warsaw: Łośgraf, 2001.

Jasiewicz, Krzysztof. *Pierwsi po diable. Elity sowieckie w okupowanej Polsce 1939–1941 (Białostocczyzna, Nowogródczyzna, Polesie, Wileńszczyzna)*. Warsaw: Instytut Studiów Politycznych PAN and Oficyna Wydawnicza 'Rytm', 2002.

—— ed. *Tygiel narodów: stosunki społeczne i etniczne na dawnych ziemiach wschodnich Rzeczypospolitej, 1939–1953*. Warsaw: ISP PAN, Oficyna Wydawnicza Rytm, and Polonia Aid Foundation Trust, 2002.

Die Judenpogrome in Russland. Cologne and Leipzig: Jüdischer Verlag, 1910.

Judge, Edward H. *Easter in Kishinev: Anatomy of a Pogrom*. New York: New York University Press, 1992.

Kalyvas, Stathis N. *The Logic of Violence in Civil War*. Cambridge and New York: Cambridge University Press, 2006.

Kappeler, Andreas. *The Russian Empire: A Multiethnic History*. London and New York: Pearson Education, 2001.

Karjahärm, T., Ia. Krastyn, and A. Tila. *Revolutsiia 1905–1907 godov v Pribaltike*. Tallin: Akademia Nauk Estonskoi SSR, 1981.

Kaufman, Stuart J. *Modern Hatreds: The Symbolic Politics of Ethnic War.* Ithaca, NY, and London: Cornell University Press, 2001.

Kielmansegg, Peter Graf. *Deutschland und der Erste Weltkrieg.* Frankfurt am Main: Akademische Verlagsgesellschaft Athenaion, 1968.

Kirsh, Iu. *Agrarnaia revolutsiia v Pribaltike.* Moscow: Mezhdunarodnyi agrarnyi institute, 1931.

Klier, John, and Shlomo Lambroza, eds. *Pogroms: Anti-Jewish Violence in Modern Russian History.* Cambridge: Cambridge University Press, 1992.

Kőhrer, Erich, ed. *Das wahre Gesicht des Bolschewismus! Tatsachen—Berichte—Bilder aus den baltischen, Provinzen, November 1918–Februar 1919.* Berlin: Verlag für Sozialwissenschaft, n.d.

Kołakowski, Piotr. *NKWD i GRU na ziemiach polskich 1939–1945.* Warsaw: Dom Wydawniczy Bellona, 2002.

Kołodziejczyk, Ryszard, ed. *Społeczeństwo polskie w dobie pierwszej wojny światowej i wojny polsko-bolszewickiej 1920 roku.* Kielce: Kieleckie Towarzystwo Naukowe, 2001.

Kõll, Anu Mai, ed. *The Baltic Countries under Occupation: Soviet and Nazi Rule, 1939–1991.* Stockholm: Acta Universitatis Stockholmiensis, 2003.

Kolstø, Pål, ed. *National Integration and Violent Conflict in Post-Soviet Societies: The Case of Estonia and Moldova.* Lanham: Rowman & Littlefield, 2002.

Kostyshyn, S. S., et al. *Bukovyna: istorychnyi narys.* Chernivtsi: Chernivets´kyi derzhavnyi universytet im. Iu. Fed´kovycha, 1998.

Kozłowski, Maciej. *Zapomniana wojna: walki o Lwów i Galicję Wschodnią, 1918–1919.* Bydgoszcz: Instytut Wydawniczy Świadectwo, 1999.

Krausnick, Helmut, and Hans-Heinrich Wilhelm. *Die Truppe des Weltanschauungskrieges: Die Einsatzgruppen der Sicherheitspolizei und des SD 1938–1942.* Stuttgart: Deutsche Verlags-Anstalt, 1981.

Laar, Mart. *War in the Woods: Estonia's Struggle for Survival, 1946–1956.* Washington: Compass Press, 1992.

Landau, Zbigniew, and Jerzy Tomaszewski. *W dobie inflacji.* Warsaw: Książka i Wiedza, 1967.

Lazarev, A. M. *Moldavskaia Sovetskaia gosudarstvennost´ i bessarabskii vopros.* Chişinău: Kartia Moldoveniaske, 1974.

Levene, Mark. *The Rise of the West and the Coming of Genocide.* London and New York: I. B. Tauris, 2005.

Levin, Nora. *The Jews in the Soviet Union since 1917: Paradox of Survival.* 2 vols. New York: New York University Press, 1990.

Lewandowska, Stanisława. *Życie codzienne Wilna w latach II wojny światowej.* Warsaw: Wydawnictwo Neriton-Instytut Historii PAN, 1997.

Lieven, Anatol. *The Baltic Revolution: Estonia, Latvia, Lithuania and the Path to Independence.* New Haven: Yale University Press, 1993.

Lieven, Dominic. *Empire: The Russian Empire and its Rivals.* New Haven: Yale University Press, 2000.

Litvin, Aliaksei. *Akupatsyia Belarusi (1941–1944): pytanni supratsivu i kalabaratsyi.* Minsk: Belaruski knigazbor, 2000.

Liulevicius, Vejas Gabriel. *War Land on the Eastern Front: Culture, National Identity and German Occupation in World War I.* Cambridge, Mass.: Cambridge University Press, 2000.

Livezeanu, Irina. *Cultural Politics in Greater Romania: Regionalism, Nation Building, and Ethnic Struggle, 1918–1930.* Ithaca, NY: Cornell University Press, 1995.

Lohr, Eric. *Nationalizing the Russian Empire: The Campaign against Enemy Aliens During World War I.* Cambridge, Mass.: Harvard University Press, 2003.

Łossowski, Piotr. *Konflikt polsko-litewski 1918–1920.* Warsaw: Wydawnictwo Książka i Wiedza, 1996.

Lubny-Gertsyk, L. I. *Dvizhenie naseleniia na territorii SSSR za vremia mirovoi voiny i revolutsii.* Moscow: Izdatel'stvo Planovoe khoziaistvo, 1926.

Machcewicz, Paweł, and Krzysztof Persak, eds. *Wokół Jedwabnego.* 2 vols. Warsaw: Instytut Pamięci Narodowej—Komisja Ścigania Zbrodni Przeciwko Narodowi Polskiemu, 2002.

MacMillan, Margaret, *Peacemakers: The Paris Conference of 1919 and its Attempt to End War.* London: John Murray Paperbacks, 2002.

Madajczyk, Czesław. *Faszyzm i okupacje, 1938–1945: wykonywanie okupacji przez państwa Osi w Europie.* 2 vols. Poznań: Wydawnictwo Poznańskie, 1983.

Magosci, Paul Robert. *The Shaping of National Identity: Subcarpathian Rus', 1848–1948.* London and Cambridge, Mass.: Harvard University Press, 1978.

—— *A History of Ukraine.* Toronto: University of Toronto Press, 1996.

—— *The Roots of Ukrainian Nationalism: Galicia as Ukraine's Piedmont.* Toronto and London: University of Toronto Press, 2002.

Makarchuk, S. A. *Ukrains'ka Respublika Halychan: narysy pro ZUNR.* L'viv: Svit, 1997.

Mańkowski, Zygmunt, ed., *Niepodległść Polski w 1918 roku a procesy państwowotwórcze w Europie środkowo-wshodniej.* Lublin: wydawnictwo Uniwersytetu Marii Curie-Skłodowskiej, 1996.

Marples, David R. *Stalinism in Ukraine in the 1940s.* New York: St Martin's Press, 1992.

Martin, Terry. *The Affirmative Action Empire: Nations and Nationalism in the Soviet Union, 1923–1939.* Ithaca, NY: Cornell University Press, 2001.

Matsko, A. *Revolitsionnaia bor'ba trudiashchikhsia Pol'shi i Zapadnoi Belorussii protiv gneta burzhuazii i pomeshchikov, 1918–1939 gg.* Minsk: Izdatel'stvo Belarus, 1972.

Mędrzecki, Włodzimierz. *Niemiecka interwencja militarna na Ukrainie w 1918 roku.* Warsaw: Wydawnictwo DiG, 2000.

Mel'tiukhov, Mikhail. *Osvoboditel'nyi pokhod Stalina: Bessarabskii vopros v sovetsko-rumynskikh otnosheniiakh (1917–1940 gg.).* Moscow: 'Iauza'-'Eksmo', 2006.

Mendelsohn, Ezra. *The Jews of East Central Europe between the World Wars.* Bloomington: Indiana University Press, 1983.

Merkis, V. *Razvitie promyshlennosti i formirovanie proletariata Litvy v XIXv.* Vilnius: Mintis, 1969.

Mikoda, Janina, ed. *Zbrodnicza ewakuacja więzień i aresztów NKWD na Kresach Wschodnich II Rzeczypospolitej w czerwcu-lipcu 1941 roku: Materiały z sesji naukowej w 55. rocznice ewakuacji więźnów NKWD w głąb ZSRR, Łódź, 10 czerwca 1996 r.* Warsaw: Główna Komisja Badania Zbrodni przeciwko Narodowi Polskiemu-Instytut Pamięci Narodowej, 1997.

Mints, I. I, A. A. Drizul, Iu.I. Zhiugzhda, and V. A. Maamiagi, eds. *Bor'ba za Sovetskuiu vlast' v Pribaltike.* Moscow: Nauka, 1967.

Misiunas, Romuald J., and Rein Taagera. *The Baltic States: Years of Dependence, 1940–1990.* Berkeley, University of California Press, 1983.

Motyl, Alexander J. *The Turn to the Right: The Ideological Origins and Development of Ukrainian Nationalism 1919–1929.* New York: Columbia University Press, 1980.

Musial, Bogdan. '*Kontrrevolutionäre Elemente sind zu erschiessen': Die Brutalisierung des deutsch–sowjetischen Krieges im Sommer 1941.* Berlin and Munich: Propyläen Verlag, 2000.

Mykhailiuk, O. H., ed. *Istoriia Volyni z naidavnishykh chasiv do nashykh dniv.* L'viv: vydavnytstvo pry L'vivs'komu derzh. Universyteti vydavnychoho ob'iednannia Vyshcha shkola, 1988.

Myllyniemi, Seppo. *Die Neuordnung der baltischen Länder 1941–1944: Zum nationalsozialistischen Inhalt der deutschen Besatzungspolitik.* Helsinki: Vammalan Kirjapaino, 1973.

Navitskas, K. *Litva i Antanta (1918–1920 gg.).* Vilnius: Izdatel'stvo Mintis, 1970.

——, ed. *Aparat represji a opór społeczeństwa wobec systemu komunistycznego w Polsce i na Litwie w latach 1944–1956.* Warsaw: Instytut Pamięci Narodowej-Komisja Ścigania Zbrodni przeciwko Narodowi Polskiemu, 2005.

Niwiński, Piotr, ed. *Aparat represji a opór społeczeństwa wobec systemu komunistycznego w Polsce i na Litwie w latach 1944–1956.* Warsaw: Instytut Pamięci Narodowej-Komisja Ścigania Zbrodni przeciwko Narodowi Polskiemu, 2005.

Nowak, Zenon Hubert, and Zbiegniew Karpus, eds. *Studia i szkice z dziejów Żydów w regionie Bałtyku.* Toruń: wydawnictwo Uniwersytetu Mikołaja Kopernika, 1998.

Pajewski, Janusz. *Budowa Drugiej Rzeczypospolitej, 1918–1926.* Krakow: nakładem Polskiej Akademii Umiejętności, 1995.

Palmer, Alan Warwick. *The Lands Between: A History of East-Central Europe since the Congress of Vienna.* New York: Macmillan, 1970.

Panayi, Panikos, ed. *Minorities in Wartime: National and Racial Groupings in Europe, North America and Australia during the Two World Wars.* Oxford: Berg, 1993.

Pedosov, A. D., G. I. Volkova, L. Ia. Zile, A. K. Pankseev, K. Z. Surblis, I. M. Tikhonova, B. A. Toman and R. Ia. Sharmaitis, eds. *Postroenie sotsializma v Sovetskoi Pribaltike: istoricheskii opyt kompartii Litvy, Latvii, Estonii.* Riga: Avots, 1982.

Petersen, Roger D. *Understanding Ethnic Violence: Fear, Hatred, and Resentment in Twentieth-Century Eastern Europe.* Cambridge: Cambridge University Press, 2002.

Petrovych, Ivan. *Halychyna pid chas rosiis'koi okupatsii, serpen' 1914-cherven' 1915.* L'viv: Politychna Biblioteka, 1915.

Piotrowski, Tadeusz. *Poland's Holocaust: Ethnic Strife, Collaboration with Occupying Forces and Genocide in the Second Republic, 1918–1947.* Jefferson, NC: McFarland & Co., 1998.

Pistohlkors, Gert, ed. *Baltische Länder.* Berlin: Siedler Verlag, 1994, series Deutsche Geschichte im Osten Europas.

Plieg, Ernst-Albrecht. *Das Memelland 1920–1939: deutsche Autonomiebestrebungen im litauischen Gesamtstaat.* Würzburg: Holzer Verlag, 1962.

Pohl, Dieter. *Nationalsozialistische Judenverfolgung in Ostgalizien, 1941–1944: Organisation und Durchführung eines staatlichen Massenverbrechens.* Munich: R. Oldenbourg Verlag, 1997.

Poluian, I. V. *Zapadnaia Belorussiia v period ekonomicheskogo krizisa 1929–1933 gg.* Minsk: Navuka i tekhnika, 1991.

Popoff, George. *The Red Plague: Soviet Rule in a Baltic Town.* New York: E. P. Dutton & Co., 1932.

Porter, Brian. *When Nationalism Began to Hate: Imagining Modern Politics in Nineteenth-Century Poland.* New York: Oxford University Press, 2000.

Prokopovych, Erich. *Kinets' avstriis'koho panuvannia v Bukovyni.* Chernivtsi: Zoloti lytavry, 2004.

Prusin, Alexander Victor. *Nationalizing a Borderland: War, Ethnicity, and Anti-Jewish Violence in East Galicia, 1914–1920.* Tuscaloosa: University of Alabama Press, 2005.

Pushkash, Andrei. *Tsivilizatsiia ili varvarstvo: Zakarpat'ye 1918–1945.* Moscow: Izdatel'stvo 'Evropa', 2006.

Rauch, Georg. *The Baltic States: The Years of Independence. Estonia, Latvia, Lithuania, 1917–1940.* Berkeley: University of California Press, 1974.

Raun, Toivo U. *Estonia and Estonians.* Stanford, Calif.: Hoover Institution Press, 1991.

Röhr, Werner, ed. *Okkupation und Kollaboration (1938–1945). Beiträge zu Konzepten und Praxis der Kollaboration in der deutschen Okkupationspolitik.* Berlin: Hüthig Verlagsgemeinschaft, 1994.

Roshwald, Aviel. *Ethnic Nationalism and the Fall of Empires: Central Europe, Russia and the Middle East, 1914–1923.* London: Routledge, 2000.

Rostunov, I. I. *Russkii front pervoii mirovoii voiny.* Moscow: izdatel'stvo Nauka, 1976.

Rothschild, Joseph. *East Central Europe between the Two World Wars.* Seattle: University of Washington Press, 1974.

Rubliov, O. S. and Iu. A. Cherchenko. *Stalinshchyna i dolia zakhidnoukrains'koi intelihentsii, 20–50-ti roky XX st.* Kiev: Naukova Dumka, 1994.

Rudnicki, Szymon. *Obóz Narodowo Radykalny: geneza i działalność.* Warsaw: Czytelnik, 1985.

Sakowicz, Kazimierz. *Ponary Diary, July 1941–November 1943: A Bystander's Account of a Mass Murder,* ed. Yitzhak Arad. New Haven: Yale University Press, 2005.

Sambuk, S. M. *Politika tsarisma v Belorussii vo vtoroi polovinie XIX veka.* Minsk: Nauka i Tekhnika, 1980.

Sannikov, Georgii. *Bol'shaia okhota: razgrom vooruzhennogo podpol'ya v Zapadnoi Ukraine*. Moscow: Olma-Press, 2002.

Salomon, Ernst. *The Outlaws*. London: Jonathan Cape, 1931.

Sambuk, S. M. *Politika tsarisma v Belorussii vo vtoroi polovinie XIX veka*. Minsk: "Nauka i Tekhnika," 1980.

Sannikov, Georgii. *Bol'shaia okhota: razgrom vooruzhennogo podpol'ya v Zapadnoi Ukraine*. Moscow: "Olma-Press," 2002.

Schall, Jacob. *Żydostwo galicyjskie w czasie inwazji rosyjskiej w latach 1914–1916*. L'viv: nakładem Księgarni I. Madfesa, 1936.

Schiper, Ignacy. *Dzieje handlu żydowskiego na ziemiach polskich*. Warsaw: nakładem Centrali Związków Kupców, 1937.

Semenov, Iu. I., ed. *Natsional'naia politika v imperatorskoi Rossii. Tsivilizovannye okrainy (Finlandiia, Pol'sha, Pribaltika, Bessarabia, Ukraina, Zakavkaz'ye, Sredniaia Aziia)*. Moscow: Staryi sad, 1997.

Sherstobitov, V., et al. *Istoriia natsional'no-gosudarstvennogo stroitel'stva v SSSR, 1917–1978*. 2 vols. Moscow: Mysl', 1979.

Shkliar, E. N. *Bor'ba trudiashchikhsia Litov.-Beloruss.SSR s inostrannymi interventami i vnutrenniei kontrrevolutsiyei (1919–1920gg)*. Minsk: Gosudarstvennoe izdatel'stvo BSSR, 1962.

Shvahuliak, Mykhailo. *'Patsyfikatsiia': pol's'ka represyvna aktsiia u Halychyni 1930 r. i ukrains'ka suspil'nist'*. L'viv: Akademiia Nauk Ukrainy—Instytut Ukrainoznavstva, 1993.

Simon, Gerhard. *Nationalism and Policy toward the Nationalities in the Soviet Union: From Totalitarian Dictatorship to Post-Stalinist Society*. Boulder, Colo.: Westview Press, 1991.

Sīpols, V. *Die ausländische Intervention in Lettland 1918–1920*. Berlin: Rütten & Loening, 1961.

Śleczyński, Wojciech. *Zajścia antyżydowskie w Brześciu nad Bugiem 13 maja 1937 roku*. Białystok: Archiwum Państwowe w Białymstoku, 2004.

Smele, Jonathan D., and Anthony Heywood, eds. *The Russian Revolution: Centenary Perspectives*. London and New York: Routledge, 2005.

Snyder, Timothy. *The Reconstruction of Nations: Poland, Ukraine, Lithuania, Belarus, 1969–1999*. New Haven and London: Yale University Press, 2003.

Sobolev, Ivan G. *Bor'ba s 'nemetskim zasil'yem' v Rossii v gody pervoi mirovoi voiny*. St Petersburg: Izdatel'stvo Rossiiskaia natsional'naia biblioteka, 2004.

Solov'yev, A. K. *Belorusskaia Tsentral'naia Rada: sozdanie, deiatel'nost', krakh*. Minsk: Navuka i tekhnika, 1995.

Sorokin, Pitirim A. *Man and Society in Calamity: The Effects of War, Revolution, Famine, and Pestilence upon Human Mind, Behavior, Social Organization and Cultural Life*. New York: E. P. Dutton, 1943.

Spector, Shmuel. *The Holocaust of Volhynian Jews, 1941–1944*. Jerusalem: Yad Vashem–Federation of Volhynian Jews, 1990.

Spivak, B. I. *Narysy istorii revoliutsiinoi borot'by trudiashchykh Zakarpatttiia v 1930–1945 rokakh*. L'viv: vydavnytstvo L'vivs'koho universytetu, 1963.

Stang, Knut. *Kollaboration und Massenmord: Die litauische Hilfspolizei, das Rollkommando Hamann und die Ermordung der litauischen Juden.* Frankfurt am Main: Peter Lang, 1996.

Stankiewicz, Witold. *Konflikty społeczne na wsi polskiej, 1918–1920.* Warsaw: Państwowe Wydawnictwo Naukowe, 1963.

Stasiuk, Andrzej and Iurii Andrukhovych. *Moia Evropa: dva esei pro naidyvnishu chastynu svitu.* L´viv: Klasyka, 2005.

Stražas, A. *Deutsche Ostpolitik im Ersten Weltkrieg. Der Fall Ober Ost 1915–1917.* Wiesbaden: Harrassowitz Verlag, 1993.

Sukiennicki, Wiktor. *East Central Europe during World War I: From Foreign Domination to National Independence.* 2 vols. Boulder, Colo.: East European Monographs, 1984.

Suny, Ronald Grigor and Terry Martin, eds. *A State of Nations: Empire and Nation Making in the Age of Lenin and Stalin.* New York: Oxford University Press, 2001.

Swain, Geoffrey. *Between Stalin and Hitler: Class War and Race War on the Dvina, 1940–1946.* New York: RoutledgeCurzon, 2004.

Sword, Keith, ed. *The Soviet Takeover of the Polish Eastern Provinces, 1939–1941.* New York: St. Martin's Press, 1991.

Szarota, Tomasz. *U progu zagłady: zajścia antyżydowskie i pogromy w okupowanej Europie: Warszawa, Paryż, Amsterdam, Antwerpia, Kowno.* Warsaw: Wydawnictwo Sic!, 2000.

Tennenbaum, Samuel Lipa. *Zloczow Memoir.* New York: Shengold Publishers, 1986.

Tomaszewski, Tadeusz. *Lwów 1940–1944: pejzaż psychologiczny.* Warsaw: WIP, 1996.

Tory, Avraham. *Surviving the Holocaust: The Kovno Ghetto Diary.* Cambridge, Mass.: Harvard University Press, 1990.

Torzeski, Ryszard. *Polacy i ukraińcy: sprawa ukraińska w czasie II wojny światowej na terenie II Rzeczypospolitej.* Warsaw: Wydawnictwo Naukowe PWN, 1993.

Turonek, Jerzy. *Białoruś pod okupacją niemiecką.* Warsaw: Książka i Wiedza, 1993.

Ulam, Adam B. *Expansion and Coexistence: The History of Soviet Foreign Policy, 1917–1967.* New York-Washington: Frederick A. Praeger, 1968.

Vakar, Nicholas P. *Belorussia: The Making of a Nation.* Cambridge, Mass.: Harvard University Press, 1956.

Valakhnovich, I. A. *Antisovetskoe podpol'ye na territorii Belarusi v 1944–1953 gg.* Minsk: BGU, 2002.

Vardy, Steven Béla, and T. Hunt Tooley, eds. *Ethnic Cleansing in Twentieth-Century Europe.* New York: Columbia University Press, 2003.

Vardys, Stanley V. and Romuald J. Misiunas, eds. *The Baltic States in Peace and War, 1917–1945.* University Park: Pennsylvania State University Press, 1978.

Vaupshasov, S.A. *Na trevozhnykh perekrestkakh: zapiski chekista.* Moscow: Izdatel´stvo politicheskoi literatury, 1974.

Vital', Luba, ed. *Bezhanstva 1915 hoda*. Białystok: Prahramnaia rada tydnvika Niva, 2000.

Volgyes, Ivan, ed. *The Peasantry of Eastern Europe*. 2 vols. New York: Pergamon Press, 1979.

Yefremov, P. N. *Vneshniaia politika Rossii, 1907–1914*. Moscow: izdatel'stvo Instituta Mezhdunarodnykh Otnoshenii, 1961.

Yevreinov, G. A. *Natsional'nye voprosy na inorodcheskikh orkainakh Rossii. Skhema politicheskoi programmy*. St. Petersburg: Tipographiia A. Benke, 1908.

Waite, Robert G. L. *Vanguard of Nazism: The Free Corps Movement in Postwar Germany 1918–1923*. Cambridge, Mass.: Harvard University Press, 1952.

Wardzyńska, Maria. *Sytuacja ludności polskiej w Generalnym Komisariacie Litwy, czerwiec 1941–lipiec 1944*. Warsaw: Agencja Wydawnicza MAKO, 1993.

Weeks, Theodore R. *Nation and State in Late Imperial Russia: Nationalism and Russification on the Western Frontier, 1863–1914*. DeKalb: Northern Illionois University Press, 1996.

Weiner, Amir, ed. *Landscaping the Human Garden: Twentieth-Century Population Management in a Comparative Framework*. Stanford, Calif.: Stanford University Press, 2003.

Weinzierl, Erika, and Karl R. Stadler, eds. *Justiz und Zeitgeschichte*. Vienna: J. H. Pospisil, 1977.

Weiss-Wendt, Anton. *Murder without Hatred: The Estonians and the Holocaust*. Syracuse, NY: Syracuse University Press, 2009.

Wells, Leon Weliczker. *The Janowska Road*. New York: Macmillan, 1963.

Wilhelm, Hans-Heinrich. *Die Einsatzgruppe A der Sicherheitspolizei und des SD 1941/42*. Frankfurt: Peter Lang, 1996.

Wspomnienia Rudolfa Hoessa, komendanta obozu święcimskiego. Warsaw: Wydawnictwo prawnicze, 1956.

Wynot, Edward D. *Caldron of Conflict: Eastern Europe, 1918–1945*. Wheeling, Ill.: Harlan Davidson, 1999.

Zaprudnik, Jan. *Belarus: At a Crossroads in History*. Boulder, Colo.: Westview Press, 1993.

Zapolovs'kyi, Volodymyr. *Bukovyna v ostannii viini Avstro-Uhorshchyny 1914–1918*. Chernivtsi: Zoloti lytavry, 2003.

ARTICLES

Altenberg, A. 'Die Besetzung Memels durch die Russen (18.–21.März 1915)'. *Ostpreussische Kriegshefte* 3 (1916): 25–34.

Altshuler, M. 'Russia and her Jews:The Impact of the 1914 War'. *Wiener Library Bulletin* 27, 30–1 (1973–74): 12–16.

Ancel, Jean. 'The Romanian Way of Solving the "Jewish Problem" in Bessarabia and Bukovina, June–July 1941'. *Yad Vashem Studies* 19 (1988): 185–232.

Angelus, Oskar. 'Die ersten bolschewistischen Deportationen aus Estland'. *Baltische Hefte* 91 (1962): 2–13.

Antosiak, A. V. 'Revolutsiia i kontrrevolutsiia v Bessarabii v 1917–1918 godakh'. *Voprosy istorii* 12 (1988): 47–58.

Atamukas, Solomonas. 'The Hard Long Road toward the Truth: On the Sixtieth Anniversary of the Holocaust in Lithuania'. *Lituanus* 47/4 (2001): 19–21.

Baran, Oleksandr. 'Uhors'ka administratsiia na okupovanomu Zakarpatti (1939–1944)'. *Ukrains'kyi istoryk* 35/1–4 (1998): 172–190.

Birn, Ruth Bettina. 'Collaboration with Nazi Germany in Eastern Europe: The Case of the Estonian Security Police'. *Contemporary European History* 10/2 (2001): 181–98.

Borodziewicz, Wincenty. 'Rozmowy polsko-litewskie w Wilnie 1942–1944'. *Przegląd Historyczny* 80/2 (1982): 317–37.

Brubaker, Rogers, and David D. Laitin. 'Ethnic and Nationalist Violence'. *Annual Review of Sociology* 24 (1998): 423–452.

Brűggemann, Karsten. 'Defending National Sovereignty against Two Russias: Estonia in the Russian Civil War, 1918–1920'. *Journal of Baltic Studies* 34/1 (2003): 22–51.

Chinn, Jeff and Steven D. Roper. 'Ethnic Mobilization and Reactive Nationalism: The Case of Moldova'. *Nationalities Papers* 23/2 (1995): 291–325.

Dąbrowski, Roman. 'Die social-wirtschaftliche Tätigkeit der litauischen Minderheit in der Zweiten Republik (1918-1939)'. *Studia Historiae Oeconomicae* 21 (1994): 101–12.

Danylenko, V. M. 'Likvidatsiia pol's'koi derzhavy ta vstanovlennia radians'koho rezhymu v Zakhidnii Ukraini'. *Ukrains'kyi Istorychnyi Zhurnal* 3/468 (2006): 111–25.

Dean, Martin. 'Poles in the German Local Police in Eastern Poland and their Role in the Holocaust'. *Polin: Studies in Polish Jewry* 18 (2005): 353–66.

Dumin, Tadeusz. 'Nacjonalism i antysemitizm w programie Obozu Narodowo-Radykalnego'. *Studia na faszyzmem i zbrodniami hitlerowskimi* 3 (1977): 337–52. Wrocław: Wydawnictwo Uniwersytetu Wrocławskiego.

Filimoshin, M. V. 'Desiatkami strelial liudei tol'ko za to, chto … vygliadeli kak bol'sheviki'. *Voenno-Istoricheskii Zhurnal* 2 (2001): 43–8.

Finder, Gabriel N., and Alexander V. Prusin. 'Collaboration in Eastern Galicia: The Ukrainian Police and the Holocaust'. *East European Jewish Affairs* 34/2 (2004): 95–118.

Friedrich, Klaus-Peter. 'Spontane "Volkspogrome" oder Auswűchse der NS-Vernichtungspolitik? Zur Kontroverse um die Radikalisierung der antijűdischen Gewalt im Sommer 1941'. *Kwartalnik Historii Żydów 4/Jewish History Quarterly* 212 (2004): 587–611.

Gasparaitis, Siegfried. ' "Verrätern wird nur dann vergeben, wenn sie wirlich beweisen, dass sie mindestens einen Juden liquidiert haben": die "Front Litauischer Aktivisten"

(LAF) und die antisowjetischen Aufstände 1941'. *Zeitschrift für Geschichtswissenschaft* 49/10 (2001): 886–904.

Goldin, Semen. 'Deportation of Jews by the Russian Military Command, 1914–1915'. *Jews in Eastern Europe* 1 (2000): 40–73.

Haberer, Eric. 'The German Police and Genocide in Belorussia, 1941–1944', Part I: 'Police Deployment and Nazi Genocidal directives'. *Journal of Genocide Research* 3/1 (2001): 13–29;

Hamm, Michael F. 'Kishinev: The Character and Development of a Tsarist Frontier Town'. *Nationalities Papers* 261 (1998): 19–37.

Hellmann, Manfred. 'Der Staatsstreich von 1926 in Litauen: Verlauf und Hintergründe'. *Jahrbücher für Geschichte Osteuropas* 28/2 (1980): 220–42.

Heydenkorn, Benedykt. 'Ukraińska polemika o Berezie Kartuzskiej'. *Zeszyty Historyczne* 62 (1982): 205–9.

Himka, John-Paul. 'Western Ukraine in the Interwar Period'. *Nationalities Papers* 20/2 (1994): 347–64.

Hroch, Miroslav. 'Nationalism and National Movements: Comparing the Past and the Present of Central and Eastern Europe'. *Nations and Nationalism* 2/1 (1996): 35–44.

Ilarionova, T. S. 'Obmen naseleniem mezhdu SSSR i Germaniei nakanune i v nachale vtoroi mirovoi voiny'. *Otechestvennaia istoriia* 4 (2004): 54–62.

Iljuszyn, Ihor, and Grzegorz Mazur. 'Utworzenie i działalność czekistowskich grup operacyjnych NKWD w zachodnich obwodach Ukrainy w latach 1939-140 (na podstawie materiałów Państwowego Archiwum Służby Bezpieczeństwa Ukrainy)'. *Zeszyty Historyczne* 135 (2001): 49–74.

Ioffe, G. Z. 'Vyselenie evreev iz prifrontovoi polosy v 1915 godu'. *Voprosy Istorii* 9 (2001): 85–97.

Jasiński, Alfred. 'Borysławska apokalipsa'. *Karta* 4 (1991): 98–114.

Jundziłł, Zygmunt. 'Z dziejów polskiej myśli politycznej na Litwie historycznej'. *Niepodległość* 6 (1958): 61–77.

Kersten, Krystyna. 'The Polish–Ukrainian Conflict under Communist Rule'. *Acta Poloniae Historica* 73 (1996): 135–51.

Koehl, Robert Lewis. 'A Prelude to Hitler's Greater Germany'. *American Historical Review* 59/1 (1953): 43–65.

Kołakowski, Piotr. 'NKWD-NKGB a podziemie polskie: Kresy Wschodnie 1944–1945'. *Zeszyty Historyczne* 136 (2001): 59–86.

Kopchak, V. 'O nekotorykh strukturnykh izmeneniiakh naseleniia Zakarpat´ya za sto let (1869–1970)'. *Ekonomika Sovetskoi Ukrainy* 14/6 (1972): 66–9.

Krzepkowski, Mieczysław. 'Wspomnienia dziennikarza z czasów okupacji (Wilno 1939–1941)'. *Zeszyty Historyczne* 45 (1978): 139–70.

Kuznetsov, S., and B. Netrebskii, eds. 'Pod maskoi nezavisimosti (dokumenty o vooruzhennom natsionalisticheskom podpol'ye v Latvii v 40–50-kh gg'. *Izvestiia TsK KPSS*, 11 (1990): 112–23.

Kuznetsov, S., I, Kurilov, B. Netrebskii, and Iu. Sigachev, eds. 'Vooruzhennoe natsionalisticheskoe podpol'ye v Estonii v 40–50–kh godakh'. *Izvestiia TsK KPSS*, 8 (1990): 166–177.

Leidinger, Hannes. 'Der Einzug des Galgens und des Mordes: die parlamentarischen Stellungnahmen polnischer und ruthenischer Reichsratsabgeordneter zu den Massenhinrichtungen in Galizien 1914–1915'. *Zeitgeschichte* 5/33 (2006): 235–60.

Levin, Dov. 'Jewish Autonomy in Inter-war Lithuania: An Interview with Yudl Mark'. *Polin: Studies in Polish Jewry* 14 (2001): 192–211.

Lohr, Eric. 'The Russian Army and the Jews: Mass Deportation, Hostages, and Violence during World War I'. *Russian Review* 60 (2001): 404–19.

Łossowski, Piotr. 'Rządy dyktatorskie w państach bałtyckich, 1926–1934–1940: studium porównawcze'. *Studia na faszyzmem i zbrodniami hitlerowskimi* 8 (1982): 3–31.

Lowentnal, Leo. 'Terror's, Atomization of Man'. *Commentary* 1/3 (1946), 1–8.

Lysenko, V. G. 'Utvorennia i rozvytok Moldavs'koi ASSR u skladi USSR (1920–1940)'. *Ukrains'kyi Istorychnyi Zhurnal* 9 (1974): 46–54.

MacQueen, Michael. 'The Context of Mass Destruction: Agents and Prerequisites of the Holocaust in Lithuania'. *Holocaust and Genocide Studies* 12/1 (1998): 27–48.

Malinovskii, B. V. 'Avstro-Vengriia i agrarnaia reforma v Ukrainie, 1918 r'. *Voprosy germanskoi istorii: sbornik nauchnykh trudov* (2003): 194–212.

Matthäus, Jürgen. 'German Judenpolitik in Lithuania during the First World War'. *Leo Baeck Institute Yearbook*, Yearbook 43 (1998): 155–74.

Motyl, Alexander J. 'The Rural Origins of the Communist and Nationalist Movements in Wołyń Województwo, 1921–1939'. *Slavic Review* 37 (1978): 412–20.

Musielak, Michał. 'Narodowy socjalizm w myśli sanacyjnej'. *Studia na faszyzmem i zbrodniami hitlerowskimi* 20 (1997): 5–40.

Nelipovich, S. G. 'Repressii protiv poddanykh 'Tsentral'nykh Derzhav': deportatsii v Rossii, 1914–1918 gg'. *Voenno-istoricheskii zhurnal* 6 (1996): 32–42.

Pagel, Jürgen. 'Der polnisch-litauische Streit um Wilna und die Haltung der Sowjetunion, 1918–1938'. *Jahrbücher für Geschichte Osteuropa* 40/1 (1992): 41–75.

Parming, Tönu. 'The Jewish Community and Inter-Ethnic Relations in Estonia, 1918–1940'. *Journal of Baltic Studies* 10/3 (1979): 241–62.

'Polacy znad Wilii, Niemna, Narwi i Bugu w łagrach sowieckich w latach 1944–1947 (praca anonimowa)'. *Zeszyty Historyczne* 67 (1984): 155–87.

'Pribaltiiskii krai v 1905 godu'. *Krasnyi arkhiv: istoricheskii zhurnal* 11–12 (1925): 259–84.

Prusin, Alexander V. 'The "Stimulus Qualities" of a Scapegoat: The Etiology of Anti-Jewish Violence in Eastern Poland, 1918–1920'. *Simon Dubnow Institute Yearbook* 4 (2005): 237–56.

Remeikis, Thomas. 'The Impact of Industrialization on the Ethnic Demography of the Baltic Countries'. *Lituanus*, 13/1 (1967): 29–41.

Rieber, Alfred J. 'Changing Concepts and Constructions of Frontiers: A Comparative Historical Approach'. *Ab Imperio* 1 (2003): 23–46.

—— 'Civil Wars in the Soviet Union'. *Kritika: Explorations in Russian and Eurasian History* 4/1 (2003): 129–62.

Rink, Friedrich. 'Expulsion of the German Colonists from Wolhynia, 1915–1916'. *Heritage Review* 25/1 (1995): 19–22.

Roman, Louis. 'The Population of Bessarabia during the 19th Century: The National Structure', *Romanian Civilization* 32 (1994): 53–66.

Rőskau-Rydel, Isabel. 'Polnisch–litauische Bezihungen zwischen 1918 und 1939'. *Jahrbücher für Geschichte Osteuropas* 35/4 (1987): 556–81.

Rossino, Alexander. 'Polish "Neigbors" and German Invaders: Anti-Jewish Violence in the Bialystok District during the Opening Weeks of Operation Barbarossa'. *Polin: Studies of Polish Jewry* 16 (2003): 431–52.

Ruffmann, Karl-Heinz. 'Deutsche und litauische Memelpolitik in der Zwischenkriegszeit: ein Vergleich'. *Nordost-Archiv* 2/2 (1993): 217–33.

Sanborn, Joshua A. 'Unsettling the Empire: Violent Migrations and Social Disaster in Russia during World War I'. *Journal of Modern History* 77 (2005): 290–324.

Sarunas, Liekis. 'The Transfer of Vilna District into Lithuania, 1939'. *Polin: Studies in Polish Jewry* 14 (2001): 212–22.

Savchenko, V. N. 'Vostochnaia Galitsiia v 1914–1915 godakh (etnosotsial'nye osobennosti i problema prisoyedineniia k Rossii'. *Voprosy istorii* 11/12 (1996): 95–106.

Senn, Alfred E. 'Die Besetzung Memels in Januar 1923'. *Forschungen zur Osteuropäischen Geschichte* 10 (1965): 334–52.

Sha'ari, David. 'The Jewish Community of Cernăuţi between the Two World Wars'. *Shvut: Studies in Russian and East European Jewish History and Culture* 7/23 (1998): 106–46.

Simoncini, Gabriele. 'The Polyethnic State: National Minorities in Interbellum Poland'. *Nationalities Papers 22*, suppl. 1 (1994): 5–28.

Snyder, Timothy. 'The Causes of Ukrainian-Polish Ethnic Cleansing 1943'. *Past & Present* 179 (2003): 197–234.

Solonari, Vladimir. '"Model Province": Explaining the Holocaust of Bessarabian and Bukovinian Jewry'. *Nationalities Papers* 34/4 (2006): 471–500.

—— 'Patterns of Violence: The Local Population and the Mass Murder of Jews in Bessarabia and Northern Bukovina, July–August 1941'. *Kritika: Explorations in Russian and Eurasian History* 8/4 (2007): 749–87.

Staliūnas, Darius. 'Anti-Jewish Disturbances in the North-Western Provinces in the Early 1880s'. *East European Jewish Affairs* 34/2 (2004): 119–38.

Stola, Dariusz. 'A Monument of Words'. *Yad Vashem Studies* 30 (2002): 21–49.

Strods, H. P. 'Deportatsiia naseleniia Pribaltiiskikh stran v 1949 godu'. *Voprosy Istorii* 9 (1999): 130–5.

—— and Matthew Kott. 'The File on Operation "Priboi": A Re-Assessment of the Mass Deportations of 1949'. *Journal of Baltic Studies* 33/1 (2002): 1–36.

Sužiedėlis, Saulius. 'The Military Mobilization Campaigns of 1943 and 1944 in German-Occupied Lithuania: Contrasts in Resistance and Collaboration'. *Journal of Baltic Studies* 21/1 (1990): 33–52.

—— 'The Burden of 1941'. *Lituanus* 47/4 (2001): 47–60.

Sycz, Mirosław. 'Pierwsze dni II wojny światowej na Kresach Wschodnich RP'. *Dzieje Najnowsze* 26/1 (1994): 121–5.

Tokc´, Siargej. 'Barac´ba za belaruskuju dziarzhaunasc´ na absharakh Garadzenskaj (Bershtauskaj) pushchy u 1920-kh gadach'. *Belaruski gistarychny zbornik* 15 (2001): 133–67.

Tomaszewski, Jerzy. 'Lwów, 22 listopada 1918 roku'. *Przegląd Historyczny* 75/2 (1984): 279–85.

Urbaniak, George. 'Lithomania versus Panpolonism: The Roots of the Polish–Lithuanian Conflict before 1914'. *Canadian Slavonic Papers* 312 (1989): 107–27.

Vais, A. 'Otnoshenie nekotorykh krugov ukrainskogo natsional´nogo dvizheniia k evreiam v period Vtoroi mirovoi voiny'. *Vestnik evreiskogo universiteta v Moskve* 2/9 (1995): 104–13.

Vitkovskii, A., and V. Iampol´skii, eds. 'Vchera eto bylo sekretom (dokumenty o litovskikh sobytiiakh 40–50–kh gg'. *Izvestiia TsK KPSS*, 10 (1990): 129–39.

V.N. 'Ukraińskie wspomnienia z Berezy'. *Kultura* 9/12 (1955): 78–85.

Wapiński, Roman. 'Kształtowanie się w Polsce w latach 1922–1939 poglądów na ruchy faszystowskie w Europie'. *Studia nad faszyzmem i zbrodniami hitlerowskimi* 9 (1985): 89–127.

Weiner, Amir. 'Déjà Vu All Over Again: Prague Spring, Romanian Summer and Soviet Autumn on the Soviet Western Frontier'. *Contemporary European History* 15/2 (2006): 159–94.

—— 'The Empires Pay a Visit: Gulag Returnees, East European Rebellions, and Soviet Frontier Politics'. *Journal of Modern History* 78/2 (2006): 333–376.

Wróbel, Piotr. 'Barucha Milcha galicyjskie wspomnienia wojenne, 1914–1920'. *Biuletyn Żydowskiego Instytutu Historycznego* 2/158 (1991): 87–98.

—— 'The Seeds of Violence: The Brutalization of an East European Region, 1917–1921'. *Journal of Modern European History* 1 (2002): 125–49.

Żbikowski, Andrzej. 'Inny pogrom'. *Karta* 6 (1991): 130–3.

Zemskov, V. N. 'Prinuditel´nye migratsii iz Pribaltiki v 1940–1950 gg'. *Otechestvennye arkhivy* 1 (1993): 4–19.

Zgórniak, Marian. 'Polskie ultimatum do Litwy w 1938 roku'. *Annales Universitatis Mariae Curie-Skłodowska* 51, section F: Historia, 14 (1996): 161–71.

Żyndul, Jolanta. 'Zajścia antyżydowskie w Polsce w latach 1935–1937—geografia i formy'. *Biuletyn Żydowskiego Instytutu Historycznego* 159 (1991): 57–70.

UNPUBLISHED MATERIALS

Gracheva, Sofia, ed. 'Shchodennyk Viktora Petrykevycha (1883–1956)—Stanislav 1939–40, Buchach 1941–1944, Drohobych 1944, Kolomyja 1944–1956'.

Holquist, Peter. 'Forms of Violence in the First (1914–1915) and Second (1916–1917) Russian Occupations of Galicia'. Conference paper.

Ponarski, Zenowiusz. 'Konferederacja Wielkiego Księstwa Litewskiego 1915–1916: pytania i odpowiedzi'. Manuscript in author's possession.

Index